Contents

Book

Chapter 1 Introduction: making the transition from AS to A2

How to use this book ... 12
1.1 What is sociology like at A2 level? ... 14
1.2 What are the main differences between the AS and the A2 level? ... 16
1.3 What is the specification like for OCR sociology? ... 18
Frequently asked questions ... 20

PART 1 TOPIC AREAS – UNIT 2536

Chapter 2 Crime and deviance ... 21

2.1 Key issues in crime and deviance ... 22
2.2 How does crime and deviance link to the AS course? ... 24
2.3 How can we find out about crime and deviance? ... 26
2.4 What is crime, what is deviance? ... 28
2.5 Are criminals born or made? ... 30
2.6 Do official statistics give a true picture of crime? ... 32
2.7 The structuralist approach to crime and deviance: functionalism ... 34
2.8 The structuralist approach to crime and deviance: Marxism ... 36
2.9 How is neo-Marxism different from Marxism when discussing crime? ... 38
2.10 What do interactionists say about crime and deviance? ... 40
2.11 What do feminists say about crime and deviance? ... 42
2.12 What is realism? ... 44
2.13 Is crime just a different route to common goals? ... 46
2.14 What do postmodernists say about crime? ... 48
2.15 Patterns of crime: class ... 50
2.16 Patterns of crime: ethnicity ... 52
2.17 Patterns of crime: gender ... 54
2.18 Patterns of crime: age ... 56
2.19 Patterns of crime: region ... 58
2.20 What are agencies of social control? ... 60

CD

Introduction

What is sociology like at A2 level?
What is the specification like for A2 sociology?
What are the main differences between the AS and A2 level?

Crime and deviance

Crime and deviance case studies
Crime and deviance webquest
Crime and deviance revision cards
Crime and deviance multiple-choice questions
Crime and deviance test your evaluation skills
Crime and deviance key word quiz

Contents

2.21 What is control theory? 62

2.22 What are the solutions to crime? 64

2.23 How does the mass media portray crime and deviance? 66

2.24 What does the study of drugs tell us about crime and deviance? 68

2.25 How can we make crime and deviance synoptic? 70

2.26 Pushing your grades up higher 72

Frequently asked questions 74

Chapter 3 Education 75

3.1 Key issues in education 76

3.2 How does education link to the AS course? 78

3.3 How can we find out about the sociology of education? 80

3.4 What do we mean by 'education'? 82

3.5 What do we mean by 'intelligence'? 84

3.6 What is the tripartite system? 86

3.7 What is the comprehensive system? 88

3.8 What is vocationalism? 90

3.9 What impact did the 1988 Educational Reform Act have? 92

3.10 What is 'Curriculum 2000'? 94

3.11 What other types of education are there? 96

3.12 What do structuralists say about education? Functionalism 98

3.13 What do structuralists say about education? Marxism 100

3.14 What do structuralists say about education? Feminism 102

3.15 What do interactionists say about education? 104

3.16 What do postmodernists say about education? 106

3.17 How does education socialise pupils? 108

3.18 What do sociologists mean by 'in-school' and 'out-of-school' factors? 110

3.19 What is the relationship between education and class? 112

3.20 What is the relationship between education and gender? 114

3.21 What is the relationship between education and ethnicity? 116

Education

Education case studies

Education webquest

Education revision cards

Education multiple-choice questions

Education test your evaluation skills

Education key word quiz

Heinemann
SOCIOLOGY A2
for OCR

Warren Kidd   David Abbott   Gerry Czerniawski

www.heinemann.co.uk

✓ Free online support
✓ Useful weblinks
✓ 24 hour online ordering

01865 888058

Heinemann Educational Publishers
Halley Court, Jordan Hill, Oxford OX2 8EJ
Part of Harcourt Education

Heinemann is the registered trademark of
Harcourt Education Limited

First published 2004

09 08 07 06 05 04
10 9 8 7 6 5 4 3 2 1

British Library Cataloguing in Publication Data is available
from the British Library on request.

ISBN 0 435 46707 7

There are links to relevant websites in this book. In order to ensure that the links are up-to-date, that the links work, and
that the sites aren't inadvertently linked to sites that could be considered offensive, we have made the links available on the
Heinemann website at www.heinemann.co.uk/hotlinks. When you access the site, the express code is 7077P.

Typeset by 𝍔 Tek-Art

Original illustrations © Harcourt Education Limited, 2004

Cover illustration by Matt Buckley

Printed in the UK by Bath Press

Picture research by Thelma Gilbert and Bea Ray

Acknowledgements
Every effort has been made to contact copyright holders of material reproduced in this book. Any omissions will be
rectified in subsequent printings if notice is given to the publishers.

Page 14, Hulton Archive; page 16, Rex Features; page 28 (top), Rex Features; page 28 (bottom), Topham
Picturepoint; page 30, The Wellcome Trust; page 40, Corbis; page 47, Rex Features; page 50, Rex Features; page 52,
Photofusion/Paul Doyle; page 54, Carlton TV; page 56, Rex Features; page 58, Rex Features; page 66, John Frost
Newspaper Services; page 68, Rex Features; page 83, Photofusion; page 85, Corbis; page 88 (top), John Walmsley;
page 88 (bottom), John Walmsley; page 95, Photofusion; page 101, Photofusion; page 103, Peter Gould; page 107,
Hulton Archive; page 111, Photofusion; page 115, Kobal Collection; page 118, Stephen Ball; page 126, Corbis; page
130 (top), Rex Features; page 130 (bottom), Corbis; page 134, Alamy; page 142, Corbis; page 146, Getty; page 154,
Corbis; page 160, IPC Media; page 166, Corbis; page 185, Sally & Richard Greenhill; page 206, Hulton Archive; page
212, Charles Murray; page 214, Rex Features; page 220, Erik Olin Wright; page 221, Rex Features; page 222, Rex
Features; page 224; Sally & Richard Greenhill; page 235, Rex Features; page 247, Topham Picturepoint; page 254,
Topham Picturepoint; page 274, Rex Features;

Contents

3.22 What changes are taking place in education policy and provision?
3.23 How can we make education synoptic? 118
3.24 Pushing your grades up higher 120
Frequently asked questions 122

Chapter 4 Popular culture
4.1 Key issues in popular culture 125
4.2 How does popular culture link to the 126
AS course?
4.3 How can we find out about the sociology of 128
popular culture?
4.4 What is culture? 130
4.5 What do we mean by popular culture? 132
4.6 What is the Marxist view on popular culture? 134
4.7 What are neo-Marxist views on popular 136
culture?
4.8 What are feminist views on popular culture? 138
4.9 What is the pluralist view of popular culture? 140
4.10 What is the poststructuralist view on popular 142
culture?
4.11 What is the postmodernist view on popular 144
culture?
4.12 How do sociologists connect youth subcultures 146
and the culture industries?
4.13 How do sociologists connect class, ethnicity, 148
gender and leisure?
4.14 What is the relationship between class and 150
culture?
4.15 How can culture be a commodity? 152
4.16 What is the relationship between ethnicity and 154
culture?
4.17 How do sociologists connect femininity with the 156
culture industries?
4.18 What is the relationship between masculinity 158
and the culture industries?
4.19 What is postmodern about leisure and 160
tourism?
4.20 What do sociologists mean by global culture? 162
4.21 What do sociologists mean by proto 164
communities?
4.22 What are symbolic boundaries? 166
4.23 How can we make popular culture synoptic? 168
4.24 Pushing your grades up higher 170
Frequently asked questions 172
174

Popular culture

Popular culture case studies
Popular culture webquest
Popular culture revision cards
Popular culture multiple-choice questions
Popular culture test your evaluation skills
Popular culture key word quiz

Contents

PART 2 SYNOPTIC SKILLS – UNIT 2539

Chapter 5 How to be synoptic   175

5.1   Key issues in synopticity   176
5.2   How will your synoptic skills be tested?   178
5.3   How can we make good use of synoptic tools? 180
5.4   How can we write in a synoptic fashion?   182
5.5   How do theory and methods allow us to be
       synoptic?   184
5.6   Pushing your grades up higher: what ways are
       there to demonstrate synopticity?   186
Frequently asked questions   188

Chapter 6 Social inequality and difference   189

6.1   Key issues in social inequality and difference 190
6.2   How does social inequality and difference
       link to the AS course?   192
6.3   How can we find out about social inequality
       and difference?   194
6.4   What is social inequality and difference?   196
6.5   How do sociologists define wealth and
       income?   198
6.6   Who has the most wealth?   200
6.7   How do sociologists explain inequalities in
       wealth and income?   202
6.8   How does work affect inequality and
       difference   204
6.9   How do sociologists define poverty?   206
6.10   How is poverty linked to class, ethnicity and
       gender?   208
6.11   How are the poor excluded from society?   210
6.12   Changes in the class structure: is there an
       underclass?   212
6.13   How can we measure social inequality?   214
6.14   What do Marxists and functionalists say about
       social inequality and difference?   216
6.15   How does Weber explain social inequality and
       difference?   218
6.16   How do neo-Marxists and the New Right
       explain social inequality and difference?   220
6.17   Does social mobility exist?   222
6.18   What is the class structure like now?   224

How to be synoptic

What tricks are there to demonstrate synopticity?
How can we make crime and deviance synoptic?
How can we make education synoptic?
How can we popular culture synoptic?
How can we make theory and methods synoptic?
How can we make social inequality and difference
synoptic?

Social Inequality and Difference

Social inequality and difference case studies
Social inequality and difference webquest
Social inequality and difference revision cards
Social inequality and difference multiple-choice
questions
Social inequality and difference test your evaluation
skills
Social inequality and difference key word quiz

Contents

6.19 What has happened to class: are we all middle class now?   226
6.20 What has happened to class: are we all working class now?   228
6.21 How does ethnicity shape our life chances?   230
6.22 What are gender differences and inequalities in life chances important?   232
6.23 Is feminism still relevant?   234
6.24 What are the links between class, gender and ethnic inequalities?   236
6.25 How does social inequality and difference affect our identity?   238
6.26 How can we make social inequality and difference synoptic?   240
6.27 Pushing your grades up higher   242
Frequently asked questions   244

PART 3 SKILLS FOR SUCCESS IN SOCIOLOGY

Chapter 7 A2 Personal study: a practical guide (Unit 2538)   245

7.1   Key issues in the personal study   246
7.2   How is the personal study written up?   248
7.3   What does each of the chapters do?   250
7.4   How do you decide what to do?   252
7.5   How do you decide what method to choose?   254
7.6   What goes in the rationale?   256
7.7   How do I build a brief background focus?   258
7.8   How and where do I explain my methodology?   260
7.9   How do I show my results? What goes in the research section?   262
7.10 Where and how do I make conclusions?   264
7.11 What goes in the evaluation chapter?   266
7.12 Pushing your grades up higher   268
Frequently asked questions   270

Chapter 8 A2 examination skills   271

8.1   Key issues in developing good exam skills. What will the exam look like?   272
8.2   What skills are needed for the A2 course?   274
8.3   How should I divide up my time in the exam?   276
8.4   How do I write good essays?   278
8.5   How can I show good evaluation skills?   280

Exam and revision tips
Margin boxes
    Key ideas
    Key definitions
    Key facts
    What, when and why?
    Who is this person?
    Synoptic links
    Methods links
    Classic study
    Coursework suggestions
    Top exam hints

Pushing your grades up higher:
    Protest and social movements
    Education
    Theory and methods
    Crime and deviance
    Social inequality and difference
Revision tips
Webography

Contents

8.6 How can I write good introductions and
conclusions? 282

8.7 How can I get my essays to flow? 284

8.8 How will my essays be assessed? 286

8.9 What makes good revision? 288

Frequently asked questions 290

Bibliography 291

Index 295

Theory, methods and methodology

Theory, methods and methodology chapter

Theory, methods and methodology margin boxes

Theory, methods and methodology case studies

Theory, methods and methodology webquest

Theory, methods and methodology revision cards

Theory, methods and methodology multiple-choice questions

Theory, methods and methodology test your evaluation skills

Theory, methods and methodology key word quiz

Foreword

This book has been written as the follow-up to *Heinemann Sociology AS for OCR* (2003). It is intended to be used in the second year of an A Level course, ideally as a follow-up to the AS course book, but it can also be accessed if the AS book was not used for the previous year.

Sociology A2 for OCR is designed to take off from the point where the AS course, and book, halted. What does it mean to be a student of A2 sociology and how does the A2 course extend, develop from and differ to the previous AS one? What are the challenges of the A2 year? What are the differences in terms of knowledge, both in breadth and depth?

This book seeks to strip A2 sociology down to its essentials; to show students how all the ingredients of sociology work together. We aim to get students thinking about the relationships between theory, key words and studies, and how the ideas from their previous AS year relate to the topics studied in the A2 year. The book also seeks to unite subject content with skills development and examination advice and technique. We have written the book with the examination in mind, yet at the same time tried to show how sociology as a discipline works, and how evaluation skills can be developed by thinking in a sociological fashion.

We hope you like this book, and we wish you every success with your examinations.

Warren Kidd
David Abbott
Gerry Czerniawski
2004

Foreword

Author biographies

Warren Kidd is the Senior Tutor for the Social Sciences at Newham Sixth Form College ('New Vic') in East London, where he teaches sociology. Warren is an accomplished textbook author for the AS and A level market and has previously been a vice president of the Association for the Teaching of the Social Sciences (ATSS). He is an experienced provider of teacher INSET and contributor to student sociology conferences. He is the series editor for both this book and *Heinemann Sociology AS for OCR* and has written the introduction, synoptic skills, coursework skills and examination skills chapters of this book.

David Abbott teaches at Hills Road Sixth Form College in Cambridge. He has written several textbooks and articles for AS/A2 level sociology. David has written the crime and deviance and social inequality and difference chapters of this book, as well as the theory, methods and methodology chapter on the CD-ROM.

Gerry Czerniawski teaches sociology at Newham Sixth Form College. A former member of the executive of the ATSS, Gerry is an associate lecturer in social sciences for the Open University and tutors in sociology at the London School of Economics and Political Science (LSE) on the Saturday School programme for A level students. As well as producing resources for the ATSS, Gerry has provided INSET courses in sociology and is also a teacher trainer on the City and Guilds teacher-training course. Gerry has written the education, and popular culture chapters of this book.

Dedication

Warren dedicates this book to his family, his friends, his loved ones and his students. He would like to thank Jane, for making it all so much easier, and the students at Newham Sixth Form College, who provided the inspiration for so many of the ideas behind this book.

David dedicates this book to Rosie, Christopher and Olivia.

Gerry would like to dedicate this book to Patrick Chamberlayne, 'La Garrigue' and family and Paul Stephens at Stavanger University College, Norway.

Chapter 1

Introduction: making the transition from AS to A2

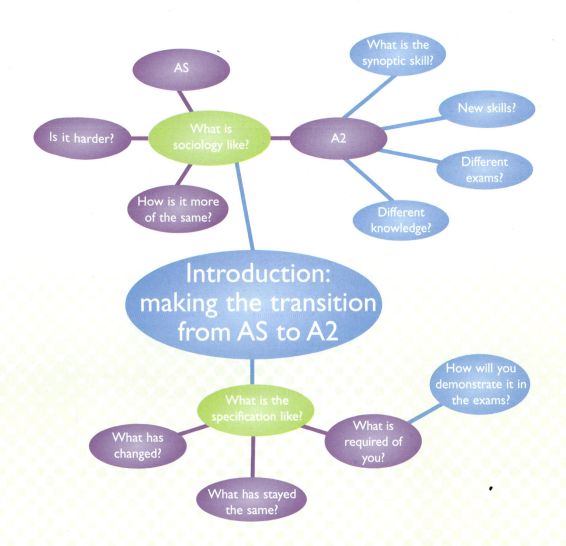

How to use this book

This book aims to help you to be successful on your sociology course. Exam success is not simply a case of knowing the subject content, it is also a case of being able to apply what you know in the way the exam and the examiners require. You will find this book helpful in the following ways:

- It contains a lot of knowledge, but also provides you with support for the exam.
- It focuses on what the OCR Awarding Body specification says about the course you are following.
- It shows you what sociology is all about and what the tricks and shortcuts are to learning the subject.
- It breaks sociology down into manageable sections, focusing on the idea that there are four essential or key ingredients that you have to use in order to 'do' sociology well.
- It provides both classic and up-to-date sociological studies and theories.

What features does this book have?

This book provides the following features:

- Coloured pages which indicate the exam advice in each chapter. You will also notice that the contents page is colour-coded in the same way to give you a quick exam advice guide.
- Each section contains information to help you think about the exam, and also to try and push your grades up as high as possible.
- Margin boxes that give you tips and advice.
- Each chapter begins with a look back at the AS course, showing how synoptic links can be made. Plus, at the end of every chapter, you will find information on the synoptic exam (Unit 2539) and links between each topic. In this sense, we have tried to be synoptic both forwards and backwards.
- Each chapter ends with some frequently asked questions that you may need to know the answers to.

What do the boxes in the margin do?

In the margin of every section, you will come across a variety of different boxes. They each do a slightly different thing, and they are there to help you.

- Top exam hint: this box gives you some very quick exam tips (AO1/2).
- Synoptic link: this will help you to think about your sociology course as a whole, rather than as a series of separate topics or options (AO1).
- Methods link: this box integrates methods into every topic (AO1) – this is a very important synoptic skill, and is central to thinking like a sociologist.
- Coursework suggestion: handy hints or an actual proposed idea for linking topics to coursework at A2 level are provided (AO1/2).
- Key definition: this box contains a key term and its definition (AO1).

- Key idea: this box contains an important sociological idea explained (AO1).
- Key fact: this provides a relevant statistic, to give your exam answers that bit more depth (AO2).
- Classic study: these boxes focus upon a really important or well-known piece of research to help you support your arguments in the exam (AO2).
- What, when and why?: this box will help you to locate the ideas and people you are reading about within the historical period they come from. This is useful for evaluation purposes (AO2).
- Who is this person?: when studying sociology, you will find that you come across many different sociologists who all have different ideas. This will help you to understand a bit more about the people behind the ideas you are learning (AO1).

How is the book divided up?

This A2 book is divided into distinct areas:

- **Introduction** – The introduction focuses on the requirements of the specification and gives an introduction to Sociology at A2 level.
- **Section 1 Topic areas** – This section looks at three of the topics for unit 2536.
- **Section 2 The synoptic unit** – This section covers social inequality and difference, the topic for unit 2539. There is also a complete chapter giving advice on the important skill of synopticity.
- **Section 3 Skills for success** – This section looks at important skills such as essay writing and evaluation skills. There is also a separate chapter on the unit 2538 coursework, providing ideas, advice, hints and tips.

The CD-ROM

The CD-ROM that accompanies this book gives you the opportunity to print off the margin boxes in specific combinations to suit your own needs. These will be invaluable for revision and for coursework so make good use of this facility throughout your course.

Along with exam and revision tips, the CD-ROM also contains new case studies for your revision, web activities, handy revision cards and key word exercises, multiple-choice assessment tests, evaluation skills exercises and a bibliography of useful websites. You will also find a chapter on the theory, methods and methodology topic which will be useful throughout your course. A CD-ROM symbol will appear throughout the book and will direct you to the relevant sections of the CD.

 **CD-ROM**

What is sociology like at A2 level?

Auguste Comte 1798–1857. Comte was lucky. He invented sociology, so he did not have to learn about many new ideas or harder theories as they did not exist. For you, however, this A2 year will be both easier and harder. There are many new ideas to learn, but also plenty of opportunities to use ideas from last year again.

✓ Top Exam Hints

- **Do not forget that sociology is still made up of the same ingredients as it was before: theory, key words, named examples and evaluation. These are still the 'tool-kit' that you need in order to think in a sociological fashion.**

- **Remember that what you learned last year can still be used this year. Do not throw away those notes or revision cards. Bring your revision cards into lessons since they are more portable than your class notes. Make use of them this year as background information.**

Welcome to sociology

First, welcome to A2 sociology. The aim of this book is to try to help you to be as successful as possible by giving all you need to know in manageable-sized pieces. The aim is not to provide a great long list of ideas to learn, but rather to show you how sociology works as a way of thinking about society, and to show you how the sociology examinations work. This book continues where the AS book left off; showing you what you need to know, explaining what it means, and trying to show you how to develop the necessary skills you will need in order to pass the final examinations successfully.

Sociology at A2 level is both the same and different to sociology at AS level. It is both easier and harder.

How is sociology at A2 easier?

- Sociology has not changed much. We have not re-interpreted any of the theories you learned at AS. Nothing in the world of sociology has changed so much that you will not recognise it when you see it again in these pages.

- This means, sociology is actually easier this year. You do not need to worry about what you are getting yourself into as you already know. There are still the four important ingredients of sociology to focus on: theory, key words, named examples and evaluation.

- You can use much of what you learned in your AS year again this year. In fact, this will actually save you time, as you do not need to learn again what you learned last year. There are theories from last year that you now know, and so you will not need to spend time re-learning them, just take a little time to remind yourself of them. This is also true for the language that sociologists use. Most of the key words from last year will also be used this year. You will be familiar with what sociologists say and how they say it, but this time around it will not seem as strange and unfamiliar as it might have at the start of last year.

- There is also possibly more time this year. You will certainly find yourself going at a quicker pace once you start the course, as your teachers can proceed faster because of your existing knowledge base of sociology. They do not have to progress slowly to make sure you understand the basics because you already have them. The A2 exams are also a little bit later in the year than the AS exams are. Again, this means a few more lessons; a little bit more time.

How is sociology at A2 harder?

At the same time as it gets easier, it also gets a bit harder – a typically confusing sociological statement!

- There will be some new theories that you will have to learn; theories that you will not have been taught at AS level.
- You might need to go into more depth for some of the theories you learned last year. There might be more case studies to know, or slightly different interpretations to learn. However, the important thing to remember is that you always have the basics from last year's work.
- Arguably, the A2 examination is harder than the AS one. Obviously, this depends on the individual, but the A2 examination does ask you to be much more evaluative than the AS exam.
- The A2 examination also requires you to write essays (referred to in the specification as an unstructured essay question) for the unit on power and control (2536) – very different from the AS exams last year. The exam also requires you to demonstrate the important skill of 'synopticity' – to be able to show links to all the units you have studied in the final unit 2539 on social inequality and difference.
- Finally, coursework at A2 sociology is much more demanding than at AS, especially in terms of the time it might take to complete it. But, all you have to do is start it early, and follow the advice of your teachers and the guidance in this book.

What is sociology at A2 level like?

As you can see, nothing much has changed except the nature of the examinations and the skills you are required to demonstrate. Sociology is still sociology. The ideas remain the same, but at A2 you are expected to do more with them. It is not sufficient just to learn the ideas, you need to show that you can manipulate them, and that you really understand how sociology works inside and out. This is also the aim of this book.

Key points to remember
- Sociology as a subject has not changed between AS and A2 levels.
- A2 sociology is harder since there is more to learn and harder skills to master.
- A2 sociology is also easier since you are starting A2 with a whole year's worth of sociology behind you.

✓ Top Exam Hint

Remember in the AS book we encouraged you to make revision cards of all the studies that you needed to know in the AS year? This year, early on in the course, go through these cards and sort out those that might link to the topics you are doing at A2. Consult your teacher if you are unsure. Now you have the cards, use them. Use them in class and in essay answers – try to establish connections between this year and last year.

✳ Key Idea

Being synoptic means being able to show links and connections between things. This is a major skill in the second year of your sociology course – as it is for all A2 subjects.

● Synoptic Link

Go through your AS folder early on in the course – consider how what you did in the AS year might relate to what you will be doing this year. Take pages from your notes and insert them at the beginning of this year's class, ready for the skill of synopticity.

1.2 | What are the main differences between the AS and the A2 level?

What does this mean?

Think back to the start of your AS year. One of the big concerns you might have had then was understanding what AS level was. Also, in the case of sociology and perhaps some other subjects that do not often get taught at GCSE level in schools, you might have wondered what the new subject would be about.

This year you will not have these concerns. You know already what to expect from sociology. You may have already sat AS examinations and you have already begun to learn the basics of the subject. You now need to concern yourself with how the A2 level might differ from the AS.

What are the differences of knowledge?

The AS course is like an introduction to the ideas of sociology. The A2 course takes these same ideas, but asks you to apply them to different topics and, while doing so, to develop new skills.

The AS theories will still be used at A2, although some new theories might be added. Most theories are still either 'macro' or 'micro', or they are either 'consensus' or 'conflict' in their approach to viewing society. You might find that the number increases, but you will also find that many new theories seem very similar to the old ones you already know.

You will still need to know all the key concepts you learned last year. The way you speak and write sociology has not changed, but for the essay questions in the exam you will really need to be able to manipulate these technical and conceptual terms. They are a priority in order for your essay answers to have depth.

What are the differences of examination?

Like the AS exams, the A2 exams are either one hour (unit 2536, power and control) or one hour and 30 minutes long (unit 2537, applied social research skills, which is optional, and unit 2539, social inequality and difference, which is the end of the course 'synoptic' paper).

Although the AS exam asked for two-part structured essay questions, for A2 in unit 2536, power and control, the exam requires you to write an unstructured essay question. This starts with the key phrase 'outline and assess' and is what we might imagine a more 'traditional' extended essay question would be like.

Start this year with confidence – you already have a whole year of sociology behind you.

✓ Top Exam Hints

- In the AS book we encouraged you to keep a vocabulary book – dust it down and get it out for this year's course too. Since you will have lots of words in it already, it means you start this year much better off than you did last year. Just make sure that you refer to it and use the words in your exam answers for depth.

- Look at Chapter 8 in this book for detailed advice on how to write good-quality essays.

What are the differences of skill?

The greatest difference is in the weighting of the skill of evaluation. For the A2 course it is much more important than in the AS year.

You will also be required to demonstrate your ability to think and to manipulate information synoptically. In other words, your ability to be able to draw on other areas of sociology in order to make connections. Sociology always used to ask students to think like this, but now it is actually tested on the unit 2539 social inequality and difference exam paper. This lasts for one hour and 30 minutes and it is worth 20 per cent of the overall two-year mark.

Key points to remember

- There will be more theories to learn this year, and some will be harder than in the AS year.
- The exam will require much more detailed pieces of writing from you.
- You will need to demonstrate both synoptic and evaluation skills in the exam at A2 level.

✓ **Top Exam Hints**

Look at Chapter 5 in this book to seek advice on how to master the skill of synopticity.

1.3 What is the specification like for OCR sociology?

What does this mean?

As with all qualifications, the Awarding Body, in this case OCR, lays out what it wants students and teachers to do unit by unit, year by year.

- The AS exam is made up of three units.
- The A2 exam is made up of a further three units, making a total of six units in all. This is what is known as a 'six-unit award'. Universities often talk about three units, six units, and twelve units (the vocational qualifications that are worth two A Levels since they do twice as many units).
- For sociology, at AS you would have either taken two exams and produced a piece of coursework or you would have taken three exams.

What has changed and what has stayed the same?

The A2 sociology course follows the following pattern.

- You will have already studied three units last year for the AS. For the A2 you will have either three exams or two exams and a piece of coursework. This coursework is called 'the personal study' since you develop, carry out and evaluate an independent and personal piece of original sociological study.
- The units for this year are titled:
    o Unit 2536 power and control
    o Unit 2537 applied sociological research skills or unit 2538 the personal study
    o Unit 2539 social inequality and difference; this is called the 'synoptic unit'.
- It is important to remember, like the AS year, that the fourth unit you study is referred to as a general 'theme' leading to more specific actual topic areas studied under each theme: Under the theme of power and control you will be examined in either crime and deviance, education, health, popular culture, social policy and welfare or protest and social movements.
- For the sixth and final unit, social inequality and difference, you will be tested on three key areas and you will be required to understand all three, and how they link together: dimensions of workplace inequality, poverty as a dimension of inequality, and different explanations of inequality and difference. The OCR specification also says that the exam will focus upon issues of class, gender and ethnicity under the above three headings.
- For the power and control unit you will sit a one hour examination and will be required to answer what the specification calls an 'unstructured essay question'. These are different from the two-part structured essay questions for the second unit last year on culture and socialisation (unit 2533). You have a choice of two questions for each of the six options on the paper and you answer one question only. This exam is worth 15 per cent of the overall two-year grade – the same as the personal study or the methods exam this year.

✓ Top Exam Hint

Do not forget what you already know about sociological theory. You might like to keep a list in the front of your folder of all the key words associated with each of the theories you know so far. This might help you when you come to write essays as you can use the words to create depth and detail.

● Synoptic Link

Synopticity will be tested formally on the last, sixth unit, but good students are always synoptic – even in the other units. Always try to make connections; try to see sociology as a whole world view rather than simply as a series of unrelated topics. Since everything in society is connected somehow, so too is everything in sociology!

The synoptic exam paper (unit 2539) opens with the following quote.

'You will be assessed on your understanding of the connections between sociological thought and methods of enquiry as they apply to the study of social inequality and difference. You should therefore take every opportunity to include references to aspects of social inequality that you have studied throughout your course.'

As you can see, you are being asked to make links or connections based around the theme of inequality and difference from everything that you have been taught, from any topic, and to consider how both theories and methods deal with and relate to the issue in question.

- For the methods unit you will either complete a one hour and 30 minutes exam, or the 2500 word personal study. The exam (unit 2537) continues where the unit on 'methods' or research skills left off last year on the AS course. The exam covers three issues, all of which are inter-related: research design and theory, techniques of data collection and how to interpret and to report data. The written exam asks you to answer two questions: a data response question and a question covering a more practical evaluation of research design.
- Finally, the last exam, your sixth unit (unit 2539) on social inequality and difference is what we refer to as the synoptic paper. In other words, even though this paper has a theme or a 'topic' you will also be expected to illustrate how the topic might link to all the other topics you have studied both at AS and at A2. This is why the paper is the 'synoptic' paper.
- The synoptic paper lasts for one hour and 30 minutes and it gives you a choice of one from two possible multi-part data response questions. The marks for this paper for the individual questions are always 6, 6, 12, 22 and 44. The last question, worth 44 marks, asks you to 'outline and assess' and in this sense is like the essay questions in unit 2536 on power and control.

What will the A2 year be like?

The Awarding Body says that the units can be taken in any order, although they recommend that the synoptic unit (unit 2539) is taken at the very end since it is a summary for the whole course. Technically speaking, you could do the units in whatever order your teachers choose, but most teachers will probably teach them in order.

You might start the year with a re-cap of the AS work, and you might also start the year looking at the unit 2538 coursework option, if you are taking this. Most schools and colleges will probably try to get you started on this quite early on as it is a sizable piece of work, although it is worth remembering that is it worth only 15 per cent of the total A2 level marks. Having said this, if you can get a high grade for coursework it might take some pressure off you for the final two examinations.

Key points to remember

- The skill of evaluation is more important at A2 than in the AS exam.
- The 'methods' unit might be either an exam on theory and methods or a piece of coursework.
- The last, sixth unit, is the 'synoptic' unit.

✓ Top Exam Hint

Essay questions always start with 'outline and assess'. Make sure you think about what this means. You are being asked to describe arguments and different points of view and then to assess these views against each other and against evidence that you know.

Do not forget that for the sixth exam paper, the synoptic paper, you are being asked to see connections between theory, methods and the topic in question – social inequality and difference. This is a formal requirement of the last exam, but do not forget that theory and methods link to every topic, and there will always be an opportunity to use them in question (c) of the exam paper.

Frequently asked questions

Q. How much harder does sociology get at A2?

A. This depends upon who you are and what you may or may not be good at already. For some people, it is the thought of having to write full essays, for others it is having to be much more evaluative than before. The ideas do not really get any more difficult, but there are more of them, and you will need to remember a lot more, especially since unit 2539 is synoptic and requires you to make connections and links with other ideas and topics.

Q. What is the most challenging thing about A2 sociology?

A. Most students think that the ideas will be harder at A2 than at AS, but it is more the case that the skills get more challenging. In fact, sociology is sociology – the ideas in A2 are the same as the ideas and theories in AS. What is challenging is what you are now required to do with them. You will also find however, that there is a greater emphasis on theory at A2 than at AS level.

Q. What skills do I now need to develop?

A. The most important skill for A2 sociology is that of evaluation. You really need to be able to do things with the ideas you are given, rather than just repeat them. You need to be able to say what is good or bad about an idea or a theory; to say if you think a theory does or does not have any real evidence to support or disprove it. You will most notice the need for this skill in essay answers, and in coursework, if you do it. You can develop this skill by following the advice in Chapter 8 on exam skills.

Chapter 2

Crime and deviance

 **CD-ROM**

2.1 | Key issues in crime and deviance

◆ **What, when and why?**

Sociological views and explanations of crime change over time, as do laws and other aspects of society, such as technology. In an article published in 2002, researchers at the Harvard University Medical School (see Denscombe 2003) argued that murder rates in the USA are lower than would otherwise currently be expected, given the high rates of violence, because of improvements in emergency medical care. They argue that this is 'masking' what they describe as an 'epidemic of violence'. This indicates one of the ways in which crime is socially constructed.

✳ **Key Idea**

Power, control and social inequality are key ideas running throughout this topic. Power is vital because some people have more power than others in defining crime and in enforcing law and order. This is also clearly linked to stratification, so sociologists are keen to investigate how crime and deviance and law and order are linked to differences of class, race, gender, and age.

What are the important issues in crime and deviance?

The sociological study of crime and deviance is a fascinating topic which challenges our 'common sense' views about right and wrong. Sociologists bring their usual approach to studying society to this topic, and aim to ask provocative, searching questions in order to identify the truth about crime and deviance. The following are the sorts of questions posed by sociologists.

- What counts as crime? Do some groups have more power in defining crime and deviance than others?
- How can we measure crime?
- Are some people more likely than others to acquire a criminal identity? Is this the result of natural or social factors? Is it a matter of choice or the result of powerful structural forces beyond individual control?
- Do criminals come from particular social groups? Are men more criminal than women, black people more criminal than white people, and the poor or those from lower social classes more criminal than the middle classes? Alternatively, are some important social processes shaping our picture of crime and criminals?

Why are sociologists interested in crime and deviance?

The study of crime and deviance is currently of great interest to sociologists. Criminology courses (a multi-disciplinary subject, but one which involves much sociological theory and research) are increasingly popular in universities, and crime has a high profile in the media. There are several reasons why sociologists have such an interest in crime.

- We are currently living through a period of great social change. This involves changes in the types and levels of crime. Understanding how crime is changing can help to shed light on how society is changing and vice versa.
- In a period of change, society's rules (its norms and values) change a great deal. Durkheim argued that shared rules are one of the things that hold society together (integrate it). Sociologists are therefore interested in studying crime and deviance as a way of understanding what holds society together.
- In a time of rapid social change, we tend to look back and compare our society with the past. Sociologists are interested in finding out whether crime really is worse now than in the past.
- Whether or not there is now more or less crime compared with the past, it is indisputable that crime is currently a big social problem. Sociologists want to conduct research in order to contribute to solving the social problem of crime.

What are the key ideas we can use to think about crime and deviance?

Some of the concepts, theories, and studies you will learn about in crime and deviance will be new to you. Sociological definitions of crime and deviance themselves, and the concept of sanctions (rewards and punishments), social order and social control are a few key examples, and they will help you to understand how crime is socially constructed. Other ideas though will be familiar from previous topics and the core themes. Chief among these ideas are the following.

- Power and social inequality: sociologists aim to find out how the social construction of crime and deviance is influenced by power relations and stratification. This raises the question of whether social rules and the law represent the interests and views of all members of society or of some social groups in particular.
- Social inequality also involves gender and ethnicity. Sociologists are interested in whether crime and deviance are gendered, that is, whether defining crime and deviance also involves any processes of differentiation and division on the basis of gender. Similar questions are raised with regard to ethnicity and crime.
- Another useful key idea is labelling theory (see section 2.10), which you may have learned about in education. Sociologists use this theory in a similar way when studying crime and deviance, aiming to see whether criminal and deviant identities are imposed on some people through labelling.

What does the Awarding Body say about crime and deviance?

The OCR examiners will expect you to know about:

1. the social nature of crime and deviance, including definitions of crime and deviance, their social construction and relativity; social reactions to crime and deviance and their consequences including the mass media.
2. patterns of crime and victimisation, including measuring crime and the fear of crime together with criminal statistics, self-report and victim surveys; patterns of crime and victimisation by social profile (class, ethnicity, gender, age and region); theories and explanations of crime and deviance.
3. power, control and the problem of crime, including agents of social control and the role of the law, the police, criminal justice system and penal systems, the mass media and the state, criminalisation and control; solutions to the problems of crime including the relationship between sociology and social policy.

The exam for this unit will be one hour in length and will be composed of two unstructured essay questions from a choice of twelve, from the module 2536 options, of which candidates must answer one question.

Key points to remember

- Sociologists aim to challenge commonsense views of crime and deviance and show how these phenomena are socially constructed.
- There are several key ideas to use in understanding crime and deviance, but it is important to remember to link your study of crime and deviance to the core themes of social differentiation, power and stratification.
- You will improve your understanding of crime and deviance if you link it to your study of sociological theory and methods and methodology.

✓ Top Exam Hint

- Use CW Mills' idea of the relationship between the public and private to demonstrate your sociological imagination when discussing crime. For example, show how crime and deviance, and the acquisition of a criminal identity, vary depending not simply on the seriousness of the offending behaviour, but on who is carrying it out, and where and when it is taking place.

- As with all of the OCR units you have to show competency or ability in the assessment objectives of AO1 (*knowledge and understanding and presentation and communication*) and AO2 (*interpretation and analysis and evaluation*).

  For AO1 you need to show *knowledge and understanding* of the names of sociologists and their case studies; the relevant theories; the key concepts (for example, globalisation); evidence to support the claims sociologists make and a keen awareness of the research methodologies used by sociologists.

- For AO2 you need to show how you can actually interpret, apply and evaluate this knowledge when putting forward a particular argument and evaluate continuously throughout any answer you are writing. There is a greater emphasis placed on AO2 at A2 than at AS. This might mean, for example, that you choose to draw on the ideas of a study and see how it might (or might not!) be relevant to an area of crime and deviance. You might also identify trends from the past and see to what extent that particular trend is present today.

How does crime and deviance link to the AS course?

❝❞ Key Definition

The word **synoptic** means to summarise or form an overview. It is part of the nature of an overview or summary that it shows the links between different ideas or events. This is exactly what synopticity in sociology should do. In sociology you cannot fully understand topics such as 'families and households' or 'crime and deviance', unless you also have a good understanding of theory and method, so you will have to use your knowledge synoptically, and show how it illuminates our understanding of a particular topic area.

Why are links to AS important for sociology?

At A2 level, your examination will involve **synoptic** questions in unit 2539. The word 'synoptic' simply means that you will be asked to make links to other topics you have studied in sociology. In unit 2539 you will be asked questions which require you to demonstrate that you understand the links between the various types of social inequality you have studied, such as inequalities in the workplace, poverty, class, race and gender inequalities, and the nature of sociological thought and methods of sociological enquiry. This chapter is devoted to both of the last two elements, but you also need to think back to your work for AS and the chapter on methods in *Heinemann Sociology AS for OCR*.

What links can be made to families and households?

Some theories and studies of the family can provide explanations of crime. For example, Parsons' theory about sex role socialisation, and various studies of conjugal roles, could be used to tell us why crime is a gendered activity. All of these show that female identities are structured towards domestic roles and this is one way of explaining the lower rates of recorded crime committed by women.

Bowlby's theories about maternal deprivation offer another explanation of the link between family and crime, maintaining that single parent families are less stable and lead to higher rates of juvenile delinquency (1946). A study by Farrington (1994) suggests that criminal careers develop within problem families. Such families are characterised by poor parenting skills and consequently children develop an anti-social personality.

What links can be made to education?

Criminal behaviour is often associated with low levels of educational attainment. Therefore, explanations of educational attainment can provide us with insights into crime. Bernstein's studies of language differences (1971), or the various studies on cultural deprivation, indicate that different cultural values such as a focus on instant gratification could help play a role in crime. Paul Willis's famous study, 'Learning to Labour' (1977) shows how working-class boys actively create a macho anti-school subculture which, ironically, prepares them for a life of unfulfilling manual labour. It could be argued that anti-school subcultures of this sort can also explain juvenile delinquency.

How does crime and deviance link to theory and methods?

- Sociological theory is important because the way sociologists define and study crime and deviance will be strongly shaped by the theoretical and methodological approach that they take.
- A sociologist's theoretical approach will be crucial because of the different theoretical approaches to power and stratification, and because of the different approaches to the structure/action debate. Also, remember that theories can be categorised in terms of conflict and consensus, and this too has an important influence on how a theory explains crime and deviance.
- Methodology is also relevant as a choice of a macro or micro approach, and adoption of either a positivist or an interpretive methodology will lead to very different types of findings about crime.
- A good example of the importance of methods occurs in the debates about the usefulness of official statistics on crime. This draws very much on material that you will have examined previously in the debates between positivist and interpretivist approaches to methodology, so you will need to be sure that you have a good understanding of that part of the specification.

Key points to remember

- The concepts, studies, theories and topics you learned about in your AS year are relevant to crime and deviance.

∞ Methods Link

Your work for AS sociology will have taught you about the different methodological approaches used by sociologists, for example positivists and interpretivists. These are very important and if you use these ideas carefully you can quickly go to the heart of some of the key questions in this topic, such as whether certain social groups commit more crime than others. This will enable you to produce high-level evaluation.

✓ Top Exam Hint

Make sure you have revised a few examples from families and households, education, theory and methods, or the other topics you have studied, to use in synoptic questions. You do not have to revise the whole topic again, but you should be able to remember about half a dozen relevant studies, or half a dozen examples of how education, say, is linked to crime and deviance.

How can we find out about crime and deviance?

How have sociologists tried to measure crime and deviance?

The measurement of crime and deviance has led to a great deal of controversy in sociology. Sociologists have tried to measure crime in several main ways:

- through the use of official statistics of recorded crime rates
- by using **self-report studies** which invite those who have committed offences to admit to their activities
- by using **victim surveys** which ask a large sample of people to say whether they have been victims of crime and to provide details of these crimes.

There are advantages and disadvantages with all of these methods of trying to measure the extent of crime and deviance.

What methods do sociologists tend to use to study crime and deviance?

Sociologists have used the methods indicated above to try and measure the extent of crime and deviance. However, measurement is only one aim of sociological research into crime and deviance. Sociologists also wish to find out why people commit crime, how certain actions come to be seen as criminal, as well as how the criminal justice system functions. This means that sociologists may draw on many methods, both quantitative and qualitative, primary and secondary, in order to investigate crime and deviance.

What problems with definition and measurement are encountered in crime and deviance?

Although sociologists are keen to point out that definitions of crime and deviance are socially constructed, there are relatively few disputes in sociology about the meaning of either term, in the way in which, for example, there are disagreements about how the term 'the family' should be defined.

There is, however, debate about how crime is best measured. Official statistics measure recorded crime, which comprises crimes that are known to the police, either because they are detected by the police or because other people report the offence to the police. Clearly this means that crime statistics cannot give a comprehensive picture of all crime in any time or place, and do not tell us how much crime is unreported. While all sociologists recognise the limitations of official statistics, there is disagreement as to exactly how useful official statistics are.

What other problems are there in studying crime and deviance?

There are several other methodological issues in this topic which concern sociologists. Three main issues stand out:

- the value of qualitative methods in studying crime and deviance
- ethical concerns
- the issue of bias in sociological research.

Qualitative methods have been used extensively in studying crime and deviance by researchers who have taken the view that the reality of crime can only be understood by taking an interpretive approach. However, such methods have received widespread criticism for their alleged lack of validity. It can be argued that people participating in criminal activity have an interest in exaggerating and glorifying their activities, or in concealing the true nature and extent of them, or in rationalising (defending) their activity. All of this may mean that researchers do not gain a true insight into crime. The other common disadvantages of the method, such as the Hawthorne effect, also have to be considered.

Ethical issues are important in all sociological topics, but there are perhaps some especially difficult issues in crime and deviance. The British Sociological Association advises researchers to keep to the principle of informed consent and to avoid deceiving respondents and participants wherever possible. Nevertheless there are well-known cases where sociologists have not obeyed these principles, such as James Patrick's research (1973) into gangs using covert participant observation, and Laud Humphreys, who deceived participants by not revealing his identity as a researcher. Researchers are also put in a difficult position if they become aware of crimes which have been committed.

Perhaps most important of all, some sociologists have claimed that the dominant approach in sociology which depends on quantitative (positivist) methods, has led to the incorporation of systematic biases into the sociological study of crime. Marxists, for example, have argued that positivist sociology most commonly identifies criminality with the working class, and crimes committed by other social groups are relatively (but not completely) neglected (Sutherland 1933). Feminist sociologists have argued that our views of crime are strongly gendered, and that the dominant view of crime in sociology reflects a malestream approach (Abbott and Wallace 1990). Finally and more recently, some researchers have argued that the dominant view of criminals in contemporary society is also highly racialised and is the result of a form of racism called institutional racism (Fitzgerald and Hough 2002, see section 2.16).

Key points to remember

- Official statistics provide details of the extent of crime, but they only measure recorded crime.
- Sociologists can also use qualitative methods to study crime, but these raise issues of validity.
- Research into crime and deviance raises especially difficult questions about research ethics.

What is crime, what is deviance?

Which of these people is committing a crime? Which acts are deviant?

What does this mean?

Sociologists think about **crime** and **deviance** in ways which are subtly different to those used in everyday conversation. It may seem unnecessary to agonise over what we mean by these terms, but sociologists argue that they are more complex than we realise. Looking at crime and deviance in a more sociological way enables us to think about who defines crime and deviance and who benefits, thus raising important questions about power, control, and social inequality.

What is crime and what is deviance?

Crime can be simply defined as any act which breaks the law, and deviance can be defined as any action which departs from 'normal' behaviour. Sociologists make some critical points about these definitions.

- To say that crime is any act which is against the law is a circular definition, and it just tells us that crime is anything that the law says it is. This certainly describes crime, but it does not explain how and why certain acts become defined as crimes, and it seems to carry the implication that crime is a natural and universal category.
- To define deviance as any behaviour that departs from normal behaviour immediately begs the question of what normal behaviour is and how (and by whom) it can be identified and defined. Furthermore, the idea of normal behaviour is usually made in contrast to behaviour which is 'abnormal'. Abnormal behaviour is often considered to be a sign of disease or illness. Are we to define crime and deviant behaviour as a type of illness?

Sociologists are highly sceptical of the ideas that crime and deviance are natural and universal, or forms of illness.

Can sociologists offer anything better?

Sociologists argue that crime and deviance are both socially-constructed concepts. This means that our ideas about crime and deviance vary between different cultures and different periods in history. Neither crime nor deviance are natural or universal categories. This means that our views of what is criminal or deviant behaviour are influenced by the values and norms of the society we live in and which we have absorbed through socialisation. The evidence from cross-cultural studies and historical studies of our own society shows instead that views about what counts as criminal or deviant are remarkably flexible.

- Homosexuality, for example, was a criminal offence in the UK until 1963, whereas in 1994 the age of consent for homosexual relations was reduced to 18. Michel Foucault's historical study of sexuality (1977) is one of many studies which have mapped out changing attitudes to sexuality, showing that homosexuality and other practices have been tolerated in different societies at different times.

- Steven Box (1983) points out that our own society does not have entirely consistent views about the criminality or deviant nature of killing. He argues that only some types of killing are counted as murder. In other cases where death results from human actions, such as drink driving or work-related fatalities due to inadequate safety standards, the actions are not defined as murder.

Deviance can also depend very much on the situation where actions occur. Ken Plummer (1979), for example, distinguishes **situational deviance**. For example, walking about naked is deviant in a shopping centre, but not in a sports centre changing room.

Lastly, it is important to understand that some actions can be criminal but not deviant, and some may be deviant but not criminal, such as smoking cannabis, shouting in a library. The fact that these distinctions can occur, reinforces the notion that crime and deviance are socially constructed, and therefore that relationships of power are important in determining whether an action is deviant or criminal.

How are definitions of crime and deviance maintained?

These social definitions of crime and deviance are upheld through the process of social control. Sociologists argue that all of our behaviour is subject to **sanctions**. Sanctions are responses to our behaviour, but they may be rewards or punishments. The general idea is that people are less inclined to act in ways which are punished and more likely to follow rules when they are rewarded in some way.

There are two types of sanctions, formal and informal. Formal sanctions are imposed by governments or legitimate political authorities, whereas informal sanctions are imposed by other groups, such as friends or neighbours. Thus all our actions are locked into a web of relationships which guide our behaviour in terms of society's norms and values.

Conclusion

- Crime and deviance are socially-constructed categories.
- Crime and deviance are not universal categories of behaviour. They change according to time and place.
- Power relationships determine which actions are defined as criminal or deviant.

For consideration

1. Which social groups have the power to define actions as criminal or deviant?

2. Many young people now smoke cannabis. Does this mean it is not deviant?

✳ Key Idea

It is vital to grasp the idea that crime and deviance are socially-constructed categories. Sociologists argue that crime and deviance vary considerably between different societies and different times. This indicates that crime and deviance must be seen as being defined by social judgements and reactions to people's actions, rather than to any universal quality of the nature of an action. This concept allows sociologists to distance themselves from moral judgements about crime and deviance.

✓ Top Exam Hint

It is vital to grasp the idea that crime and deviance are socially constructed categories. Sociologists argue that crime and deviance vary considerably between different societies and different times. This indicates that crime and deviance must be seen as being defined by social judgements and reactions to people's actions, rather than to any universal quality of the nature of an action. This concept allows sociologists to distance themselves from moral judgements about crime and deviance.

☐ Key Fact

According to the 2002 British Crime Survey, 52 per cent of all people between the ages of 20 and 24 have smoked cannabis.

Are criminals born or made?

1. Trococéphale violateur, de Ravenne.

2. Voleur milanais, condamné 13 fois.

Lombroso started a long tradition in criminology which maintained that criminals were abnormal, and either psychologically or physiologically different to 'normal people'. This view is no longer considered as offering a satisfactory explanation of crime.

∞ Classic Study

Lombroso's study, *L'uomo Delinqente*, was based on phrenology – the belief that character could be assessed from the shape of the skull. The study aimed to show how abnormal features were linked to criminal behaviour. Lombroso believed that criminals were less evolved than 'normal' people, and even argued, for example, that female prostitutes could be identified through the possession of prehensile feet (the big toe widely separated from the other toes).

☐ Key Facts

- Mednick's sample consisted of 14,427 adoptions in Denmark between 1924 and 1947.
- Lombroso's sample included some 3839 living criminals, and he examined the crania (skulls) of 383 dead criminals.

What does this mean?

It has been argued that some people are naturally inclined to be criminals. This means that it is part of their nature, or that they have a 'criminal gene'. An alternative view is that people are shaped much more by the environment that they are raised and live in, and it is this which will determine whether they turn out to be a criminal. The debate between these two views is called the 'nature/nurture debate'.

What evidence is there that criminality is innate?

A study published in 1876 claimed that criminality was the result of biological factors and could be identified through characteristic physical features. This research was conducted by an Italian doctor, Cesare Lombroso, who studied a large sample of prisoners as well as anatomical samples. Although this might seem far-fetched and old-fashioned, the idea that biological factors are important in determining whether a person will exhibit criminal behaviour persists today. Psychologist Sarnof Mednick (Mednick et al 1987) has argued that studies of adopted children appear to show that criminality can be inherited. Mednick argues that findings from his study of adoption in Denmark show that adopted children's behaviour shows more similarity to their biological parents than to their adopted parents, especially where there is persistent offending behaviour.

What criticisms have been made of this evidence?

Several important methodological criticisms have been made of these research studies.

- Lombroso's study used a sample drawn from the prison population. This cannot be used to generalise on the wider population. There may have been similar proportions in the wider population with the physical features which Lombroso identifies and associates with criminality, and this would mean that the association was a false one. Lombroso's study therefore cannot be said to be representative of either the whole population or the whole criminal population.
- Mednick's study provides some interesting findings, based on a very large sample. However, this only measures the relationship between parents and children in terms of recorded crime rates. It may therefore not provide a valid measure of criminality, since many crimes go unrecorded.

Are criminals born or made?

In trying to answer this question, it is worth noting that Mednick's views have sometimes been distorted in textbook accounts of his work. Mednick has commented that an understanding of *'biological factors **and their interaction with social variables** may make useful contributions to our understanding of the causes of criminal behaviour'* (1987, page 91 editorial emphasis). This comment indicates that both biological and social factors have a role to play in explaining crime and deviance.

As geneticist Steve Jones has argued, genes should not be seen as determining our behaviour (1994). Genes are complex sets of 'chemical instructions' which shape (rather than determine) our lives, our physical characteristics, and our behaviour; but they do this in interaction with the environment. Individuals may have genetic coding that predisposes them to be taller than other individuals, or likely to develop certain diseases, but precisely how tall they will grow, or whether a disease will develop, will also depend on environmental factors.

Steven Rose argues that biology, psychology and sociology offer different levels of explanation (1984). Biology and psychology can tell us about why particular individuals are predisposed to commit crime. Crime, though, is socially defined and constructed, and to understand how this happens we have to examine social factors, and not see crime as just the activities of unusual, abnormal or sick people, nor reduce it to an individual phenomenon. These characteristics may typify some crimes, but not all, nor are they exclusive to certain social groups. What sociologists emphasise is how an action, such as killing, can be seen in very different ways depending on when and where it takes place, and who does it.

Conclusion

- Crime is clearly caused by both biological and social factors.
- The task for sociologists is to examine how crime and criminals are socially constructed.
- Explaining crime only in terms of individual factors is reductionist.

✳ Key Ideas

- Reductionism (see also section 2.8) is a form of explanation which boils the causes of an event down to one factor. Sociologists are highly critical of the idea that the cause of crime can be reduced to an explanation in terms of the discrete characteristics of an individual, for example, 'he was insane', 'he cannot control his temper'. This does not explain the regularity and structured nature of what we know about crime, for example, the relationships between different groups as indicated by crime statistics.

- The nature/nurture debate is crucial to understanding a sociological approach to crime. Sociologists generally claim that human behaviour cannot be reduced to and understood in terms of biological drives or instincts. Any such influences of biology are always developed in a culture or a social context. Therefore, attempts to explain human behaviour only in biological terms will never provide a complete answer.

For consideration

1. If criminality is innate, what are the implications for the punishment of criminals?

2. Are biological explanations of the relationship between crime and gender, age and ethnicity, convincing?

Do official statistics give a true picture of crime?

What does this mean?

Official statistics on crime are collected by the government through the recording of crimes by the police and courts and through the British Crime Survey (BCS), a large-scale victim survey. The problem with both of these sources is that they lack validity and obscure the true extent of crime – the so-called 'dark figure' (unknown) or the 'tip of the iceberg' (only one-seventh of an iceberg is visible on the surface, the rest is hidden beneath the water). Sociologists therefore need to understand how crime statistics are constructed in order to evaluate how useful they are as sources of data.

What problems are there with using official statistics?

The problem with police recording of crime is that it only shows 'crimes known to the police'. This depends both on police activity and the public's willingness to report crime. Clearly the police are unable to identify all criminal offences, but research by Holdaway shows that the police work selectively (1983). In doing this they reflect public views of crime as well as shaping and reinforcing public attitudes. Holdaway conducted participant observation on the occupational culture and working practices of the police. He found that the occupational culture led to police officers creating their own view of the priority and seriousness of offences and a strong belief that police officers had the right to exercise 'discretion' over how they dealt with offences. In practice, Holdaway argues that this also means that officers would apply the law in ways which were to their own benefit. This might mean for example that minor offences were neglected, possibly to avoid extra paperwork, or arrests were made in order to be able to return to the police station instead of remaining outside in unpleasant conditions. Senior officers may try to exercise control over these processes, but they too will have 'discretion'. The whole process of policing therefore contributes towards the social construction of crime.

The public too will not have a simple response to crime. People may have many reasons for not reporting crime to the police, ranging from a lack of trust to a belief that a crime is too minor or can best be dealt with privately, or they may not realise that they have been a victim of a crime.

So, crime is socially constructed and this is why official statistics lack validity and only show us a part of the picture about crime. Official statistics possibly tell us more about this process of construction than about crime itself.

Why do sociologists use official statistics?

Despite these problems, official statistics on crime are still a useful resource as long as they are used critically. Official statistics provide a cheap and easily-available resource, they provide some ability to analyse change over time, and they consist of a large number of cases. Sociologists can therefore gain some insights into crime using this resource. They can combine official statistics with the results from victim surveys and self-report studies to estimate the 'real' rate of crime.

What other methods can sociologists use to measure crime?

There are several other methods that researchers can use in addition to the official crime statistics. The two most important methods are victim surveys and self-report studies. Victim surveys aim to encourage members of the public to reveal whether they have been the victim of a crime and other relevant details, such as why they did not report the crime. Self-report studies attempt to persuade respondents to confess to offences they have committed but which may not be known to the police. There are, however, disadvantages with both of these methods.

- Not all respondents take part in victim surveys, and those who do not may be aware of crimes that would change the overall picture of crime.
- Respondents may not report all crimes for various reasons.
- Views about crime change so people's willingness to report or confess may change over time.

Conclusion

- The picture of crime provided from official statistics lacks validity.
- However, crime statistics can be useful if combined with self-report and victim surveys.
- If official statistics lack validity, then sociological theories of crime and deviance based on such theories may be flawed.

⌐⊕ Classic Study

Hobbs, '*Doing the Business*', 1986: Hobbs argues that there was a reciprocal relationship between the police and people in the East End of London. Hobbs argues that both police and criminals needed each other, and they developed complex relationships involving the trading and bartering of information and favours. This study therefore helps to reinforce the criticisms made of official statistics by showing the context in which they are constructed.

✳ Key Idea

According to official statistics, the typical criminal is young, male, working class, black, poorly educated, and likely to have had a disturbed childhood. However, the implication of this section is that before trying to provide sociological explanations of this, we should consider carefully whether official statistics in fact provide us with a valid picture of crime and criminals.

For consideration

1. If official statistics lack validity, should sociologists avoid using them?
2. What sort of crimes are people likely to report? Why?

The structuralist approach to crime and deviance: functionalism

What does this mean?

Functionalists say that we should look at society as an organic system. This means that all the components or parts of society fulfil a particular function, which helps the whole society to work efficiently and effectively. The classical sociologist, Emile Durkheim, argued that crime actually plays a useful role in maintaining social order, provided it does not reach a harmful level.

What does Durkheim say about crime and deviance?

Durkheim argued that crime increases during periods of rapid social change characterised by anomie (no norms, normlessness). Durkheim therefore suggested that we can best understand crime and deviance by seeing how it is linked to social order. Durkheim claimed that all societies require social order if they are to function effectively. Social order requires rules, laws, and shared norms and values. However, Durkheim recognised that social order is a fragile thing. It would be impossible, he felt, to imagine a society where social order had reached a level such that nobody ever broke the law. Durkheim therefore believed that crime and deviance are inevitable. However, Durkheim also believed that a society without crime would not be very desirable, and he saw crime as having several useful functions in society.

- All societies respond to the breaking of rules and laws by attempts to enforce formal sanctions (punishment), and this leads to collective ideas about social morality being reinforced. This sends out a strong message, which helps to reinforce shared norms and values, and therefore social order.
- In societies where there is very little crime or deviance, there will be little challenging or questioning of social order. Durkheim argues that this is bad, because it can prevent questions about social order and morality being debated and discussed. It also means that social change is less likely, since societies change by responding to challenges and questioning the existing social order.
- Crime and deviance can be seen as providing society with a safety-valve; too much crime and deviance indicates that social integration is too weak, while too little indicates a society where the forces of integration are so strong that they will prevent the challenging of social order and the innovation needed for further evolution.

Durkheim took the view, therefore, that both crime and the punishment of crime were necessary to maintain a healthy society.

✳ Key Idea

Durkheim's belief that crime and deviance are closely related to the regulation of social integration is clearly reflected in this quotation from his book *The Division of Labour in Society*.

'*We can say, without being paradoxical, that punishment is above all designed to act upon law-abiding people. For since it serves to heal wounds inflicted upon the collective sentiments, it can only fulfil this role where such sentiments exist and to the extent that they are active.*'

Source: *Readings from Emile Durkheim*, K Thompson (ed and transl), London, Routledge, page 45.

What does Robert Merton say about crime and deviance?

Not all functionalists would agree completely with the following view of crime and deviance. Robert Merton (1949) argued that functionalists need to pay more attention to inequalities in society. Merton's so-called strain theory argues that, as a result of inequalities, not all social groups will have the same ability to achieve the common cultural goals of a society, so there is a strain (tension) between the cultural goals of a society and the means of achieving them. Merton claims that some groups will have less access to the means of achieving cultural goals by, for example, not having an equal chance of gaining entry to higher education and top professions.

Merton contends that this means that social groups will adapt or respond to cultural goals in different ways, and he identified five main adaptations to common goals.

1. Conformists accept the goals and the means of achieving them.
2. Ritualists lose their belief in the goals, but stick to the means or rules in society.
3. Retreatists withdraw from society having given up on the goals and the means.
4. Innovators accept the goals but reject the means.
5. Rebels reject the means and the goals and replace them with alternative means and goals.

Merton says that crime and deviance are therefore likely to occur when there are unequal opportunities for achieving common social goals. Merton's idea of strain reflects his functionalist approach, since he is claiming that crime and deviance are the result of a lack of balance between goals and the means of achieving them during periods of social change. This reflects the functionalist idea of the **organic analogy**, and the idea that societies have to be based on consensus and harmony if they are to function effectively.

Conclusion

* Functionalists assume that society is based on shared values.
* It is possible that the law could benefit some groups more than others.
* Functionalism neglects actors' reasons for committing crime.

☞ Who is this person?

Robert K Merton (1910–2003) was strongly influenced by functionalists such as Durkheim, and was taught by Talcott Parsons at Harvard University. Merton had a wide range of interests; students may be surprised to learn that he was the originator of the idea of self-fulfilling prophecy (often thought of as an interactionist concept). Merton argued for a more complex notion of functions, including dysfunctions and manifest and latent functions, the last referring to the unintended consequences of actions.

🗩 Key Definition

The functionalist concept of the **'organic analogy'** means that we should examine society as if it is an organism or living being. An analogy is a comparison. Crime can therefore be seen as a disease. However, just as a small amount of a disease can be used to inoculate a body against further infection, so a degree of crime can be useful.

✳ Key Idea

Durkheim's analysis of crime is important, even to sociologists who are not functionalists, because it suggests that crime is created by society. Durkheim shows us that crime is related to social order and social integration, and it varies with them. Crime is therefore not 'natural', it is socially constructed. Other sociologists, for example Marxists, may disagree about how crime is constructed, but they would agree with Durkheim that it is socially constructed.

For consideration

1. Is there a consensus on which crimes help reinforce social order and which do not?

2. What assumptions does Durkheim make about power?

The structuralist approach to crime and deviance: Marxism

Key Facts

The National Prison Survey (Walmsley 1992) found that the prison population of the UK was disproportionately working class:

- 41 per cent of male prisoners had unskilled or partly skilled jobs before coming to prison.

- the proportion of the general UK population with unskilled or partly skilled jobs was 18 per cent.

- 13 per cent of male prisoners were homeless before going to prison.

What does this mean?

Marxist views of crime and deviance, unlike other theories, put a much greater emphasis on the role of economic inequality and inequalities of power in creating crime and deviance. Marxist theory therefore prompts sociologists to examine the political structures and institutions responsible for maintaining law and order, and to raise the question of which social groups control these institutions and which groups benefit most from capitalist law and order.

How does Marxism explain crime and deviance?

In order to understand how Marxism can be applied to explain crime and deviance, it is worth reminding ourselves of some of the key ideas in Marxist theory.

- Marxists argue that capitalist societies consist of two classes with opposing interests. This means that class conflict is an inevitable feature of capitalist societies.
- Marxists claim that the state in capitalist societies always works in the interests of the capitalist ruling class (bourgeoisie).
- The dominant ideas of society are always those of the dominant class (the bourgeoisie).

Taken together, these points lead Marxists to argue that law and order in capitalist society reflects the ideas of the dominant class, and that it is their definitions of crime and deviance which are the dominant ones. Marxists therefore argue, in contrast to functionalists, that law and order does not function to the benefit of everyone in capitalist society. On the contrary, it reflects the interests and views of the dominant social class. It is in fact a form of social control, which enables the bourgeoisie to control and coerce the working class. In the 1970s, Marxist-influenced theories of crime and deviance were particularly popular, and a number of American studies elaborated Marxist views.

Does the law reflect class interests?

David Gordon (1976) argues that law and order fulfils a number of vital functions for capitalist society. Gordon argues that crime comes to be associated with the working classes, and this helps the bourgeoisie to control the working class. Crime is seen to be a working class 'problem' and this helps to justify the need to control them and imprison those who break the law. It also justifies the need for a strong police force and the use of force where necessary. Law breaking in capitalist society is therefore seen to be the result of 'bad' or 'unruly' members of the working class. Gordon argues that this also helpfully distracts attention from the misdeeds of the bourgeoisie.

William Chambliss (1976) and Frank Pearce (1976) echo these views. Chambliss investigated organised crime in Seattle in the 1960s, and argued that most organised crime was controlled by a small elite group that included senior members of the business and political communities and even reached into the police force. While this was going on, though, Chambliss argues that most police time was spent dealing with minor public order offences. Pearce also studied organised crime in the USA and claimed that such crime was conducted on a bigger scale than crimes committed by working-class offenders.

Steven Box (1983) has argued that the implications of views such as these for the way we must view crime are radical. Box argues that law and order in capitalist societies is applied in a highly selective way. Selective law enforcement means that those identified as criminals tend to be predominantly young, male, working class, and, disproportionately, black. Box argues that law and order in capitalist society is a process of mystification, whereby the evils of society are seen to emanate from a small and relatively powerless group. This mystifies the mass of the population, precisely because it identifies crime in such a selective way, while carefully neglecting the crimes of the powerful. This process is one which criminalises certain sections of the population. Crime therefore is ideologically defined, in a highly distorted way, which acts as a powerful mechanism of social control.

The idea of 'criminalisation' refers to the way that particular activities come to be defined as criminal. The term can also be applied to the activities of particular groups of people. Box and others influenced by the Marxist approach, consider that it is the working classes and many of their activities which are criminalised in capitalist society. Their cultural values are also likely to be criminalised, and the identities which they can construct are more likely to be stigmatised criminal identities. Those from other social groups committing similar activities are less likely to be criminalised (for example, dope smoking in inner city areas such as Brixton has been policed quite strictly, whereas this activity taking place in middle-class suburbs or student halls of residence does not receive similar police attention).

Conclusion

Use these points to evaluate Marxist approaches to crime and deviance.

* Marxist theory is economically **reductionist**.
* Marxism neglects race and gender.
* Consider what empirical evidence there is to support the Marxist approach.

For consideration

1. Identify working-class activities that have been criminalised.

2. What is the evidence for selective law enforcement?

☀ Key Idea

The idea of criminalisation acknowledges that crime is socially constructed, and suggests that members of some social groups are likely to be seen by others as more prone to having a criminal identity. Marxist-inspired sociologists have argued that the criminal justice system criminalises the working class, and others, such as Hall, suggest that it also criminalises ethnic minorities. Criminality can therefore also be 'racialised'.

● Synoptic Link

Marxism is a structural theory, so in evaluating this approach you need to remind yourself about the importance of the structure/action debate. You can consider whether Marxist accounts need to give more weight to the explanations people give for their actions and to the idea that people have agency (freedom). Apply these points to the studies discussed here and those in section 2.9, such as Hall's.

66 99 Key Definition

The term **reductionism** refers to arguments which reduce complex social processes to one or a limited number of causes. Marxism is thus often criticised for 'economic reductionism', that is, reducing the cause of crime to economic inequality.

How is neo-Marxism different from Marxism when discussing crime?

What does this mean?

Marxism has been criticised for appearing to say that all crime has an economic cause and is related to the persistence of economic inequality and class conflict. Marxism was also criticised for its economic determinism – the idea that all our actions are caused by economic factors and that people have no free will. These criticisms have led some sociologists to try and overcome the weaknesses of Marxist explanations of crime.

How have Neo-Marxists explained crime?

A group of sociologists based at the Centre for Contemporary Cultural Studies at the University of Birmingham have argued that Marxists need to pay much more attention to factors such as culture and ideology. Stuart Hall's study, *Policing the Crisis* (1978), is one of the most well-known examples of this version of neo-Marxism.

These sociologists have been strongly influenced by the ideas of Italian Marxist Antonio Gramsci. Gramsci was aware of the need to address the criticism that Marxism was economically deterministic. He developed the idea that capitalism did not simply depend on the use of force or economic power to prevent the working class from rebelling. Instead Gramsci argued that the role of ideology and **hegemony** was crucial in legitimating the capitalist system. In capitalist society, the dominant or hegemonic ideas are capitalist ideas. These ideas are therefore widely accepted by the working class.

Hall used Gramsci's theory of hegemony to argue that the moral panic over 'mugging' that arose in the 1970s was amplified by the media, and was in fact a reflection of the economic crisis at the time (during the 1970s Britain's economy declined following the long post-war boom). The moral panic soon took on racial undertones following a focus on certain stories in the press, so that mugging became linked with black youths. The panic distracted the mass of the population from the economic crisis, providing another social problem to concentrate on and a group that was politically weak was then blamed for the existence of that problem. The whole process therefore worked as a sort of ideological smokescreen, distracting people's attention from the more serious issues, and created a 'myth' of black criminality (see section 2.16).

Gramsci argued that there are always struggles over ideas and culture in capitalist society, and ideas are always being contested. Sociologists such as John Clarke (1975) have further developed these views, arguing that working-class crime and deviance is best seen as an oppositional subculture, as those in marginal social positions respond to their position by rejecting some of the values of the wider, capitalist society.

❝❞ Key Definition

By **hegemony** Gramsci was referring to the ability of the state to persuade the masses into believing or consenting to the rules and values of the elite that dominated them.

How else has Marxism been developed in order to explain crime?

In a book entitled *The New Criminology* (1973), Ian Taylor, Paul Walton and Jock Young tried to adapt Marxist views to changing circumstances in the 1970s. They attempted to maintain Marxism's emphasis on the importance of economic factors, but also wanted to argue that criminals were free to choose whether to commit crime or not. The authors wished to make use of insights from interactionist theory and they believed that it was important to consider the role of non-economic factors. Thus they contended that there were several key elements of any sociological explanation of crime:

1. Inequalities in wealth and power.
2. The factors and circumstances leading to the decision to commit a crime.
3. The meaning that deviance has for the person committing the act.
4. How other members of society react to the deviant act.
5. An understanding of which social groups have the power to make the law.
6. The effects of labels and labelling.
7. The authors emphasise that all of these elements, and the relationship between them, must be studied in order to create a complete theoretical explanation.

Points 3, 4, and 6 are drawn from interactionism, while points 1, 2, and 5 reflect the Marxist approach to crime and deviance. *The New Criminology* (sometimes called 'critical criminology', see section 2.12) aimed to provide a complete theory of crime and deviance by combining the strengths of both Marxism and interactionist theory. In doing this, the 'New Criminology' approach argued that sociologists had to be critical of the established capitalist order that created the conditions which allow crime to develop, that is social inequality and deprivation. The New Criminologists were arguing that criminals were, in a way, rebelling and protesting against an unequal society, where there was one law for the rich and another for the poor. They argued that this allowed the crimes of the powerful to be neglected.

Conclusion

Use these points to evaluate neo-Marxist theories.

- What evidence is there for interpreting crime as a way of resisting capitalism?
- Some critics (see section 2.16) would say that the high rate of black street crime in the 1970s was not a myth.
- Neo-Marxism appears to say little about how crime and deviance are gendered.

For consideration

1. Do criminals try to justify their crimes, and if so, how?
2. Can criminals' justifications of crime be seen as explanations of crime?

⌐⊙ Classic Study

Policing the Crisis (1978) is regarded as a key text in Marxist explanations of crime and race. It is a highly theoretical account of the development of the moral panic over 'mugging' by young black men in the 1970s. The study draws on Cohen's theory of moral panics (see section 2.3) as well as Gramsci and uses secondary media sources and statistics to place the events of the 1970s into the social and historical context of race relations in Britain. Despite its sophistication, critics might point to its relative lack of empirical detail.

● Synoptic Link

Paul Willis's study, *Learning to Labour*, is a good example of subcultural Marxism, and is an excellent study to use as a synoptic link between crime and education. Willis's study shows how a group of working-class boys actively create an 'anti-school subculture'. This is an act of deviance. Willis explains this deviance in terms of a subcultural resistance to the dominating authority of school and work.

◆ What, when and why?

The development of the New Criminology was a response to the criticisms made of the more standard versions of Marxism in the 1960s and 1970s but also to the overwhelmingly positivist study of crime in the UK in the late 1960s. The authors of *The New Criminology* were also involved in the creation of the National Deviancy Conference, formed in 1968, which aimed to provide a sociological alternative to the functionalist-inspired views of crime dominant amongst policy-makers and researchers at that time.

✓ Top Exam Hint

Where it is relevant to the set questions, it is a very good idea to show that you have a high level of knowledge and understanding by indicating that there are several types of Marxism. You can say that this shows that theoretical ideas are always changing. Willis provides a good example of a Marxist trying to resolve the structure/action debate. Remember, no single theory can provide all the answers.

2.10 | What do interactionists say about crime and deviance?

✳ Key Idea

'Social groups create deviance by making the rules whose infraction constitutes deviance, and by applying these rules to particular people and labelling them as outsiders. From this point of view, deviance is not a quality of the act the person commits, but rather a consequence of the application of others of the rules and sanctions to an offender. The deviant is one to whom the label has successfully been applied; deviant behaviour is behaviour that people so label.'

(Becker 1963, page 9)

Howard Becker is one of the key sociologists in the field of labelling theory, and has conducted research on medical students, teachers, drug users and jazz musicians.

What does this mean?

Interactionist theory focuses on how people's actions are motivated and the meaning that social action has for those participating in it. As such it offers a very different view of crime and deviance to that offered by functionalism and Marxism. They are structural theories and see crime as the result of forces that people have no control over. Interactionists, by contrast, argue that social order is constantly being negotiated and constructed. This means that what counts as crime and deviance are much more open to negotiation.

How do interactionists define crime and deviance?

Howard Becker has made one of the most important contributions to understanding crime and deviance through the development of **labelling** theory. Becker's theory starts with the assertion that no act is criminal or deviant until it has been labelled as such. So, whether an action is criminal or deviant has nothing to do with the act itself, but has much more to do with the social reaction to the act. Becker therefore agrees with the idea that crime and deviance are socially constructed, but he interprets this in a much more radical way than structural theorists. For labelling theorists, crime and deviance is much more about the social reaction to certain types of behaviour, rather than about the meaning that the activity has for the person who commits the act.

What does this tell us about crime and deviance?

Labelling theory provides sociologists with a number of fresh insights into crime and deviance.

Becker's studies show that being labelled as a deviant can have important consequences for a person's identity. If the label of criminal or deviant is successfully applied, the negative label becomes a master status, which cancels out the other statuses that an individual has. This can effectively exclude the individual from many social activities, such as work. Excluded from mainstream society, deviants find support with other similar individuals. This is likely to reinforce a deviant lifestyle, and the development of further deviant activities may lead to a deviant career. All of these processes can culminate in the creation of deviant subcultures.

How can we evaluate labelling theory?

Many criticisms have been made of labelling theory. The following are just a few of the most important ones.

- It does not explain why people commit deviant acts in the first instance.
- It is deterministic (denies that people have free will and the power to act).
- It neglects power and social structure and therefore cannot explain why certain types of people are regularly and repeatedly identified as criminal.

British sociologist Ken Plummer has defended labelling theory against these criticisms (1979). As he reasons, labelling theory is not a perfect theory, but it can provide convincing responses to all of the above points. First, labelling theorists identify individual deviant acts as ways of gaining status and self-esteem. The theory is not deterministic, as it puts great stress on the way that labels are always the outcome of negotiation. Certainly, concepts such as self-fulfilling prophecy can be interpreted as being deterministic, but they can be used more cautiously, without involving that implication. The most serious criticism is that labelling theorists neglect questions of power and structure. Undoubtedly, as action theorists, interactionists are bound to place less emphasis on action than structure. However, as Plummer has pointed out, the whole point of labelling theory is to show the inequalities in the operation of the law, and it was labelling theory that helped sociologists begin to raise questions about this.

Is interactionism still relevant?

Interactionist theory was developed in the 1960s and 70s. In contemporary sociology very few sociologists would wish to align themselves narrowly to only one perspective. Interactionism therefore has a more general influence in contemporary sociological research, as researchers synthesise a range of theoretical and methodological influences. However, Interactionism and labelling theories are still highly relevant in contemporary society and policies. Interactionist theory implies that crime would be reduced through declassifying certain types of behaviour. Equally, removing the criminal 'label' by cautioning rather than arresting would avoid imposing a self-fulfilling prophecy. A good example of this can be seen in the 2004 reclassification of cannabis from a Class B to a Class C drug in Britain. This means that although you can still be arrested in some instances (ie using cannabis near schools or dealing), police now 'presume against arrest' for personal cannabis use or possession of small amounts.

On the other hand recent public attempts to 'name and shame' offenders, such as the *News of the World's* 2000 campaign to make paedophiles publicly known following the death of 8-year old Sarah Payne, can be seen as examples of continuing labelling. A recent study by Sarah Thornton (1995) into club cultures however, examines the idea of labelling in a new light, suggesting that sometimes people actively seek to acquire a negative label because it provides status amongst deviant sub-cultural groups (see also section 2.23).

Conclusion

- Crime and deviance can only be understood by examining how people define actions as criminal or deviant.
- What counts as crime is continually being negotiated and constructed.
- Criminality or deviance is not a characteristic of any activity. Actions

For consideration

1. Can labelling theory tell us why some people are more likely to be labelled than others?

2. Would it be useful to synthesise labelling with a structural theory? If so, why and which one?

✎ Classic Study

Becker's study *The Outsiders* (1963) introduced a range of important concepts and approaches to sociologists in the 1960s. The book consists of a selection of essays explaining the interactionist view that deviance is best thought of in terms of social reaction to actions. The book includes a famous study of 'dance musicians' and how people 'learn' to become marijuana users. The book gives some indications on how Becker conducted his research but, like much interactionist work, positivists may criticise it for its apparent lack of rigour and openness to subjective interpretation.

∞ Methods Link

Sociologists interested in labelling theory and interactionism take an Interpretivist approach to social behaviour and favour studying on the micro level. This means that they will use qualitative methods such as observation and informal interviews. Of course, this also leads their work to be criticised as being unrepresentative, subjective, and liable to distortion through the interviewer/Hawthorne effect.

✓ Top Exam Hint

If you are evaluating labelling theory it is a good idea to link it to the structure/action debate. A good point to make is that the weaknesses of labelling theory in relation to power and structure simply reflect its position in that debate. This does not mean that sociologists such as Becker ignore power and structure, just that they explain it more at a micro level.

| # What do feminists say about crime and deviance?

Key Definitions

- **Malestream:** a play on words hinting at the word 'mainstream'. Feminists feel that mainstream sociology is male dominated – conducted by and focusing on men.

- **Gender blind:** unaware of differences based on gender.

- **Essentialism:** the idea that there is some essential core of fixed or natural characteristics defining certain types of people, either on the basis of gender, or class, or ethnicity. For example, the 'essential' man is tall and strong, and heterosexual. This form of thinking helps to obscure the reality that social characteristics such as class, ethnicity and gender are socially constructed and helps to justify the social exclusion of those who do not conform.

◆ **What, when and why?**

Heidensohn argues that malestream sociology neglected gender for a long time for several reasons. Sociology has been dominated by men (and in many ways still is) who have set a 'malestream' research agenda and who have 'vicariously identified' with male criminals (this implies that they have gained excitement by studying male criminals). In addition, a positivistic approach to sociology and criminology has not encouraged a questioning of women's role in crime, since it seemed clear that few women were involved. The influx of more women sociologists, from the late 1960s onwards, however, has meant that these assumptions are gradually beginning to be challenged.

What does this mean?

Feminists have argued that women's role in crime has traditionally been treated in two ways, both of which have been unhelpful. Firstly, **malestream** sociology has been **gender blind**. It has therefore ignored the role of women in crime, either as victims or as perpetrators. Secondly, many malestream theories have tended to explain female deviance as the result of physiological or psychological abnormalities or illness, offering an **essentialist** view of women. This has simply helped to reinforce stereotypes of female offenders as, for example, evil monsters or fallen women. Feminists have therefore argued that new theories are needed to explain women's role in crime and deviance.

Malestream theories

Feminists have argued that all malestream theories are incapable of fully explaining the relationship between gender and crime.

- Functionalist theory argues that gender differences in criminal behaviour are the result of differential socialisation (sex-role socialisation). This seems unconvincing, though, as it cannot explain why all men do not become criminals, and why some women do become involved in crime.
- Marxist theory, when linked with feminist insights, offers a useful focus on the economic causes of crime and women's economic position in society. However, not all crime has economic causes. Marxist-based explanations tend to neglect the cultural origins and aspects of patriarchy.
- Labelling theory also offers insights, e.g. women may be less likely to be labelled deviant, but it neglects the structural sources of power.

What alternative explanations do feminists offer?

Feminists argue for the need to develop new theories of crime and deviance which focus on gender as a key explanatory variable.

Heidensohn argues that women as criminals have been given less priority in the study of crime and deviance for a number of reasons. Traditional female crime, such as shoplifting, is less interesting than male crime. Female crime may be less of a social threat as it tends to be less violent and official statistics show a big gap between the number of male and female offences, so it is of less interest.

Heidensohn is influenced by control theory (1986, 2002) and has argued that in patriarchal society women are controlled ideologically. As such, sociologists should investigate why women conform more, and why they are less criminal. Patriarchal ideologies operate at home, in public and at work (see section 2.17).

Pat Carlen, while also influenced by control theory, suggests that it remains important to explain why some women do become involved in crime (1988). She argues that working-class women in particular are required to make 'the class deal' and 'the gender deal'. 'The class deal' is the idea that rewards come to those who conform and work. 'The gender deal' is the idea that rewards come to those who conform to the feminine role that of the housewife and mother, subordinate to the male breadwinner. Carlen argues that women will conform to these 'deals', but this is most likely for women brought up in 'respectable' working-class homes with a male breadwinner and a female carer.

Women as victims

Although women should not be solely portrayed as victims, sociologists influenced by radical feminism, such as Dobash and Dobash 1980, Radford 1987 and Stanko 1988, have suggested that the law is biased against women. As a result of this, sociologists have ignored issues such as domestic violence and male violence in general. Heidensohn refers to this as gendered crime, where women are the victims of men, and where such crimes often go unreported. This has led to the 'normalisation' of male violence, while the scale of it is underestimated. Moreover, patriarchal ideology constructs women not always as the victims, but rather as the causes of such violence (for example, 'she was asking for it'). This leads to the control of women's use of public space by, for instance, creating informal social rules about where women can go, at what times, and what they should be wearing. The fear of violence therefore has a powerful control over women's lives.

Contemporary Feminism and Crime

Lorraine Gelsthorpe (1997) can be broadly described as a 'liberal feminist' and her recent research demonstrates the way that magistrates can tend to view female offenders in terms of the categories of 'troubled' or 'troublesome' and therefore blame women for men's crimes (i.e., the wearing of certain clothing may 'invite' rape or 'bad' behaviour may incite abuse) (see section2.17).

Sociologists influenced by postmodernism, such as Carol Smart (1995), have argued that sociologists need to focus on 'deconstructing' feminine identities and the dominant views of crime in order to show how they are socially constructed. She questions how feminine identities are constructed and how these relate to criminal activity. However, critics would argue that this is contradictory; postmodernists claim that there is no such thing as truth and that no general theories are possible – yet they seem to be offering one themselves.

Conclusion

Feminist contributions are valuable for several reasons.

- They demonstrate the importance of gender as an explanatory variable.
- They demonstrate the role of patriarchal ideologies in shaping (biasing) the way crime is socially constructed.
- A focus on gender should involve studying femininity *and* masculinity. Recent studies by Connell (1995) and Messerschmidt (1993) have attempted to do this.

For consideration

1. Are feminist sociologists biased?
2. Is a total theory of crime possible?

✳ Key Idea

Sociologists such as Campbell (1981) have argued that 'chivalry' exists within the criminal justice system, meaning that women receive less harsh punishments for criminal activity, often leading to cautions rather than imprisonment (see section 2.17).

∞ Methods Link

Pat Carlen conducted her research with a sample of 39 females with convictions using unstructured interviews. Carlen's own identity as a woman would have given her various advantages in conducting the research. Bear in mind, though, that this is a small sample and so questions of representativeness are raised. Also, while feminists have argued that there are advantages to feminist-conducted research, there are also threats to validity involved, such as interviewer effect.

☐ Key Fact

Official statistics of crime, such as the British Crime Survey, show a large difference between male and female fear of crime. The 2002/3 BCS showed, for example, that one quarter of women were 'very worried' about being raped or physically attacked and women were four times more likely to worry about being attacked at night than men. This therefore reinforces the traditional view of the family.

✓ Top Exam Hint

Gender involves examining both masculinity and femininity, as both are defined in contrast to each other. Use these points and the following information to evaluate feminist explanations of crime. Connell argues that there are many masculine identities and only some are criminal identities. Messerschmidt argues that not all males have the same opportunities to achieve the dominant status of normative hegemonic masculinity. Those excluded from the usual means of achieving this, for example career success, may opt for a subordinate form of masculinity based on opposition to dominant norms, for example, it may put a higher value on physical toughness.

◆ **What, when and why?**

An unusual mixture of New Left realist and Right realist thinking is reflected in Labour's slogan 'Tough on crime, tough on the causes of crime'. This was developed by Tony Blair in the early 1990s (Blair T, 1993) at a time when crime rates were rising despite the policies (considered harsh by some) of a Conservative government which aimed to reduce crime. Labour's slogan enabled them to sound simultaneously tough and progressive.

❝❞ Key Definition

Marginalisation is a term used by sociologists to refer to the way some groups in society are disadvantaged either culturally or economically. This deprivation (lack) is said to place such groups in an inferior position compared with other social groups. Some sociologists argue that groups in such social positions may develop distinctive subcultures.

☞ Who is this person?

Jock Young (born 1942) has been a key figure in British criminology. In the 1970s he was one of the co-authors of *The New Criminology*, and in the 1980s he was a co-author of other publications which led to the development of New Left realism. Apparently, Young's views on crime were affected when he witnessed a particularly unpleasant assault on the underground railway in London. There is some tension between the two approaches, and Young's shift shows that sociologists can change their views in the light of experience.

What does this mean?

Realist approaches to crime were developed in the 1980s when crime appeared to be rapidly increasing. There are two versions of realism: Left Realism and Right Realism. These reflect different political and sociological approaches to crime. Left wing views in politics are those which are associated with a broadly socialist outlook on life, and put a particular emphasis on equality. Right wing views are usually associated with a broadly conventional or 'conservative' outlook. They emphasise the need for authority, order and hierarchy, and generally view social change as disruptive and negative. They also argue for the need to present 'real' solutions to a real problem,

What was New Left realism?

New Left realism developed as a critical response to the New Criminologists (see section 2.9). The New Left Realists (NLRs) argued that the New Criminologists had romanticised crime, portraying crime as the justifiable response of oppressed working-class people desperately trying to survive in an unequal society. The NLRs argued that this was a highly prejudiced view of crime, which neglected the harsh realities of crime.

One of the key NLR authors was Jock Young, who had also co-authored *The New Criminology*. In the 1980s Young became disenchanted with what he saw as 'Left idealist' views of crime. Young argued that such views were based on the assumption that crime would simply not occur in a more equal society. This led the 'Left idealist' criminologists to argue that the only solution to crime was the creation of a socialist society. Young and his fellow NLRs argued that, as the creation of a socialist society was highly unlikely in 1980s Britain, the task for sociologists was to develop a more realistic understanding of crime. Young argued that sociologists should provide practical policy recommendations to reduce and prevent crime.

The New Left Realists believed that crime was the result of relative deprivation, **marginalisation**, and the development of subcultures, but they made the following key claims about the nature of crime.

- Street crime was a real social problem, and official statistics were broadly correct in showing that most crime was committed by young, black, working-class men.
- It is young working-class men who are predominantly the perpetrators of crime, and, at the same time, their victims are usually other working-class people. Crime is not necessarily a working-class struggle against capitalism and should not be 'romanticised' as a political protest.
- The majority of solved crimes are reported by the public, yet police clear up rates have not risen alongside rising crime rates, leading to public distrust of the police system. This leads to a reduced flow of information between the public and the police.

- Distrust of the police and fear of crime can lead to a rise in actual crime, as the public fear rises, presence on the streets and willingness to testify lowers, and crime becomes easier to commit. This crime is then exacerbated by its portrayal in the media.

The policy recommendations of the New Left realists moved far away from the idea of reducing inequalities, and suggested developing community organisations in the administration of criminal justice through citizens' juries and neighbourhood-watch type schemes. Police relations with the community should also be developed to improve the flow of information.

What is Right realism?

At around the same time that the New Left realist view was being developed, other sociologists with a more right-wing approach to politics were developing Right realism. These sociologists believed that crime rates were rising as society was fragmenting due to the decline of community and a consequent lack of respect for authority.

James Q. Wilson (1982) argues that crime occurs as a result of a rational choice or calculation. Individuals will be likely to commit crime if the benefits of the crime outweigh the disadvantages or costs. This does not mean that harsh punishments will not act as a deterrent; what counts is the likelihood of being caught. Wilson is therefore arguing that criminals make a rational choice as to whether to commit crime. Wilson has also joined forces with New Right advocate Richard Hernstein (who has worked with Charles Murray) to argue that some individuals are innately more likely to commit crime. This seems to suggest that biological or natural factors have a key role, though Wilson and Hernstein argue that socialisation and parenting are a vital influence. If children who are inclined towards criminal activity are not disciplined early in life, Wilson and Hernstein believe that it is more likely that they will become involved in criminal activity. This carries echoes of Murray's arguments about 'welfare dependency' and the development of anti-social cultures among the poor. This theory has some similarities with control theory, but the emphasis on the ability of criminals to make rational choices and the idea of an innate predisposition towards crime are features which make it distinctive. (See also What, when and why margin box.)

Conclusion

Both Left and Right realism have had a strong influence on law and order policies introduced by Labour governments elected in 1997 and 2001. However, both views are open to similar criticisms.

- Do official statistics provide a generally accurate picture of the scale and nature of crime?
- Both views neglect the crimes of the powerful.
- Both views (arguably) neglect the role of inequality in creating crime.

For consideration

1. Is the NLR view closer to Merton's view of crime than Marx's?

2. Is it acceptable for sociologists to change their views?

☐ Key Fact

The Policy Studies Institute found in a 1983 study that 75 per cent of young black Londoners felt police fabricated evidence, and 82 per cent thought violence was used against suspects.

☀ Key Idea

New Left realists also argued that crime is not equally distributed and not everyone is likely to become a victim. By speaking to victims, sociologists can find out why these people are targets for crime. In doing so, sociologists can uncover the relationships between the age, gender and ethnicity of the perpetrator and the victim.

∞ Methods Link

New Left and Right realists both assume that official statistics provide a broadly accurate picture of crime. This is contested by sociologists who remain influenced by a more radical approach. Here we can see once again how sociologist's values shape their methods and how these in turn both reflect and shape their view of crime.

✓ Top Exam Hint

It can be argued that both types of realist theory neglect the crimes of the powerful and white-collar crime, due to their overriding focus on 'street crime'. Crime committed by working-class offenders is real enough, but the point made by those like Steven Box, that law enforcement is selective, still remains the case.

Is crime just a different route to common goals?

- A **subculture** is a group which shares some of the norms and values of mainstream culture, but which adapts and distorts those values in order to symbolise their rejection of mainstream norms and values. Groups develop oppositional subcultures as a collective response to the problems which they experience.

- **Illegitimate opportunity structure**: Deviance is a collective solution to problems imposed by society. This means that certain individuals and groups are denied access to the goals of society and some form their own opportunity structures because they cannot access legitimate opportunities.

- **Techniques of neutralisation**: Matza uses the term 'techniques of neutralisation' to refer to the excuses people use to justify what the wider society sees as deviant or criminal acts.

✳ Key Idea

Cohen argued that although working-class males want to achieve the same goals as the rest of society, their access to these goals is restricted by society. This can be seen through education where working-class pupils may be excluded from receiving an education because the language structures used are middle-class (for example, see section 3.19). Equally, interactionists such as Keddie (1971) argue that teachers base their judgement on what is a good student on what they think is 'ideal' rather than on performance. As such, they teach in a different way depending on what set or stream pupils are placed in. Cohen argues that subcultures form as working-class boys reject these values and turn to crime to achieve 'success'.

What does this mean?

Functionalist explanations of crime are based on the idea that crime and deviance will increase when shared culture and social controls are weakened. However, some functionalists have argued that there is not simply one set of shared values. They argue that all societies will contain groups who develop their own distinctive **subcultures**. Such groups will share some of the values of the mainstream culture, but they will develop some of their own values. These groups are called subcultures.

What do functionalist subcultural theorists say about crime and deviance?

The work of American sociologists Walter Miller (1962), Cloward and Ohlin (1961) and Albert Cohen (1955), provide good illustrations of the functionalist subcultural approach. All of these sociologists were influenced by Robert Merton's approach to crime and deviance (see section 2.7), but unlike Merton, they did not agree that there was one set of cultural values that all deviants adapted to.

- Walter Miller argued that what he called the 'lower class', in contrast to Merton's view, did have a distinctive set of norms and values which set them apart from the rest of society (1962). Miller argued that lower working-class culture focused on the values of 'toughness', being 'smart' in appearance, and put a great emphasis on the need for 'excitement'. Miller argues that these subcultural values inevitably mean that young lower-class males form gangs and get into trouble with the police.

- Cloward and Ohlin contended that there were in fact three types of subculture; criminal, conflict, and retreatist. A criminal subculture develops where there are already many adult criminals, and this provides **an illegitimate opportunity structure** which enables young people to be drawn into criminal activities. Conflict subcultures, though, involving vandalism, hooliganism and gang violence, develop where there is little adult criminal activity, and so there are few opportunities for young people to get involved in more serious crime. Retreatist subcultures, characterised by high levels of drug use but relatively little other crime, develop where young people have failed to succeed in mainstream society, but they have also failed to become criminals in any of the other two subcultures mentioned. Cloward and Ohlin see this last subculture developing in certain lower-class areas.

- Albert Cohen argues that Robert Merton's approach seems to assume that all crime is committed for some material gain. He also argues that Merton's analysis only explains why particular individuals get involved in crime and deviance. Cohen argues that deviant action has to be seen as a collective phenomenon, something which social groups rather than just individuals commit. Cohen uses the concept of status frustration to explain why young working-class males are often involved in crime. Cohen argues that the ability of young working-class men to achieve the goals which bring high status in modern society is blocked by their social position (they are culturally deprived). Such young men therefore reverse or replace the dominant cultural goals by getting involved in delinquent activities. Activities such as fighting, vandalism, and 'joyriding' do not make criminals rich, but they do bring prestige and status within a subculture.

Does this mean that criminals do have different values to everyone else?

Functionalist subcultural theories do suggest that criminals have different values to other members of society. However, sociologist David Matza argues that criminals actually have the same cultural values as others (Matza 1964). Matza claims that we can deduce this because delinquents, criminals, and deviants frequently use what he calls **techniques of neutralisation** to justify their actions. They may, for example, deny that what they have done is wrong; justify themselves by arguing that they only steal from shops, do not use violence, do not steal from old people, or they may appeal to higher loyalties, for example, 'I had to steal to get clothes for my children'.

Matza concludes that criminals are not that different from other people, and reasons that criminals just drift into crime due to circumstances. He claims that all societies have what he calls 'subterranean values'. This means that there are many activities that many people will indulge in when they think they can get away with it. These values coexist with mainstream values. For example, aggressiveness may be expressed during a football match. Delinquents and criminals simply express these values in the wrong places and times, whereas those in other social groups manage to conceal their 'subterranean values' more effectively. A delinquent may express aggressiveness in a social situation for example, or look for excitement by stealing, or skipping school.

Conclusion

Use the following points to help evaluate functionalist subcultural theories.

- Subcultural theorists still believe that there is a dominant set of shared values.
- The theories are still structural and see action as determined.
- The theories still appear to neglect differences of race and gender.

For consideration

1. Do criminals have the same values as other people?

2. Are there such things as 'subterranean values'? Discuss some examples.

∞ Methods Link

Radical sociologists would argue that sociologists' own cultural values can distort their views of crime, and that it is significant that subcultural functionalists focus on working-class crime and appear unaware of crimes committed by the powerful. Our views about crime are inevitably shaped by our culture, and this criticism highlights the difficulty of studying crime in terms of cultural values. It also raises the issue of whether sociologists can avoid making value judgements.

✓ Top Exam Hint

In evaluating these approaches, remember that functionalist theories are still open to the criticism that they do not adequately explain power relations since they neglect the economic bases of power differences. They also only focus on particular types of crime, such as delinquency, and neglect crimes of the powerful. Make the point, therefore, that subcultural functionalist explanations can be seen as being based on a narrow view of crime and deviance.

Are joyriders trying to resolve status frustration?

2.14 | What do postmodernists say about crime?

What does this mean?

Postmodernism is a relatively new theory in sociology which claims that society is fragmenting. Postmodernists claim that key social structures such as class, and ethnic and gender differences are fragmenting, leaving people much freer to create their own identity in contemporary society. Although postmodernists have not often written directly about crime and deviance, many other sociologists have used some insights and ideas from the theory to explain crime and deviance.

How can postmodernism help us understand crime?

Sociologists influenced by postmodernism have argued that society is undergoing changes which may be contributing to shifts in the type and extent of crime. Postmodernists argue that contemporary society is fragmenting. This means that social groups are less important, and postmodernists claim that now the most important influence on individual identity is consumption. They argue that it is through our spending patterns that we try to create an identity and distinguish ourselves from others. Several key points can therefore be made by sociologists who are influenced by postmodernist ideas.

- Lash and Urry (1994) argue that contemporary societies are fragmenting, and this has led to the creation of 'wild spaces' where the normal rules no longer apply. They are thinking here of the many urban areas of severe deprivation in Britain and the USA, where ethnic minorities and other socially-excluded groups develop a criminal lifestyle and identity.
- A postmodernist-influenced view of contemporary cities can point to the way that the very rich and the very poor now often live in very close proximity. This can lead to an increased fear of crime on the part of the rich, who isolate themselves in gated communities. As American academic Mike Davis notes (1994), city authorities may employ security features ranging from private security guards and closed circuit television to architectural security features such as water sprinklers in parks which prevent 'down and outs' sleeping rough in public places.
- Other sociologists have developed the postmodernist idea that we now live in a consumer culture, where people are free from constraints and there is, therefore, less social control. However, not all individuals have an equal chance to create their identity. There is a **polarisation of identities**, as increasingly individuals distrust those who appear to be different to themselves. This leads to a 'culture of resentment' as inequalities increase.
- People come increasingly to think of themselves as individuals rather than as members of social groups. This means that they have fewer obligations to other people. This process is called individualisation. This can mean that there are fewer constraints preventing people from committing crime, and it can also lead people to the view that crimes committed against others are to be ignored, therefore enabling a tolerance of crime to develop.

This last concept is one which is closely associated with French thinker Michel Foucault (not best described as a postmodernist). Foucault explains the term in more detail arguing that individualisation means crime is seen as an individual problem and an individual responsibility. Foucault believed that since it is very difficult for modern states to monitor and control all citizens, they have to try and develop other forms of discipline or social control. Modern societies see the creation of a culture whereby individuals monitor or control themselves. Professional experts (police, psychiatrists, legal experts, and criminologists) make what Foucault calls 'normalising judgements' about what sorts of people are criminals. These definitions become influential, but they also create the illusion that crime and deviance are purely individual matters, and do not acknowledge that the 'normalising judgements' by which some come to be seen as insane or criminal, for example, are socially constructed.

Conclusion

Postmodernist-influenced views of crime and deviance may seem very persuasive. However, use the following points to critically evaluate postmodernist views.

- A 'culture of resentment' and 'polarisation of identities' may not be an entirely new phenomena. Postmodernism, therefore, exaggerates the extent of social change.
- The social changes identified by postmodernist theory may be better explained by other theories, such as functionalism, Marxism, or control theory.
- It is hard to see how postmodernist theories can be operationalised and tested.

For consideration

1. Is there a culture of resentment?
2. Are all social groups fragmenting?

Patterns of crime: class

How many crimes can you see being committed here? Sociologists argue that white-collar crime is an important, but frequently hidden, form of crime.

✳ Key Idea

The idea of white-collar crime was first explained by Edwin Sutherland in the following terms. Sutherland claimed that

'persons of the upper socio-economic class engage in much criminal behaviour ... this criminal behaviour differs from the criminal behaviour of the lower socio-economic class principally in the administrative procedures which are used in dealing with offenders'.

(E Sutherland 1949)

∞ Methods Link

White-collar crime is hard to research, due to the difficulties in identifying it, and the unwillingness of individuals and organisations to discuss it. However, white-collar crime is also important because its existence and relative neglect suggests that sociological theories of crime, which focus on 'street crime', neglect the crimes of the powerful and therefore provide a biased image of crime.

What does this mean?

The idea of white-collar crime refers to crimes committed by professionals or members of the middle classes. The term is interesting because it seems to imply that white-collar crime is somehow unusual and that criminals are usually from a different class, such as blue-collar or manual workers. Investigating white-collar crime may lead us to revise our views about what sort of social groups criminals come from and which theoretical explanations of crime we find most convincing.

What is white-collar crime?

The concept of white-collar crime was invented by American sociologist Edwin Sutherland in the 1940s. Sutherland defined white-collar crime as *'crimes committed by persons of respectability and high social status in the course of their occupations'* (1949). Sutherland had in mind crimes such as fraud and embezzlement. However, white-collar crime can also include a range of other activities, some of which may be considered by some people to be normal business practice. An example of this might be the fairly common practice of not paying bills until well after the agreed credit terms, or salvaging waste from a job and re-selling it, or dumping toxic waste into the environment. Critics of Sutherland have taken different views of this definition. Some have argued that it is simply an anti-capitalist and business bias. Others have argued that Sutherland's definition is too vague, and does not, for example, distinguish between those who commit crime in the course of their occupations for their own benefit, and those who commit it for the benefit of their employer. This has lead several sociologists, including Hazel Croall (1992), to distinguish between two types of white-collar crime.

- Occupational crime: this refers to crimes committed by professionals, senior or junior executives or others, in the course of their occupation. This could include fraud; for example, various types of electronic or computer crimes are increasingly common.
- Corporate crime: this refers to crimes committed by corporations or businesses. It can include a wide range of activities from pollution, fraud, breaking health and safety regulations, to negligence or corporate manslaughter.

Croall would argue that we can broaden this further. She claims that what is at issue is in fact 'crimes of the powerful', and suggests that we can also use the term 'organisational crime' to refer to crimes committed by governments or public organisations. Muncie and McLaughlin in a similar way refer to 'crimes of the state'.

Is there much white-collar crime?

Michael Clarke (1990) points out that white-collar crime is difficult to research because it is easily concealed and disguised. Many firms are embarrassed to acknowledge that their employees can act criminally and therefore do not report incidents. Clarke also points out that as white-collar crime such as fraud or accounting scams can be complex and hard to investigate, requiring highly specialist knowledge and skills, the police are not likely to prioritise it. Clarke notes that in 1987 only 5 per cent of British detective manpower was allocated to fraud squads.

It is hard to estimate the extent of white-collar crime, but recent research by Professor Susanne Karstedt and Stephen Farrell (University of Keele) suggests that white-collar crime is increasingly common and could be costing around £14 billion per year, which is five times more than the cost of burglary (Radford 2003). This is a finding which bears out the views of Steven Box, who argues that white-collar crime is important because it shows us how relations of power are vital in shaping our perceptions of crime. The ability of the powerful to avoid criminalisation and the low number of convictions for white-collar crime help increase the focus on the crimes of the less powerful. This process is therefore an ideological device which distracts our attention from the reality of crime. It is another example of selective law enforcement.

Conclusion

- The difficulties in measuring white-collar crime remind us once again of the methodological difficulties in studying crime.
- White-collar crime can lead us to reflect on the validity of theoretical explanations of crime. Perhaps theoretical explanations should focus more on what makes people obey the law than what makes them break it.
- White-collar crime may also lead us to reflect that the differences between so-called 'criminals' and those from higher social groups are exaggerated and distorted.

☐ Key Facts

In a cross-cultural study with a sample of 4000 people aged 25–65 in England and Wales and West Germany, Karstedt and Farrell (2003) found that many respondents admitted to exaggerating insurance claims (7 per cent in England and Wales, 22 per cent in Germany), or paying cash to avoid taxation (34 per cent and 54 per cent). Karstedt and Farrell argue that contemporary society is aptly described as 'predatory' (people prey on others, like animals), and that market societies are not necessarily moral societies.

✓ Top Exam Hint

White-collar crime raises important questions about the nature of crime and challenges the view implicit in many sociological theories, that crime is mainly a working-class activity. Use this insight to evaluate the sociological theories which have been discussed so far.

For consideration

1. What methodological criticisms might be made of the findings of Karstedt and Farrell?
2. Give examples of crimes of the state.

| # Patterns of crime: ethnicity

Why are young black people eight times more likely to be stopped and searched than whites?

Key Facts

- 19 per cent of male prisoners are from ethnic minorities

- 25 per cent of female prisoners are from ethnic minorities.

As ethnic minorities form around 6–7 per cent of the UK population, ethnic minorities are disproportionately represented in the prison population.

Source: Morgan 2002

- In 2001–02, The Home Office found that black people were eight times more likely to be stopped and searched than white people.

Source: Home Office, *Race and the Criminal Justice System*, 2002

What does this mean?

A major concern for sociologists and others has been whether there is any evidence that crime is more prevalent among certain ethnic minority groups. This issue arises from the data produced by official statistics showing British prisons having a disproportional number of ethnic minority inmates. This finding raises the question of whether ethnic minorities really are more criminal, or whether there is bias and selective law enforcement.

How do sociologists explain the relationship between crime and ethnicity?

Official statistics show that a high proportion of offenders come from ethnic minority groups. Sociologists can explain this pattern by applying any of the theories discussed in this chapter. In the 1980s, however, sociological explanations came to focus on one key question and debate which still concerns sociologists and criminologists today.

- On the one hand, neo-Marxist influenced researchers such as Stuart Hall (see section 2.9), argue that black criminality is a myth. Black people are no more criminal than any other group in society, but are seen as such because of distorted media reporting and inadequate statistics.
- On the other hand, researchers generally associated with the New Left realists (see section 2.12) such as Lea and Young (1993), argue that official statistics are generally accurate, and young black men really are committing more offences than other groups.

In trying to choose between different theoretical explanations, sociologists have to combine theory with empirical evidence, so let us now examine the research evidence on crime and race.

What evidence is there of racial discrimination in the criminal justice system?

Since recorded crime only provides a partial view of crime, trying to investigate whether the criminal justice system is racist is very difficult. The criminologist Robert Reiner (1994) has argued that it would require much more self-report data and other comparable data to make a judgement, and given that this is not available it is probably impossible. However, this has not prevented some sociologists from trying, and several pieces of recent research can provide evidence from which tentative conclusions can be drawn.

- In 1983 the PSI published a reported entitled *Police and People in London*. Researchers used a range of qualitative methods, including non-participant overt observation ('shadowing' police officers) and interviews to investigate the attitudes of Metropolitan Police officers. The researchers found that the use of racist language and jokes was common and had become part of the institutional culture.

- Simon Holdaway has conducted qualitative research into the occupational culture of the police, and he has also found evidence of the widespread use of racist language and attitudes.
- A large multi-method research project carried out in 2001 by Marion Fitzgerald and Michael Hough, *The Policing For London Survey* (PFLS), found that although many people stopped by the police were satisfied with their treatment, there had been a decline in confidence in police effectiveness. Dissatisfaction with the police was highest among young people, black suspects, and those living in poor areas. The study found that the best predictors of being stopped by the police were 'being young, being male, being black, being working class and being single' (2002).

The evidence of these research findings seems to give considerable support for the view that policing practices are often institutionally racist. (See What, when and why box for more examples.) However, as indicated above, there are methodological problems with all research in this area. Other researchers, while acknowledging the existence of racism in British society, express a note of caution. Phillips and Bowling (2002), for example, point out that the structural context of ethnic minorities in British society cannot be neglected, while Smith (a co-author of the 1983 PSI report) argues that the over-representation of black people is so great that it cannot all be explained as the result of **institutional racism**. Others might well argue that while structural factors (inequality) may lead some ethnic minorities towards crime, the evidence of institutional racism simply underlines the selective nature of law enforcement and suggests there is a high probability that black people are no more likely to be criminal than other sections of the population (see sections 2.16 and 2.21). This in no way justifies any law breaking, but it does put it into a different context.

Conclusion

Remember the following points when evaluating debates on crime and ethnicity.

- Official statistics lack validity and researchers need to use a range of evidence in examining race and crime.
- Ethnicity may just be one element in a complex web of causes.
- Sociologists should never neglect power relations. Consider which social

For consideration

1. Do only some ethnic groups have criminalised identities? If so, why?
2. What is the best way to research race and crime?

 What, when and why?

A concern over the issues of policing, crime and race relations has been a long-running theme in British society. This concern was heightened following the racist murder of Stephen Lawrence in 1993 while he was waiting at a London bus stop. The Macpherson Enquiry in 1999 argued that the Metropolitan Police was institutionally racist in its actions concerning the investigation of his murder. As a result his killers have not been held accountable. The murder of ten-year-old Damilola Taylor in 2001 was seen as the Metropolitan Police's first big test on the murder of a black youth since the Stephen Lawrence case. However, the trial collapsed in 2002 due to police and Crown Prosecution failings, according to official investigations.

Key Idea

In *Policing the Crisis: Mugging, the State and Law and Order* (1978), Stuart Hall et al criticise what they argue is the distorted and often racist reporting of black crime in the British media. They argue that, in times of economic crisis, crime statistics can be politically manipulated to provide reason for the failure of the economy. Using the example of the mugging crisis in the 1970s, Hall et al argue that this results in the scapegoating of a particular group of people – in this case, black youths (see section 2.9).

Key Definition

Institutional racism refers to the way in which the rules and procedures of an institution can work. Where institutional racism occurs, there are systematic biases in the way that they are applied to people. These biases do not have to be intentional or involve a deliberate attempt to discriminate on the part of individuals or an institution.

Methods Link

The PFLS research provides a good demonstration of the complexity of professional research. The researchers used a multi-strategy approach that involved qualitative and quantitative methods and a sample of 5700 Londoners. The study involved a survey (which had a response rate of 49 per cent) and also used focus groups with members of the public and with police officers, depth interviews, and observation. See the web activity on the CD-Rom for further details.

Patterns of crime: gender

Are women naturally less criminal than men?

∞ Methods Link

Feminists have been critical of the malestream bias of sociology and have argued that feminists can use different approaches to produce more valid research. Perhaps one of the key biases is that, until fairly recently, sociologists have failed to question and investigate the highly gendered nature of crime.

What does this mean?

Official statistics show that far fewer women are convicted of criminal offences than men. This raises the question of whether women are really less criminal than men, and if so, why. It also raises the question of whether women are fairly treated by the criminal justice system, or whether biases exist in the way it operates.

What evidence is there that women are less criminal than men?

In a review of research into this issue, Heidensohn (2002) argues that the overwhelming conclusion to be reached is that women do indeed commit less crime than men. However, the situation is more complex than this fact suggests.

- Self-report studies indicate that, while women are less involved in criminal activity than men, the difference is not quite as large as official statistics suggest. Heidensohn reports that the ratio of male compared with female offending was around 6:1 in 1999, but that self-report studies revealed a figure nearer to 3:1.
- Moreover, Heidensohn notes that the share of crime committed by women is slowly increasing, and that women do commit all types of crime. However, the proportion of offences committed by women varies considerably between different offences.

How do sociologists explain women's role in crime?

Biological explanations

Developing Lombroso's original research (see section 2.5), Lombroso and Ferrero (1895) argued that women's biology prevented them from becoming criminal, as they were more passive and naturally more inclined to childrearing than aggressive physical activity such as crime. Other researchers have seen biological differences leading in a different direction. Otto Pollak (1950) argued that women were by nature devious and manipulative. Pollak concluded that women committed more crime than was apparent from official records; were more skilled at concealing their crimes; and that they focused their efforts on particular types of crime, such as shoplifting.

The chivalry thesis

In the 1980s, some researchers argued that women offenders gained more lenient treatment from the police and courts; Campbell (1981), Allen (1987). Carol Smart, however, has argued that women can be treated more harshly or unsympathetically by courts in some cases (1989). Women who are seen to be particularly deviant may therefore be stigmatised with a negative identity, for example, 'monster'. Recent research by Gelsthorpe and Louck (1997), based on 197 interviews with lay (part time, unpaid) and stipendiary (paid) magistrates from five courts in England and Wales, found no evidence of deliberate discrimination by magistrates. However, the researchers did find that magistrates were more inclined to take account of family circumstances in cases involving women, and women were more likely than men to be treated with leniency when they had dependants. Also, in finely balanced cases where the magistrates were unsure whether the sentence should be custodial or non-custodial, personal circumstances were more important for female offenders.

Control and the gendering of crime

Frances Heidensohn (1996, 2002) argues that women have a gendered identity in British society, and that crime is a gendered activity. She argues that women's identity in British society is constructed in such a way that criminal activity is not seen as a desirable feminine activity. Socialisation into gender roles and patriarchal social control in the family and household limits the opportunity that women have to become involved in crime. Heidensohn therefore uses control theory (see section 2.11), as well as feminism to explain gender and crime. This supports Gelsthorpe and Louck's findings, suggesting that women's treatment in the criminal justice system is gendered, and that this reflects the gendering processes in the wider society. However, Heidensohn makes the important point that women have the ability to choose how to act, and that they actively construct their gender activities. Sociologist Bob Connell (1985) makes the same point about male gender identities. For Heidensohn the implication of this is that sociologists, rather than posing the question of why female crime rates are so low, should instead be asking what it is about masculinity that leads so many young men into crime. Moreover, women's ability to go out to public places is controlled by strongly held sets of norms which determine what is and what is not suitable behaviour for women; for example, drinking alone in pubs, wearing certain sorts of clothing, walking home alone at night. Women are also closely controlled in the workplace by male superiors and the sexism of the workplace such as sexual harassment, pinups, wolf whistles and so on. All of these, Heidensohn argues, mean that there is a control of women's activities in public and private spaces, and this constrains women's behaviour, making crime and a criminal identity 'unfeminine'.

Conclusion

In evaluating competing explanations of the evidence showing that women are less criminal than men, bear in mind the following key points.

- Crime is a gendered activity.
- Explaining the relationship between gender and crime has to involve examining both masculinity and femininity.
- People actively create their identities, but in doing this they are constrained by structural forces.

66 99 Key Definition

The **chivalry thesis** is the idea that women are treated more leniently by the police and courts, reflecting the view that women are not 'naturally' criminal, and therefore the occasional lapse can be more easily forgiven.

✳ Key Idea

By gendered crime, Heidensohn refers to crime in which women are the victims of men, such as rape and domestic violence. She argues that such crimes are often 'hidden' in official statistics and many go unreported as they occur in the home and may be committed by family or friends.

● Synoptic Link

Issues of gender and criminality can be linked to other areas in sociology. You might, for example, link crime and deviance to issues of social inequality and power within family and households, such as the 'dark side' of the family, where crime is committed against women in the home to a larger degree than men. These gendered crimes can also be linked to issues of power as Heidensohn (1989), for example, argues that crimes such as rape can be linked to the exertion of male power over women.

✓ Top Exam Hint

Use your knowledge of other theories to evaluate explanations of women's role in crime, for example, Marxism, functionalism, labelling theory, as well as key feminist concepts such as patriarchy. Remember that biological explanations fail to address why it is that only some women commit crime. Once again this underlines the point that crime has to be seen as being caused by many factors.

For consideration

1. What structural conditions might encourage women to commit crime?

2. Why and how could criminality be seen as a positive feature of male identity?

Patterns of crime: age

What does this mean?

According to official statistics, crime is strongly associated with youth, and sociologists are interested in investigating why this is the case and whether it is a valid portrayal of crime.

Is youth crime a modern phenomenon?

Sociologist Geoffrey Pearson has pointed out that while crime by young people is nothing new, the way it is seen and the type and extent of crime and deviance by young people, is a modern phenomenon (1983). The concept of 'youth' is socially constructed and varies over time and place. Industrial capitalism has constructed a child-centred society, where the role of children is such that they are sheltered from the labour market until reaching adult status and often until well into their twenties. From the 1950s onwards, sociologists have been particularly interested in the creation of youth cultures, and have noted that such cultures are often seen as being a social problem for the wider, adult society. Youth cultures have, therefore, often been associated with crime and deviance and constructed as '**folk devils**' (see section 2.23), and sociologists have applied all the theories discussed in this chapter to explain this relationship. The rest of this section therefore focuses on some of the more influential and recent explanations of youth crime.

What are the more current explanations of youth crime?

As is indicated in sections 2.14 and 2.23, many contemporary views of crime have been strongly influenced by the idea that modern society is increasingly consumerist and individualistic. Also related to this view is the idea that most crime is committed by a dysfunctional underclass. Some of these views are reflected in American sociologist James Coleman's concept of **social capital** (Coleman 1987), which has come to be increasingly influential in recent years among some researchers and policy makers. Although published in 1987, these ideas currently provide a strong focus for policy makers.

Coleman uses the term social capital to refer to the relationships within a family, the networks of support, and the structures of relationships between individuals and groups within a community. The presence of social capital can therefore be indicated by:

- strong family relationships and low levels of single-parent families
- high levels of interaction between parents and children
- clear and firmly-held sets of norms and values.

Coleman argues that these factors are associated with very low rates of juvenile crime, and the lack of social capital is correspondingly associated with high rates of juvenile crime. Coleman therefore concludes that youth crime is the result of low levels of social capital.

Are young people just more likely to be seen breaking the law or are they really more criminal?

☐ Key Facts

- 25 per cent of all recorded crime is committed by children aged between 10 and 17.
- 40 per cent of all crime is committed by persons under the age of 21.

Source: Criminal Statistics (2000)

According to the National Prison Survey (Walmsley et al 1992):

- 40 per cent of male prisoners left school before the age of 16, compared with 11 per cent of the male population
- over a quarter of prisoners had been in local authority care at some time, compared with 2 per cent of the general population.

💬 Key Definition

- **Folk devils**: the largely exaggerated or even fictitious group that moral panics are linked to. (See page 66).
- **Social capital** refers to the social advantages and resources which a person has access to. The concept was devised by James Coleman and it refers to the social relationships and bonds which confer advantages on individuals and groups by providing networks and structures of support.

As Newburn has pointed out (2002), views based on this theory have been taken up by policy makers and politicians in power in the UK since 1997. A social capital approach to youth crime has helped to promote the idea that juvenile crime and delinquency is the result of disruptive families or dysfunctional families and poor parenting.

What criticisms can be made of social capital theory?

Social capital may seem to provide an analysis which fits well with the images of crime which we all see through the media and perhaps even in our own lives. However, sociologists have to be careful of generalising from their own experience, and from the media whose information-gathering processes are based on the principle of 'newsworthiness' (see section 2.23). Accordingly, we can draw on a range of theories and concepts to critically evaluate Coleman's theory.

- The idea of social capital appears vague and hard to operationalise. It also seems likely to involve value judgements on the part of the researcher. Single-parent families, for example, can provide very secure environments for childrearing.
- This leads to an alternative suggestion that the key association is the link between social class and juvenile crime. Poor parenting may also occur as much, perhaps in different ways, in middle-class families, and it may be that it is their social class position which helps rule out the need or inclination for crime.
- It is also important to recall Steven Box's claim that criminal activity is not restricted to the lower social classes (see section 2.8).

Conclusion

- There is a strong relationship between youth and crime in official statistics.
- Official statistics lack validity.
- Many youth identities are constructed as 'delinquent' by adults.

◆ What, when and why?

In the 1990s, a range of social policies had been devised to tackle youth offending. One policy was the creation of ASBOs (Anti-Social Behaviour Orders) created by the 1998 Crime and Disorder Act. This gives new powers to the police and other agencies such as local councils. It shows the reflection of Right realism and control theory on current policy (see sections 2.12 and 2.21). Sociologists (influenced by Beck and Foucault) have noted how this reflects a view to the individualisation of crime.

✓ Top Exam Hint

Do not forget to apply your knowledge of other theories of crime to the issue of youth and crime. They are invaluable, but do need to be linked up with the more recent material that is discussed here. All the main theories discussed in this chapter make relevant comments, especially functionalist and Marxist subcultural theories, and control theory. Review your notes and look through sections 2.7, 2.8 2.9.

For consideration

1. What other value judgements is social capital theory making?
2. How would other sociological theories explain youth crime?

Patterns of crime: region

Is inner city crime a result of social disorganisation?

Key Fact

Evidence from the 1998 British Crime Survey found huge differences in the risk of being a victim of violent crime for adults from different social groups.

- 4.8 per cent of men from high-income, rural households were victims of violent crime in 1997, compared with 9 per cent of men from low-income, inner city households and 18.9 per cent of men from private rented accommodation in inner city areas

- the corresponding figures for women were 2.9 per cent, 7 per cent and 8.9 per cent respectively.

(Mirrlees-Black et al 1998)

Key Definition

Value consensus: functionalist Talcott Parsons used the term 'value consensus' to describe the common moral values that society holds and agrees on, and by which society conducts or governs itself. These values are passed on through generations through socialisation.

What does this mean?

A number of research studies have found a strong relationship between crime and region. In the UK, the most recent research has found that those living in inner city locations are more at risk of being victims of crime than people living in rural areas (Mirrlees-Black et al 1998). Sociologists have therefore been concerned to investigate this relationship and find out how it can be explained.

How have sociologists explained the relationship between crime and region?

Some of the most well known research on the relationship between crime and locality was conducted in the 1930s and 1940s by American researchers Shaw and McKay. Shaw and McKay were based at the University of Chicago, and their work helped develop the ecological approach to crime, which argued that the best way to study crime was by examining the environment in which it occurred. Shaw and McKay (1942) conducted a detailed statistical examination of crime rates in the various boroughs of Chicago. They found a strong statistical pattern. The highest crime rates occurred in the centre of the city (called the central business district or CBD), and as one moved further away from the CBD, crime rates fell.

Shaw and McKay explained that the CBD was a 'zone of transition', or an area characterised by a constantly changing population. The central area would also have a high proportion of immigrants, of families living on low incomes, and a high level of people moving in and out of the area. Shaw and McKay argued that this led to 'social disorganisation'. By this, they meant that there were few community relationships and organisations, little social control (or **value consensus**), and therefore more opportunities for crime. It was this, they argued, that could explain the patterns of criminal activity revealed by crime rates.

What criticisms can be made of these studies?

Several studies in the UK have led to criticisms of Shaw and McKay's explanation of the relationship between crime and region.

- Morris's study of crime levels in Croydon (1957) argued that the highest rates of crime were actually found in particular council estates, not the CBD. Importantly though, his study raises the issue of how the concept of social disorganisation should be operationalised. Morris points out that the estates he studied were tightly knit communities where everybody knew everyone else, in contrast to the middle-class areas where neighbours kept themselves to themselves. More critical, Morris argued, in creating high crime rates in particular areas was the policy of the council to house 'problem families' in the same area.

- Baldwin and Bottoms' (1976) study of crime in Sheffield argued that it was not social disorganisation which caused high crime rates, but the council's segregating of 'problem families'. However, Baldwin and Bottoms say that other tenants also contributed to this pattern, since they would refuse to accept housing on a 'problem' estate. The result was that particular estates filled up with those who had been in trouble with the law, tipping an estate into lawlessness and creating 'sink estates' that law-abiding residents did not want to live in.
- Even more critically, Owen Gill's observational study of a poor area in Liverpool suggested that some areas are labelled (1977). This leads to increased levels of police monitoring, and even a self-fulfilling prophecy, as residents adopt a tough self-image and identity.

Social disorganisation then, is a difficult concept to operationalise accurately, and studies and findings such as those from Shaw and McKay may lack validity.

Is location still an important factor?

Despite these criticisms, the relationship between locality and crime remains a key focus for contemporary sociologists and policymakers. Recent attention has focused on 'wild spaces' where normal social rules are suspended (Lash and Urry 1994). Some sociologists, such as Muncie and McLaughlin (1996), have argued that the geographical distribution of crime reflects the way some areas are criminalised, marginalised, and socially excluded. Others, such as Amitai Etzioni (see section 2.21), have argued that high rates of crime in decaying urban areas reflect the decline of community bonds, and that policies need to foster the regeneration of community ties. In some quarters this has led to calls for a tougher response to crime, which can include the so-called zero tolerance approach whereby all breaches of the law are treated seriously (see also section 2.21).

Conclusion

In order to evaluate the relationship between crime and region, focus on the following points.

- The research here focuses on a narrow definition of crime.
- Social disorganisation is difficult to operationalise accurately and reliably.
- The validity of official crime statistics can be questioned.

Methods Link

Shaw and McKay operationalise social disorganisation using indicators such as the proportion of immigrants and numbers of owner-occupiers. Baldwin and Bottoms' study also identified factors such as the number of rooms, number of inhabitants per dwelling, and whether the property was owner-occupied or rented, as being significant indicators. Use of these indicators can be questioned. Morris, for example, claims that 'social disorganisation' was most common in middle-class areas where people did not even know the names of their neighbours.

Synoptic Link

This point can be linked to the theme of social inequality and difference. As Gill's (1977) study indicates, it is not simply a matter of the inhabitants of an area deciding that they want to be seen in a certain way. The identity an area acquires will be strongly influenced by the way it is seen by others. This may be based on key social factors such as the class or race of the people living there.

✓ Top Exam Hint

The concept of social disorganisation is very similar to Durkheim's concept of anomie. You can criticise this from a Marxist viewpoint and point out that perhaps crime levels and perceptions of crime and locality are best explained in terms of power and the ability of some groups to criminalise others. Does more crime really occur in inner city areas, or is this just labelling?

For consideration

1. How would you operationalise 'social disorganisation'?
2. Do Shaw and McKay give a valid picture of crime? Explain your answer.

2.20 | What are agencies of social control?

66 99 Key Definition

An **agent** is simply a person or an entity, such as an institution or a group, which is able to exercise power or produce an effect. Sociologists therefore speak of actors (people) or groups or institutions, as having **agency**.

✳ Key Idea

The idea of 'criminalisation' refers to the way in which certain groups or actions become defined as criminal. For example, many sociologists say that certain groups become criminalised, so that all members of that group are seen as having a criminal identity. This process can be gendered (women are less likely to be identified as criminal or to adopt a criminal identity) and ethnicised or racialised (criminals are disproportionately likely to be associated with particular ethnic groups). It is also a process which links crime to certain social classes, particular regions or areas, and to particular age groups. However, some activities can be criminalised if the law changes and is enforced more rigorously (see section 2.16 and Key Fact).

☐ Key Fact

In January 2004, cannabis was reclassified from a Class B to a Class C drug in Britain. This put it in the same category as tranquillisers. Although you can still be arrested for repeat offences, for using cannabis near schools or for possessing and dealing large amounts, police were advised to presume against arrest when stopping people for personal cannabis use or possession of small amounts of the drug. The aim was to free police time to concentrate on more socially-harmful drugs such as heroin and crack cocaine. As a result, cannabis use is now less criminal than it was in the past merely because the 'label' has changed. The Conservative Party has stressed however, that if it gains power in the next elections, it would revert this reclassification and cannabis use would become a crime once again.

What does this mean?

Sociological theories of crime and deviance stress the view that crime and deviance are socially constructed. This implies that some social groups have more power and ability to define activities as criminal or deviant, and to create and uphold dominant norms and values to control crime. This ability is referred to as social control; the process by which dominant norms and values are enforced by positive and negative, formal and informal sanctions. However, this process does not happen unless certain **agents** or **agencies** are active in defining and punishing actions as criminal or deviant.

What are the agencies of social control?

There are several key agents of social control.

*   The law (created by Acts of Parliament).
*   The Criminal Justice System (courts, prisons, probation service, all administered by the Home Office).
*   The police force (administered by Chief Constables, local Police Authorities, and by the Home Secretary).
*   The media.

All of these agencies have considerable influence in defining what is criminal or deviant and in responding to criminal and deviant behaviour. Of course, these agencies have differing degrees of power; the law is created through formal sanctions such as Acts of Parliament, and sociologists have shown how political processes and institutions are dominated by elite social groups. However, other more informal groups also have a role to play and, as has been claimed by Cohen's study (see section 2.23), police, courts and political organisations can be influenced or panicked into action by the media.

How do the agencies of social control function?

Most of the key agencies, which are agencies created by the state, will function by classifying and identifying criminal and deviant activity, and will try to prevent or limit such behaviour by creating punishments (formal negative sanctions) and rewards (formal positive sanctions). Sociological theories will view social control in different ways.

Functionalists, such as Durkheim, argue that the exercise of social control through official laws is necessary as crime acts against the beliefs of society. An act is therefore criminal because it breaks these rules or beliefs. Furthermore, punishment acts to reinforce social values and therefore helps to integrate society.

Marxists, in contrast, see social control and official sanctions as nothing more than devices for maintaining the rule of the wealthy and powerful who create laws to serve their own interests. Marxists see power as something that is monopolised by the capitalist class rather than shared.

Interactionists have argued that social control is a much more fluid process and came about through complex negotiations between different groups. Both Marxism and interactionism suggest that the process of identifying criminals is a structured process, which favours some groups and identities, and discriminates against others. This process is referred to as '**criminalisation'**.

Phenomenologists: Aaron Cicourel looked at the treatment of delinquency in two Californian towns (1976). He used phenomenology to study delinquency by looking at the way acts and individuals are labelled as deviant, and so become deviant. This is also referred to as ethnomethodology. He found that this labelling is a process of negotiation. The police have a certain picture of what is considered deviant, based on locality, what is unusual or suspicious. Young people are stopped if they fit this picture, and are more likely to be charged with a crime if their background fits the picture (bad attitude, poor education, bad neighbourhood), and so become labelled as deviant. As such, Cicourel argues that delinquent behaviour is a result of the forces of social control and that the criminal justice system treats and labels offenders differently. He does not, however, argue that labelling a person makes them commit more offences.

How has social control changed?

Recently Stan Cohen (1995) has argued that the forms of social control used by the state have changed. He argues that, historically, punishment has moved through various changes, from an increased involvement by the state (police force, prisons) and specialist agencies such as psychiatrists to label deviants, to a reduction in physical punishment in prisons and asylums (decarceration). Although this may seem liberal and humane, it actually serves to blur the boundaries between deviant and non-deviant groups. He argues that with agencies such as community care, education, social work and the medical professions, more individuals can be controlled. Meanwhile technology provides methods of surveillance of individuals, such as electronic tagging and CCTV. Cohen suggests that the effect of such policies will be to increase the marginalisation of those seen as criminal or deviant.

Conclusion

- Crime and deviance are socially constructed. Definitions are created and enforced by agents of social control.
- Criminal identities are gendered and ethnicised, and also identified with class and region.
- However, some sociologists, such as Cohen, argue that social control is now much more subtle but will increasingly marginalise criminals and deviants.

✳ For consideration ✳

1. How can social groups resist criminalisation?

2. Are some social groups or categories constructed as victims rather than as criminals or deviants? How does this occur?

☞ Classic Study

In his 1976 study, *The Social Organisation of Juvenile Justice,* Cicourel found a high number of the young people convicted were from low social classes. He argued this was because of the idea of what is deviant held by the authorities. He found middle-class youths were less likely to be charged with a crime when arrested. They had 'good' backgrounds and their parents and lawyers could offer cooperation and argue for their release.

✓ Top Exam Hints

- A criticism of Cicourel might be that he does not explain how these labels or meanings are produced, unlike Marxists, for example. However, phenomenology does not try to produce reasons, but to discover what a particular phenomenon (deviance in this case) is.

- Use the key concepts of power and social control to discuss the social construction of crime and deviance. These concepts demonstrate how dominant views of what crime is are constructions, and how certain groups are criminalised, and how crime and deviance is itself gendered and ethnicised.

◆ What, when and why?

The sorts of policies Cohen refers to have become increasingly popular in the UK since the 1980s. This is probably because they sit well with neo-liberal views of society, which tend to focus the blame for crime on the individuals who commit it, and also because it places responsibility upon individuals to prevent themselves from becoming victims of crime, rather than expecting it to be provided by the state. Such views and policies provide governments with solutions which reflect a dominant ideology (neo-liberalism) and also provide cheaper solutions to social problems.

2.21 | What is control theory?

✳ Key Idea

The key idea of control theory is nicely summed up in this comment from Hirschi.

'The question "Why do they do it?" is simply not the question the theory is designed to answer. The question is, "Why don't we do it?"'

(Travis Hirschi 1969, page 34)

◆ What, when and why?

Control theory developed in the late 20th century in the USA (see Key Idea above), as crime rates in the USA rose. Arguably, it was particularly popular from the 1980s onwards. Some of the ideas of control theory came to be reflected in 'zero tolerance' policies in the 1980s. These policies were devised in response to the growing rates of disorder and crime in American cities, particularly New York in the 1980s.

What does this mean?

Most sociological theories on crime and deviance start from the point of trying to explain what makes people act in criminal or deviant ways. Control theory cleverly works from the belief that we should instead invert this question, and ask what prevents most people, most of the time, from breaking the rules.

What is control theory?

Control theory has its origins in Durkheim's ideas about the relationship between crime and social control. Durkheim argued that rapid social change led to a lack of integration, anomie, and thus weak social controls and higher rates of crime and deviance. Control theorists take this idea and develop it further.

Travis Hirschi, for example, has argued that crime levels are related to the degree to which social bonds exist (1969). Hirschi identifies four types of bond: attachment, commitment, involvement, and belief.

- If people are attached they will care about others.
- If people have some stake in society and the social order they will be committed.
- If people are involved in their society, through membership of social and community groups and indeed through employment, they will feel involved.
- If strong social bonds on these bases exist, a fourth bond, that of belief in social values and rules, will also be evident.

The four elements of social bonding are needed to control behaviour and prevent crime.

Wilson and Kelling (1982) argue that when control is absent, crime can spiral and areas fall into decline. This is likened to the situation where a window is broken in a disused building (hence this is sometimes known as the 'broken windows thesis'). If no repairs are made and no attempts made to stop the damage recurring, gradually more vandalism occurs. As this happens, so further minor crimes occur, and gradually an area will gain a reputation and crime will become an increasingly bigger problem. Wilson and Kelling draw the conclusion that the control of disorderly behaviour in public places, even for minor offences, is vital in order to prevent the escalation to more serious crime. This view was one of the most important influences that led to the policy of a 'zero-tolerance' approach to crime, which was developed and applied in New York City in the 1980s.

How has control theory influenced social policy on crime?

Amitai Etzioni is an American sociologist who has applied some of these ideas to social policies aimed to reduce crime. Etzioni (1995) maintained that policies need to develop community organisations, such as Neighbourhood Watch schemes, or youth development projects. Etzioni argues that schemes need to bind people into a range of community networks. This helps to create social integration and that will create the controls that prevent crime. This sort of approach closely reflects Hirschi's views about social bonds. Etzioni is referred to as a 'communitarian', and he believes that modern societies need to rebuild a sense of community. His ideas have some similarity with Giddens' notion of the 'third way'. The influence of all of these ideas can be seen in the policies of recent New Labour governments with their catchphrase 'tough on crime, tough on the causes of crime' (see 2.12). Some theorists have developed control theory and applied it to gender and crime, and to age.

Jock Young has noted that control theory is closely related to the demands of 'administrative criminology' (1988), a term used to refer to studies of criminality sponsored by and conducted on behalf of the state. Critics argue that this approach often avoids asking more difficult and interesting questions about crime, for example about the nature of and definition of crime, and contents itself with narrowly empirical studies. However, a mix of control theory and administrative criminology has led to the development of current policies, such as installing CCTV in shops, malls, car parks and town centres, with the idea that this will make it harder to commit crime in these crime 'hot spots'. This is sometimes known as 'target hardening'.

Another policy closely related to control theory is 'zero tolerance'. Zero tolerance was devised in New York in the 1980s. The idea is that if even the most minor breaches of the law are punished, then gradually crime will be reduced. Zero tolerance therefore shares the Right realist assumption (see section 2.12) that minor criminal acts lead to a downward spiral of lawlessness, but it also reflects the views of control theorists and communitarians such as Etzioni, who believe that stronger controls and community organisations make it harder for crime to take hold in an area.

Conclusion

Control theory provides some interesting insights into crime and deviance, but numerous criticisms have been made of it. Use the three criticisms below to help you evaluate control theory. The points for consideration give clues to two further issues.

- Control theory has a selective view of crime, mainly focusing on violent offences, theft, delinquency, and street crime.
- Control theory cannot adequately explain fraud and white-collar crime since, arguably, white collar criminals are embedded in exactly the sort of social networks which should exert control on such activities (see section 2.15).
- Marxists, radical criminologists, interactionists, and feminists, would argue that this view neglects the role of the state and the criminal justice system in actively constructing crime and criminals.

For consideration

1. Does control theory assume that consensus is attainable? Does it neglect the fact that there may be conflict over values and rules?

2. Are all people naturally selfish?

✳ Key Idea

Communitarianism is the idea developed by American sociologist Amitai Etzioni, which argues that, in the late 20th century, many of the problems of modern society could be solved by policies that focus on rebuilding a sense of community in mass society. Communitarians believe that modern society is fragmented and therefore aim to recreate social integration by strengthening institutions such as the family, and emphasising the importance not just of rights, but also of responsibilities.

☞ Who is this person?

Amitai Etzioni was born in Cologne in 1929. He survived the upheavals of the Second World War and was educated at the Hebrew University in Jerusalem, and gained his PhD from the University of California, Berkeley, in 1958. Etzioni has acted as a consultant and adviser on a multitude of government and think tank committees in the USA, and believes passionately that sociology can contribute to social policy.

What are the solutions to crime?

What does this mean?

Crime and deviance are not only sociological problems, but are also defined by society as a social problem. Many different groups discuss social problems and their possible solutions, including the government, the media, religious groups, etc. By defining or labelling something as a 'problem', you are obliged to then think about how to solve or to stop it. Many sociologists wish to use their insights to help influence government decision-makers and help create social policy that limits crime and deviance.

What are non-sociological theories of crime and deviance?

Non-sociological theories have offered a whole range of interpretations in order to explain the criminality of the individual:

- biological inferiority
- nutritional deficiency
- extreme introversion or extroversion
- a dominant sexual drive.

The implication of these ideas is that you can solve crime by treating the individual. This is very much an anti-sociological view. Sociology tends to take the stance that the social environment needs to change, not the individual. This explains why sometimes sociology is accused of 'siding with the criminal'.

What solutions do sociologists offer?

This depends on which sociologists you ask and there are several main solutions.

Traditional Marxism: Traditional Marxism assumed that the solution to crime was relatively simple. The creation of a Communist society would make crime unnecessary. In the Communist state there would be few inequalities and everybody would have their basic needs catered for, therefore crime would not exist. Interestingly, since the end of Communism in Russia in 1991, a notable feature has been the rapid development of a criminal underworld and high crime rates.

New Left Realism: Lea and Young (1990) argue for a return to community policing (in contrast to recent moves towards a military approach that they blame for riots in inner-city areas). They also advocate the development of 'consensus policing', i.e. the creation of a consensus within communities and between police and communities. They feel these would establish trust between the police and community and increase reporting of crime. Both of these require social change, by which Lea and Young refer to a more equal and open, and less marginalised society (see also 2.12).

Control Theory: Control theorists argue that the solution to crime is to increase the risk of criminals being caught. They advocate 'target hardening' - the development of highly visible deterrents to crime, such as alarms, CCTV, or even Neighbourhood Watch schemes. Etzioni advocates the development of strong community organisations to reduce isolation and create strong social bonds. Initial research into CCTV schemes appears to indicate that these schemes, while not reducing the number of crimes committed, have had an effect on arrest rates and clear-up rates (see also 2.21).

Right Realists: Wilson and Kelling's 'Broken windows thesis' (1982) advocates the rapid repair of any criminal damage and a rapid response from police to tackle crime problems. This has led to the development of '**zero-tolerance'** policing, which entails the belief that if minor criminality is tackled swiftly and firmly, more serious crime does not develop. There is some overlap between policies developing out of control theory and right realism (see also 2.21).

In recent years New Labour's policy on crime can be seen to reflect elements of all three of these views, briskly summarised by Tony Blair's famous quote 'tough on crime, tough on the causes of crime'. This soundbite also echoes the familiar Conservative Party slogan *'strong on law and order'*, both of which suggest that crime will not be tolerated. The number of police in the community has been increased, and recent ideas such as 'restorative justice' where offenders have to apologise to their victims draw upon control theory and New Left Realism (Braithwaite, 1994), for example. Equally, Reiner (1996) argues that government policy is now concerned less with the ultimate solution to crime (if such a thing actually exists) and more with target-hardening. Anyone likely to be a potential victim of crime must undertake better crime-prevention measures, echoing right realism.

Many social ideas and policy suggestions from the New Labour Party since the mid-1990s, have been based on a call for individual and family responsibility, giving them common ground with the New Right realists. Policy on continued school truancy introduced in November 2000, for example has enabled courts to fine or imprison parents for not ensuring their child is at school. This idea places the responsibility for juvenile criminal activity and delinquency firmly in the hands of the parents. It is therefore up to the family to police itself.

Conclusion

1. The policies examined here all derive from theories which tend to see crime as linked to economic factors in various ways.
2. However, crime is socially constructed, and not all crime is economically motivated or perpetrated by the poor or working class.
3. As Durkheim argues, whatever policies are adopted it may be that crime is inevitable (see section 6).

For consideration

1. Can you think of examples of crimes which are not economically motivated?

2. How could these and other crimes be best prevented or reduced?

⌖ Classic Study

Lea and Young suggest not all working-class crime is a fight against capitalism, as they claim left idealists suggest. They argue that the working classes *do* commit the most crime; but equally, they *suffer* from the largest amount of crime, as they tend to live in inner-city and urban areas. They don't wish to reject totally the notion of crime as a politically motivated activity, and understand that the motivation for some crime is from a sense of deprivation; but they also argue that this is inadequate. They argue that the causes of crime are:

- **Social deprivation** including poverty, unemployment and poor living conditions.

- **Poor political representation of the working classes**. Frustration at the inability to solve problems through political channels leads to an increasing sense of hostility.

- **The nature of working-class subculture**. Some working-class people choose to solve their problems of living in a capitalist society through antagonism against the police and authority.

✓ Top Exam Hint

Sociologists such as Cohen see the value of sociology in that it takes up issue with what we might call 'common-sense' views on crime, and tries to show these as being unresearched and often based on a lack of clear facts. Cohen goes further and suggests that the medical/ psychological models of criminality fit easily within society's commonsense understandings of deviance. Over time, through the mass media in particular, the ideas associated with these theories such as criminality representing sickness, mental ill-health, a response to disturbing childhood experiences etc. have become part of the lay persons or publics frame of reference, which makes them difficult to resist. Use and develop this idea in the exam in order to gain evaluation marks.

How does the mass media portray crime and deviance?

Does the mass media portray a realistic picture of crime? Or do sensational headlines such as this contribute to moral panics and a social construction of crime?

✎ Classic Study

Stan Cohen, *Folk Devils and Moral Panics:* the research on which this study is based was conducted between 1964 and 1966. Cohen used primary and secondary sources and a wide range of methods. He used newspapers and many documents, questionnaires, interviews, participant observation, non-participant observation, and a survey on attitudes to delinquency among councillors, lawyers, magistrates and similar official figures. This is interesting because it shows that although strongly influenced by interactionism, like most other sociologists, Cohen has used a complex mix of methods.

What does this mean?

Sociologists argue that our knowledge of crime and deviance is socially constructed. This means that our views of what crime is, what causes it, and what should be done about it, are ideas which we learn from institutions and other people in society. One of the key institutions through which dominant ideas about crime and deviance are transmitted is the mass media. Sociologists argue that the mass media can have a powerful influence on our views about crime and deviance.

How does the mass media contribute to the social construction of crime?

A range of research into the content of the mass media suggests that a highly selective view of crime is transmitted by the media. Research by Williams and Dickinson (1993) indicated that 12 per cent of the content of current affairs coverage was devoted to crime, and that over 60 per cent of this focused on crimes involving violence. In the early 1990s, however, violent crime represented only some 5 per cent of all crime recorded by the police. This indicates a highly selective view of crime. Sociologists have made various explanations for this phenomenon. Chibnall's study (1977) put crime reporting firmly into the context of news production. As Chibnall found, news production follows the principal of 'newsworthiness' according to which news is defined in terms of five factors.

- It must be highly visible and spectacular.
- Sexual and political implications are highly desirable.
- Graphic presentation is essential (dramatic pictures).
- It must involve individual pathology (sickness, abnormality).
- It must involve deterrence and repression.

Certain types of crime 'stories' provide these elements, and these are the type journalists will be most likely to publicise. It is for this reason that violent crimes involving innocent young victims, spectacular crimes involving risk, excitement and violence, or crimes which are particularly shocking or sickening will gain a high media profile. The more mundane cases of crime, which are the vast majority, will attract little interest.

How do audiences react to the mass media's portrayal of crime and deviance?

Stan Cohen has argued that the media plays a crucial role in constructing the social reaction to crime and deviance. In a key study, *'Folk Devils and Moral*

Panics' (1973), Cohen argued that exaggerated and distorted reporting by the media was able to create a public reaction to crime and deviance which could lead to the public labelling of a group as deviant. Cohen argued that this process involved several stages, but it concerned a problem being identified and seen as being caused by one group, who were then stigmatised and labelled. The media focus on this deviant group leads to further reporting, but Cohen's study showed that this only led to further public outcry, and the attention of what he calls 'moral entrepreneurs' – public officials such as editors, senior police officers, members of the legal profession, and politicians. This interest in turn leads to both further reporting by the media, who see a developing story that must be reported, and a determination to tackle the perceived problem by the forces of law and order. The media interest and exaggerated reporting therefore leads to a social reaction and amplification (or a deviancy amplification spiral), as more interest in fact leads to the identification of more of the offending behaviour.

Cohen uses the example of the moral panic over the 'mod and rocker' riots of the late 1960s to illustrate this. Other sociologists, such as Fishman (1978) and Chibnall (1977) argue that in fact 'crime waves' are nothing but moral panics. Other examples of moral panics would include the response to dance music and ecstasy use in the last twenty years. However, Sarah Thornton (1995) has used this example to criticise aspects of Cohen's concept. Thornton argues that the idea of one social reaction to deviance is oversimplified, and that in contemporary society there may be many reactions to such exaggerated reporting. She also uses the idea of reflexivity, arguing that, in fact, many deviant and subcultural groups, such as the ravers of the 1980s and 1990s, actively sought to gain media and public notoriety. It is through such means that some groups and subcultures can shock and create a distinctive identity in what Thornton sees as a fragmented and postmodern world.

Conclusion

In evaluating the role of the mass media it is useful to remember the following points.

- Giddens argues that people are reflexive. This means they interpret media output rather than just accept it.
- As Thornton contends, it is more accurate to talk about social reactions in the plural, not just social reaction.
- Study of the mass media indicates that crime is a social construction.

What does the study of drugs tell us about crime and deviance?

Sociologists argue that whether an action is seen as deviant or not depends on the social reaction.

❏ **Key Fact**

According to the British Crime Survey in 2000, about half of all those aged between 16 and 29 have tried an illicit drug during their lifetime.

What does this mean?

The way that drugs are used in society, and the way that society responds to drug use, provides a good case study of what sociologists mean when they say that crime and deviance are socially constructed.

How do drugs affect people?

Howard Becker (1963) interviewed marijuana users and claimed that drug use cannot be explained simply in biological terms. Becker found that users have to learn how to feel the effects of smoking marijuana, for example, by learning how to respond to the drug, how to recognise the symptoms of a 'high', and the correct ways to signify enjoyment.

Those who use the drug may not necessarily become regular users, but using marijuana is likely to lead them to commit themselves to the outlook of those they share the activity with. Becker argues that regular users may develop a deviant career as marijuana use becomes a more important part of their identity and becomes a 'master status'.

How does society react to drug taking?

Jock Young (1971) argues that it is the way in which society responds to drug taking that is of chief importance. Young's research into drug users in London led him to conclude that what mainstream society disliked about drug users was not so much their drug use, but rather their cultural values. The drug users Young studied in the late 1960s were critical of the work ethic and placed higher value on leisure. Young also argued that the stigmatisation and marginalisation of drug users was counter productive. Young argued that excessive police attention in fact led to deviance amplification, as drug users found it difficult to shed their master status. This was therefore a process of criminalisation and fears about drugs often lead to the creation of moral panics (see section 2.23). Young claims that the media created a fictional account of drug takers and their world, but these processes led to the fiction becoming a reality, as a powerful self-fulfilling prophecy was set in motion.

Becker's and Young's studies are therefore good illustrations of the way that crime and deviance are socially constructed. Other drugs, such as alcohol and tobacco, do not meet with such strong social disapproval, even though they cause more deaths than other drugs (South 2002). In January 2004, cannabis was reclassified from a Class B to a Class C drug in Britain. This means that, although you can still be arrested in some instances such as using cannabis near schools or dealing, police now 'presume against arrest' for personal cannabis use or possession of small amounts. This policy aims to free police time to concentrate on more socially-harmful drugs such as heroin and crack cocaine, and shows how crime and deviance has been socially constructed (or deconstructed).

How is society and crime changing?

Drug use has changed since Becker's and Young's studies in the 1960s and 1970s, with the use of different drugs and increased levels of use (see margin items). As Jock Young has shown, sociologists have also begun to look at society in different ways, with new theoretical frameworks and new concepts. Jock Young draws on a number of these in his recent work, and argues that crime, in general, is increasingly seen in terms of social exclusion (2002). Young suggests that many policy makers, government officials, and politicians, now explain crime in the following terms.

- In a fragmented and diverse society, crime is caused by social exclusion (see section 2.12).
- Crime is predominantly caused by a small number of people, living in close proximity (see sections 2.12 and 2.14).
- Crime is largely the result of the development of a socially-excluded underclass in a dependency culture (see section 2.12).
- Crime is the outcome of these factors, which lead to social disorganisation and a chaotic lifestyle centred around drug use (see section 2.13).

However, Young counters this picture by arguing that it is, in fact, neo-liberal policies which have caused fragmentation, inequality, and social exclusion, by promoting the idea that government should not interfere in the process of wealth creation by initiating social policies. Young argues that this inevitably means that the gap between rich and poor increases, and an 'underclass' develops. Neo-liberal policies also promote globalisation, and this is essential to understanding the rapid increase in drugs use from the 1970s onwards (South 2002). Young argues that so-called 'third way' policies on crime, as advocated by Giddens, by communitarians such as Etzioni, and politicians such as Tony Blair, neglect the power of neo-liberal policies to create huge inequalities. Inequality is an inevitable consequence of such policies, and leads to a situation where crime and the drugs trade become alternative career paths for those without the resources to compete in more socially acceptable ways.

Conclusion

- Globalisation has led to an increase in drug use in the late 20th century.
- Drug use and other crime and deviance, can be seen as the outcome of social exclusion.
- Sociologists have to consider critically what factors cause social exclusion.

For consideration

1. Has drug use become normal?
2. Why are alcohol and tobacco acceptable drugs in the UK?

✳ Key Idea

This extract from the classic study 'Outsiders' illustrates Becker's view that becoming a drug user and experiencing the effects of drugs is a social process.

'See, like I didn't know the first thing about it – how to smoke it, or what was going to happen, or what. I just watched him like a hawk – I didn't take my eyes off him for a second, because I wanted to do everything just as he did it. I watched how he held it, how he smoked it, and everything. Then when he gave it to me I just came on cool, as though I knew exactly what the score was. I held it like he did and took a poke just the way he did.'

(Becker, Outsiders, 1963, page 48)

☞ Classic Study

Jock Young's 'The Drugtakers' is one of the first key studies of drug use and how it comes to be socially constructed as a deviant activity in British sociology. Most textbooks describe it as a study, and while the book is based on participant observation of a group of drug users in Notting Hill between 1967 and 1969, the reader is hard pressed to find much detail of how the study was carried out. This makes the study a rather easy target for the common criticisms levelled at qualitative research.

◆ What, when and why?

Neo-liberal policies argue in favour of letting countries and businesses trade wherever they like, without government restrictions. Many sociologists see these policies as being one of the causes of globalisation (see Chapter 4, Popular culture). Nigel South points out that the production, sale, and consumption of drugs now has to be seen in its global context. Events in a distant place can affect our own lives, but, because this is a global phenomenon, it is hard for governments to control these events. Third way policies have been devised in the late 1990s by sociologists such as Giddens and taken up by politicians such as Tony Blair. These argue that crime is a serious and real problem, which can only be solved by a mixture of firm punishments and improved welfare provisions to help young people in deprived areas.

How can we make crime and deviance synoptic?

Why is synopticity important for crime and deviance?

Synopticity is all about making links between the different component parts of sociology. By learning about the way that crime and deviance is linked to other topics in sociology, you will improve your understanding of all topic areas and of sociology in general. In a way then, you cannot really understand crime and deviance without also understanding about key areas in sociology, such as culture, identity, inequality, social inequality and difference. This section therefore helps you to identify the way that crime and deviance are linked to these key course themes.

How does crime and deviance link to methods?

As we have seen throughout this chapter, the way sociologists define and measure crime has a strong influence on their findings. As we have discussed, there are many debates about the validity of official statistics, but it is important to remember that the more positivist inclined researchers also question the validity of qualitative research methods such as participant observation (see the case studies on the CD-Rom for more useful examples on this topic).

How does crime and deviance link to issues of culture?

Sociologists have always been interested in culture, but in recent years there has been renewed interest in it. Sociologists have been keen to demonstrate that our ideas about crime and deviance are cultural constructions. This means that different societies define crime and deviance in different ways and also that these definitions change over time. Linking culture to power helps us to realise that cultural norms and values are often the values of particular social groups. Cultural values are upheld through social control, so powerful groups can ensure that the dominant culture is their culture. They can use this power to criminalise other cultures or aspects of other cultures.

How does crime and deviance link to issues of identity?

Crime and deviance is central to the way that our identities are constructed. Even if we are not criminal or deviant, we are marked out as a certain sort of person, for example, 'law-abiding citizen', 'normal', or 'honest'. This will help define our identity, our status and the roles which we are able to adopt in society. These sorts of identity will be positively sanctioned. On the other hand, if our activities lead us to be labelled as criminal or deviant, we will find our identity is more likely to be what Goffman has called a stigmatised identity. This too will mark our particular status and role for us in society, a predominantly negative identity, which will be most likely to lead to negative sanctions being applied.

How does crime and deviance link to issues of deviance?

It is important to remember that not all criminal acts are deviant, and equally that not all deviance is criminal. Deviant behaviour can be concerned, for example, with alternative cultural values and practices. Ethnic minority groups, for example, may often find themselves labelled as deviant and be portrayed as having a stigmatised identity. Homosexuality is widely regarded as being deviant by many people in British society, and gay identities are frequently stigmatised by the wider society, though there is perhaps growing tolerance.

How does crime and deviance link to issues of inequality?

Inequality features as a key focus in many sociological explanations of crime and deviance, particularly in terms of class, ethnicity and gender. Marxists and those influenced by them, argue that law and order is selectively enforced. Sociologists also point to the relative neglect of white-collar crime and the more lenient approach which the law appears to take towards white-collar criminals, corporate crime, and even crimes of the state. A slightly different focus on inequality suggests that the effect of large inequalities in capitalist societies is a direct cause of crime. This comes about because inequality leads to despair, envy, and crime.

How does crime and deviance link to issues of social inequality and difference?

Social inequality refers to the structured inequalities of class, ethnicity, gender, and societies can be stratified by other criteria, such as age. A key issue running throughout this theme is power, and many sociologists would argue that power varies according to an individual's or group's position in society. In the middle of the 20th century, sociologists devoted most attention to the relationship between class and crime and deviance. More recently, though, interest has shifted to consider how all of these forms of stratification are interrelated.

Key points to remember

- To fully understand crime and deviance it has to be linked to other topics in sociology.
- It is particularly important to link crime and deviance to social inequality and difference. This key topic and course theme shows us how crime and deviance is linked to issues of power, and to class, race, and gender differences.
- We also have to link crime and deviance to culture and identity, as we can only understgand how some actions are defined as criminal or deviant if we understand how a particular culture constricts these definitions.

☀ Key Idea

Power is an absolutely vital concept to grasp if you are to demonstrate a real understanding of sociology. It is important in this topic as it will shape your answer to questions such as 'Who has most power to make the laws and rules?' and 'Who benefits most from law and order?' It will also influence which questions you think worth asking about crime and deviance.

2.26 | Pushing your grades up higher

✓ Top Exam Hints

The different skills your exam will test you on are referred to as AO1 and AO2.

- AO1 refers to knowledge and understanding of sociological theories, concepts and methods.

- AO2 refers to your ability to identify, interpret, analyse and evaluate your knowledge.

Use 'signpost' phrases or words to link together your paragraphs in long answers. These enable the reader to follow your argument clearly and easily. A simple example of a link word is 'however', but short, direct phrases or sentence constructions do the same job.

- 45 per cent of your marks will be for AO1.

- 55 per cent of your marks will be for AO2.

These are marks for the whole AS and A2 exams. This shows that at A2 your focus must be on analysing, interpreting and evaluating your knowledge. You will not do well if you simply regurgitate material which you have rote learned (learned by heart without understanding it).

1. Practise writing introductions and conclusions for long answers and get friends or your teacher to look at what you have written. This exercise forces you to summarise your thoughts on debates and theories in a very compressed way.

2. Get copies of past question papers and work through the questions. Also consult the chief examiner's report on the most recent sitting of the examination. This will contain useful advice and tips on what to do and what not to do in the exam.

3. Make a spider diagram or a list of the links between crime and deviance and other topics, sociological theories, and methods and methodology. Use your diagram/list to write down the names of key studies, concepts, or sociologists that you can use in the exam.

4. Make a list of key 'link' or 'signpost' words, phrases or constructions. These will help you show readers how paragraphs in your essays are linked together. They will help you to make your argument flow logically by explaining your points and reasoning in careful detail. Examples of signpost words or phrases are: 'however', 'it can be argued that', 'this view is supported by evidence from'.

5. Make your own glossary of key terms and concepts in crime and deviance. Review, revise and test yourself by using it regularly.

6. Avoid 'restricted evaluation'. This means that you have tried to evaluate, but have not explained your points in sufficient detail or elaborated (spelt out) why your argument is a good one and why it is preferable to alternative views. A brief, one sentence justification for your views in a long essay answer will not be sufficient. If it is not supported by reasoned argument and some evidence, it is just an assertion.

7. Remember to show an awareness of current debates and social change, where they are relevant, in your work. This does not mean waffling on about some obscure report you have read in the local newspaper or TV news. It means that you might argue, for example, that the changing climate of opinion regarding drug use is a good example of the way in which crime and deviance are relative to time and place. It also means that you should try to use an understanding of current theories, such as postmodernism or globalisation, where you can see the relevance of such theories to your answer. These theories, debates, and aspects of social change may be helpful in critically evaluating older theories or studies.

8. This is a synoptic paper, so remember to integrate your general sociological knowledge. You can do this throughout the exam, but pay particular

attention to the links which each question requests you to make. Use a direct style to draw the reader's (examiner's) attention to these links. You can use constructions such as, 'in studying this area, sociologists have to be aware of a number of theoretical issues…', or 'the idea of deviance is also relevant in other topics such as the family…'

9. Do not quote large chunks of textbook material in the exam. It is always better to put things in your own words, as this shows that you have a genuine understanding of the ideas you are discussing.

10. Remember to write as clearly as you can and to set your answers out neatly in the exam. It does not matter if you forget something and want to add it later. You can write your extra comments and put an asterisk or maybe a letter or number by the material. Then just repeat the symbol where you want the extra material to be joined and add a brief margin note, and it should be clear that you want the material to be read.

Key points to remember

- Use your knowledge and understanding carefully and appropriately the exam is not simply a test of how much you have remembered.
- Evaluate and present well-reasoned arguments in response to the longer questions.
- Relate your knowledge about crime and deviance to other relevant concepts and theories. Material from units 2532 and 2533 may be relevant to some questions.

✳ Key Idea

Evaluation is one of the key AO2 skills and it is vital to understand it in order to maximise your marks in the exam. In order to evaluate, you must show that you can use sociological theories, concepts, and research findings critically. You must identify strengths and weaknesses, and weigh up the strengths and weaknesses of different studies, theories, and findings, and then show how you can reach a conclusion.

Frequently asked questions

Q. Why are sociologists more interested in male criminals than in female ones?

A. Some sociologists would say that this is because most crimes are still perpetrated by male offenders. However, feminist sociologists would take a more critical view of this. They would argue that there is a bias within mainstream sociological studies on crime and in criminology, towards viewing crime as a predominantly male activity. So, feminists argue, not only is crime gendered, but so is our understanding of crime. Feminist sociology has forced researchers to look at this issue more critically, and investigate those women who are involved in crime, as well as studying the way the criminal justice system deals with female victims and offenders.

Q. Can sociologists ever really know about crime?

A. Positivist sociologists would argue that scientific methods will indeed present the truth about crime, but interpretivists would be more sceptical. However, many sociologists would be cautious in answering this question and would agree that sociological knowledge about any topic is always partial and provisional. This does not mean that it is pointless to attempt sociological research, but rather that knowledge is always partial and therefore it can only help make a contribution to understanding. This is not the same as the postmodernist view that no such thing as the 'truth' exists; it just means we cannot be absolutely certain that we always know what the truth is.

Q. Will we ever live in a society without crime?

A. Marxist-inspired sociologists can argue that crime will decline in a more equal society. However, possibly the most convincing answer comes from Durkheim, who argued that crime was inevitable and would never be eradicated. Durkheim points out that no matter how tolerant societies are, all will have rules and there will always be occasions when the rules are broken. In an imaginary society of saints, Durkheim says, what seem to us minor misdemeanours will come to be regarded as more serious breaches. Rules and laws will always change, but they will never be abolished, and therefore crime, or law breaking, will always take place.

Chapter 3

Education

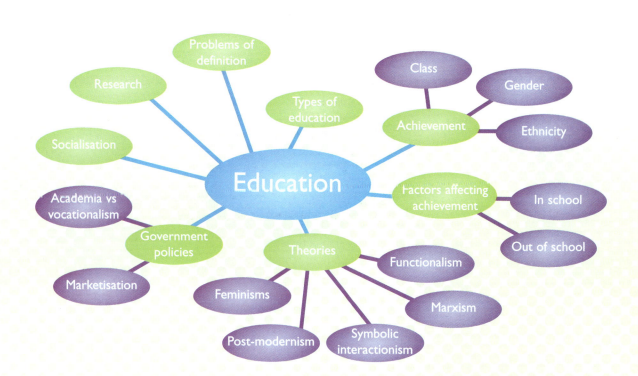

 **CD-ROM**

3.1 | Key issues in education

✏️ **Coursework Suggestion**

One of the joys of carrying out sociology coursework on education is that there is no shortage of material, resources or people to either research or ask for help. Nearly everybody has got an opinion on education be it positive or negative. You also have great experience about this topic area (after all, you have spent the last few years in it) and can use part of your time researching while you study.

There are dangers to watch out for, however. Your own values might get in the way of your research. The fact that you are 'in' education may also mean that you take things for granted and therefore overlook something that could be worth investigating (for example, why are so many senior managers of schools male when the majority of teachers are female?). You may also feel 'I can do this tomorrow' and then leave things to the last minute. Nevertheless this is an ideal topic for coursework and allows you to develop your knowledge gained in the AS year.

● **Synoptic Link**

Sociologists of education examine how education in its various forms might be a source of 'power' for some groups and individuals and not for others. Sociologists can examine why this might be the case and finally explore the effects of that power on different classes, ethnicities and genders.

Why are sociologists interested in education?

The sociology of education grabs the attention of all types of sociologists, whatever their theoretical background. For some, education manages to act as a way of socialising people into the norms (for example, eating food with the correct cutlery) and values (for example, 'ambition' or 'honesty') that are seen to be important for a particular society. For others it can be seen as a source of conflict, particularly when issues surrounding gender, class and ethnicity are put under the sociologist's 'microscope'.

What are the key ideas and concepts in education?

- To answer the key debates, students need to be aware of the views on education of the classical sociologists, functionalists, Marxists, neo-Marxists, Max Weber, postmodernists, symbolic interactionists, interpretive sociologists and feminists. You will learn all about these theories in this chapter.
- You need to know about the connection between the education system and the economy. You also need to be clear about differences between private and state education along with the five major policy changes since 1944: namely the introduction of the tripartite system; comprehensive systems; new vocationalism; the 1988 Educational Reform Act; and 'Curriculum 2000'.
- Finally, you need to be aware of the many processes and concepts that exist when focusing on explanations to do with educational attainment by class, gender and ethnicity and the interplay between the three.

What does the Awarding Body say about education?

The OCR examiners will expect you to know about:

- the relationships between education, socialisation and identity
- institutional processes within education
- patterns and trends in educational achievement including those of class, gender and ethnicity
- macro and micro theories of educational achievement (materialist, culturalist, structuralist and social action theories)
- power and control and their relationship to education
- the relationship between education and the economy
- the transition from school to work;

and to have an understanding of:

- key educational policies and implications for their provision.

The exam for this unit (2536) will be one hour and will be composed of two unstructured essay questions of which candidates must answer <u>one</u> question.

As with all of the OCR units you have to show competency or ability in the assessment objectives of AO1 (*knowledge and understanding* and *presentation and communication*) and AO2 (*interpretation and analysis* and *evaluation*).

For AO1 you need to show *knowledge and understanding* of the names of sociologists and their case studies; the relevant theories; the key concepts (for example, 'cultural capital'); evidence to support the claims sociologists make.

For AO2(a) you need to show how you can actually *interpret and apply* this knowledge when putting forward a particular argument and for AO2(b) *evaluate* continuously throughout any answer you are writing. There is a greater emphasis placed on AO2 at A2 than at AS. This might mean that you choose to draw on the ideas of a theory or case study that was carried out 30 years ago and see how it might (or might not!) be relevant to an area of power and control. You might also identify trends from the past and see to what extent that particular trend is present today.

It will also help if you learn all possible synoptic links as you progress through this unit (look out for the Synoptic Link box in the margins). You must also examine this topic area in relation to the core theme of social differentiation, power and stratification.

Key points to remember

1. The sociology of education raises a variety of synoptic possibilities with social inequality.
2. This topic makes for an exciting option in coursework due to the availability of resources and your own personal experience.
3. Identify, practise and perfect the skills required for AO1 and AO2 described above (the many examples in this chapter will help you do this).

✓ **Top Exam Hint**

- Looking at the debates mentioned on this spread, make sure that by the end of this chapter you can clearly write one sentence about each debate using the following theories: functionalism, Marxism, neo-Marxism, Weberianism, postmodernism, symbolic interactionism and feminism. Make revision even easier by turning these sentences into a revision table or by creating cards that you can then use to revise from.

- Evaluation in the sociology of education exam means that you question how data was gathered and when it was gathered (for example, ethnicity statistics on exam pass rates). You question to what extent the empirical data (what sociologists use as evidence, i.e. events that can be observed, measured or tested) can be verified for its accuracy. You analyse the argument to see if it 'holds together' logically (i.e. that no wild claims are being made). Finally, you identify to what extent the theory, study or claim is 'comprehensive', that is, it can be used to explain other situations in a different culture, time or place.

3.2 How does education link to the AS course?

Why are links to AS sociology important for A2 sociology?

Being 'synoptic' is about being a good sociologist. In other words, you look across a variety of different areas when attempting to explain why something might take place. For example, if a child is performing badly in school a sociologist will not just look at what is taking place in the classroom but might also be interested in what is taking place at home or the area where the child lives. The same sociologist might also be interested in the class or ethnic background of the child or perhaps even explore the subcultures and peer groups the child is involved with. Performing well in sociology exams is similar, in that examiners reward students who can combine different areas of sociology when answering exam questions. The sociology of education can be linked to a variety of AS topic areas as shown below.

What links can be made to the family?

There is a direct link between the family and education in that sociologists refer to the family as 'primary socialisation'. By this they mean that we learn the norms and values of society or the culture we mix in via our families first. We then go on to other forms of socialisation (through education, the media and work) where these norms and values are reinforced. This makes education a form of 'secondary socialisation'. Much research that you will read about in this chapter offers explanations about how well or badly pupils do based on their family and home conditions.

What links can be made to religion?

For some sociologists, religion acts as a way of integrating (and socialising) people into the norms (accepted ways of behaving) and values that are seen to be of importance for a particular society. Many schools belong to religious communities that provide networks which reinforce the socialisation process. Some religious schools are selective, both in terms of what they may perceive as academic ability but also in the expectation that the pupils (and families) follow the religion the school supports.

As a subject taught in schools, religion has been criticised by many sociologists as being 'ethnocentric' in nature. This means that the religion that is taught tends to overwhelmingly reflect a white Christian understanding of religion rather than reflecting the variety of religious perspectives that exist in multicultural England.

What links can be made to mass media?

As an institution of social control, there are a variety of theories which argue that the media has enormous influence on how we perceive other institutions in society such as religion, the family and, of course, education. The media has at various times reflected (or created) various 'discourses' (ways of thinking) about education. These discourses end up being 'internalised' (i.e. accepted as being true) by many who read them. Thus we read about A level exams getting easier, pupils truanting from schools and turning to crime as a result, and league tables that supposedly show that schools at the top are better than schools at the bottom. One of the jobs of the sociologist of education is to explore to what extent such discourses are true. In your exam you can use these stories as part of your evidence for particular arguments contained within the theories you will explore in this chapter.

What links can be made to youth and culture?

Much of the work that you have covered in this unit will provide wonderful insight into a study on education. Not only have you covered many of the names and theories that can be brought into this unit (something the examiners appreciate) but cultural explanations form a significant set of explanations within education. Your coursework at A2 will also benefit from your own experience in education, your knowledge of the unit and your study of youth and culture.

Key points to remember

1. Good sociology *is* synoptic. Get into the habit early by continuously relating what you read in this chapter to as many other areas of sociology as possible. This will develop your sociological imagination and will, in turn, be reflected by the quality of your writing.
2. Whenever you come across a new case study, jot it down and add one sentence to identify what *other* areas of sociology it could be applied to.
3. When planning your coursework this year try to combine education with one area you have studied in AS, such as youth culture and education. In this way you will have a variety of theories and studies at your fingertips that you can use when analysing the data you collect.

✍ Coursework Suggestion

You can always 'replicate' a study when carrying out sociology coursework. This means that you can choose one of the famous studies carried out, preferably one that is slightly dated, such as Paul Willis's 1977 study on working class 'lads' in which he explored why working class males chose to 'opt out' of the education system and enter low status jobs when they left school, and see if the findings are still applicable today. This is fun because you can use the sociologists' ideas to formulate your own version of your chosen study, while at the same time discovering new developments by following in their footsteps.

☞ Who is this person?

Paul Willis studied English at Cambridge before gaining his doctorate at the famous Centre for Contemporary Cultural Studies in Birmingham. Willis's work is fascinating because as a Marxist he is looking at the big macro issues of class, identity and education but his methods reflect an 'ethnographic' edge normally associated with micro or interpretive methods.

How can we find out about the sociology of education?

✓ Top Exam Hints

- What do sociologists mean by 'unstructured' interviews? How often is an interview really 'unstructured'? The moment a sociologist is exploring a particular issue in an interview then automatically there is some sort of structure. Tell the examiner that most interviews are to a certain extent structured because they reflect the interests and values of the researcher. One of the few examples of truly unstructured interviews would be when the patient is talking to a psychiatrist or counsellor about their problems. This means that in the sociology of education all interviews will vary between being 'semi-structured' and 'structured'.

- Gain evaluation marks by drawing to the examiner's attention the fact that the work of Paul Willis confuses the debate about whether sociology should be 'macro' or 'micro'. His work certainly has a 'macro' element to it (i.e. he is a Marxist and interested in how 'class' shapes the lives of the pupils he is researching). But his 'interpretive' research methods focus on the attitudes of the 'lads' he talks to. Using interviews and observations this is a small, in-depth study that is definitely 'micro' sociology at its best. Mention this when you get to the concluding paragraph of your exam answer.

How have sociologists tried to measure 'education'?

Sociologists can approach education from a macro perspective (i.e. how school pupils are shaped by the processes that they experience both inside and outside the school). They can also study education from a micro perspective (i.e. examining close up how pupils experience education). Sometimes they combine both macro and micro elements in their research. Either way, this area of sociology provides huge possibilities for the sociology student to show off their knowledge of sociological **methodology**.

Apart from their own particular theoretical interests, sociologists choose their methodology as a result of issues that include:

1. *The nature of the research problem* for example, are you researching documents or people; is the research 'overt' (research that is carried out with the full knowledge of all those involved) or 'covert' (research that is carried out 'under-cover' from those being studied); or is the researcher looking back over time and comparing past with present?
2. *The traditional research strategies, methods and data sources* thought to be appropriate for a particular problem (for example, looking at school records to assess which pupils are excluded from school).
3. *How available or accessible the data is* that the sociologist requires (for example, how willing would some schools be to have sociologists roaming around in their midst!).
4. *The resources at the researcher's disposal* (for example, funding, time, equipment and assistance).

Values also determine how a particular sociologist approaches the sociology of education, i.e. are they a Marxist, feminist or symbolic interactionist? The aim or particular focus of their research will reflect the theoretical interest of the sociologist.

Such values will also determine whether or not the sociologist is gathering quantitative data or qualitative data. This might depend on whether the researcher considers themselves to be positivist (i.e. scientific) or interpretive (i.e. more interested in how the respondent feels about what is being researched) in their approach to the sociology of education.

What methods do sociologists tend to use to study education?

Methods vary depending on what the sociologist is trying to find out. Questionnaires that are highly structured provide useful broad-ranging data although their completion rate is low. They also do not allow pupils to open up, and tell it like it is. Observation is a fabulous method to use in the classroom but is time-consuming and the presence of the researcher can change and/or affect what they are looking at. Interviews allow the researcher to probe and 'fish' out particular trains of thought but children can sometimes not grasp the particular issues the researcher is examining.

Three sociologists who have used a variety of methods to study education:

1. Ethnographer Valerie Hey (1997) used a variety of qualitative methods when exploring girls' friendships in two London schools. Her methods included participant observation, and analysing girls' notes written to each other in class, and an examination of girls' personal diaries.
2. Interactionist David Gillborn (1990) used classroom observation to explore how ethnic differences influenced how teachers perceived their students.
3. B Davies (1989), in exploring gender roles within literature and the perceptions of these stories from young children, spent hundreds of hours over a period of two years reading different types of stories to children to assess their responses.

What problems with definition are encountered in education?

Remember that whatever definition (or 'operationalisation') we use to start our research will then affect what we look for and what we uncover as a result.

To start with, the word 'education' is problematic. Do we mean 'informal education', i.e. learning to cook or learning to drive, or 'formal education', i.e. learning sociology! But if we define 'formal' education as something that is 'examinable' do we mean that learning to drive is formal education – see the difficulty? Even the word 'intelligence' is difficult to 'operationalise' because, as you will see in this chapter, the tests used to evaluate intelligence can sometimes reflect the values of the people who wrote the tests rather than assessing the abilities of the person being tested.

Key points to remember

1. There are a variety of reasons why sociologists choose the methods they do – these must be learned for the exam.
2. Memorise not only the key names of sociologists associated with the sociology of education, but also the method of research they adopted.
3. Do not forget the importance of definition or 'operationalisation' when discussing any research that takes place. Evaluating somebody else's research is impossible unless we know what they mean.

✓ Top Exam Hints

- Nowadays sociology students should not need to argue whether or not interviews produce 'qualitative' data and questionnaires produce 'quantitative' data. Technology has come a long way in recent years with the aid of extremely sophisticated software. Questionnaires, observations and interviews can all generate quantitative data that can be analysed in an extremely sophisticated and efficient way. Make the examiner aware of this but be careful – do not imply that quantitative data is better than qualitative data. Each has its own specific uses for the sociologist.

- Remember that when you are evaluating writers and research it really helps to remember the concept 'historical perspective'. This means that what one thing means in one culture at one point in time may have a completely different meaning in another culture, at another point in time. This is really useful when discussing girls' attitudes to education in the exam. What girls might have thought about education and work in the 1970s is probably very different to that of today!

3.4 | What do we mean by 'education'?

☀ Key Ideas

- Education is seen by sociologists as a form of socialisation. By this they mean that there is an ongoing process whereby individuals learn how to conform to norms and values and learn the behaviour expected from certain roles (i.e. the role of a pupil, son, daughter, worker, teacher etc.). Many sociologists argue that this is initially carried out through 'primary socialisation' the main agency of which is the family. However, at a later stage of the child's development, other types of 'secondary socialisation' carry out this function via religion, the mass media, peer groups and, of course, education. As you will see later on in this chapter, Talcott Parsons, a functionalist, argues that the school acts as a bridge between the socialisation of the family and that of work.

- Three points you can make in the exam are:

  1. Functionalists (sociologists who see the world working in consensus/harmony) argue that education should equip pupils with the right skills to 'fit' into the work place, the most gifted students taking their place high up within the career structure.
  2. Marxists (sociologists who argue that society is based on conflict between classes, for example, working and middle classes) argue that the economy shapes the education system to serve its needs rather than the needs of the individual pupils who attend school.
  3. As you will see in this chapter, despite the very different views held by functionalists and Marxists, both theories argue that education is directly linked to the economy.

What does this mean?

If you stop and ask somebody 'what is education?', the chances are they will mention school books and teachers and noisy playgrounds. And yet if you were to ask that same person what the most useful thing they had ever learned was, they might reply in a completely different fashion. They would probably mention learning to cook or to drive or learning about a particular hobby. Does this mean that learning to cook is not a type of education? Sociologists make a distinction between 'formal' and 'informal' education.

What is the difference between informal and formal education?

Informal education is exactly the kind of education mentioned above but for which we receive little reward other than the enjoyment taken from the activity itself. You may learn to cook but, unless you have studied cookery in a school or a college, you may not receive any certificates for it. By 'formal' education sociologists refer to different types of schools and learning environments where, in one way or another, pupils will be taught, assessed and accredited with an exam award, certificate or merit.

Sociologists are fascinated by formal education because we spend so much of our time being educated. You will have spent probably twelve years of your life within some sort of formal education institution by the time you read this page. Many sociologists refer to this type of 'socialisation' as secondary socialisation ('primary socialisation' taking place within your family). Education interests sociologists for two reasons.

- There are a variety of ways that education affects the individual.
- There are a number of ways in which education affects society as a whole.

What is state education?

Think about the primary school you went to if you were educated in England. The chances are you are imagining a building of orange bricks and big windows. The building is probably quite old and there are many of them all over the country. The playground gates are probably black and of heavy metal and the entrance to the building has probably got 'boys' or 'girls' above the doorway.

The reason for this is that the 1880 Education Act provided, for the first time, compulsory education for most children from the ages of five to ten. That is why many primary schools all date from the same period. The school-leaving age was gradually raised (to twelve in 1889, to fourteen after the First World War and finally to sixteen in 1973). State education refers to the free provision of education for all people who live in England. It is paid for by tax-payers, for example, employees. State education does not include 'independent' schools (sometimes referred to as 'private' or '**public**' schools) for which fees are paid in order to study. Sociologists are interested in 'state education' because of what different governments have argued should be taught, and how.

Is there a connection between formal education and the economy?

Many sociologists would argue that there is an extremely strong connection between state education and the economy. This is also quite often the focus of exam questions. This chapter will explore this relationship between state education and the economy when we look at the different theories. By studying the history of education sociologists have shown that major changes within the education system have always come about when there is a fear about how well the British economy is doing compared to other economies. This has enormous implications for what happens in the classroom and why. This chapter will explore these processes.

Conclusion

So when you look at your old primary school again or see one of those old Victorian buildings, you might consider that perhaps it was built not only for the needs of the children inside it, but also to provide educated workers for a country that was facing international competition within a globally competitive business world.

Victorian primary schools were built from 1870 onwards and compulsory 'state' education was introduced from 1880 for the first time in England and Wales.

66 99 Key Definition

Be careful when talking about 'state' education and using the word '**public**'. In America 'public' education means the same as 'state' education here, i.e. it is provided free to residents of the country. The term 'public education' in England has a different meaning and refers to the most famous 'private' or 'independent' fee paying schools, such as Harrow, Eton and Rugby. Do not confuse these terms.

◆ What, when and why?

It is interesting to note that whenever there has been great concern expressed over the economy, major changes within education have soon followed. In the 1870s there was concern over Britain's competitive 'edge' over other countries, and in 1870 state education started. After the economic crisis created by the Second World War, there was the introduction of a new educational system called 'The Tripartite System'. In the 1970s there was an economic recession and this gave rise to the vocational qualifications of the 1980s.

For consideration

1. How many connections can you make between education and the economy?

2. Do you think formal or informal education is more important? Why?

What do we mean by 'intelligence'?

What does this mean?

When you hear somebody being referred to as really 'intelligent' what do you actually think? Perhaps they are good at maths, or tests, or have an amazing memory. Perhaps they are extremely good problem solvers or can speak five different languages. They probably have got lots of qualifications and attended a well-known university.

Yet the idea that there is an intelligence that you can measure, test and grade, is actually only one particular theory or view as to the nature of intelligence in general. Unfortunately, not only has this view dominated much of educational thinking throughout most of the 20th century but it is also an idea that has led to a way of sorting children into taking certain subjects at school and, in some cases, then jobs that affect the rest of their lives. In this sense it has added to the patterns of inequality of educational achievement according to class, gender and ethnicity that you will discover in this chapter.

What do we mean by 'IQ'?

An intelligence test is a standardised test where the score is given as an 'intelligence quotient' or 'IQ'. It is a way of numerically measuring somebody's intelligence. Such tests were first constructed in France by Alfred Binet (1857–1911) to assess children's 'educability' in schools. Psychologists and educationalists in the 1920s and 1930s developed these ideas to argue that there were different 'types' of children that could be identified by such tests. As we shall see in this chapter, such tests were used to allocate different types of schooling to these students on the basis of how well they performed in the test.

Such tests can be criticised because they assume that there is only one intelligence and that intelligence can be measured. They are also attacked because the tests are culturally biased, i.e. they reflect the ideas and ways of thinking of the people who wrote them. The following example shows this.

Q. Which item is the odd one out? Tumbler; Acrobat; Flute; Shot
A. Acrobat (the other three are names for different types of glasses).

Many writers argue that the results of such tests favour middle-class children in the UK. These culturally-biased tests discriminate against all those who have English as their second language, or those children whose normal English is very different from the English of those who wrote the tests. In many cases such tests were/are written by middle-class, white males.

✳ Key Idea

The idea that people have 'innate' or born intelligence can be taken to quite racist assumptions. Herrnstein and Murray (1994) argued that there are differences in intelligence between black Americans and white Americans and that this could be shown using IQ testing. They argued that the evidence of black Americans scoring 10–15 points below whites on average proved their case. Critics however argue that such tests only go to show that the IQ test is 'culturally biased' in favour of the people who wrote the tests in the first place – namely middle-class whites.

✐ Coursework Suggestion

Explore the effects of IQ testing on individuals by carrying out your own 'focus group' in which you administer an IQ test and then get the group to discuss the difficulties they faced when carrying out the test. Use their opinions to critically assess the explanations about intelligences that you have read about in this section.

Are there other ways of defining intelligence?

There are other ways of defining intelligence although the problem is that most education systems and exam assessments do not recognise alternative ways of conceptualising intelligence.

American psychologist, Howard Gardner, argues that rather than having an intelligence defined by somebody's 'IQ', humans are better thought of as having nine intelligences.

American psychologist, Howard Gardner, challenges the idea of a single measurable intelligence.

- *Linguistic* – the ability to learn and develop language or languages.
- *Logical/mathematical* – the ability to be good at mathematical problems.
- *Musical* – the ability to remember a song or piece of music on only one hearing or the ability to pick up a musical instrument and play melodies without instruction.
- *Spatial* – the ability to map read, recall and describe places by picturing them in your mind.
- *Bodily kinaesthetic* – athletes, dancers and other physical performers have the ability to control and move their bodies in ways that others cannot.
- *Naturalist* – the most recent of Gardner's intelligences, this refers to the ability to recognise and categorise natural objects like plants, or rocks or animals.
- *Interpersonal* – the ability to read other people's moods, feelings and motivations.
- *Intrapersonal* – the ability to understand one's own moods, feelings and motivations.
- *Existential* – the ability to raise fundamental questions about existence, life, death and the universe.

Conclusion

Gardner's ideas of multiple intelligences challenge the idea that one test is enough to classify pupils and students into different types of education. Much more is needed than that. Gardner also argues that many teachers teach in the style that reflects their own sets of intelligences rather than those of the students in the classroom. This means that when children do not do well in subjects this may well be the fault of the teacher rather than the inability of the student.

For consideration

1. Think of examples to show how you possess each of Gardner's intelligences.

2. To what extent do you think your education meets the needs of each of those intelligences?

What is the tripartite system?

◆ **What, when and why?**

The 1944 Education Act came at a time when Europe was coming to the end of the Second World War. People in those countries had experienced war at first hand and in many cases were disillusioned with the policies and the politicians that had allowed such a war to take place. There was also general enthusiasm to create a new and better society when the war had finished. The Education Act needs to be seen in this light because of the powerful role education has within society – particularly in relation to the economy. Not only can the level and standard of education affect what status individuals may have later on in life, but it also can determine the status of countries internationally in terms of their economic success and status.

✓ **Top Exam Hint**

- Three points you can make in the exam are:

  1. Remember that any IQ test can be said to be culturally-biased in favour of those that wrote it.
  2. The allocation of grammar schools discriminated against girls because in the early years of the system figures were readjusted to make more boys gain places at grammar schools.
  3. The schools were unequally funded, i.e. grammar schools gained more money per student than the other two schools.

- Remember that examiners will expect you to be fully conversant with key educational policies – especially new educational policy. This means that you must not only be able to describe them but also show that there are many conflicting views as to whether they have been successful or not.

What does this mean?

The tripartite system of education was set up as a result of the 1944 Education Act. 'Tri' meaning three, it referred to three types of schools that children could attend: the technical school, the secondary modern and the grammar school.

The aim of the 1944 Education Act

The years 1939 to 1945 had witnessed widespread destruction, mass killing and human suffering on an enormous level. Policy makers and the general public in many Western European societies wanted a new and better society to replace the one that had been partially responsible for the Second World War taking place. Education as an institution was seen as one vehicle for change.

The Act aimed to offer an equal chance to develop the talents and abilities of all pupils in England and Wales. This was to be done within a free system of compulsory state education that was to be completely reorganised into primary education (nursery, infant and junior education) to the age of eleven; secondary education from the ages of eleven to fifteen; and then post-compulsory education, i.e. that of free choice that could take children into further and/or higher education at university level. These were exciting and ambitious aims.

A psychometric or IQ test was given to children in their last year of primary school. The test would be used to measure intelligence and was known as the 11-plus exam. It would be used to 'determine' which type of secondary school in the tripartite system these children would attend once they had completed their primary education.

What were the three schools?

- *The grammar school* – accepted what it considered to be academically bright pupils who had done well in the 11-plus exam. Such schools taught a wide range of academic subjects including Latin and in some cases Greek. These schools entered their pupils for public examinations ('O' and 'A' levels) which were needed for any pupil that wished to attend university. Twenty per cent of the population at that time attended these schools.
- *The secondary modern* – accepted most students in the country. Such children would not have performed as well in the 11-plus exam as those who went on to grammar schools and as a result they would receive a basic education with a more practical emphasis. Up to the 1960s there was very little opportunity for public examinations to be taken in such schools meaning that the opportunity to go to university was effectively ruled out if you went to such a school.

- *Technical schools* – only accepted about 5 per cent of students in the country at that time. Such schools were designed for pupils that excelled in technical subjects and consequently emphasised vocational skills and knowledge.

Criticising the tripartite system

Despite its ambitious and exciting aims, there were many problems with the tripartite system of education.

1. The problem with IQ tests, as we have seen, is that they can be culturally biased in favour of middle-class pupils. This meant that the majority of grammar school pupils came from the middle classes. Far from providing an equal education for all, the tripartite system reflected the existing social divisions in society.
2. **'Parity of esteem'** (the idea that one school should be considered to have the same 'status' as another) did not exist between these three types of school. Parents, teachers and students saw the grammar school as superior to the other types of school. This could mean that some parents, some teachers and some students could see themselves as failures if they were involved in any school that was not a grammar school.
3. Despite the aims of the 1944 Education Act to provide better education for all, the tripartite system did not include those pupils whose parents or guardians paid for their education, i.e. independent or private school education. At that time, 7 per cent of the population of school children attended such schools.

Conclusion

Far from providing an equal education for all, the existence of both the tripartite system of education and private schools meant that an extremely small percentage of the population were gaining the opportunity to go to university and to have life chances in general that most others could not. 'Most others' in this case tended to be working-class families.

For consideration

1. Can you see a similarity between the tripartite system of education in the 1940s and 1950s and the system today?
2. Why do you think that many parents argue that grammar schools should not be abolished?

● **Synoptic Link**

Functionalists argue that societies should be meritocratic, i.e. that those that possess ability to work hard and do well academically need an education system that recognises both these traits. Marxists are critical of whether this is in fact the case arguing that people do not start on a 'level playing field' as functionalists suggest. The tripartite system can, in A2, be used in any discussion you have about social inequality and its connection to education.

✳ **Key Idea**

'Parity of esteem' means that two or more objects have the same status. This phrase comes up again and again in education, for example to refer to whether or not comprehensive schools and grammar schools have had the same 'status' (or 'parity of esteem'). We can use this term here to discuss whether or not 'vocational qualifications' are viewed by the public as having the same 'status' or 'parity of esteem' to A-levels. This phrase must be memorised for any education exam question.

3.7 | What is the comprehensive system?

What does this mean?

In 1965 the then Labour government, led by Harold Wilson, requested that all local education authorities in the country run secondary education along comprehensive lines. Comprehensive schools were set up to provide *one type* of school for all types of student, inclusive of all types of ability regardless of gender, class or ethnicity. This meant that there was also no requirement for an entrance exam, 11-plus result or interview. Students were placed in **streams** or **sets** based on ability.

Is there or has there ever been a 'comprehensive' system?

When looking at the British education system it is extremely difficult to talk about one particular system lasting over any length of time. There are two main reasons for this.

1. Due to the nature of British politics and what is effectively a two-party system, what one political party works hard to set up, the other party will work equally hard to change, modify or destroy when it gains power. Traditionally the Conservative party has favoured the tripartite system while the 'old' Labour party supported the idea of a fully comprehensive system. Until the Blair government came into power, the Conservative party largely dominated post-war politics in England and Wales. Consequently they worked hard to destroy or attack any idea that comprehensive schools could be a success. Tony Blair's New Labour is encouraging a variety of different types of education and continues to push the idea of parental choice, formerly associated with the Conservative party.
2. The idea of any system is that it works in the same way for a large group of people. However, in the case of comprehensive schools they took their pupils from what are referred to as catchment areas, i.e. pupils had to live in the immediate area around the school. That means that it is very difficult to compare, for example, a comprehensive school in an inner-city area to one in the leafy green suburbs. In the first case, the majority of students will be from a variety of cultural backgrounds and will probably be mainly working-class; and in the second, students will probably be white and there will be a larger percentage of middle-class children.

These two reasons can be used to explain why it is very difficult to evaluate the comprehensive system or any other system of education that has been put in place by each successive government.

Evaluating the success of comprehensive schools

There are a number of difficulties in trying to measure how well comprehensive schools have performed in the past.

Why is it difficult to evaluate the comprehensive system?

❝❞ Key Definition

'**Streams**' and '**sets**' are terms that students often confuse in the exam. Streaming means being placed in one class for all subjects based on ability (for example, top 'stream' or bottom 'stream'). Setting was considered an improvement because instead of staying in the same class/stream over a long period of time, it allowed students to be placed in different sets for different subjects (for example, Top 'set' for maths, middle 'set' for French and bottom 'set' for geography).

- Stop-go policies have meant that no one comprehensive system has been in place long enough to evaluate its success.
- With a small minority of rich children attending private schools it is impossible to know how well comprehensive schools might have performed had these children attended them.
- Measuring the 'performativity' (how well a school performs) of any school depends on what you are actually measuring, i.e. exam results, the ability to take children from very low ability to a significantly higher one, or in fact, the creation of a warm supportive and caring environment.
- Although comprehensive schools were extremely popular, there were always a significant number of grammar schools around to 'attract' high-achieving students. Had the grammar schools not been there, these students would have attended the comprehensive schools and boosted the schools' overall exam pass rates.
- Some comprehensives broke down the barriers between class, gender and race by educating pupils from different classes, genders and races. However, this is dependent on the locality of the school. A comprehensive in a predominantly white, middle-class area for example, will not include pupils from different ethnic backgrounds if they do not live in the catchment area.

Conclusion

The popular complaint, voiced by parents, that comprehensive schools lowered standards for high-achieving students was used by the Conservative party as an excuse to attack and restrict the number of comprehensive schools that existed. However, a study carried out by the National Children's Bureau refuted such an idea. By taking 16,000 pupils all born in the same week of 1958, it explored how children performed in different types of secondary school. It showed (by exploring maths and reading tests) that high-achieving children made the same level of progress regardless of whatever different type of secondary school they attended.

✳ Key Ideas

- Policies that change when one government loses and another one wins are often referred to as 'stop-go policies'. This idea explains why many excellent policies have never really been given a proper chance because when a new government is elected they will probably attempt to change or stop the policies of the previous government. Use this as an evaluative tool when referring to any educational policy that you discuss in the exam.
- Three criticisms you can make about comprehensive schools are:

  1. Heath (1992) argues that class differences in education have largely remained unchanged since the introduction of comprehensives in the 1960s.
  2. The streaming system that many comprehensives use results in social class segregation, i.e. working-class children tend to be labelled and placed in lower streams.
  3. Comprehensive schools tend to be 'single' rather than 'multi' class institutions. Pupils come from the 'catchment' area where the school is. This might mean a working-class catchment area, such as Newham, or a middle-class catchment area, such as Kensington.

● Synoptic Link

There are a variety of concepts that would enable you to make links with Social inequality and education. These concepts include 'locality', 'social control', 'identity' and of course 'class', 'gender' and 'ethnicity'. Make sure that your folder has got these links highlighted before you start A2. Show your folder to your teachers and get them to check that these synoptic links are correct.

For consideration

1. To what extent do you think it mattered to teachers or students which type of school they attended?
2. How might the views of teachers about the type of school they work in affect the methods and ways in which they teach their pupils?

3.8 | What is vocationalism?

⁂ Key Idea

The exam will want you to make a connection between education and the economy. As a result of the British economy not doing well in the 1970s, British politicians changed the traditional way in which people were educated in England and Wales. By encouraging teachers to focus on skills required for the workplace, it was hoped that a newly trained work force would increase British business competitiveness. In this way it also placed the emphasis (and blame) on teachers to increase employment (by equipping pupils with the right skills) rather than on economic policies that could lead to more jobs in the first place.

What does this mean?

Vocational training refers to any type of training that is preparing people for the world of work. In many countries in Europe throughout most of the 20th century, vocationalism was very much part of the school curriculum. However, in England in the 1960s, vocational training was viewed by the government as something that should be tackled in the workplace rather than in school. 'New Vocationalism' refers to the change in view by the government that vocational training should also take place in schools and colleges. It emerged in Britain in the late 1970s and is still something that is continuously being developed within schools and colleges across the country today. In January 2003 the government announced that a complete overhaul of education would need to take place for 14–19 year-olds which would have to take into consideration the employment needs of industry.

Why was 'new vocationalism' introduced by the government?

During the 1970s the British economy (as well as many other European economies) went into recession, i.e. it became very weak. British politicians were concerned about the rising unemployment that this created and, in particular, the rising youth unemployment. Rather than accepting any responsibility, in 1976, at Ruskin College, Oxford, the then British Prime Minister James Callaghan blamed teachers for the lack of skills that young people possessed. Schools, he argued, should improve vocational training and education to meet the requirements of industry.

What government educational policies and organisations have been inspired by 'new vocationalism'?

- The Manpower Services Commission became the main agency in developing youth training in the 1970s.
- In 1978 the Youth Opportunities Programme was introduced to offer young people six months of work experience and 'off the job' training.
- In 1983 the Youth Training Scheme was introduced to offer school leavers a year of training in a variety of different occupations.
- In 1986 the National Council for Vocational Qualifications was set up to offer a nationally recognised system of qualifications.
- General National Vocational Qualifications (GNVQs) were quickly introduced as alternative ways for young people to gain qualifications that were work-orientated.
- With Curriculum 2000 came the introduction of Advanced Vocational Certificates of Education (AVCEs) which were to replace GNVQs and offer a qualification equivalent to two A-levels.

Four criticisms of 'new vocationalism'

1. Professor Dan Finn (1987) argued that it was the poor economic management of the British government that was responsible for unemployment rather than the lack of skills of young people.
2. Philip Cohen (1984) argued that in many vocational training programmes young people were used as cheap labour rather than being trained in the workplace to learn new and valuable skills.
3. Paul Stephens (2001) argues that in Britain there has always been a class snobbery between those that are 'trained' and those that are 'educated'. He argues that in many other countries no such snobbery exists. This accounts for why, in the UK, many people see A-levels as being socially more acceptable than the vocational qualifications.
4. Richard Pring (1990) ironically refers to a 'New Tripartism' consisting of those with A-levels, those with BTEC/GNVQs and those who have received some sort of youth training. The qualification can be connected to class, occupation and pay.

Conclusion

Remember that state education was set up in the 19th century primarily as a result of a realisation by the government that there was a direct relationship between education and the economy. By teaching children how to read they were being prepared to be efficient workers at a time when international economic competitiveness was a national concern. The conception and gradual introduction of new vocationalism took place during a period of economic decline (the late 1970s and 1980s). You, the student, can make the connections between schooling, employment and the economy that have been raised in this section.

✓ Top Exam Hint

Evaluating any theory or concept in education means that you question how the data was gathered and when. Question to what extent the empirical data (the research data that has been collected) can be 'verified' for its accuracy. Analyse the argument to see if it holds together logically. Identify to what extent the theory, study or claim is 'comprehensive', i.e. that it can be used to explain other situations in a different culture, time or place. Use these points to structure an evaluative paragraph about the writer, theory or concept you are criticising.

● Synoptic Link

You might like to consider how those in power have the ability to effectively control the destiny of so many young people through the decisions they take as professionals. Teachers effectively 'stream' children when they advise that they either take an academic or vocational route in education. Teachers may well have fixed ideas about the type of students that may fit better in academic rather than vocational subjects, and vice versa. You can also see from the work of Richard Pring how a case can be made that there are disproportionately more working-class and ethnic minority children on vocational courses. In this way you are connecting the concepts of power, control and social inequality and difference.

For consideration

1. Is the purpose of education to get a job?
2. Do you think 'parity of esteem' exists between A-levels and vocational qualifications? Justify your answer.

3.9 What impact did the 1988 Educational Reform Act have?

✍ Coursework Suggestion

Carry out two **focus groups** with teachers to explore how their feelings change about education the longer they work within the system. Do this first of all with a group of teachers who have just qualified or who are in the process of training (ask your teacher for help in how to contact them) and then with a group of teachers in your school who have been working for a few years. See how their reactions vary (or not) to some questions you pose to them. Then you can try to come up with reasons for their differences in opinions.

💬 Key Definition

A **focus group** is a small sample of people gathered together by the researcher. Focus groups are often used as an initial method of research to explore issues of interest to the sociologist. In doing so they can gain valuable information in a way that is not too threatening to the respondents. The aim is to introduce a question or questions that the group can discuss possible answers or solutions to. Sometimes the researcher will then carry out 'follow-up' interviews with one or two of the members of the focus group to explore particular issues raised.

✓ Top Exam Hint

Tell the examiner that the National Curriculum did not affect all students in the country. It did not affect private schools within the independent sector nor did it affect the variety of specialist schools that existed for children with special education needs. You should also remember that the 'National Curriculum' only affected the English and Welsh education systems. Scotland has continued to have a completely different education system. In OCR sociology you will not be expected to know anything about the Scottish system.

What does this mean?

The 1988 Educational Reform Act (known as the ERA) was the largest change in educational policy-making since the 1944 Butler Act and reflected the New Right ideas of the Conservative party who led the country at the time. By taking its ideas from the ideas of business, the ERA attempted to increase parental choice and introduce market forces into education, i.e. that by competing with each other, schools would raise standards.

What changes did the ERA introduce?

- State schools were to be inspected in a more thorough fashion than at any time since their creation.
- A 'National Curriculum' of subjects was introduced for all pupils within the state primary and secondary education system and was composed of maths, science, English, history, geography, technology, music, art, physical education and a modern language (in secondary schools).
- Compulsory testing at Key Stages in these subjects was required at the ages of seven, eleven, fourteen and sixteen within the state sector.
- The ERA also introduced league tables of local education authority schools listed in order of performance based on the national curriculum assessment (exams). Parents, as a result, would have the right to send their children to the school of their choice. Schools, for the first time, were in competition with each other.
- Local Management of Schools (i.e. where schools themselves have the major responsibility in saying how they should be run) replaced the previous system where LEAs (local education authorities) had control over how the schools were run. The new system gave greater power to individual heads of schools.
- Many schools (including a large number of grammar schools) could opt out of local funding. This meant that the complete budget for running the school from the government was given to the headmaster/mistress. Such schools believed that they would have greater freedom in how they might use their resources.
- Private industry was to play a bigger role in English education by the setting up of City Technology Colleges (CTCs). Once again independent of LEAs, these institutions focused on maths, science and technology and were generally located in inner-city areas.

Conclusion

Parental choice sounds like a wonderful idea and league tables may well show how well some schools are doing but they also hide three processes of social marginalisation (the process whereby some people become 'left out' of mainstream society) outlined below.

1. David Gillborn (2001) argues that in the pressure to be successful in the league tables some teachers and heads of schools may not accept certain types of pupil because of the stereotypical ideas they may have about some pupils' performances. Such prejudice may mean that some students may not be accepted because of their ethnicity, gender or class backgrounds.

2. Parental choice affects how much money a school may receive. Every extra pupil means more money for a school and if a school performs well in the league tables then more parents will want to send their children there. This can have disastrous consequences for some excellent inner-city schools. A school that is slightly selective, or is in a predominantly middle-class area may well perform better than an inner-city school that attracts a greater share of pupils with social problems. It is these schools that need extra money. However, they may well not perform highly in the league tables and, as a result, miss out on much needed cash.

3. While the introduction of a National Curriculum has definitely helped to increase female educational performance (i.e. girls for the first time study the same subjects as boys and therefore have more opportunity to out-perform them than ever before), the key stage tests have been strongly criticised. The tests are tiered according to ability, resulting in teachers having to judge which tier pupils should be entered for. Both post-structuralist, Stephen Ball (1999), and interactionist, David Gillborn (2001), argue that there is a disproportionate percentage of working-class and ethnic minority pupils in lower tier groups.

For consideration

1. Do you think business ideas of competition and market choice can be applied to education?

2. What evidence can you see in your school or college that these ideas exist?

● Synoptic Links

- The concept of 'identity' makes a useful synoptic link between education and social inequality. David Gillborn (2001) has shown that some teachers make damaging generalisations about class and ethnic identities. With the increase in testing that the ERA has brought about he shows how pupils from working-class ethnic minority backgrounds may be entered for lower tiered tests. As a result these pupils are stratified into lower paying jobs and career opportunities later on based on the decisions made for them by their teachers.

- The concept of 'power' can be used to show how any group (for example, those based around age, gender, class, ethnicity, sexuality) can lack power over others or be 'exploited' by others because of their status. Use the concept of 'power' and highlight how, as a result of the education system, groups can be stratified within English society (for example, the power of some teachers to not enter certain students for exams!). Equally, some parents have more power than others to influence where their child goes to school, through the ability to move house to live in the catchment area of a good school. Parents with less money are less likely to be able to do this.

☀ Key Idea

Three criticisms you can use in the exam are:

1. The Education Reform Act does not cover those children attending private schools.

2. The league tables create 'sink schools', i.e. those schools that people see at the bottom of the tables, a position from which it is very difficult to recover.

3. The information in the league tables does nothing to reward those schools that, although at the lower end of the tables, accept children with special needs, language difficulties or from very low income families. It is these schools that require extra funding.

3.10 | What is 'Curriculum 2000'?

◆ **What, when and why?**

Sir Ron Dearing, the former head of the School Curriculum and Assessment Authority (SCAA), was appointed in 1993 by the government in London to review the provision of post-16 education in England and Wales. He was already highly critical of the level of testing and the highly prescriptive National Curriculum (i.e. one that told teachers exactly how to teach the subjects listed by government). He was also critical of the level of educational provision for 16–19 year-olds. The report suggested that students should take on a larger common component of core subjects along with grading that no longer separated the 'academic' from the 'vocational', i.e. that both academic and vocational subjects should be graded using the same grading scale of A–E.

✓ **Top Exam Hints**

- When trying to evaluate any concept, idea, theory or writer in sociology exams, always memorise and remember the ten sociological variables (age, class, cross-cultural perspectives, gender, globalisation, ethnicity, historical perspectives, region, religion, and sexuality). You can use any one of these 'variables' (hopefully you will use more than just one!) and write a single sentence – the examiners will have to award you extra marks for doing this.

- 'Parity of esteem' (see section 3.6) is an expression that means that something has equal status to something else. You can use this expression to argue that while Curriculum 2000 was meant to help bring 'parity of esteem' between academic A-levels and vocational AVCEs, the unequal way in which the exams have been levelled (see this section) means that no such equality exists. The system works against vocational students and therefore working-class and ethnic minority students.

What does this mean?

The chances are, if you are reading this book, that you are a product of Curriculum 2000, an entirely different way of organising what was once the A-level system of exams. Curriculum 2000, named after the year the policy came into force, has been the biggest reorganisation of post-16 education since the 1950s and has introduced AS- and A2-levels (the equivalent to a full A-level) which have replaced the A-level system.

What was the aim of Curriculum 2000?

As a result of the Dearing Report in 1998, it was found that while students in France and Germany experienced 30 hours of 'taught' time per week, sixth-formers in England studying A-levels were taught between 15–18 hours a week. European students were also seen to study a much broader range of subjects than English students, who specialised very early on in a narrow range of subjects. In response to the Dearing Report's findings, the aim of Curriculum 2000 was to broaden the curriculum for 16–19 year-olds to include a mixture of arts and sciences, vocational and academic subjects and to increase the skills awareness that industry required in maths, communication and IT.

How can we criticise Curriculum 2000?

- Before Curriculum 2000, teachers and pupils could use a lot of the third term to prepare for any exam that might have been set. Chris Savory (2002) from the Institute of Education argues that the 'two-term' dash that all AS students now face when preparing for the summer AS exams means that there is too much to learn in too little time, particularly for less able students.

- Jacky Lumby (2002) from Leicester University argues that it has created too much work for both staff and students and has reduced the possibility of doing other non-curriculum related subjects that add so much to some pupils' lives, for example, the Duke of Edinburgh award and work experience.

- While the AS examination has been constructed to be significantly easier than the A2, students taking Advanced Vocational Certificates in Education (AVCEs, i.e. vocational A-levels) have a completely different experience. Their first year exams are pitched at the same level as their second. Therefore no parity of esteem (see section 3.6) can be seen between the vocational and the academic.

- The introduction of examinations in the Key Skills of numeracy, communication and IT has been also criticised for offering exams that are too difficult for the level they are meant to be testing. They have also added to the exam load of students making the UK the most exam-orientated country in the world.

- While the aim was to increase student take-up of the arts and sciences, in reality students have been choosing the subjects that reflect their own strengths. In addition to this, although the expectation was for students to take five AS subjects in their first year, hardly any are actually doing this.

Conclusion

Can we identify any implications for policy and provision? It is too soon to explore the effects of this educational policy on working-class and ethnic minority pupils although much research is currently being carried out. For many less able students, the increased work pressure along with the reduced amount of teaching time available in the AS year means that certain students are suffering. The final term is now a term of examination rather than teaching.

With a greater share of working-class and ethnic minority students being channelled by teachers into an AVCE route, and, with the current situation where AVCE year one exams are harder than AS exams, it would seem likely that the system will increase rather than narrow the divide between classes and between the majority and ethnic minorities.

In January 2003, New Labour announced that another complete overhaul of the education system will be taking place. According to the Tomlinson Interim Report in February 2004, the changes will almost certainly involve the 14–19 age group and will possibly result in the creation of a diploma system and the removal of the AS/A2 system altogether.

Three evaluations you can use in the exam are:

1. Curriculum 2000 has only been around for a few years and this has not given enough time for sociologists to gather data about its 'success' or 'failure'.
2. If we are talking about its 'success', what are we comparing its success to?
3. By combining the old fashioned A-level with the European idea that students should study more broadly, the government has not really created a 'new' system of education but taken existing ideas from two very different systems – the British and the French/German models.

Curriculum 2000 – increasing the levels of education or the levels of stress?

✎ Coursework Suggestion

Use the Internet and email system to contact the heads of different schools in Europe (many European teachers will speak very good English). Carry out interviews to find out information on the different educational systems that exist. Use your data to evaluate how successful the English system is, from an international perspective. Remember that when deciding what questions you are posing you will have to be extremely clear about the definitions you deploy, the sample you use and the theoretical framework that you adopt. You will also need to bear in mind that, when evaluating your work, you can revisit these issues and discuss them as 'methodological problems'.

For consideration

1. What benefits can you see from the introduction of Curriculum 2000?

2. To what extent do you think that teachers have had to change the way they teach as a result of the introduction of Curriculum 2000?

What other types of education are there?

What does this mean?

When thinking about formal education, it is so easy just to consider different schools within the state educational sector (for example, grant-maintained schools, grammar and comprehensive schools) and those schools that are in the independent sector (i.e. private schools). However there are a variety of other types of schooling that you need to be aware of when answering questions in the exam. In this way, you are adding to your knowledge of educational achievement based on differences in class, gender and ethnicity.

Is there really an education system?

The sociology student should immediately challenge any question in the exam that refers to an education system by arguing that no one system exists. Do this by pointing out the variety of different 'systems' that are on offer.

- *Primary schools*: schooling for children aged 5–11.
- *Comprehensive schools*: schooling for children of all abilities aged 11–18 (up until the age of 16 if the school has no sixth form).
- *Lower/middle/upper schools*: a different way of organising the age range found in schools. Originally associated with private and grammar schools, many comprehensive schools are splitting the age ranges into these three groupings.
- *Special schools*: Provided by local educational authorities (LEAs) and some voluntary organisations, these schools are for children with special educational needs (for example, children with Down's Syndrome).
- *Education Otherwise*: With well over 1000 families in England and Wales taking part in this very distinct type of education, EO is where parents educate their children at home. Families who join EO are sent guides in how to provide adequate education for their children. This type of education is on the increase.
- *Pupil Referral Units (PRUs):* These are special institutions set up for disruptive students where their problems can receive special help. Not all LEAs have these units. A debate exists as to whether such children should be allowed to study in normal schools, be excluded or be allowed to study in PRUs. The majority of pupils in these units tend to be working-class white youths.
- *Grammar schools*: Originally dating back to the 14th century, these schools tend to accept academically bright children. After the 1944 Education Act such schools formed part of the tripartite system of education. Grammar schools are state schools and, as such, do not charge fees.
- *Independent/fee paying/private schools*: Independent schools (the term generally preferred by private and public schools) are schools that charge fees to the parents/guardians of the pupils who study there. There are

approximately 200 of these schools in England and Wales with the majority being boarding schools or having a boarding facility. The best known of these schools (Harrow, Eton, Marlborough, Westminster, Rugby and Sherborne) are referred to as public schools. These schools have had a tradition of sending many pupils into public office, i.e. pupils have become members of parliament or high-ranking figures within the legal profession. The term public school in the United States has the opposite meaning to that used here. In America public schools are free state schools for the public.

- *Religious schools*: In recent years a variety of religious groups have been forming their own full-time schools, particularly in the Jewish and Islamic communities.

Postmodernists versus Marxists

Many **postmodernists** argue that **postmodern** society is a pic'n'mix society where diversity and choice exist to a degree that they never did before. Looking at the diversity of education listed above and, perhaps, the degree of choice on offer, would seem to confirm the opinions that postmodernists share.

However, examining the list of schools above from a Marxist perspective might paint a different picture. The poverty that some working-class families share, along with extremely poor housing conditions, might well account for the high proportion of working-class children to be found in PRUs. Alternatively, how many working-class families could actually afford to have one parent at home, full-time, to provide the education to follow the Education Otherwise package?

Conclusion

As you can see, any question that asks you to assess how successful the educational system has been needs to be instantly unpacked in the exam. It is not enough to talk about the secondary education system without realising that the concept itself is too simplistic. It is also important to realise that the variety of education packages that exist may well represent those from a particular class, gender, ethnicity, region or religion.

66 99 Key Definition

Postmodernist theory talks about 'diversity' (many different types) and 'fragmentation' (the breaking up of established ways of doing things) in what it describes as a 'postmodern' society. Postmodernists argue that there are so many conflicting needs of individuals that it is impossible to provide one single type of education to meet all the needs. The variety of different types of education that are listed in this section can be used to support the post-modern argument of diversity and fragmentation.

● Synoptic Link

A synoptic link can be made here with social inequality and difference. By highlighting the role that education plays in maintaining the class system you will gain high evaluation marks for synopticity. Marxists argue that education not only acts as an 'ideological tool of the state' (i.e. making us think/do what it wants) but also allows people to forget they are living in a class-ridden society (the Marxist idea of false consciousness) by believing that it is a 'meritocracy' (the idea that you get to where you are in life based on 'merit' i.e. intelligence, hard work, commitment, and so on), exam certificates being 'merits'.

For consideration

1. What do you think about the idea of parents educating their children at home?

2. Why do you think that this type of education is increasing?

What do structuralists say about education?

☀ Key Ideas

- Emile Durkheim believed that the main function of education was to socialise children by teaching collective values. While primary socialisation occurred in the home, secondary socialisation was undertaken in school.

- Talcott Parsons (1964) argued that the school system is a microcosm of the adult occupational world. By this he meant that the rules and regulations that exist in school, along with the various power relationships that exist with other friends and teachers 'mirror' those to be found in later life when we start working. This is how, as part of 'secondary socialisation' (remember that 'primary socialisation' takes place in the family), the school teaches and prepares students for their work roles in life.

✓ Top Exam Hint

Many students in the exam wrongly argue that Marxism and functionalism 'are two completely different theories'. They are not and in fact they share many similarities that you will need to be able to spell out in the exam. They are both 'deterministic', i.e. they argue that education shapes and forms us. They argue that there is a strong connection between the needs of the economy and how the education system has been formed to meet those needs.

Functionalism

What does this mean?

Functionalist theory was the dominant sociological theory in the UK and the United States during the 1950s and early 1960s. Functionalists talk about how society creates shared norms and values and therefore tend to highlight the positive functions or contributions that education offers to society. They examine how schools promote a consensual society (i.e. individuals, groups and institutions in general are not in conflict) by *socialising* people in its norms and values. This theory is one of many that highlight the relationship between schooling, employment and the economy.

Education and a 'meritocratic society'

American functionalist, Talcott Parsons, argued that society was a 'meritocracy', i.e. that the social position you achieved in society as an adult (he called this 'achieved status') was based on your ability. This idea would suggest that the best people get the best jobs. For Parsons the education system acted as a bridge between the ascribed status you received at birth (for example, your gender or ethnic background) and your achieved status. In this way the education system could be seen to act as a sieve or mechanism for allocating different roles to people in society based on their ability.

Functionalists argue that education performs two functions

1. *An economic function* – in which the education system contributes to economic growth by training its pupils to be a skilled and hardworking future work force.
2. *A socialising* function – in which societies' norms and values are transmitted to pupils from one generation to the next.

How do education systems fulfil these two functions?

- *They integrate young people into their roles as loyal adult citizens*. This is done through many subjects in school (for example, the teaching of citizenship), but also through the **'hidden curriculum'** by teaching students to be obedient in class.
- *They integrate young people into their roles as workers*. By giving students qualifications you reward them for their hard work in the same way that wages are a reward for the labour process (this idea is also called the 'correspondence theory', see section 3.13).
- *They promote a sense of national identity*. This is done by the teaching of subjects like history, English, and religious education.

- *They transmit the norms and values from one generation to another.* It is not only by teaching the above subjects that such norms and values are transmitted, but also by educating future teachers who in turn will pass on the values they have learned within the education system.
- *They meet the economic needs of societies by creating a literate, hardworking work force.* This is done through the National Curriculum and the teaching of both A-levels and vocational qualifications. How effective this is would depend on how good the disciplinary system within a particular school or college might be in ensuring its pupils work hard.
- *They select and allocate roles for people based on ability within the classroom.* Closely associated with the functionalist idea of a 'meritocratic' society, this means that education helps to ensure that the most suitably qualified people get the most important and best-paid jobs.

Another way in which education acts as a form of secondary socialisation is through the process of role allocation. For Davis and Moore, writing after the Second World War, school and the education system allocates roles to people, which they then go on to perform as a functionally 'useful' member of the adult world. This process of role allocation is criticised by others such as Marxist sociologists since they argue that the meritocracy in Davis and Moore's ideas is little more than a myth. The education system seems fair, and this legitimates the idea that role allocation is fair. Instead, class divisions and difference is continued from one generation to the next.

Conclusion

As you can see, functionalists argue that education, as an institution, acts as a secondary form of socialisation, where young people are allocated roles within society depending on their ability in a variety of different ways. Such an idea is strongly criticised by other theorists (for example, feminists, Marxists and interactionists) who argue that society is not 'meritocratic' and that pupils of different classes, ethnicities and genders face prejudice within a system that is unfair and unjust.

66 99 Key Definition

The **'hidden curriculum'** is analysed by sociologists as an important form of socialisation that affects class, gender and ethnicity. It refers to the many different ways that students pick up messages about class, gender and other expectations, for example, who possesses authority. This is done in a variety of ways, for example, when teachers ask pupils to 'stand up' when they enter a classroom. Such actions enforce the idea of 'respect' for authority even if, as feminists argue, that 'authority' is patriarchal.

The language that some teachers and books use when talking about girls and boys can also form part of the hidden curriculum (for example, the way that some teachers might use the words 'managing director' and then immediately refer to the managing director as 'he' when talking to the class).

✳ Key Ideas

Cultural or social reproduction refers to the functionalists' and Marxists' argument that education is an agency of socialisation. For functionalists this means that it is the job of education to transmit societies' norms and values from one generation to the next. However for Marxists, education is seen as 'culturally reproducing' the class system from one generation to the next.

For consideration

1. What evidence is there to show that functionalists are correct when they believe that the education system is 'meritocratic'?

2. In what ways might Curriculum 2000 have affected the idea that education is meritocratic?

3.13 | What do structuralists say about education?

Marxism

What does this mean?

Marxists are highly critical of the role that education plays in people's lives. They completely disagreed with the functionalist idea that society was meritocratic by arguing that education systems automatically work against the interests of the working classes. By providing the rich and powerful with educational qualifications, the working classes could be exploited by those in power above them. This structural/macro theory highlights inequality of educational achievement and the relationship between education and the economy.

What is the 'myth of education'?

Bowles and Gintis', 'Myth of education' (1976) argued that the functionalist meritocratic idea that education offers everybody an equal chance is in fact a myth or story that all of us blindly believe. They believed that education systems worked against the interests of the working classes.

In their 'correspondence theory' they argued that there was a correspondence between social relationships in the classroom and the workplace. By this, they meant that the hierarchies, certificates, and discipline systems that can be found in schools are actually very similar to the world of work. In school you are paid in certificates, while in work you are paid in wages.

Education as an agency of social control

Louis Althusser (1971) believed that education as an institution socialised working-class children into accepting their subordinate position to the middle classes. He argued that education socially controls people in two ways.

- It convinces pupils that the capitalist system that we live in is fair and just.
- It prepares people for their later 'exploitation' in the workplace.

It does this in three ways.

1. *The hidden curriculum* means that students learn to follow instructions in an unquestioning way (e.g. folding arms; referring to teachers as 'miss' or 'sir'). This is preparing them for their exploitation in the workplace as they automatically accept the instruction and authority of those above them even if it means that they are 'used' in the process.
2. *'Alienation' of schoolwork* means that many children become bored or 'alienated' with schoolwork but are rewarded with marks or certificates. Alienation in this sense means that pupils cannot see the point of much of what they study or do not feel that they have a real say in what they

☀ Key Idea

Neo-Marxist Louis Althusser (1971) focused on the ways that the state can exercise 'power' in a variety of different ways. He argued that any nation can use what he called 'repressive state apparatuses' such as the police, the law and the army to control people. But he also referred to 'ideological state apparatuses' such as the media, culture, religion and education. These institutions can be used by the state to convince people that the society they live in is just and fair. He argued that education has replaced religion as the most powerful ideological state apparatus.

should study. This situation is similar to the world of work where **alienation** becomes something not to be questioned.

3. *Textbooks* that show how western societies might be 'advanced' give the impression that capitalism is the only successful economic system. Pupils may, as a result, start to look down on other, non-capitalist ways of organising an economy, for example, some Islamic states, or parts of China.

Education as 'alienation'

Paul Willis' work (1976) (see also section 3.2), though now dated, throws up fascinating issues for the sociologist of education. He focuses on how working-class children opted out of what they considered to be boring school work, even though many realised that by doing so they would enter equally boring jobs. Interviewing twelve 'lads' during their last year at school and first year at work, Willis highlighted how they rejected the values and attitudes they saw in school. They did this through their behaviour to other pupils and teachers but also by 'bunking' off lessons. Willis argued that this showed how, far from being helpless victims within the school, their rebellious attitude was evidence that working-class children could resist the middle-class values that schools encouraged.

Education as a system that reproduces social inequality

Marxists argue that education has a cultural reproduction role. Bourdieu has argued that schools, along with the staff that work in them are generally middle-class institutions. Working-class children simply do not possess the cultural capital (the ideas, tastes, values and lifestyle associated with a particular class) required for success in such establishments. This means that middle-class children will generally do better than working-class children. As such, school ensures middle-class dominance from one generation to the next.

Conclusion

Traditional Marxists are highly critical of the fact that education prepares us for our acceptance of the values of society. They argue that education socialises children into possessing a false consciousness which fails to see the inequalities of the capitalist society.

Kellner (2003) argues that the type of structuralist Marxist theories of capital and schooling that began circulated in the 1970s (e.g. Willis' work on his working class 'lads' in *Learning to Labour* or Stephen Balls' *Beachside comprehensive*) have been largely replaced by more poststructuralist versions of Marxism (e.g. Stephen Ball's recent work – see section 3.19). Kellner argues that neo-Marxist theories have sought to overcome a too-narrow focus on class and economics by stressing the importance of developing theories of agency and resistance and incorporating dimensions of gender, race, and sexuality into an expanded notion of multicultural education, democratisation,

Working-class boys making the choice to opt out, or victims of the system?

66 99 Key Definition

'Alienation' – this Marxist concept refers to the inability of individuals to relate, or identify with the work that they do. Marx argued that as societies became more and more modernised (i.e. working on production lines) they lost the traditional satisfaction that many areas of work had offered (for example, carpentry and farming). The meaninglessness of modern day work can produce feelings of frustration, anger and in some cases lead people to acts of crime or deviance.

● Synoptic Link

A synoptic link made between education, crime and deviance and social inequality and difference allows sociologists to explore how schools can 'alienate' some groups causing them to 'kick back' against the values being taught and create their own 'subcultures'. One reaction to alienation might be truancy. The current debate in the media about truancy shares the concern that disillusionment in school can lead to crime at a later stage. Sociologists explore these synoptic links.

For consideration

1. What activities are you involved in within education that you consider to be 'alienating' to you?

2. To what extent do you agree with Bowles and Gintis that the school 'corresponds' to the workplace?

What do structuralists say about education?

- Sylvia Walby (1999), a feminist sociologist, talks about a 'triple systems theory' of patriarchy. Arguing that 'patriarchy' is a useful concept she believes that experiences of ethnicity and class complicate how we think about what it is to be 'female'. She therefore argues that we have to combine three structures of power and difference when talking about gender-related issues: patriarchy, capitalism and racism. Applying these ideas to education, we need to consider how girls' educational experiences are affected by both their class and ethnicity, both in and out of the schools they attend.

- Walby's six social structures are as follows:

  1. The patriarchal mode of production where women's labour is exploited within the household by men.
  2. Patriarchal relations in paid work where women are segregated and paid less.
  3. Patriarchal relations in the state where the state operates in the interests of men rather than women.
  4. Male violence against women through rape, sexual, emotional and physical assault.
  5. Patriarchal relations in sexuality where men's sexuality is viewed completely differently to that of women.
  6. Patriarchal relations within cultural institutions and the creation through the media, education and religion, of masculine and feminine identities.

Feminism

What does this mean?

Feminists argue that education helps to enforce 'patriarchy', i.e. the belief that society is structured to meet the needs of males more than females and is, in fact, dominated by males. Feminists take a keen interest in the role that education plays as a 'secondary' form of socialisation. There are however a variety of 'feminisms' that students need to be aware of. They all highlight patterns of inequality and show how patriarchy is culturally transmitted and reproduced through education.

Feminism or feminisms?

Remember that 'feminisms' reflects the idea that there are many different opinions about how patriarchy affects women. In addition to the triple systems theory of Walby (see Key Idea) the key feminist theories are:

Liberal feminists argue that patriarchy will be ended by changes in equal opportunities and educational policies. For example, they would argue that the introduction of the National Curriculum has played a significant role in bringing about equality of education by making sure that both genders study the same subjects in school.

Marxist feminists argue that women's role in society is shaped and determined by the needs of the economy. They blame the capitalist system for allowing women to be forced into a situation where they are socialised into supporting men both in the home and the workplace. Education is seen as enforcing these expectations both on men and women.

Black feminists argue that to be black and female is a very different experience to that of being white and female. These very different experiences can be seen in schools and colleges and the way teachers and books treat both groups of students differently.

Radical feminists argue that patriarchy can only end when women are freed from the negative influence (and violence) that men inflict on women – both physically and emotionally. The school classroom and playground are seen as prime sources of such violence.

Post-feminists argue that there is no single meaning to what it means to be a 'woman' but rather that women possess multiple identities. Women can be 'black', 'white', 'gay', 'straight', 'working-class', and so on. They can be any or most of these at the same time. This lack of a single meaning as to what 'female' means confirms the postmodern idea that no single theory or concept can explain anything, including that of gender differences.

How does the 'hidden curriculum' operate?

Heaton and Lawson (1996) argue that feminists point to the hidden curriculum (see Key Definition, section 3.12) as a main source of gender socialisation in schools. They argue that it operates in five different ways.

1. *Through books* – Feminists claim that many children's books and school text books portray women as dependent on men. Kelly (1987) argues that women are largely 'invisible' in science texts.
2. *Through students* – Many female students are made to feel uncomfortable in the presence of male students when studying certain subjects. For example Culley (1986), when studying computing, showed how boys liked to 'colonise' the space around computers. In many cases teachers did not intervene leaving many girls to feel excluded from what was wrongly perceived as a male activity.
3. *Teachers' expectations and attitudes* – Although much has changed in recent years Heaton and Lawson argue that many teachers still possess strongly sexist ideas about certain tasks within the classroom, for example, boys are still asked to move furniture while girls are still asked to clean and wash surfaces (for example, in the laboratories).
4. *Through a patriarchal curriculum* – despite the introduction of the National Curriculum, many feminists argue that what is taught in schools still creates gender inequalities in education. The way that sport is still taught in many schools tends to focus more on the achievements of boys than girls for example, football and cricket. The choices made by boys and girls in A-levels are still strongly gender-specific in some areas (look around your own sociology class!)
5. *Through a lack of positive role models* – Despite the fact that there are more female teachers in England and Wales than male teachers, more men than women still occupy the senior management levels of schools and colleges. There are also remarkably few black female teachers. Feminists argue that this creates an expectation that positions of power and authority are automatically associated with men more than women.

Conclusion

Education is seen as a major source of gender socialisation by feminists. Different feminisms highlight different aspects of the education system that enforce an ideology that males are somehow naturally in positions of power and authority. The hidden curriculum shows a variety of ways that these processes work. However, you need to remember that despite the many problems that female students face in schools they are, in general, out-performing males in all areas of education.

Girls and boys in science, but who is asked to wash up afterwards?

✳ Key Idea

'Cultural transmission' is a really useful idea to use in the exams (and coursework). It refers to how one culture can be transmitted or 'passed on' from one generation to the next. This can happen with education and for example with the teaching methods of some teachers. Teachers will themselves reflect the ideas and beliefs they have gained throughout their lives and then 'transmit' those ideas to a new generation of students – one or two of whom might become teachers, and so the process goes on. This idea can be used to show how cultural expectations of the genders can be passed on from one generation to the next.

For consideration

1. Which branch of 'feminism' do you find the most convincing in its approach to gender socialisation?
2. How might you suggest an alternative approach to education that would challenge many of the criticisms offered by feminists?

3.15 | What do interactionists say about education?

What does this mean?

George Herbert Mead's (1934) theory of symbolic interactionalism starts with the idea that we develop who we are, or 'our self' by interacting with other people. By encountering 'significant others' such as parents, teachers, religious leaders and friends we start to see the world from their eyes. It should therefore come as no great surprise that this theory plays a very significant role when examining issues of class, ethnicity and gender in education. This micro theory of social action helps the sociologist understand the inequalities that exist through institutional processes by allowing the researcher to 'get up close' to that which is being studied.

The influence of Howard Becker

The following quote is taken from research carried out by Howard Becker in 1952 on 60 Chicago teachers: *Said one teacher: "Of course, it's not their fault, they aren't brought up right . . . parents in a neighbourhood like this aren't really interested"'*. Such a quote showed how teachers held strong stereotypical ideas of pupils from certain socio-economic backgrounds. Becker has strongly influenced the work of David Gillborn, Stephen Ball and many other contemporary sociologists when looking at how teachers label students and the effects this may have on them.

Labelling and the self-fulfilling prophecy

W. I. Thomas (1909) argued that if people defined social situations as real, they were real in their consequences. In what has now become known as the 'self-fulfilling prophecy' he was referring to how people can start to believe, and make possible, situations they would otherwise have thought could not happen. The following three examples show how this happens.

- Interactionists Rosenthal and Jacobson (1968) showed how teachers responded to being told that some of their students were brighter than others. In their experiment, teachers were told that a randomly picked sample of their pupils were actually intellectual 'bloomers'. Despite the fact that this was not true, these pupils, they argued, outperformed others in their class. Rosenthal and Jacobson used this to show how, when labelled, both those that are labelled and those that do the labelling start to bring about a 'self-fulfilling prophecy', i.e. that subconsciously teachers will start to respond to those students in a very different way. Such accounts can be used to show how teachers who hold stereotypical views about race, class and gender may actually have a major effect on pupils they teach.
- Post-structuralist Stephen Ball's (1981) study, *Beachside Comprehensive*, showed how teacher expectations of some students led to the banding or

☀ Key Idea

The work of Howard Becker is highly influential in the exploration of labelling and self-fulfilling prophecies within education. Although his work is strongly associated with criminology and deviance, it has been applied to the way that pupils and teachers interact with each other. His work showed how teachers applied labels to students, for example, 'rebellious'. He argued that teachers constantly reinforced their initial negative judgements in all subsequent interactions with students, resulting in the pupil being 'trapped' in that perception.

streaming of certain pupils in a comprehensive school. His work showed how teachers varied their expectations and teaching methodology depending on the band pupils were in.

- Over the last thirteen years, interactionist David Gillborn has continued to be influenced by the work of Howard Becker as he explores the experience of ethnic minority pupils at the hands of some teachers. His work has shown that some teachers 'blame' African-Caribbean students more than white students for poor behaviour even when the behaviour is identical. In what he describes as 'the myth of the black challenge' he shows how teachers perceive certain types of behaviour as 'threatening' and then go on to punish students accordingly. He found that these pupils were disproportionately placed on report, put in detention or excluded compared to other ethnic minorities in schools.

Conclusion

Had it not been for this type of interactionist research, the experiences of pupils at the hands of some teachers within the education system would never have become discovered. These experiences show, through the concept of a self-fulfilling prophecy, how pupils themselves along with teachers can affect the educational careers of different genders, ethnicities or classes. There are, however, two criticisms that need to be noted.

1. The small-scale nature of much of interactionalist research can sometimes ignore larger macro dimensions to the classroom experience such as government policy (for example, the introduction of Curriculum 2000) and funding (greater funding would mean more teachers to fewer students and therefore a more meaningful learning environment for all concerned).
2. Paul Willis' (1976) study on working-class 'lads' has shown how some pupils do not passively accept the labels or expectations that others have for them.

For consideration

1. To what extent do you think the 'labelling process' is a useful explanation for male underachievement?

2. What other theories can you use, in combination with interactionist theory, when explaining the educational under-achievement of pupils?

3.16 | What do postmodernists say about education?

✳ Key Idea

The period of modernity stretched from the late 18th century through to the 1970s. During this period many writers argue that life was far more predictable than it is now. Science was seen to provide some of the answers that in previous times only religion could address (for example, if it rained in medieval times it was because 'god' or 'the gods' permitted it whereas in 'modern' times we can explain this 'scientifically'). By the 20th century scientific theories and other theories were used in the hope that the quality of life would improve. Jobs were 'for life' and identities were 'fixed' by class, race or gender. Postmodernists argue that this 'golden' age started to come to an end from the 1960s onwards.

✓ Top Exam Hint

Remember that postmodernism is itself a theory that attempts to offer an explanation for what education is and how it works. Many postmodernists argue that all theories are just stories or 'metanarratives' (the word for big theories that postmodernists use). However, does this not equally make 'postmodernism' a story or theory? Say this in the exam as a way of evaluating postmodernist claims and the examiners will award you marks for your evaluative skills and knowledge of sociological theory.

What does this mean?

Postmodernists argue that the period that we are living in now is very different from that of any other time in history. They argue that the 'modern' era of the 18th, 19th and 20th centuries has ended and that education needs to adapt to the enormous changes that are taking place within societies at a global level. They refer to what was once a 'golden age' of certainty, and contrast that with today's society that is risk-laden and diverse.

The risks include the dangers of genetically-modified food, chemical warfare and the possibility of global destruction. The diversity includes the variety of languages and the ethnic mix of people who live together in towns and cities; changes in music, fashion and lifestyle; and changing patterns in the way we work. These have huge implications for education systems. This theory highlights issues to do with the transition from school to work, along with the changing relationship between schooling, employment and the economy. It also helps in an understanding of educational policy-making and provision.

What are some of these changes that have taken place?

1. *A change from 'fordism' to 'postfordism'* – 'fordism' takes its name from The Ford Motor Company, where cars were mass produced on production lines. Throughout much of the 20th century, 'fordist' methods of production meant that people were trained in a particular skill and then gained jobs that were quite often on a production line or associated with one particular way of working. The expectation was that these were jobs for life. Nowadays, the concept of a job for life no longer exists. 'Postfordism' is the idea that production methods quickly change to meet the needs of consumers/customers whose tastes quickly change from one fashion to the next. This means that any future work force must be trained in schools to be multi-skilled. They must also expect to change jobs throughout their lives.

2. *Societies are become increasingly fragmented and diverse in make up* – traditional institutions like the family and religion have gone through immense changes over the last 50 years. Single parent families make up almost half the families in Britain. Gay couples are becoming accepted in mainstream society. Increasingly the role that religion plays in the formation of schools is changing to address the needs of a multi-cultural England. In all cases this means that any attempt to impose a common or national curriculum on all pupils is unlikely to meet the needs of all concerned.

3. *A 'collapse of the economy of truth'* – Hebdige (1989) argues that any particular theory or 'expert knowledge' is in fact a 'metanarrative' or big story. Such stories cannot claim to be a 'truthful' portrayal of how the world actually is. What you believed to be true yesterday is likely to be

proven untrue today. Knowledge is just a 'social construction,' i.e. something that powerful groups in society say we should know. Evidence of this distrust in expert knowledge can be seen in the way that many people no longer hold the same trust in doctors or priests that they once did.

4. *An increase in all types of 'surveillance'* – postmodernists argue that in today's societies we are continuously being 'observed'. They point not only to the increase in CCTVs in operation but also to the increase in record-keeping paperwork and the use of targets so that we can 'monitor' people in schools, jobs and in society in general.

Conclusion

- Moore and Hickox (1994) argue that because of the rapid changes that are taking place in most societies it is impossible to provide a curriculum (national, vocational or otherwise) that can address the challenges that such changes create.

- As a result of the increase in monitoring, record-keeping and target setting that postmodernists argue is a symptom of today's education, pupils suffer because they are increasingly asked to take tests and exams. Thus stress loads increase along with widespread disillusionment about what education really is.

- If there are, as postmodernists argue, no longer right or wrong pieces of knowledge, where does that leave the status of teachers who are supposed to be 'experts' in the classroom? Does this account for why there is a current shortage of teachers in the profession?

Blue-collar workers in the 1950s with a job for life – what defines somebody's class today?

● Synoptic Link

Apply the ideas presented here synoptically to social inequality and difference. Postmodernists challenge traditional explanations of social inequality based on class, gender and ethnicity. They argue that while these old-fashioned concepts belonged to an era where 'production' was what defined an identity (for example, you were a builder, metal worker, engineer, and so on) and these jobs were invariably linked to your class background, now it is what we consume that defines who we are – therefore these old labels are no longer appropriate.

For consideration

1. What evidence can you collect that proves the postmodernist argument that 'experts' are no longer treated with the respect they once were?

2. What certainties can you find that characterise what postmodernists refer to as 'modernity'?

3.17 How does education socialise pupils?

What does this mean?

Understanding the nature of 'power' and 'control' is the central concern of most sociologists. The majority of pupils in England spend a minimum of eleven years being formally educated in primary and secondary schools. Whether in the classroom, canteen or playground, a variety of 'interactions' take place that many sociologists argue can affect or socialise our identities. The effect of this socialisation process depends enormously on who has the power to control the socialisation process in the first place.

What does education do to pupils?

The following list identifies some of the ways in which schools might socialise pupils into the adult roles they later take on.

1. *Alienation* – Many Marxists argue that education alienates working-class children (see section 3.13). The curriculum, textbooks and even the way some teachers talk is far removed from the desires and lifestyles of working-class children. Rising rates of truancy in British schools would be evidence to show this is the case.

2. *Ideological control* – Whether we are talking about patriarchal ideology or capitalist ideology, schools have a variety of ways of making pupils believe society's values should go unquestioned. One example of this process is standing up when teachers come into the class, and calling them 'miss' or 'sir'. In this way pupils learn to 'respect' authority and not challenge those in power regardless of whether or not they are correct.

3. *Labelling* – By allowing teachers and pupils to 'label' each other, many children are being placed in an educational 'pathway' that determines their life chances later on (see section 3.15). One example of this is when some teachers place children in lower sets or streams which, if leading up to GCSEs, can drastically affect their exam results. David Gillborn (1990) has shown how quite often it is members of ethnic minorities that get placed in these lower sets or streams.

4. *Relationships of power* – Pupils are confronted in school by different authority figures from their teacher, to tutor, to year head and all the way up to the headmistress or headmaster. They are also confronted with their own peer groups and the various subcultures that exist within any school. These can leave lasting impressions on children. Some sociologists argue that male under-achievement can be traced to the fact that many primary school teachers are female which in turn socialises male pupils into believing that studying is not 'macho'.

5. *Cultural reproduction* – Schools have the capacity to culturally reproduce the dominant culture in the society the school exists in. This can be done through subjects within the National Curriculum (for example, History

where English history is taught from an English perspective) but also through the way that teachers themselves have been educated and then go on to teach new generations of pupils who, one day, may become teachers themselves!

6. *Role allocation* – By placing children in classes and setting them up within a system of tests and certificates, students can be 'sifted' into a role, be it doctor, engineer or road sweeper. Schools also have the ability to 'culturally reproduce' gender roles by persuading male or female pupils to take on specific subjects (although after the introduction of the National Curriculum this has decreased).

7. *The structure of the organisation* – Many feminists would argue that from an early age children are, without realising it, forced to accept that regardless of how many women may be in an organisation, in most cases men dominate the powerful positions in working life. Schools are one very good example of this 'social fact' with most heads and senior management positions being occupied by males.

8. *School sports* – Sociologists argue that sports in schools can be a way of socialising pupils into values of competitiveness, discipline, conformity and loyalty. While many functionalists would argue that this is in fact a positive function of the education system, some Marxists would argue that these values help sustain the capitalist system – a system that they are highly critical of.

Conclusion

As you can see, there are a variety of ways that schools, and the teachers who work in them, socialise pupils into particular ways of thinking and acting. Whether you believe that this is a positive or negative process will depend upon which particular theory is used to explain why these processes take place.

✓ **Top Exam Hint**

Remember to apply the ideas of George Mead's symbolic interactionism when referring to how children are socialised. He argued that the 'play' and 'game' stages of socialisation are crucial to forming a child's 'sense of self' or 'identity'. Both these stages quite often take place in the playgrounds at schools.

● **Synoptic Link**

Remember that by using the concept of 'socialisation' you can make direct links to the experience that children have in schools and the lives as adults they will be 'socialised' into. As a result this can be tied to social inequality and difference. In both cases choose case studies that show how teachers, the classroom or the make up of the school directly influences where pupils end up as adults.

For consideration

1. Draw up a list of any other ways that schools socialise pupils into particular norms and values.

2. How would the major sociological theories explain the processes of socialisation you have listed?

What do sociologists mean by 'in-school' and 'out-of-school' factors?

What does this mean?

When examining differences in educational achievement based on class, gender or ethnicity, sociologists focus on what they call 'in-school' and 'out-of-school' factors. In other words, sociologists have to look both within and beyond the immediate environment of the school to explain why students do well or badly within different educational systems.

What are 'in-school' factors?

- *Type of school* – is the school a comprehensive or grammar school?
- *Structure of the school* – is the school made of up of streams or sets or are the classes mixed ability?
- *Leadership of the school* – is the school well managed by the head/principal or senior managers? To what extent are the managers of the school white/black/male/female/working-class/middle-class?
- *Staffing of the school* – to what extent do the staff of the school reflect the cultural make up of its students, i.e. if the school is in a predominantly black or working-class area, how many black or working-class teachers are employed by the school?
- *Funding of the school* – does the school have enough money for resources (for example, books, desks, rooms, computers, teachers, and so on)?
- *Entry requirements* – does the school accept students with a variety of abilities or does it select on the basis of past exam performance?
- *Labelling* – to what extent do teachers label students and how might that affect which classes and ultimately which exams they may or may not sit?
- *Self-fulfilling prophecies* – as a result of labelling and being placed in a particular set, tier or stream, how might a pupil start to believe the label and then become the label, i.e. 'bright', 'not-so-bright', and so on?

What are 'out-of-school' factors?

- *Poverty* – to what extent are pupils materially deprived of certain essential requirements if they are expected to succeed within the educational system? These requirements might include a room of their own at home to study in, sufficient money for books, a healthy diet, sufficient clothes, and so on.
- *Parental interest* – often (wrongly) associated with middle-class parents, this might refer to taking an interest in homework, attending parents' evenings, encouragement and support for their child's studies in general and making sure that their child regularly attends school.
- *Language differences* – whether because of class or ethnic differences, a

culture clash can sometimes exist between the language used at home and outside the school with the language found in text books and used by teachers.

- *Cultural capital* – Neo-Marxist Bourdieu argues that the cultural capital of the middle classes is rewarded by exam success whereas that of the working classes is not. By this he means that the everyday bits of knowledge that many young middle-class children soak up from their parents (for example, names of classical musicians; names of theatre plays; knowledge of holiday destinations; certain newspapers) is the kind of knowledge that teachers unintentionally reward. Working-class cultural capital is, according to Bourdieu, not rewarded by teachers.

- *Positional theory* – Positional theorist Boudon argues that the difference in class position of both working-class and middle-class pupils impacts on how well both do. A lack of friends, relatives or neighbours coming from professional backgrounds along with less money to invest in education will place restrictions on children from the working classes in considering entering higher status jobs.

Conclusion

Different types of sociologists focus on different factors to explain why some people do better than others at school. In general (although not always) interpretive sociologists look at in-school factors, while in general (but also, not always), structural sociologists focus on out-of-school factors.

To what extent is deviancy a product of the education system?

● **Synoptic Link**

Education and social inequality and difference can once again be linked synoptically through ethnicity by referring to the concern that black males are under-achieving within the education system. David Gillborn's (1990) research shows that in many cases this is as a result of institutional racism within English schools. However, with rising crime rates and the wave of shootings that have been taking place in recent years, the government has been blaming 'rap' music and aspects of 'black male culture' rather than educational policies. Stuart Hall (1979), writing over 20 years ago, emphasised the way that ethnic minorities are almost invariably presented as a 'problem' within the media – often blamed for social disorder rather than the government.

For consideration

1. How might labelling theory be applied to all factors above?

2. How might a 'self-fulfilling prophecy' be associated with all factors above?

3.19 | What is the relationship between education and class?

◆ What, when and why?

New Labour was elected in 1997 and continued most of the educational policies that existed under the previous Conservative party's regime. Grammar schools and grant-maintained schools were kept and in March 2000 New Labour announced that grammar schools were 'here to stay'. The 'naming and shaming' of schools that the league tables encouraged has also continued under New Labour. However, with financial assistance being offered for the first time to the long-term unemployed and single parent mothers who wish to continue further education, some things have changed. 'Excellence in Cities' is a £350m programme that has created 'education action zones' targeting under-achievement in schools in major inner-city areas across the country.

✳ Key Ideas

- Sociobiologists hold the view that all social behaviour is shaped/determined by your natural instincts which are biologically created. The two most important of these are the desires to survive and reproduce. Sociologists challenge these ideas arguing that culture and the environment are more important than biology.

- The ideas of the New Right have had a great influence in the creation of educational policies over the last 20 years in England and Wales. Using ideas generally associated with the right wing of the Conservative party, the policies stress the need for individual freedom, responsibility and very little government involvement in public services (for example, education systems).

What does this mean?

Despite all the different government policies since the 1944 Education Act, students from working-class backgrounds, on average, achieve less within formal education than their middle-class counterparts. Evidence of this can be seen in exam results, lower reading scores in primary schools, higher leaving rates from school at the age of sixteen, and the fact that wherever streaming, setting or tiering takes place, working-class children can be seen to be disproportionately in the lower bands. There are a variety of explanations for this.

Structural explanations for working-class under-achievement

Some sociological explanations argue that it is structures within society that produce inequality within it. Below is a range of structural explanations that can be used to explain working-class under-achievement.

- Sociobiologists and many New Right thinkers argue that IQ tests show that working-class children have lower abilities than their middle-class peers.
- Basil Bernstein (1990) argues that the structure of the language that middle-class children use is the same as the language that teachers expect for exam success. He argues that working-class children's use of **restricted code** does not allow them to perform well in the school system, which is *culturally-biased* in favour of middle-class children.
- Positional theorist Boudon (1974) argues that it is harder for working-class children to aim for university and high status jobs while at the same time easier for middle-class children. When middle class, the expectation from friends, teachers and family is that you must enter a high status profession. Boudon argues the opposite is the case for working-class children.
- Bourdieu and Passeron (1977) argue, from a Marxist perspective, that the cultural capital of the middle-classes gives middle-class children an advantage over their working-class peers. By cultural capital they refer to the tastes, knowledge and ideas associated with a particular class. They argue that teachers and middle-class pupils share similar cultural capital and, as a result, teachers reward these pupils with greater educational success than their working-class counterparts.

Micro sociological explanations for working-class under-achievement

These interpretive explanations focus much more on the processes within the classroom and the individual interaction between students and teachers, and students themselves.

- Interactionist Keddie (1971) argued that teachers do not make judgements about students based on their performance but rather on their imagination as to what an 'ideal' student is. Teachers teach in a different way depending on what stream, set or tier students are placed in. This is a clear example of labelling and a self-fulfilling prophecy if the student then goes on to believe that they are bright or stupid, depending on the level they have been placed at by the teacher.

- Paul Willis (1977) argues against the deterministic explanations offered above. His research (see section 3.2) shows how values can be rejected if not relevant to pupils' lives.

Cultural explanations for working-class under-achievement

J. W. B. Douglas (1964) has argued that working-class parents are not as interested as those from the middle-classes in their children's educational success. A lack of parental encouragement along with lower levels of general knowledge, vocabulary and access to books was typical of many working-class families. However, it is important to realise that measuring parental interest is highly problematic; for example, a lack of attendance at parents' evenings may actually reflect the need to work nights to support the family rather than a lack of interest in the child's education.

Conclusion

The 'old' sociology of education focused mainly on how class played a major role in determining the educational success of pupils. However, few sociologists today hold this view, preferring to combine gender, ethnicity and class when evaluating the educational success of pupils in schools.

Increasingly neo-Marxists and other writers that have in the past focussed on class are combining identity markers like ethnicity and gender in their analysis of the education system. In a study called *Degrees of Choice,* D. Reay et al (2004) provide a sophisticated account of the overlapping effects of social class, ethnicity and gender in the process of choosing which university to attend. By the beginning of the 21st century, university education is increasingly shifting from one formed by an elite group to a mass education system for all.

Their study draws on qualitative and quantitative data to show how the welcome **expansion of higher education** has also deepened social stratification, generating new and different inequalities. While gender inequalities have reduced, those of social class remain and are now reinforced by racial inequalities in access. Students are seen to confront vastly different degrees of choice that are powerfully shaped by their social class and race. Courses such as media studies, business studies and IT tend to attract a lot of students from working class and ethnic minority backgrounds. As these courses become more popular, they become devalued and employers offer jobs to candidates with higher-status degrees, more often taken by white, middle-class students. So, while more students have the opportunity to take degrees, the chances of getting a job on graduation remains dependant on class and social position.

For consideration

1. To what extent do you accept that these explanations typify the 'working classes'?

2. To what extent is it easy to talk of class without also considering the effects of gender, ethnicity, sexuality and age?

66 99 Key Definition

Basil Bernstein (1990) talks of '**restricted**' and '**elaborated**' **codes**. The first is what, he argues, working-class children use and this consists of shortened phrases or 'slang' terms that communicate ideas well in certain circumstances but not in those of formal education. Middle-class children use both 'restricted' and 'elaborated' codes. Elaborated codes are the words that are used by teachers and found in textbooks. He argues that middle-class pupils automatically use these words and therefore perform well in the school system.

✳ Key Idea

Use Boudon, Bernstein and Bourdieu to evaluate the 'meritocratic' idea that functionalists have of a fair society. Functionalists assume that there is a 'level playing field' within the educational system and that education 'sorts out' those with ability from those without and that people are 'allocated' jobs as a result of the certificates they get from school. Boudon's theory argues that this is not the case and that the educational system automatically works against anybody who is working-class.

66 99 Key Definition

The recent **expansion of higher education** has occurred for two reasons. In the late 1990s, many polytechnics gained university status. More recently, Tony Blair has promised to get 50% of the population into higher education by 2010. While this has led to a wider range of candidates entering university, it has also created a hierarchy of universities with varying levels of entry.

In addition, changes in funding have led lower-level universities to compete for candidates by lowering entry criteria. As a result, qualifications are seen as being 'dumbed down'.

3.20 | What is the relationship between education and gender?

✳ Key Ideas

Feminist sociology has two major concerns when focusing on education systems. First, what roles do women occupy within educational institutions and second, what role does patriarchy play within the education of women? Many feminists argue that educational institutions legitimise gender inequality (for example, the way that while many teachers are women, many senior positions in schools and colleges are often held by men). By studying these institutions we can examine to what extent women's role and status is constructed through education and to what extent educational institutions oppress women.

◆ What, when and why?

By applying a 'historical perspective', i.e. considering how things might/might not have changed over time, it is possible to identify how education could be linked with social inequality and difference. During the 1970s women's status in the workplace was significantly lower than that of today. As Sue Sharpe has shown, female attitudes to education have significantly changed over the last two decades. The introduction of the National Curriculum and the fact that most females now want to stay on in education has meant that women are gaining far better jobs now than during the 1970s.

What does this mean?

It is hard to imagine that only in 1948 did Cambridge University accept full membership of women into most of its colleges. Until the 1980s sociologists of education focused on the under-achievement of females within the education system. However, this trend has completely changed over the last 25 years with women now outperforming men in most areas of education.

Traditional explanations for female under-achievement

- Sue Sharpe (1976) argues that different aspirations for females explained their lower educational achievement. Her study showed that 'love, marriage, husbands and children' were the main priorities for young women.
- Feminist Angela McRobbie (1978) argues that females in the late 1970s were influenced by magazines that highlighted the importance of romance over career.
- G. Griffin (1995) argues that some females leave school early to get out of the 'housework' role they occupy within the family.
- R. Deem (1990) focused on the role of the school curriculum during the late 1970s and early 1980s and how teachers encouraged females to take/not take certain subjects, for example, Home Economics and Science.

While the above studies are useful to sociology students, they cannot explain why females are outperforming males in the classroom today.

So what has changed?

Along with the women's movement in the 1970s, the media played a major role in promoting female individuality and ambition from the 1980s onwards (for example, Hollywood blockbuster movies at that time, such as *Working Girl*, and more recently, films like *Erin Brockovich*). Other factors were also involved.

- The introduction of the National Curriculum (a product of the 1988 ERA) that for the first time made males and females study the same subjects.
- The introduction of school initiatives in the late 1980s and early 1990s such as GIST (Girls into Science and Technology) and TVEI (the Technical Vocational Educational Initiative) that actively encouraged the role of females within these traditionally male-dominated vocational areas.
- Allison Kelly (1985) argued that as a result of an increased awareness of equal opportunities in schools, not only were books more closely monitored

for gender-biased language but also teacher training courses were modified to take into consideration the role gender plays within the classroom.

- Changes in the job market that include greater reliability on technology means that male strength is no longer a requirement within many types of manual labour.
- A report by the CBI (the Confederation of British Industry) in the late 1990s argued that if Britain were to remain economically competitive with other countries, Britain's top one hundred companies should be run by female managers. The report argued that they were better team leaders and more able to multi-task.

So why do males under-perform?

- Jane Clark (1996) showed that males were bombarded with images of the macho or anti-authority stereotypes both within and outside the media. This macho cultural stereotype associated with 'laddism' flies in the face of the image of woman as organiser or woman as carer that young males associate with the role of female teachers. This acts as a disincentive for males to be seen to focus on their studies within the school environment.
- New Right theory focuses on the increase in single-parent families and higher divorce rates to explain the lack of role models for males. The New Right often blame individuals and families for what they see as a moral decline in the values of society. The increased determination of women to be economically independent is also blamed for recent male under-achievement.
- Mac en Ghaill (1994) argues that many males experience a 'crisis of masculinity' because of the decline in traditional male jobs or professions. This identity crisis, he argues, allows some males to question the need for qualifications when the jobs they would have traditionally gone into no longer exist.

Conclusion

Despite what many commentators contend, after the introduction of the tripartite system (brought in after the 1944 Education Act), females actually achieved higher scores than males in the 11-plus exam. However, the government, concerned that more females would gain places in grammar schools than males, instructed their exams to be marked down to even up the scores.

Hollywood blockbuster films such as the 2000 film, *Erin Brockovich*, have played a role in promoting female ambition.

✓ Top Exam Hints

- Remember that when discussing gender differences in education you must also take into consideration differences in class and ethnicity, for example, the experience of a 'white', 'working-class' female in the classroom might well be very different to that of an 'Asian', 'middle-class' female. 'Triple systems feminist' Sylvia Walby (1990) argues that you must consider ethnicity, class and gender when analysing the experience of 'being female'.
- When writing for the A2 exam you must be clear that now the focus for sociologists is on male under-achievement within education and not female under-achievement. You will need to be clear about why things have changed and some of the processes involved when explaining under-achievement.

For consideration

1. Have you observed differences in the way males and females behave in the classroom?
2. Do your teachers react differently to the behaviour of males and females?

3.21 | What is the relationship between education and ethnicity?

✓ Top Exam Hints

When talking about the educational performance of a particular ethnic 'minority', you must remember that class and gender are important factors to take into consideration as are differences in language, religious belief and region. It is not enough to make generalisations about Pakistani or Bengali under-achievement but rather the social circumstances in which some Bengalis may live – whether it is in inner-city London or rural Bedfordshire.

Remember that racial categorisations such as 'white', and 'Afro-Caribbean' are 'social constructions', i.e. they have been created by individuals and have become acceptable classifications that most people use. This does not actually mean they are useful. Many statistics categorise Britons, Poles and Americans as 'white' and yet can we really make any generalisations about these three very different cultural groups? Similarly, how useful is 'Asian' when referring to the Chinese, Indians, Pakistanis, Indonesians or Malays, all of whom have distinct cultural differences? Mention this when talking about any racial categorisation or statistical comparison.

✳ Key Idea

'Cultural deprivation theory' represents a group of ideas that claim that working-class and some ethnic minority cultures fail to motivate their children adequately within education systems. As a result they fail to receive the skills and values required to succeed. It suggests that the parents of working-class children are less interested than middle-class parents in their children's success. Language differences between the classes are also used to explain differences in educational achievement.

What does this mean?

It is easy to assume that because Britain is considered to be a multicultural society there must be a relatively meritocratic education system, i.e. one that offers equal chances to all within it. When we look at the performance of Britain's ethnic minorities another picture arises in which huge differences exist between the educational performances of one ethnic minority compared to another. Sociologists explore these differences and, increasingly explore how other social variables such as class and gender help to explain why some ethnic groups seem to perform better than others.

Searching for explanations

- Intelligence cannot, as the Swann Committee (a committee appointed by the government to examine the education of ethnic minorities) showed in the mid-1980s, be a reason for differences in educational attainment between different ethnic groupings. The research showed that other social and economic factors were far more important than any differences in IQ (for example, levels of poverty, housing conditions and parental involvement).
- 'Cultural deprivation theory' states that many black children are deprived of the values needed for school success. However, this theory can be attacked by referring to how Ken Pryce (1979) showed that many Afro-Caribbean parents send their children to community-run supplementary schools.
- J. W. B. Douglas (1964) has also tried to use *cultural deprivation theory* to explain how the lack of parental involvement by many ethnic minorities explains poor educational attainment. Such evidence is based on lack of parental attendance at parents' evenings. However, this view can be criticised because quite often parents who do not attend parents' evenings are either working or feel intimidated by the formal situation.

Racism

Despite equal opportunities policies in schools, sufficient evidence exists to show that children from ethnic minorities often experience racism at schools – from teachers as well as other students. This can be seen as:

- *overt* (e.g., school playground insults)
- *covert/institutional* (e.g., teachers might exclude or unintentionally place students in lower tiers due to stereotypical views).

Most sociologists of education tend to be more interested in covert/institutional racism and its many processes and outcomes.

Confusing evidence

The Commission for Racial Equality carried out a study in 1992 ('Set to Fail') that showed how Asian students of similar ability to whites were less likely to be entered for GCSEs than their white counterparts. This would seem to show that ethnicity is a significant factor in explaining educational achievement.

However, Smith and Tomlinson (1989) argued that the class background of pupils was more important than ethnicity in explaining educational attainment. While they argue that ethnic minority groups were allocated in general to lower level courses and that many ethnic groups did worse in school tests than white students, they also argued that this was because many ethnic minorities come from working-class backgrounds and that differences in class are therefore more important than differences in ethnic background.

Some factors that explain ethnic under-achievement

1. A study carried out in 1988 by the Commission for Racial Equality showed that at 'Jayleigh' school teacher assessment meant that more white pupils were entered for a greater number of GCSEs than Asian students. More Asians were also placed in lower sets throughout their time in school.
2. Through primary-school classroom observation, Cecile Wright (1992) showed how teachers largely ignored Asian pupils particularly when it came to classroom discussion – wrongly assuming that their levels of English were not good enough.
3. Symbolic Interactionist concepts of labelling and a self-fulfilling prophecy show how teachers label some students as 'troublesome'. The frustration of experiencing this process means that some students develop 'attitude' to counteract the expectation that a teacher will pick on them. This becomes a self-fulfilling prophecy.

A recent report into education produced by Mirza and Gilborn, working for the Institute of Education, shows that while ethnic inequalities still greatly exist in the UK education system, patterns of difference in attainment between various ethnic groups themselves are changing:

- Indian and Chinese girls often outperform white girls
- Black African girls are the most rapidly improving group of students
- There are significant differences between black African and black Caribbean students
- Black boys are the most excluded groups in the system
- Girls outperform boys at all levels, within all ethnic groups
- Bangladeshi and Pakistani boys are under-achieving more than white boys.

Conclusion

There is no real clear evidence to show that ethnicity itself is a causal explanation for under-achievement. The class background of students is highly significant along with the labelling processes adopted by some teachers.

For consideration

1. Ask your college to give you a breakdown in statistics for exams over the last few years. Can you can identify differences between ethnic groups?
2. Are history text books 'culturally-biased' in favour of white culture?

☐ Key Fact

In 2003 the Department for Education and Skills reported that Indian and Chinese pupils are more likely to achieve the expected level of educational attainment, whereas Black, Bangladeshi and Pakistani pupils tend to perform less well than White pupils.

They suggest one reason for this may be due to economic disadvantage as higher proportions of Black, Bangladeshi and Pakistani pupils are eligible for free school meals (an indication of lower socio-economic level).

Source: 'Minority Ethnic Attainment and Participation in Education and Training', Research Topic Paper RTP01-03, DFES, 2003

✳ Key Idea

Trevor Jones (1993) found that members of many ethnic minorities were more likely to stay on in education than their white counterparts. His research showed that when looking at specific jobs he found that ethnic minorities were generally better qualified than whites who were doing the same job. Part of the reason for this, he argues, is that ethnic minorities perceive there to be a great deal of racism within the workplace and that therefore they will need the qualifications to 'prove' they can do the job that whites do.

David Gillborn (1995) showed how teachers in secondary schools quite often, wrongly, viewed the behaviour of Afro-Caribbean students as 'threatening'. As a result, disproportionate numbers of these students suffered greater degrees of punishment and exclusion than their white counterparts.

✍ Coursework Suggestion

David Gillborn's research is what is referred to as 'ethnographic' research, i.e. it is based on intensive firsthand investigation of small groups over a long period of time. Much educational research is carried out in this way. You could carry out your own research into education and ethnicity by 'shadowing' one or two students over a period of months to search for some evidence of institutional racism that Gillborn (1990) writes about. This could be done in break times perhaps once a week and you could ask teachers if you could observe the occasional lesson. Keep a research diary and record your findings. Carry out one interview with both students to increase the depth of your research findings.

What changes are taking place in education policy and provision?

Professor Stephen Ball is concerned about how the 'marketisation' of education affects pupils and teachers.

☞ Who is this person?

Stephen Ball is a professor of sociology and has worked at the University of Sussex and London University's Institute of Education, among others. He is also an author of several books including the famous *Beachside Comprehensive*; *The Micropolitics of the School*; and *Education Reform*. Sometimes described as a Marxist, sometimes described as a post-structuralist, his research ranges from exploring the effects of market forces on education, to families and their experience of children with cancer.

❑ Key Fact

Privately-sponsored academies
One notable feature of these developments is the emphasis placed on outside sponsors. For example, Frank Lowe represents sports stars like Anna Kournikova but he has also recently put £2m into one of the first of these schools in the London Borough of Brent. You might question why he chose to do this and what effect his sponsorship might have on the school.

What does this mean?

Sociologist Stephen Ball (1994) argues that a major change in the way that schools are managed has emerged over the last 20 years. Influenced by the ideas of the New Right, schools are managed in the same way as businesses. Hargreaves (1989) has referred to this development as a change to 'Kentucky Fried Schooling'. This 'marketisation' of education involves the belief that competition at all levels should provide a higher standard of education. However, many sociologists argue that this is not the way to run education systems.

How did the ideas of the New Right influence education?

The New Right was primarily associated in the late 1970s and early 1980s with the ideas of Margaret Thatcher, the former Conservative prime minister. Schools were to move away from being run by the local authorities to a more market-style system based on the 'language' of the commercial world of business. The idea was that this market of education would allocate resources where required. This had a number of implications for schools.

1. Schools, rather than the LEAs, were to manage their own budgets.
2. Schools had to provide freedom of choice for the consumer, i.e. the parents of the children they were trying to attract.
3. Schools had to be cost-effective as well as market themselves with an image that would attract new consumers.
4. Schools would compete with each other in the chase for new consumers, i.e. parents. Published league tables would provide parents with the information required for them to make their choices.
5. For each pupil attending a school, that school would gain a specific sum of money from the government.

In July 2004 New Labour's Education Secretary Charles Clarke announced a 5-year plan to improve state schools in England. In a final end to the traditional support for comprehensive education New Labour adopted Conservative educational reform plans. These focused on 'choice' rather than a 'one-size-fits-all' notion of education traditionally associated with Labour party educational policy.

Clarke promised that parents would have greater choice by increasing the number of **privately sponsored academies** from 12 to 200 (see key fact box). These schools were promised more financial freedom and the opportunity to specialise in subjects in certain subjects. Prior to this, choice of school existed (e.g. academies, city technology colleges, specialist schools and so-called 'beacon' schools).

It has been argued, however, that these reforms could only benefit middle class families who know how to work the system to their advantage. In an interview on BBC Radio 4, Professor Anne West, Director for Educational Research at the London School of Economics was critical of some aspects of the reforms. She argued that some schools would be able to make choices about which students they offer places to. Those that become more **autonomous** will be able to set their own admissions criteria. Schools that are more autonomous are more likely to be selective and that this could benefit middle class children more than working class (see section 3.13).

Marketisation of education as a global phenomenon?

The idea that schools should be run along business principles is not unique to England and Wales but is in line with thinking in certain other countries, namely the US, Canada, Australia and New Zealand. However, while it might be tempting to believe that such thinking is part of a global move to produce similar educational systems, this particular way of thinking does not exist in most countries in Europe.

Conclusion

The idea that schools should be run along market lines assumes that there is little inequality in society. Therefore if schools compete with each other, costs will be brought down while the standard of education will rise. There are a number of problems with this way of thinking.

- Should we really think about schools in the same way that we think about other businesses? Public services like education and health are dealing with people not consumable goods.
- If schools are forced to compete with each other, the danger is that schools will spend money on marketing the school rather than investing in resources for pupils.
- David Gillborn (2001) has shown that when schools start to compete for high positions in league tables, many students get marginalised, i.e. will not be accepted in some of the more high-achieving schools. In many cases this means that disproportionate numbers of working-class and ethnic minority students are to be found in schools lower down the league tables.
- Equality of education cannot be provided under a system that assumes little inequality. Middle-class schools in middle-class areas do not face the same problems as working-class schools in predominantly working-class areas. However, they do gain more money as a result of their higher position in the league tables.
- Charles Clarke's 2004 reforms were very similar to the Conservative party reforms produced one week earlier, confirming many social scientists argument that there is very little difference between policy making by either of the two main parties.

For consideration

1. What do you think Hargreaves meant by the phrase 'Kentucky Fried Schooling'?
2. How do schools in Europe finance and run their school systems?

❝❞ Key Definition

Autonomous mean self-governing. Some schools, such as foundation schools and voluntarily aided schools, are choosing to operate less under the control of central government. Instead, they are becoming more independent, giving them greater choice about they ways in which they manage themselves and also the students they admit.

✓ Top Exam Hints

Make sure that you have learned all the key terms and concepts in this chapter, such as alienation, marketisation and labelling, and that you can easily slot them into sentences when practising your exam answers.

● Synoptic Link

In an attempt to prepare for any synoptic component to a question in the exam go through your subject folder and highlight (this can be done with coloured pens, or labels) any handout, set of notes or photocopy where the topic of education could be connected to social inequality (for example, labelling). With each example you flag, write a sentence that explains how that particular concept of identity highlights the relationship between the individual and society. Type these up into revision notes and save this for when you start to revise for your exams.

How can we make education synoptic?

✓ Top Exam Hints

Now that you have come to the end of the unit, examine your folder. What state is it in? Do you feel that you would like to revise from it? Have you divided it into the various topics looked at in this chapter? Can you *clearly* see your class notes, handouts, homework exercises and marked work returned from your teachers? Have you placed all of these in *separate* transparent wallets or are they all bunched into a handful of such wallets making it difficult to actually know what you have in your folder in the first place? When reading through your folder, do you highlight the important bits so that you don't have to 're-read' it all again when you revise at a later stage? Organise your folder and you will find revision so much easier in the weeks leading up to the exam.

66 99 Key Definition

By using the phrase '**cultural transmission**' you can refer to how one culture can be *transmitted* or 'passed on' from one generation to the next via socialisation. This can happen via institutions such as the education system and or through the various ideologies within capitalist or patriarchal structures.

✳ Key Idea

Feminists might also argue that any dominant culture could be 'patriarchal'; Marxists might argue that any culture could be 'capitalist'; sociologists writing about race could argue that the dominant culture in the western world represents white, middle-class values. What ever dominant culture you care to discuss, this immediately allows you to talk about how some will be 'empowered' or 'disempowered' depending on who possesses more or less of the dominant culture.

Why is synopticity important for education?

If we accept that some of the key 'ingredients' to synopticity include 'class', 'gender', 'ethnicity', 'power', 'socialisation', 'culture', 'differentiation' and 'locality' *and* that we can use these ingredients to make powerful connections to social inequality, then the topic of education is an ideal tool for making these connections. Education provides an ideal chapter to use when revising your synoptic unit and examiners reward students who can combine one area of sociology with another when discussing a particular sociological issue. For example, is it really possible to talk about social inequality in the UK without including discussions about the education you receive and the type of work you do.

How does education link to issues of culture?

By 'culture' sociologists mean the set of shared values, norms and beliefs of a society or group of people. The word also refers to the shared meanings and symbols (for example, language) which people use to make sense of the world they live in. Students can talk about a 'dominant culture' to refer to the main culture in a society whose norms and values are seen to be the most powerful and generally accepted. Culture dominates any discussion on education whether it is about the pupil subcultures that exist in or outside the classroom or those of conflicting cultures embedded within student/teacher relationships.

How does education link to issues of identity?

Identity itself is an enormously complex term and yet most social scientists will agree that the constraints, challenges and opportunities you face vary depending on how 'empowered' or 'disempowered' that identity is. This chapter has shown how a variety of identities are socialised differently depending on the type of schooling or structure within a school the pupil has experienced. It has also shown how education sorts certain identities into the world of work albeit at different levels. Some writers even argue that the classroom mirrors the relationships found in the workplace.

How does education link to issues of inequality?

Now that you have almost read this chapter you will realise that far from providing equal opportunities of education to all, British education continues to treat different types of students differently. Most ethnic minority students continue to do significantly worse than their white counterparts, working-class under-achievement still exists and whereas girls were thought to 'under-achieve' the focus of concern now is on male under-achievement. Traditional Marxists argue that the economic infrastructure shapes the culture of all classes regardless of gender, age, or race. Most of the theories you have come across show in one way or another a direct relationship between education and the economy. They also show a direct relationship between education and inequality.

How does education link to issues of deviance?

A 'deviant' is somebody who 'deviates' from the norms and values associated with a particular culture. Any one dominant culture is the culture whose norms and values are seen to be the most powerful and generally accepted. Unfortunately there are many pupils that find the culture into which they are being socialised, i.e. via the secondary socialisation of education, an alien one. IQ testing and exam structures, not to mention the language of teachers and style of writing in textbooks all contribute to pushing some young people out of the classroom. Once out there is a strong likelihood that some of those alienated will drift into a world of crime or be considered 'deviant'.

How does education link to issues of social inequality and difference?

However you discuss inequality, whether in class, gender, sexuality, ethnicity or age, it can be linked to issues to do with education. The size of the classroom, the region in which the school is situated or the type of school that the child goes to, all affect how that pupil might succeed (or not) within any type of assessment. Add to that a recognition of in-school and out-of-school factors and materialist/cultural explanations, and the sociologist of education is left with a variety of often conflicting but nevertheless enlightening explanations for the inequality and difference that exists in the UK.

Key points to remember

- Remember that this unit provides a fabulous range of synoptic possibilities. Clearly label all your materials in this unit with the synoptic links mentioned in this section.
- Do not forget that the case studies quoted in this chapter (i.e. every time you see the name of a sociologist and the work they carried out) are the key to your success in the exam. Memorise them, being clear about what particular theory they relate to, and use them as evidence in the exam answers you write.
- As a matter of good practice, do not just memorise the case studies in this chapter in connection with education. For every study you come across, get into the habit of asking yourself 'how can I make a connection with social inequality and difference?' Memorise these connections and your synoptic exam will be so much more successful.

● **Synoptic Link**

Education provides a variety of links to social inequality and difference. By focusing on the way that education is seen by some sociologists to allocate 'roles' to individuals, you can examine whether this is a good or bad thing. The gap between middle-class educational achievement and working-class achievement is growing. Gender achievement has also reversed in recent years (i.e. girls are doing better than boys in all levels of education). Enormous problems exist for some members of the ethnic minorities on leaving school (gaining places at university or finding employment).

✍ **Coursework Suggestion**

Students often have problems in deciding how they can analyse the data they produce when carrying out primary research. One way to provide an analytical framework is to openly say that you will take synoptic concepts and use these as *sensitising* concepts when interpreting your data. So, for example, if you have produced interview data why not use four to five synoptic concepts as the focus point for your analysis. Some key synoptic concepts are socialisation, power, ideology, anomie, alienation, culture and social control. Why not create headings from four to five of the above concepts and then focus on your interview data in light of those concepts; this would provide a good analytical framework for your results chapter.

3.24 | Pushing your grades up higher

1. Remember that many of the broadsheet newspapers (for example, *The Times*) contain educational supplements. In the weeks leading up to the exam, buy these papers and read the headlines and stories to get a flavour for what is currently happening within government educational policy.

2. Use different named sociologists to back up any argument, theory or concept you are trying to make in the exam.

3. Try to identify either the year or the decade that the research was carried out as this will help you make the point that things may or may not have changed, for example, current female achievement compared with female under-achievement before the 1980s.

4. When referring to sociologists remember to refer to their theoretical influence, i.e. don't say 'Stephen Ball' but rather 'post-structuralist Stephen Ball'.

5. To gain extra evaluation marks try to mention the methodology of the case study you are referring to in the exam, for example, 'adopting interpretivist methodology David Gillborn found that ...'

6. By referring to whether research was quantitative or qualitative, you can link one particular study to another to build up your argument.

7. How do you start your paragraphs? Do you just mention a case study, for example, 'Sue Sharp argued that ...'? Much better to start off each paragraph with an evaluative phrase such as '*In agreement with Lees*, Sue Sharp argued ...' or you could say '*In direct challenge* to the above, Sue Sharp argued ...'

8. When an exam question asks you to discuss the contribution that a particular sociologist or sociological explanation has made to a particular issue, it is important to realise that contributions can be both positive and negative. Remember this, as this will then allow you to fully evaluate the work of the sociologist in question.

9. Always remember to use the concepts of validity, reliability and representativeness where appropriate, when discussing the work of other sociologists. By applying these terms you will show the examiners that you are extremely critical.

10. The 'A' grade student will show that they are in full command of the various theories when discussing a question. Remember that the theories are 'friends' to be called upon when you feel you cannot write any more. Say to yourself 'how might a feminist or a postmodernist analyse this particular issue?'

11. Finally, don't forget that not only are you evaluating the *case studies* you talk about but also the *theories*. Of course you will do this by contrasting one theory with another, for example, a Marxist approach to the issue with that of a functionalist or feminist approach. However, it is also useful to remember three categories when discussing theory.

- *Empirical adequacy* – i.e. what evidence is there to support the particular theory being discussed?
- *Comprehensiveness* – i.e. can the particular theory be used in all cases under all conditions?
- *Logical coherency* – i.e. does the theory logically hold together? One example where perhaps you might argue that a theory is not logically coherent is postmodernism. It attacks other theories and metanarratives for offering large-scale explanations. You could argue that there is no logical coherency here because surely postmodernism itself is a theory and therefore subject to its own critique.

Key points to remember

- You must offer evidence in support of whatever argument you are making – without it the examiners will not reward your argument with marks.
- You must show mastery of the theories when constructing an exam answer.
- Don't forget to use 'sophisticated' language when criticising the theory, case study or concept. Make sure you start those sentences or paragraphs with a key evaluative phrase (for example, 'However').

Frequently asked questions

Q. Why are so many sociologists critical of education?

A. The aim of the 1944 Education Act was to attempt to provide equality of education for all pupils within the British educational system. Sociologists over the past few decades have watched with concern how government policies have failed to live up to the aim of an act over half a century old. Many social commentators are critical of standards in education. However, sociologists have noted how the gap between middle- and working-class pupils has widened not narrowed. Gender concerns now focus on failing male pupils and/or specific groups of females within ethnic minorities who do considerably worse than their male counterparts.

Q. How many studies/names do I need to know to cope with the exam?

A. If you can, in about 50 words provide information about a named sociologist, her/his theoretical influence, her/his findings, key concepts and an evaluation. By doing this you are producing concise but fabulous revision materials. Type these up and make them into revision cards. Taking the key areas of class, ethnicity and gender it should be possible to produce 45 studies (15 for each sociological variable). In the nine weeks leading up to the exams memorise five cards a week and 'hey presto', the exam is in the bag!

Q. How much of the history of education do I need for the exam?

A. This is a sociology exam rather than one in history; however, you should know when state education first started and the reasons why it was created in the early 1870s. You then need to know about the five big educational policy changes that have taken place in the second half of the 20th century, namely, the 1944 Education Act, the introduction of comprehensive schools, vocationalism, the effects of the 1988 Educational Reform Act, and the introduction of Curriculum 2000.

Chapter 4

Popular culture

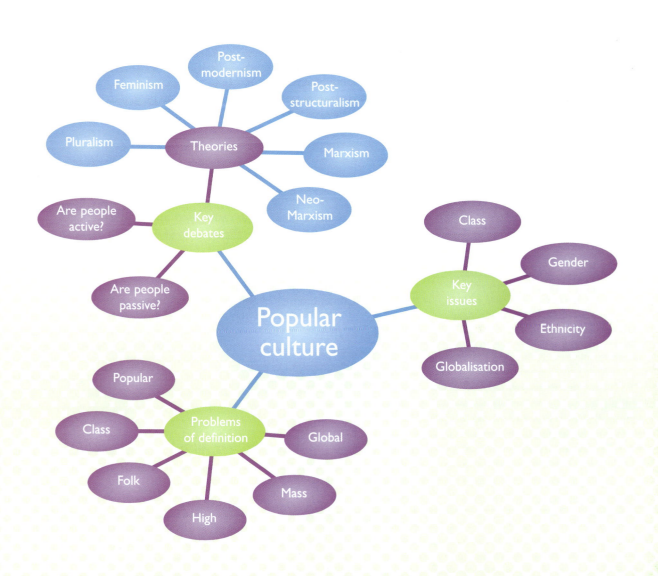

CD-ROM

4.1

Key issues in popular culture

Defining what is and what is not culture can cause enormous disagreement not only amongst sociologists but also amongst the general public.

Why are sociologists interested in popular culture?

With the term 'popular culture' sociologists refer to cultural products, such as fashion, food and music, that most people have access to and the vast majority of the population consumes. Sociologists are interested in understanding what it is that we consume, the reasons for its consumption and the effects it might have on us, the consumers.

What are the key debates in popular culture?

Debates about popular culture revolve around the following questions.

- Is popular culture less artistic or creative than other forms of culture such as ballet, opera or jazz?
- To what extent are the negative views held about popular culture elitist?
- By being popular, does it also mean it has less value?
- By being 'mass produced' is it less artistic than something that is produced in smaller numbers by fewer people?
- To what extent does popular culture encourage people to be critical about the society they live in?

What are the key ideas we can use to think about popular culture?

- Popular culture is something we buy and consume.
- Most forms of popular culture are advertised using **cultural images**.
- Often these cultural images are the creation of advertising companies hired by multinational organisations.
- **Cultural products**, such as the mobile phone and personal stereo, are seen to be used by people on a daily basis.
- The entertainment industries show images of people using cultural products to represent certain groups be they young, old, black, white, male or female.
- Individuals can sometimes adapt or change cultural products to turn them into new forms of popular culture. An example of this is the music industry as it samples tracks, instruments, fashion and vocals to create new forms of music product.

What does the exam board say about popular culture?

The OCR examiners will expect you to know:

- about different definitions of culture
- what sociologists mean by the 'cultural industries'

- what is meant by 'symbolic consumption'
- a variety of theoretical approaches to the construction and consumption of culture
- different patterns of consumption according to class, gender and ethnicity
- what symbolic communities are
- what the relationship between youth and popular culture is
- how femininities and masculinities are connected to the cultural industries and how they are socially constructed.

The exam for this unit (2536) will last for one hour and will be composed of two unstructured essay questions of which candidates must answer <u>one</u> question.

As with all of the OCR units you have to show competency or ability in the assessment objectives of AO1 (*knowledge and understanding and presentation and communication*) and AO2 (*interpretation and analysis and evaluation*).

For AO1 you need to show *knowledge and understanding* of the names of sociologists and their case studies; the relevant theories; the key concepts (*e.g. globalisation*); evidence to support the claims sociologists make; and a keen awareness of the research methodologies used by sociologists.

For AO2(a) you need to show how you can actually *interpret and apply* this knowledge when putting forward a particular argument and *evaluate* (AO2(b)) continuously throughout any answer you are writing. There is a greater emphasis placed on AO2 at A2 than at AS. This might mean that you chose to draw on the ideas of a theory or case study that was carried out 30 years ago and see how it might be relevant to an area of power and control. You might also identify trends from the past and see to what extent that particular trend is present today.

It will also help if you learn all possible synoptic links as you progress through this unit (look out for the Synoptic Link box in the margins). You must also examine this topic area in relation to the core theme of social differentiation, power and stratification.

Key points to remember

- The five key ideas that examiners use when creating questions.
- The exam lasts 60 minutes, in which time you will answer one long essay-style question.
- Understand the change in emphasis in the way you will be marked at A2 compared with AS.

● **Synoptic Link**

This unit provides a strong synoptic link to issues surrounding social inequality in any discussion about whether or not a particular form of popular culture is associated with a specific socio-economic group in society. This chapter will explore how the consumption of popular culture varies according to age, class, gender and ethnicity and how consumption can be seen as a form of difference and inequality.

✓ **Top Exam Hint**

When comparing the different theoretical approaches discussed in this chapter, tell the examiner that macro theories like functionalism and Marxism emphasise the shaping or 'determining' nature of popular culture (and society). In contrast, micro theories and postmodernism emphasise human wilfulness or free will in both the creation, adaptation and interpretation of the varieties of popular culture discussed in this chapter.

✍ **Coursework Suggestion**

Carry out a study of the CD covers used to house rap, hip-hop or RandB records. Analyse the images used and see whether or not you can support or challenge some of the theoretical viewpoints discussed in this chapter. Alternatively carry out a study of television advertisements to see whether or not they are less sexist than they used to be. You might like to set up a hypothesis along the lines that they are more sexist but in increasingly subtle ways.

How does popular culture link to the AS course?

Why are links to AS sociology important for A2 sociology?

Good sociologists do not just focus on their particular area of interest but are also able to draw upon a variety of areas within sociology to offer explanations about what is being researched at the time. For example, a sociologist interested in why people commit crimes might also look at the family, education and region of those committing crimes in an attempt to explain why crimes take place. Examiners recognise this when awarding marks and reward students for drawing upon a variety of sociological areas when answering exam questions. Below are just some of the ways you can connect popular culture to the AS units you may have covered.

What links can be made to the family?

Sociologists are interested in how different types of family structure are portrayed within the media, particularly in advertising and in soap operas, both of which are forms of popular culture. Sometimes referred to as 'cereal packet families', the nuclear family that is often portrayed by popular culture as being 'normal' comes into conflict with many people's experience of real life family situations in which increasingly single-parent, gay and step-families are the norm. Those on the New Right blame today's youth problem on the erosion of the traditional patriarchal role of the father which encouraged 'everyone to know their place'. Popular culture is often used by teenagers as they struggle to gain independence and the formation of an identity that challenges the dominant values that many families deploy.

What links can be made to mass media?

Marxists from the Frankfurt School argue that the commercialised popular culture we have today is created by the media and is therefore superficial and uncritical of the society we live in. On the other hand, Ien Ang (1991) argues that it is impossible to determine how people engage with the media and cultural products in general because in most cases this occurs in the privacy of peoples' homes. From a Marxist perspective you can also argue that the capitalist system, via the media, constructs categories, such as 'child' or 'teenager', in order to create markets and consumers for toys, clothes, records/CDs, and other forms of popular cultural products.

What links can be made to youth and culture?

Recently there has been a moral panic over the increase in gun cultures, which in turn has been linked in the press to rap music. For Stanley Cohen (1980), a moral panic is often an exaggerated (or amplified) concern over deviant behaviour of a particular youth subculture. A group is labelled or stereotyped as being a threat to social order. Press reports will demonise or create 'folk devils' such as rap musicians and, by extension, their fans. Governments can then be seen to be responding by changing licensing laws on nightclubs and the issue of firearms.

What links can be made to the individual and society?

Taking into account the speed at which people can now fly from London to Beijing or New York, or the speed with which a business deal can be concluded electronically, David Harvey (1989) argues that these factors affect national and individual identities. The media brings into our homes music, fashion, style and even religion from other parts of the world; think of the impact that MTV, McDonalds and, more recently, the Asian cultural explosion has had on the 'British way of life'.

What links can be made to sociological research skills?

Sociologists who are interested in popular culture draw upon a variety of research methods that you might have come across on your AS course. These cover both quantitative methodologies (those concerned with generalisations and statistical claims) and qualitative methodologies (those concerned with smaller-scale understandings of the meanings behind popular cultural products). Your knowledge of methodology combined with popular culture will also provide useful links to the synoptic exam at the end of your A2 year.

Key points to remember

- Examiners reward students for making connections between different areas of sociology and popular culture.
- These connections can be made in all topics covered during AS.
- Start taking an interest in how popular culture represents issues related to AS sociology; for example, how might religious or family issues be portrayed in soap operas or the tabloid press?

✍ Coursework Suggestion

By combining **content analysis** and **semiotics**, look for stories in the press about popular culture, for example rap music. Try to identify if the language used in the stories varies depending on the type of popular culture being described. Compare and contrast this with other forms of so called 'high' culture.

66 99 Key Definitions

Content analysis is the quantitative approach to analysing the media.

Semiotics is a qualitative approach where the researcher explores the deeper and often hidden meanings behind particular words, phrases or pictures.

How can we find out about the sociology of popular culture?

Britney Spears in the 21st Century.

Cary Grant in the 1940s

What do these representations say about what popular culture deems to be attractive or sexually desirable at that time in Western culture?

66 99 Key Definitions

Quantitative data is data that is statistical and that can be used to make generalisations, such as questionnaires and surveys.

Qualitative data is data which tends to be in more depth, such as observations, interviews or the study of diaries.

How have sociologists tried to measure popular culture?

You will have already learned in your AS year that methodology refers to research methods *as well as* reasons why those methods might be used. Sociologists can gather **quantitative data** or they can choose to gather **qualitative data**. Apart from their own particular theoretical interests, sociologists choose their methodology as a result of issues that include:

- the nature of the research problem: for example, are you researching documents or people; is the research covert (in secret) or overt (openly known to those being researched); or is the researcher looking back over time and comparing past with present?
- the traditional research strategies, methods and data sources thought to be appropriate for a particular problem: for example, the study of texts within newspaper coverage in an attempt to understand how different groups in society are portrayed in the newspapers.
- how available or accessible the data that the sociologist requires is: for example, how easy it is to find out what forms of popular culture are being consumed behind closed doors?
- the resources at the researcher's disposal: for example, funding, time, equipment and assistance.

Values also determine how a sociologist approaches a particular research area. While these values can vary depending on whether the sociologist is a Marxist, feminist or symbolic interactionist, they can also vary depending on whether the sociologist is male, female, black, white, middle or working class.

Such values can also determine whether or not sociologists are gathering quantitative data or qualitative data. This might depend on whether the researchers consider themselves to be positivist, that is scientific, or interpretivist, that is more interested in how the respondent feels about what is being researched, in their approach to research in general.

What methods do sociologists tend to use to study popular culture?

- Questionnaires that are highly structured provide useful broad-ranging data although their completion rate is low. They also do not allow respondents to 'open' up and give more detailed information.
- Observation is time-consuming and the presence of the researcher can change and/or effect what she/he is looking at.
- Interviews allow the researcher to probe and evaluate particular trains of thought. However, people may decide to lie to the interviewer in order to create the impression they feel the interviewer wants.

Two methodologies that are extremely common when researching popular culture are:

1. Content analysis – a form of quantitative data gathering in which measuring takes place. Examples include counting how many words of a specific type might exist in a newspaper article; measuring the size of headline space dedicated to particular stories; searching and counting specific groups of objects or people in photographs, such as the ratio of men to women in music videos.
2. Semiology – a form of analysis that looks for the hidden, deeper meanings of signs, symbols and images, such as how body posture in different photographs can drastically affect the message being sent out in the image being shown.

Sociologists have used a variety of methods to study popular culture:

- Content analysis carried out by Simon Biggs (1993) showed how, in the early 1990s, middle-aged and older characters dominated UK soap operas.
- Semiology and content analysis were combined by Sean Nixon (1996) and Tim Edwards (1997) to show how the male body is increasingly being portrayed in the media and fashion industries as an object of desire.
- Questionnaires and interviews were used by Colin Sparks (1998) to show how, despite the growth of satellite, cable and Internet usage, British audiences still preferred reading newspapers and watching terrestrial television.

What problems with definition are encountered in popular culture?

Problems exist when carrying out research in any field in having to explain the findings from such research to other sociologists. Remember that whatever definition (or operationalisation) we use to start our research will then affect what we look for and what we uncover as a result. What one thing means in one culture at one point in time, may have a completely different meaning in another culture, at another point in time. One example of this is when analysing the popular culture of teenagers before the 1940s. It is important to realise that the category 'teenager' did not exist until the 1950s and came about with the advent of American rock'n'roll making any historical research on popular culture more difficult the further back in time sociologists go.

Key points to remember

- There are a variety of reasons why sociologists choose the methods they do; these must be learned for the exam.
- Memorise not only the key names associated with this unit but also the method of research these sociologists adopted.
- Do not forget the importance of definition or operationalisation when discussing any research that takes place. Evaluating somebody else's research is impossible unless we know what they mean.

✓ Top Exam Hints

- Technology has come a long way in recent years with the aid of extremely sophisticated software. This means that so-called qualitative interviews can be analysed using computer software to generate quantitative results making the distinction between quantitative and qualitative research blurred rather than clear-cut. Make the examiner aware of this, but be careful. Do not imply that quantitative data is *better* than qualitative data. Each has its own specific uses for the sociologist.

- In the exam remember to stress the importance of sampling techniques and their influence on the findings of sociological research. Sampling refers to how the sociologist chooses the material needed for analysis, for example which magazines or songs might be used for a topic of sociological research. It is impossible to comment on how representative research might be unless you have been told how the findings were sampled in the first place. Comment on this as a form of evaluation of any research mentioned when writing your answers.

What is culture?

☀ Key Ideas

Sociologists are typically interested in four main questions when discussing culture.

1. How is culture patterned? (What are its main features?)
2. How is culture maintained?
3. Why does culture exist in a particular form?
4. How could culture exist in a different form?

Whereas many conservative and Marxist writers view mass culture in a negative way, that is believing it to be uncritical, bland and engaging little with debates on how society should be, neo-Marxists view popular culture in a positive light. The work of the Centre for Contemporary Cultural Studies (referred to as the CCCS) and many of the neo-Marxist writers working there argue that there is much in popular culture that is critical, for example street poetry, fringe theatre and rap music, about the lives we lead.

✓ Top Exam Hint

It is important to remember when studying at A2 that different writers often use terms in different ways. While the definitions of 'high', 'low', 'mass' and 'popular' cultures help *you* make distinctions between different types of culture, many sociologists use the terms interchangeably. Tell the examiner what *you* mean when using the terms and let the examiner know that these terms are open to debate or are contestable. By doing this you will gain evaluation marks.

What does this mean?

By 'culture' sociologists tend to mean a particular way of life associated with a particular group of people. It can refer to a group as small as a family but can also extend up to the populations of particular countries. We even talk about 'Western' or 'Eastern' cultures despite the confusion that this entails.

Sociologists who study culture ask questions about the way people lead their lives and the patterns of social organisation, for example the class structure, religious institutions or work environments, that might shape or determine their identities. It is possible, however, to identify two different approaches or themes that run through any description about what culture actually is.

1. A broad definition refers to a whole way of life.
2. Some definitions refer to refined behaviour or cultural achievements. This use of the term culture allows some people to refer to ways of life as 'uncultured'.

Different types of culture

- *High culture* refers to the type of culture adopted by elites or higher social classes, such as the plays of Shakespeare, the ballet, and classical music.
- *Folk culture* refers to the types of creative culture that have been passed down from generation to generation, such as folk songs, traditional recipes, woodworking and basket weaving. It does not have the same status as high culture but is nevertheless valued in its own right.
- *Mass culture* tends to have a negative image in that it is considered to be manufactured, artificial and mass produced rather than genuinely creative. Whereas folk culture is associated with something being created, mass culture is generally associated with mass consumption; for example Coca-Cola, television game shows and magazines such as *FHM* or *Hello*.
- *Popular culture* is associated by many people with working-class culture and initially seems the same as mass culture. However, while mass culture is associated with a negative view of cultural products, popular culture is generally held in a positive light and often associated with youth culture.
- *Class culture*: notions of high and low (mass) culture tend to have a class bias associated with them, in that high culture is seen to be more elitist and high class.
- *Global culture* refers to ideas, traditions, products and representations that are shared and recognised between nations, such as coffee shop culture. The idea is often described as a 'global village'.

Three approaches to defining culture

Ray Williams (1961) refers to three approaches that help when defining culture. These are:

- The ideal: culture in this sense is seen as a 'state or process of human perfection' (1961: page 57) that includes the greatest literature, opera and drama, poetry and paintings (this view coincides with the term 'high culture' described above). It is assumed that, by applying universal rules to what is or what is not culture, an overall sense of this perfection can be reached.

Williams is critical of this 'elitist' definition as he argues that only those 'in the know' have a chance to watch, criticise or create this kind of culture.

- The documentary: this approach accepts all that is in the ideal approach but extends to accept *all* types of culture that document what is taking place in any particular society. Nevertheless, Williams still argues that this is too narrow an approach when viewing what is or what is not culture. While the poems of Wilfred Owen might be considered culture in this sense, the television programme *Blind Date* would almost certainly not be. This approach, according to Williams, looks at cultural artefacts; it looks at the material and physical products of culture. (See Key Idea.)

- The social definition: this definition fits the 'way of life' description used at the beginning of this section and is one with which Williams is far happier. In this sense, the study of culture must include *'certain meanings and values not only in art and learning but also in institutions and ordinary behaviour…a whole way of life, material, intellectual and spiritual'* (Williams 1963, page 57). Finally, in this approach favoured by Williams and those in the CCCS, we see that culture refers to every undertaking, value and production created by a group. Even that seen at the time by some within the group as undesirable is still produced, and therefore, still In this sense a part of the culture that it comes from.

What factors need to be looked at when examining cultures?

Warren Kidd (2002) offers the following eight factors:

1. the dominant values of a particular society
2. the values that guide the direction that social change might take
3. shared linguistic symbols (language)
4. religious beliefs
5. what is considered to be the correct way for people to behave in their day-to-day lives
6. what is considered to be the highest intellectual and artistic achievements of a group, including science, art, literature and music
7. formal behavioural traditions and rituals
8. dominant patterns of living, including styles of architecture and patterns of land use.

This chapter will look at how these eight factors of culture dictate and maintain what we call popular culture, and how this has changed over time.

Conclusion

Culture has a variety of meanings that no one group of sociologists or people in general agree on. What some people define as being 'culture' others term 'mass culture' in a negative attack.

For consideration

1. How easy is it to be objective when deciding the quality of cultural products?

2. What criteria do you use to decide whether or not a cultural product is 'good'?

✓ Top Exam Hints

- Cultural theorist Raymond Williams (1983) says that

  'culture is one of the two or three most complicated words in the English language. This is partly so because of its intricate historical development, in several European languages, but mainly because it has now come to be used for important concepts in several distinct disciplines [subject areas] and in several distinct and incompatible systems of thought.'

  In other words 'culture' is a concept that has a variety of meanings depending on the context in which you use it. Mention this in the introduction of the exam to point out the difficulty of operationalising (defining) the concept of culture.

- When looking at Raymond Williams' three approaches, the first two approaches can be seen as being universal or absolute definitions, that is, there exists a worldwide and historically unchanging set of criteria to judge if something is 'cultural' or not.

- In Williams' third social definition approach, however, there is a more relative use of culture adopted. Relative means that one needs to look at the particular time or place in history. This allows social scientists to judge cultural products in context rather than applying an unchanging set of criteria.

✳ Key Idea

For Williams, this usage is often associated with class or status – this culture is seen to be the most valuable. The question we must ask, as sociologists, is 'valuable for what?' and 'valuable to whom?' These ideal cultural values are often defined by a ruling group which, in doing so, attempts to separate itself off from the rest of society.

What do we mean by popular culture?

Sociologists are increasingly interested in the way graffiti is used as a form of cultural expression, quite often at great risk to the artists that produce it.

☀ Key Idea

Sociologists often fall into two camps when discussing the role of the media and mass culture. Pessimists view the products of popular culture as a problem for society in that they are cheap, non-intellectual and have no artistic value. The consumption of such products is seen as damaging to those that consume them. Optimists, however, argue that there is high value in much popular culture and that just because such items may be mass-produced does not mean they are not intellectual or that they are worthless.

◆ What, when and why?

Modernity is closely linked to the philosophical movement called 'the enlightenment' or 'the age of reason'. This started around the 18th century as a number of philosophers began to question some of the dominant ideas of their day. Enlightenment philosophers argued that experimental methods and reasons were the only valid way to gain knowledge and believed that this sort of knowledge would lead to progress and the ability of humankind to control nature.

What does this mean?

As we have already seen, popular culture is associated by many with working-class culture and initially sounds the same as mass culture. But the term 'mass culture' is often used in a negative way to describe some of the cultural products, such as *EastEnders*, dog racing and fish and chips, in a way that the term 'popular culture' is not. The very same cultural products can be described as being popular culture in a complementary way. That said, opinions vary on both depending on which particular theory you adopt.

Intellectual snobbery?

A division based on snobbery between high culture and folk culture can be traced back to an elitist view of the past and a separation between two groups of people. High culture supposedly belonged to those who were well off, who were perceived to have had a good formal education and who understood and appreciated the best things in life such as fine food, a knowledge of the arts, an appreciation of good wine. This elitist view argued that folk culture belonged to 'peasants' who understood little of such things and whose culture was more suited to work with their hands rather than their minds.

How did industrialisation change such views?

Many writers argue that with industrialisation such views have quickly become outdated and redundant and, in some cases, were simply untrue in the first place. Over time industrialisation produced consumers (rather than peasant 'producers') who were interested in buying cultural products rather than making things with their own hands. What replaces the two types of culture described above is a mass culture where everybody is dealt the same diet of unoriginal material produced by large companies or 'multinational' firms.

Theories of mass culture therefore portray a passive audience who buy into a world of cultural products that keep them from realising the darker sides of the societies they live in, e.g. poverty or war.

The Frankfurt School

The ideas of the neo-Marxist Frankfurt School, such as those of Marcuse and Adorno, are highly critical of mass culture. They saw mass culture as something that constrained and controlled those who, effectively, 'fell under its spell'. This is very different from the approach adopted by the CCCS who saw popular or mass culture as offering a revolutionary source; a potential to criticise the dominant values of society.

The Frankfurt School have provided sociology with a number of key concepts when thinking about issues of popular culture:

- *mass culture*: uncritical popular products, aimed at stopping critical and therefore revolutionary thought in the majority of society
- *culture industry*: the run-for-profit capitalist businesses that produce mass culture, which ultimately stops critical thought
- *hypodermic syringe model*: this term has been used by others since the Frankfurt School to describe the image they have of passive masses 'injected' with the ideology of the capitalist class by the culture industry
- *one-dimensional man*: Marcuse describes people in this 'mass society' as being 'one-dimensional' as they are uncritical, and easily controlled by authority.

Antonio Gramsci and popular culture

The **neo-Marxist** (see 4.7) writer Antonio Gramsci argued that, in order for a more humane society to exist (for him this meant one based on socialist ideas), it was necessary to intellectually and culturally convince people that socialism was a solution to the ills in society. According to his Marxist ideas, social change had to take place with the consent of the majority of the people. Therefore popular cultural products had to be used to persuade people that such a better life was possible under socialist ideals. This was one of the reasons why the Italian Communist party chose to organise opera for the masses.

Popular culture versus mass culture

Whereas mass culture portrays a passive willing audience ready to soak up the dominant values of society, that is its many different ideologies, popular culture conveys a very different set of messages. Popular culture is seen by many to portray a notion of a far more actively critical audience. In this sense people are not a 'mass', but are active in their consumption with many cultural icons being turned around to make comments about society; think of how modern graffiti is now increasingly being recognised as a critical and powerful artistic form of expression. A great deal of present day discussion on popular culture is less concerned with what it might do to the audience and more to do with what audiences do with popular culture. This is very different from the 'top-down' image of culture held by the Frankfurt School, and the notion that the culture industry was controlling us with capitalist ideology.

Conclusion

- The pessimistic critique of mass culture is often based on Marxist theories, which suggest that mass culture creates a 'mass society' living in 'false consciousness'.
- However, others argue that mass and/or popular culture is anti-elitist in that technology enables so-called 'high culture' to be copied for the masses to see and gain pleasure from. This more positive view of mass culture also highlights the very critical nature of some mass cultures that Marxists deny exists.

For consideration

1. How might Marxists be described as elitist in their views over mass/popular culture?
2. In what ways do you feel their views might be justified?

✳ Key Ideas

- For many, the term 'mass culture' is a problem in sociology, since it was often used in a pejorative way, that is, it was used to make a negative value-judgement about the products the term referred to. A mass culture was often seen to be undesirable and less valuable. We can see issues of class here. 'Mass' is usually popular or, in other words, usually working class, which might be why it was seen in this way by some.

- The notion that audiences have power, freedom, creativity and choice can be associated with a whole range of theories that include:
  - pluralism: choice in the media reflects the variety of tastes of its audience
  - interactionism: the focus of this theory is the ability of the individual to act and change his/her environment
  - postmodernism: an acceptance of the huge variety of often conflicting products 'thrown together' to suit consumer needs
  - neo-Marxism: an assumption that some cultural products can be used to awaken people from the false consciousness they possess.

❝❞ Key Definitions

Cultural relativism refers to the idea that any definition of 'high' or 'low' culture is simply a matter of taste and value judgement. This view argues that all cultural products are as valuable as each other and value is ultimately in the eyes of the consumer.

Cultural elitism or **cultural absolutism** refers to the idea that there exists some absolute value of artistic worth to which all products can be compared in an objective and value-free way.

What is the Marxist view on popular culture?

What does this mean?

Although Marx believed that human beings have the ability to create or contribute to the culture they inhabit, he also believed that people were restricted in how they they far they could do this. That is why sociologists argue that Marxism is a deterministic theory. By 'deterministic' sociologists mean that structures in society, such as the economy, determine or shape how people think and behave. Marx did, however, take it even further by arguing that the economic system in which we live, shapes our own culture.

The relationship between work and culture

Contrary to what you might think, Marx was not against the idea of work. He was, however, against the idea of work within a capitalist system. Under such a system he argued that working-class people were exploited by being paid cheap wages while at the same time producing profits that went to a middle-class group of employers.

But he also claimed that through work people socialised and cooperated with each other, producing different types of cultures associated with the kind of work people did. In this way language, customs, traditions and even our identities could all be connected with the type of work we do. Marx argued that our identities developed through the experience of work and the different types of relationships that exist. That said, he also argued that in most cases this experience was exploitative and alienating.

How is our culture shaped by those in power?

Marx argued that the most powerful people in society shape or determine institutions such as the media, religion, law and the various culture industries, so that they promote their own economic interests. According to this way of thinking the ruling classes own and control the means of mental and cultural production – the newspapers, publishing houses, theatres, museums and even the music industry.

The rich and powerful send their children to particular types of schools where they are socialised into elitist values. On reaching adulthood they possess the cultural capital, that is the values and tastes associated with their class, that will help them 'get on in life'. As a result they gain top positions within the very institutions mentioned above that produce these values in the first place – the media, arts and entertainments industries and the business and sports worlds. Once there they preside over these cultural institutions in such a way that maintains their particular class position. The whole process starts again when their children are sent to the same types of schools they themselves attended.

There are four ways in which culture is central to the ideas of Karl Marx.

1. Ruling ideas and values are produced by a ruling group in order to maintain its power over others. In this way, social control is exercised over those who do not have access to this type of dominant culture.
2. The extent to which people are socially controlled or have freedom to act in the way they wish will, by and large, depend on the type of culture they possess or have knowledge of.
3. To break free from this dominant set of values and ideas, individuals must break free from ruling class oppression.
4. If this happens, then working-class consciousness and identity will force a revolution and the creation of a new society with its own social culture.

Marxists on popular culture

Many Marxists argue that popular culture restricts the very revolutionary thought that Marx argued the working classes needed to develop in order to free themselves from the society he was so critical about. Marx himself was extremely worried about how, through capitalist societies, cultural products such as poetry, the opera and paintings were being turned into commodities – things to be bought or sold. He described this process as one of 'commodification' where cultural products are bought because of their financial value rather than any intellectual value they have.

Marx himself wrote about what he termed 'commodity fetishism' and this idea has been picked up by the writers at the Frankfurt School in their idea of a mass culture produced by a culture industry. Marx noted how buying things was a way for people to make themselves happy. However, it was really a form of 'false consciousness' – a false need that, like a drug, only kept them happy for a short time, while still living in an exploitative society.

Conclusion

- Marx argued that the process of commodification generated a new set of needs for working-class people.
- These needs, Marx argued, were not real needs but ones which, once satisfied, created huge profits for the producers of the cultural products people bought.
- This leads to a process called 'commodity fetishism' whereby these false needs lead to people starting to worship and desire ownership of these cultural products such as modern art or designer furniture.
- Marx argued that this whole process had the effect of tricking people into believing (providing a false consciousness) that capitalism must be worth preserving if it generates these cultural products in the first place.

For consideration

1. Think about the CDs, videos and computer games you either play or buy. To what extent do you think that Marx's ideas are still applicable today?
2. To what extent do you believe that nowadays it is easy to identify a particular type of cultural product with a particular group within British society?

What does this mean?

Various forms of neo-Marxism attempt to update the ideas of Karl Marx *and* analyse why the capitalist system seems to be so successful in halting the working-class revolution and the end of capitalism that Marx predicted. Neo-Marxists are interested in the relationship between social, political and economic processes and how they shape, and in some cases are shaped by, culture.

Antonio Gramsci

Marx claimed that, under the right circumstances, the working classes would 'awake' from their 'false consciousness' and realise that the capitalist system was unfair and that they were being exploited. A working-class revolution would follow creating a new society in which the profits from capitalism would be shared among all. Writing in an Italian fascist prison during the 1930s, Gramsci was fascinated by the fact that even though the social, economic and political conditions were right for a revolution to take place in Germany and Italy at the end of the First World War (social unrest, poverty and high unemployment) no such revolution took place.

If the answer to why this had not happened could not be found in the economy then other factors including the importance of ideas and culture would need to be focused on. He argued that the ruling class in any society engages in a continuous struggle to gain support for the idea that it and the institutions it controls are 'legitimate'; in other words, there because they rightfully deserve to be. To do this, Gramsci argued that those in power have to convince everybody that their ideas are common sense and therefore there is nothing to be gained from challenging them. If it does this successfully, he argues that it has secured a 'hegemonic position'.

Gramsci argued that the dominant or ruling classes try to establish their ideas as common sense through key cultural institutions such as the media and education. However, he also argued that subordinate classes could and do attempt to resist this. This creates a struggle in which the ruling classes are continuously battling to maintain their hegemonic position.

The political economy

This neo-Marxist approach takes into consideration the ways in which structures of power shape and limit the ways in which audiences gain access to cultural products. It argues that, when considering the process of cultural production, you must focus on:

- what companies/corporations gain from an involvement in the culture industries
- what happens to culture when it is produced within the capitalist 'market place'.

In market economies Golding and Murdoch (1991) argue that it is easy to *believe* that consumers are free to choose what they wish to buy when choosing a cultural product. But in reality this is *not* the case. Consumers may consume in different ways but their choice and tastes are always determined (shaped) by the structures of capitalist cultural industries whether newspaper publishers, record companies, fashion houses or the film industry.

The Frankfurt School

Adorno and Horkheimer (1977) and Marcuse (1964) are key writers connected with this school and associated with Marxist analysis of the media. They argued that the popular culture produced for the masses represented the power of advertising and media companies' ability to shape our consciousness. As immigrants into the USA during the 1940s and 1950s, they were strongly influenced by what they viewed as the commercial exploitation of popular culture in America. They contended that the working classes had lost their ability to think critically or resist exploitation. They argued that profits drive capitalism, which in turn seeks new vehicles for profit such as what they viewed as meaningless formulaic cultural products (e.g. the pop and film industries).

The Centre for Contemporary Cultural Studies (CCCS)

The ideas of the Gramsci-influenced Centre for Contemporary Cultural Studies at Birmingham University in the UK, has a very different image of popular culture compared with that of Marcuse and Adorno. Writers such as Willis and Hebdige at the CCCS look at the way that popular culture can be what is called 'subversive': it can actually challenge those in power. Equally, mass-produced cultural products can themselves be subverted – they can be changed and customised by consumers into something very different from that originally intended. In particular, the role of music such as hip hop in many youth cultures can raise awareness of inequality and can raise critical ideas, rather than stopping them. This can be seen in the growth in recognition for black 'urban' music. In 2003, the first Urban Music Award was given at the Brit Awards, and 2004 saw 'urban' acts dominate the Grammy Award winners list.

Conclusion

- Hegemonic theorists ('cultural theorists') are critical of the political economy approach. They argue that because its arguments are economically deterministic, it reduces complex cultural patterns (tastes, creativity) to crude economics.
- They argue that the ideas of directors, designers and writers come from a variety of sources and are motivated via a variety of reasons – not necessarily just profit.
- Remember that even these sociologists have made assumptions about what is 'good' or 'bad' culture.

For consideration

1. What example of competing ideologies can you think of (see Gramsci)?

2. What criteria would you choose for evaluating whether a particular cultural product is 'good' or 'bad'?

☀ Key Idea

- Critics of Marx's ideas argue that his theories were rooted too much within explanations concerning the economy. The phrase associated with this is '**economic determinism**', that is, the economy determines or shapes the institutions in the interests of those who control its resources. (Marx called this 'the means of production'.) However, other writers, most notably neo-Marxist writers themselves, have pointed out that Marx's ideas were not constant but changed or evolved during the time he was alive and writing. Rather than explanations that were based purely around the economy, he also wrote about the complex interplay between social, cultural, political and economic processes. It is this interaction that neo-Marxists tend to focus on.

- Marx's idea of the working classes living in a false consciousness is used to show how mass culture stimulates economic demand while at the same time maintaining social control. Through advertising, appetites are wetted for different forms of entertainment (Marxists describe these as 'false needs'). Satisfaction is gained from activities such as shopping, which in turn stops people thinking about, or complaining about, the nature of society, for example unemployment, homelessness, war, famine.

What are feminist views on popular culture?

What does this mean?

Critical of the society we live in, feminist theories combine macro and micro sociologies in that, from a macro perspective, they focus on the structures within societies that shape and determine women's lives. The way that women are represented within the media is considered by many feminists to be highly ideological and yet another way of encouraging **patriarchy**. Feminists argue that quite often women are portrayed in popular culture purely and simply in the roles of sex object, mother or housewife.

What is an ideology of femininity?

Writing in 1983, Marjorie Ferguson and Angela McRobbie referred to an 'ideology of femininity' within most media products targeting women. The ideology that was being created was a manufactured view of women that focused on their needs in finding the right man, being a good wife, being interested only in romantic love, and being concerned with being a good mother. They argued that these components existed in many forms of media content and portrayed women in a particular light. By doing so it was creating an ideology that many women felt they had to live up to even if, in reality, this was far from their own ideas of what being female meant to them.

Three forms of feminism applied to popular culture

- **Liberal feminists** argue that the media reflects the sexist **malestream** values of society. They therefore claim that by promoting women into senior positions within the culture industries a change will take place in the way that women are portrayed in the media. In this way the construction of female identities will change and women will feel more empowered.
- The idea that gradual change can take place in the way that liberal feminists put forward is attacked by **radical feminists**. They argue that, whether women are in high positions or not, magazines, films and other cultural products will continue to use sex and women's bodies to sell their products. They claim that patriarchal ideology runs so deep that both men and women consume popular culture 'through the male gaze' taking it for granted that women and men are portrayed the way they are. Many radical feminists argue for a 'women's only' press – run by women for women.
- One strand of **Marxist feminism** that can be applied to popular culture is culturalist feminism, itself strongly influenced by the ideas of hegemony proposed by Gramsci. Gamman and Marshment (1988) argue that while commercialism and patriarchal values continue to dominate a great deal of popular culture, there are opportunities to question patriarchy. The interaction between characters in some television shows sometimes develops a critique of sexism; male power hierarchies are challenged.

✳ Key Ideas

Liberal feminism: this branch of feminism broadly focuses on improving rights and opportunities for women. Not overtly critical of society itself, it argues for greater representation within society as we experience it today along with an equal distribution of power.

Radical feminism attacks the very nature of patriarchal society. Radical feminists argue that there are biological and psychological differences in men and women that make men behave in the way they do. Radical feminists attempt to bring private issues, such as rape, male violence against women, sexuality, and reproduction, out of the private and into the public domain.

Marxist feminism: Marxists are critical of the capitalist system which places significance on success within the economic spheres of public and private life – both at the cheapest possible price. Marxist feminists argue that the workplace forces women into lower positions or compels them entirely into the home. Women are seen as being responsible for producing future members of the work force, namely children.

Popular television programmes have reflected this in recent years. Helen Mirren's character in the television series *Prime Suspect*, the protagonists in the 1980's American hit series *Cagney and Lacey*, or Dr Kerry Weaver, the chief of staff in *ER*, provide strong female roles in these traditionally male-dominated arenas.

The sexualisation of the male body

Angela McRobbie (1994) argues that in recent years, like their female counterparts, men's bodies are being 'sexualised' in television adverts, films and between the covers of teenage girls' magazines. This follows on from the recent growth of male lifestyle magazines that use sexist stories and images of women. However, far from contending that the sexualisation of the male body indicates a type of equality between the sexes, McRobbie argues that gender inequality and oppression continue but with both men and women now being portrayed in even more limited and oppressed ideological representations.

Conclusion

Many writers argue that in recent years there has been an 'anti-feminist' backlash against some of the ideas expressed above. Post-feminist Catherine Hakim (1995) maintains that, in reality, many modern-day women's lives have significantly improved making many feminist ideas redundant. She argues that women are free to make rational choices about what they do.

- Andrea Stuart (1990), while agreeing with many of the feminist ideas expressed above, suggests that there is no longer a feeling of 'togetherness' between women in the feminist movement – as there once was. On the contrary, she argues that many of the feminist ideas expressed are coming from popular cultural forms such as magazines, soap operas and increasing sex shops that cater for women's tastes and not just those of men. She argues that there is a gap between the popular feminism expressed in these forms and the 'professional feminism' found in universities.

- Sylvia Walby's triple systems theory (1990) argues that race, class and gender all have to be taken into consideration when analysing what is meant by 'patriarchy'. Patriarchy exists in six spheres of society: paid employment, violence, sexuality, the household, the state, and culture – none of which can be viewed in isolation from each other. See Chapter 6 Social inequality and difference for more on Sylvia Walby's theory.

For consideration

1. How does the media construct images of femininity and masculinity differently?
2. What methods of research would best be used to answer the above question?

66 99 Key Definitions

Patriarchy refers to male dominance over women. The state is seen as a patriarchical institution as it operates to legitimise male domination and power in society to the exclusion and oppression of women. According to many feminists, popular culture is one of the variety of ways in which patriarchy is enforced through its portrayal of women.

Malestream sociology is a description of sociology coming from feminists who argue that much of the subject has been written by male sociologists and represents their interests rather than those of women. Remember that the classical sociologists, Marx, Durkheim and Weber to name but a few, lived and wrote at a time, and in cultures, in which male attitudes prevailed.

What is the pluralist view of popular culture?

Is the spread of popular culture one of Americanisation, or do we have a global culture?

What does this mean?

As you can see, there is much debate about what popular culture is and the function it plays in society, be it a positive or negative one. In response to some of the more negative perceptions of popular culture are functionalist- and more pluralist-inspired writers such as Shils (1961) who argued that popular culture unifies different groups within society. Functionalist ideas can be seen to be closely influential on the pluralist ideas expressed below.

Through music, magazines, television, the film industries and the Internet such ideas are used to show how the cultural interests of everybody can be catered for in Western societies despite the increasingly multicultural nature of many of these countries. Far from being an example of commercial exploitation, popular culture is viewed as a means of incorporating the mass of the population into society.

Functionalism and global culture

Viewed in this way, functionalists argue that communication and travel have increasingly linked nearly every corner of the globe. In what is sometimes referred to as 'a global village', the view is that there is a sharing of culture, language and increasingly even money – consider the growing use of credit cards in replacement of local currencies. This particular interpretation of what is sometimes referred to as 'globalisation' is one in which the widespread increase of a global culture that incorporates and celebrates Coca-Cola, McDonalds and the Hollywood film industry is one to be celebrated rather than criticised.

Pluralism

Although influenced by functionalism, pluralism is a theory in its own right, and often applied to the media and its popular products. Pluralism adopts many of the ideas expressed by functionalists but also has much in common with Weberians and symbolic interactionists. Pluralists accept that human beings can be active agents, that is, they have free will when making decisions about what they might or might not wish to consume. Pluralists argue that:

- the media is perceived differently by different individuals
- the huge variety of cultural products available (or the huge plurality) means that individuals have an enormous range of choice available to them about what they might or might not wish to consume
- in light of the point above, this means that individuals and groups in society possess considerable power in exercising such choice
- creative individuals are free to create as many different types of cultural product as they wish

- producers of cultural products have to listen to what consumers want and need or consumers would no longer buy or be interested in the products they produce, which would mean an end to their profits.

Pluralism has a very different image of humans to that of Marxist writers, such as those of the Frankfurt School. Pluralism is associated not with a 'hypodermic syringe model' of consumers being tricked, but instead they see consumers as being active and in control through the decisions and choices they make. This is similar to the Weberian or New Right idea of market-forces (see sections 6.15 and 6.16). We have the power since we choose what we buy. Pluralist writers Katz and Blumler refer to this image of humans as a 'uses-gratifications' model; people make choices about what popular products they want, in terms of what needs, desires and wishes they think they will get out of them, and producers respond by supplying the product.

Mass production as evidence of democracy

If one argues that democracy is the ability to exercise freedom of choice in what one says, does, and purchases then many functionalists and pluralists would argue that mass production is evidence that such democracy exists. Far from devaluing or cheapening the worth of popular culture, Gans (1974) argues that mass production offers a free and democratic choice to consumers. It is worth noting, however, that Alan Swingewood (1977) attacks this notion of mass culture arguing that it is a myth. He believes that it is a term used as a value judgement by various elites in society – used to devalue the interests, activities and pleasures of ordinary people in favour of more high-cultural pursuits.

Conclusion

- The idea that mass or popular culture is evidence of a **global village** in the making is one of many different interpretations of globalisation. Other writers argue that the spread of cultural products is not evidence of a global culture but rather the Westernisation of cultural ideas across the globe. This idea is sometimes referred to as **cultural imperialism**.
- However, sociologists try to discuss the pluses and minuses of popular culture. Ien Ang (1991) argues that it is impossible to determine how people engage with the media and cultural products in general because in most cases this occurs in the privacy of peoples' homes.
- Ang also argues that despite what pluralists might claim, the opinions of ordinary viewers (and consumers of cultural products in general) are often ignored by producers and manufacturers alike.

For consideration

1. To what extent do you believe that wider choice exists for consumers of popular culture based on an increase in availability of cultural products?

2. When flicking from channel to channel on either satellite or cable television, how many truly different types of cultural product are available?

6699 Key Definitions

You can start to see that a debate is emerging between different groups of people who argue why and how different types of culture are more superior than others. This debate is termed the **mass culture debate** and refers to the various analyses that exist about the artistic or intellectual value of modern day cultural products.

A **global village** embodies the idea that people worldwide share a culture or cultures, and this unites them.

Cultural imperialism is the idea that some countries can use popular culture as a way to 'take-over' other countries.

⁜ Key Idea

The **mass culture debate** focuses around four significant issues.

1. The effect that the creation of mass communications has had on the quality of cultural products.
2. The effect that these cultural products have on audiences in general.
3. The extent to which the mass production of these cultural products either benefited or reduced the creative and artistic content of these goods based on their ability to be bought and sold.
4. The question as to whether audiences are any less critical or any less intellectual as a result of being open to the availability of these mass-produced products.

What is the poststructuralist view on popular culture?

What does this mean?

Michel Foucault took structuralism, a theory that focused on language and structures within the human mind, and developed a theory that focuses on the ways that knowledge, language, power and culture operate within society. In doing this he also attacked the more rigid structural theories of functionalism, Marxism and other macro theories for being too deterministic, that is, they do not explain how human beings can act in ways that they choose. His explanations revolved around the use of the concept of 'discourses' or 'patterns of language' and their ability to organise the way in which we relate to each other.

The theory of poststructuralism contains four elements.

1. Language shapes and controls human action.
2. 'Signs' such as certain brands of fast food or sports wear have become more important than the objects they once represented.
3. Reality is a creation of language and one in which we define ourselves as being different from others.
4. Humans are defined and determined by 'discourses' rather than 'structures'.

What are discourses?

Foucault argues that we are all caught up in a web of different **discourses**, each with their own set of concepts, ideas and words. Discourses offer particular ways of viewing the world that liberate but also restrict how we think and behave. He also argues that human beings internalise these discourses to the point that they become a common-sense approach to what is being considered at the time. One example of a set of discourses in action are those surrounding sexuality. Consider concepts such as 'male', 'female', 'gay', or 'straight'. These concepts can have a major effect upon how we organise the way that we interact with each other.

Power and culture

For Foucault, interesting questions do not revolve around 'who has power', which has been the traditional concern of most sociologists in the past, but rather 'how does power circulate?' He rejects the notion that power can be easily identified with a particular elite, group or structure. Foucault argues that power circulates through discourses or 'systems of language or knowledge'. Every kind of knowledge brings with it new forms of power relationships.

Foucault famously says, *'things are not powerful because they are true, but they are true because they are powerful'*. This means that for Foucault culture is not shaped by social class or the workings of the state (something that both Marx and Weber would have argued) but by interlinking discourses or sets of

---

☀ Key Idea

This idea comes from the writings of Baudrillard (1981) who argues that today symbols or signs have become 'commodities'; things to be bought and sold. They have taken on a reality of their own, over and above the objects they once signified or represented. An example of this is the way in which particular brands of sports wear are no longer associated with the sport item they represent but rather become a symbol for fashion or culture. In this way they become desired because of what they symbolise and not the item they represent.

66 99 Key Definition

The term **discourses** refers to ways of thinking and speaking about an aspect of social reality.

'power-knowledge relationships'. He believes that culture is created through the complex web of these discourses which circulate in society. In some cases there may be resistance to a particular set of discourses. One example of resistance might be the formation of youth subcultures in schools which are created when individuals or groups react against dominant discourses about what education might be – discourses that include competition, performance, citizenship and quality control. Of course the very creation of any subculture, Foucault would argue, brings with it its own unique set of discourses which then have the effect of both liberating and controlling those within its grasp.

Gay/lesbian cultural resistance to heterosexuality

Foucault argues that we gain our sense of self-identity from the power-knowledge relationships in which we operate. He reasons that discourses about sexuality offer a series of important concepts within which people 'position' (or think about) their own sexual identities. Today there are vibrant and fashionable lesbian and gay cultures in most European cities, which have arisen largely out of resistance to the dominant discourse that argues that white heterosexuality is acceptable and anything else is not. New forms of culture and identity have been formed as a result of resistance to some of these dominant cultural discourses.

Using the ideas of Willis, it is possible to show that 'gay subculture' has incorporated many aspects of heterosexual popular culture, and taken them on as their own. For example, many aspects of skinhead dress codes from the 1980s – often a very homophobic subculture – have now been 'submerged' into what we might associate with gay cultural dress conventions. Equally the use of the term 'gay' and, more so, the term 'dyke' have been incorporated (taken back over) by members of the gay community which, in doing so, challenges the original homophobic use of the term. In much the same way, many black people in the United States use the racist term 'nigger' in popular speak, thus reducing its meaning, and changing it. This is called 'symbolic creativity'.

Conclusion

Not everybody accepts poststructuralism. Marxist Poulantzas argues that it ignores the importance of questions that focus on who has and who has not got power. He believes that Foucault has underestimated the role that the state plays in the variety of political, economic and cultural struggles that take place on a day-to-day basis. While feminists are more sympathetic to the ideas that post-structuralists adopt, they too are concerned that 'structures' are not ignored when considering issues to do with patriarchy and the exploitation of women; for example, the so-called 'glass ceiling' where men dominate higher positions in organisations.

For consideration

1. What forms of cultural expression can you think of that can be used as examples of resistance to dominant discourses about different cultures?

2. How might Marxists argue that these cultural expressions quickly lose their value as expression and turned into commodities to be bought and sold for profit?

∞ Classic Study

Post-structuralist Stuart Hall (1992) believes that ideas in society are perpetuated by different types of discourses that are then internalised by those that accept them. He looked at the portrayal of white supremacy in literary texts. He argued that the way in which whites and non-whites have been represented have helped to create or increase differences between nations and ethnic minorities. History books completely ignore the part played by non-white peoples in the construction of the British Empire despite their prominent role. What images we do have, tend to be those connected with slavery or violence.

✳ Key Idea

Paul Gilroy (1987) argues that historically Africans exiled during slavery created their own culture in the face of exploitation and oppression. This process is also evident today in the way that ethnic minorities, oppressed or racialised, do the same thing in contemporary society. He argues that there exists a 'discourse of black criminality' that has developed since the Second World War in Britain. This has resulted in the representation of black males as criminals within the media. However, he contends that, far from being passive victims, these groups oppose many of the discourses that seek to oppress them and create their own political and cultural forms such as rap and Bhangra.

What is the postmodernist view on popular culture?

Many music tracks today are made up of a 'pick and mix' assortment. Artists, sounds and lyrics are rearranged and reformed into what, postmodernists would argue, typifies popular culture today.

✳ Key Ideas

Many postmodernist writers talk about the 'postmodern condition'. By this they mean that in today's 'postmodern world' the way we experience our everyday lives is somehow different to that of previous generations. They argue that our sense of identity is different today to that of previous generations. In the postmodern condition we no longer think about our class backgrounds as being significant in a world where the media determines most of our experiences of the outside world.

Many postmodernists borrow the term 'bricoleur' from the ideas of Levi-Strauss. This terms refers to creators of myths and stories in tribal traditions who conceive identities for the group by mixing symbolic elements of tribal tradition and culture into stories that symbolise the 'togetherness' of the group. Postmodern popular culture consumers do the same thing, they mix popular culture to make something new – to create new identities and differences.

What does this mean?

In a world where the global forces of media production allow people to learn about other people's beliefs and lifestyles, it becomes less and less possible for postmodernists to regard one lifestyle or one belief system as the 'true' one. Postmodernist writers such as Jameson (1991) and Baudrillard (1988) argue that in many advanced capitalist economies, towards the end of the 20th century, there has been a decline in engineering and manufacturing. Instead the key economic sector has become the provision of cultural and media services such as multi-channel television, globalised electronic and cable networks, radio stations, newspapers, the film industry and billboards.

A number of writers have challenged many of the assumptions held during the period of modernity. Postmodernist writers such as Jean-François Lyotard have inspired many to believe that we are in another type of world altogether. This world is a postmodern world of consumption, where none of the accepted theories or 'truths' or 'narratives' can be relied on. (For greater details about postmodernism see sections 2.14 and 3.16.)

How can you apply these ideas to popular culture?

- Jameson's (1991) negative view of a postmodern world is one where there is a 'depthlessness of culture' bringing with it a 'new kind of superficiality'. Postmodern culture picks and mixes different bits of fashion, music, lifestyles and subcultural beliefs. For example, consider how many rap and pop music tracks mix and incorporate other songs from other styles into the song you are listening to. Postmodernists would argue this is typical of the 'pick and mix' culture that they say exists today. In this sense, youth subcultures express nothing more than fashion statements rather than any deep-seated critique of the society they belong to.

- Strinati (1995) argues that films and television today are only concerned with surface style and imagery rather than the 'realities of the human conditions'. Typically postmodern, the films *Moulin Rouge*, *Run Lola Run*, *Kill Bill* and *The Matrix* series play with different and often conflicting images, geographical locations and time and space abandoning or playing with the norms of narrative structure.

- Baudrillard (1988) argues that if we are to understand today's society we need to focus on the 'political economy of the sign'. Signs (or images) like the designer labels attached to jeans, shirts or coats mean something to young people above and beyond the item of clothing the label is attached to. Certain products become status symbols, for example, so that if you do not have the right training shoes (possibly because you cannot afford them) your status is lower and you are excluded from the dominant cultural identity. In a media saturated world the 'codes' generated by various agencies of 'signification', such as radio stations, newspapers and the Internet, are so powerful that we lose the ability to distinguish between reality (the real practical value of an item compared with its image). For Baudrillard it is the job of the sociologist to find the key to understanding the principals or 'codes' governing such transactions.

- On a more optimistic note, Hebdige (1988) argues that in a postmodern world people are no longer restricted by social categories such as class, ethnicity, gender and age – they are free to choose whatever style or fashion they desire. Mixing and matching from a variety of cultural and subcultural styles, postmodern identities are diverse, pluralistic and not shaped by the constraints of any social structure. In short, there are more cultural choices available to the consumer. This is very similar to the neo-Marxist (CCCS) idea of symbolic creativity – the notion that people can use popular culture in their own way, make their own identities from the ways in which they use products and from what combinations of popular products they mix together.

Conclusion

There are a variety of writers who are critical of the postmodernist ideas expressed above.

- Philo (1990) argues that postmodernists underestimate the capacity of audiences to think critically.
- John Eldridge (1993) of the Glasgow University Media Group is critical of the **relativism** adopted by Baudrillard and others when they argue that the difference between reality and media image disappears. Eldridge believes that sociologists should continually assess the ideological content of the media (and its dangers) rather than, as postmodernists would believe, give up because it is 'all relative'.
- Kellner (1989) argues that many of the ideas postmodernists have about the media are 'media essentialism', that is they place too much importance on the role that media technology has to shape or determine society. In agreement with many Marxist writers, he argues that postmodernists ignore the social relationships that exist in the ownership and control of the media. He argues that sociologists should focus more on political connections between the media and political elites, the ways audiences use the media or how they can resist the dominant ideological messages it sometimes conveys.

◆ What, when and why?

By 'modernity' most sociologists refer to the period of the 18th, 19th and early 20th centuries – a period after the so-called 'Enlightenment' which was characterised by industrialisation, production, and the widespread belief that science contained all the 'big' answers to some of the 'big' questions. These questions included 'why are we here?', 'what is the purpose of human existence?', 'can scientific theory (or any other type of theory) lead to an improvement in the human condition?'.

❝❞ Key Definitions

The term **relativism** is often associated with postmodernist ideas. Postmodernist theory attacks other theories (they call them 'metanarratives') for attempting to offer explanatory 'truths' about how society works. Postmodernists insist that no one theory has the ability to explain how the world is. As a result, they argue that one theory is just as good as (or relative to) any other in its ability to explain things. This is referred to as relativism. Applied to culture, postmodernists argue that it makes little sense to judge the quality of cultural products by any one set of criteria or cultural standard. For postmodernists one cultural standard (and therefore product) is as good as any other – they are all relative.

Baudrillard (1988) uses the word **simulacra** to describe false or deceptive images in which we no longer even try to distinguish reality from image. The two blur together and dominate the postmodern world. Sometimes, this is called the 'hyper-real' – when things are 'more real than real', when the fabrication is seen to be more authentic than what the image is based upon.

For consideration

1. What does the music you listen to, the clothes you wear or food you eat convey about the identity that you wish the outside world to perceive you have?

2. How could you change all of the above to convey a completely different identity?

How do sociologists connect youth subcultures and the culture industries?

What does this mean?

Sociologists use the term 'youth subcultures' to mean the values, styles and cultural tastes of that particular group. While functionalists have tended to focus on the 'function' of youth subcultures they have, in the past, avoided looking at the styles and fashions associated with a particular youth subculture. This has been focused on by the work of The Centre for Contemporary Cultural Studies and symbolic interactionist theories.

Functionalist approaches to youth subcultures

Functionalists argue that youth subcultures are functional for two reasons.

1. Functionalists argue that in Western societies categories such as 'youth' or 'teenager' play a significant function allowing a gradual development from child to adult in a way not necessary in more traditional societies. Industrial societies have increasingly invested more time in formal education allowing more young people to stay on at school/college/university rather than enter employment. Membership of a close peer group means that young people gradually become more independent of their parents during this extended period of education.
2. The pressure of competition that the education system increasingly offers is offset by the more relaxed world of subcultures where friendships value the person for who they are rather than how they perform.

The Centre for Contemporary Cultural Studies (CCCS)

The early work of this organisation shifted the theoretical focus from functionalism towards making connections between social structure and youth subcultural styles being communicated. For example, what is the significance of wearing a plaster on the cheek, baseball hat, or a pair of trainers? This structural approach is sometimes referred to as a form of 'culturalism'.

Focusing on working-class culture, these ideas were used to show how working-class styles of dress (in their early work they looked at skinheads, teddy-boys and rockers) could be seen as a form of cultural resistance to the dominant ideology of capitalism. In other words, by dressing in a style of clothing that was at odds with mainstream society, teenagers were attacking its very values such as ambition, competition and meritocracy, particularly in times of unemployment when the status of being unemployed was balanced out by that of belonging to a subculture and being seen as 'cool'.

✓ Top Exam Hints

- Remember to tell the examiner that categories such as 'youth' or 'teenager' are social constructions, that is they are not based on any fixed biological criteria but are determined by different cultures for different reasons and that these reasons often change over time.

- Angela McRobbie (1991) who has worked at the CCCS has commented on the lack of focus the early work of the CCCS had on gender issues. Focusing on the language and culture of boys, she noted how this contributes to female subordination. McRobbie argued how boys 'colonise' public spaces (the streets, youth clubs and shopping centres) marginalising girls in the process. Feminist approaches like this explore connections between female adolescent culture, and how it resists ideologies of capitalism and patriarchy. She has written about the way in which black 'ragga girls' use sexually explicit dancing in a way that ridicules male sexism and reasserts female control over sexuality. In this way young black women open up public cultural space for themselves.

Class, ethnicity and bricolage

Paul Willis (1990) argues that the age of spectacular youth subcultures such as skinheads, punks, New Romantics, has gone for good. There is too much diversity today for any single youth subculture to dominate. The growth of capitalist culture and leisure industries has meant that young people have access to cultural resources in which they can be 'symbolically creative' in their leisure time, that is the mixing and merging of different ideas and styles to create new cultural meanings. Far from being fashion victims, Willis views them as 'active' agents working within the structures of the various culture industries – quite often in an active and subversive way.

Hebdige (himself a student of the CCCS) writing in 1979 developed a theoretical approach which insists that the influence of black culture and music on the white working classes is immense. He therefore argues that any analysis of youth subcultures cannot solely focus on the class background of those concerned. Subcultures involve the mixing and matching of previous subcultures to create new ones, for example black and Asian styles of music and dress being merged in rap and RandB. Bricolage refers to the way in which cultures re-use ordinary objects or commodities to create new meanings, such as the wearing of plasters on the cheek as a fashion statement rather than a sign of injury.

Conclusion

- Youth subcultures do not always appear to function in a way that some functionalists contend, that is the role of tension management (the increasing tendency of some gangs to carry guns).
- Is it really possible to assume that all youth subcultures behave the same way? For example, how might middle-class and working-class subcultures behave differently?
- Many structural theories have, in the past, been considered 'gender blind' in that they ignore an analysis of the different (or increasingly similar) roles that males and females play in these different subcultures.

For consideration

1. In what ways can you see different cultural styles, fashions and symbols being merged in the clothes you wear and the music you listen to?

2. Why do you think these particular elements have been chosen to forge new fashions?

4.13 | How do sociologists connect class, ethnicity, gender and leisure?

✓ Top Exam Hint

Use the concept of historical perspective to evaluate to what extent opinions and attitudes have changed over time. For example, how are women now perceived when they say they play football compared with 40 years ago? Tell the examiners that you are aware of these differences in attitudes and that you question the validity of the findings of case studies that perhaps were written when values and attitudes were very different.

What does this mean?

- Sociologists focus on the social, economic and political contexts in which leisure occupies people's lives. The 'leisure society' is a term that sociologists used to describe how society could be during the 1950s. It described a situation where, with increasing modernisation of work practices (production lines, technology and managerial systems), people would work fewer hours than in the previous century and therefore have more available time to dedicate to leisure.

- In practice these sociological imaginative ideas were incorrect. Extended to the 21st century with 'performance related pay', 'targets' and 'profit margins' (ideas that reflect New Right theories), people are suffering from a whole range of stress-related diseases that are far removed from the idea of a 'leisure society'.

- What leisure time people do have is very often structured by the very same types of inequalities that exist in other parts of people's lives and as such can and does affect what sociologists might say about the identities they take up, for example, class, gender or ethnic-based identities.

Class and leisure

- Glyptis (1989) studied patterns of leisure and argued that participation in sports and entertainment activities is clearly structured by social class. Glyptis claimed that 34 per cent of professional workers are involved in indoor sports such as badminton, squash, swimming, compared with only 15 per cent of unskilled manual workers. She argues that this is because most leisure centres (even those run by public authorities) charge membership or entry rates and therefore this affects who can and who cannot afford to take up such sports. Glyptis also claimed that car ownership often played a role in relation to certain activities; for example, golf courses are often placed in areas where public transport is inaccessible.

- Marxists Clarke and Critcher (1985) have commented on how leisure activities are increasingly being run as commercial or profit-making industries. For example, local sports halls used to be run directly by local councils but in recent years they are increasingly being 'farmed out' to private companies who attempt to run them at a profit.

Gender and leisure

If we assume, as many feminists do, that the amount of free time available to women is less than that available to men – women often carry out a 'triple shift' of paid work during the day time, housework in the evenings, and emotional support for the family the rest of the time – then this has enormous repercussions on the type and quantity of leisure activities that women take up.

- Delphy (1984) argues that women not only have less money to spend on leisure (women earn on average less than men) but the triple-shift lifestyle they lead structurally constrains their lives, limiting the opportunities for leisure that their male counterparts experience.
- Deem (1990) used the term 'patriarchal control' to refer to the extent and type of female involvement in leisure activities based on the reactions of males (early hostility to women playing football or women drinking in pubs alone).
- Wimbush (1986) drew similar conclusions to both Delphy and Deem in a study that focused on young mothers living in Edinburgh showing how their leisure activities were severely restricted by the lack of male involvement in childcare.

Ethnicity and leisure

It is worth telling the examiners that sociologists increasingly combine issues of class and gender when focusing on explanations surrounding ethnic identities. This is particularly true in terms of leisure where, in many cases, the lower than average levels of income of ethnic minorities have a direct impact on the type and amount of leisure activities available to them.

For many ethnic minorities, cultural and religious factors also restrict certain types of leisure. For example, many women do not go swimming or clubbing because some branches of Christian, Judaic and Islamic religions will not permit women to publicly show specific areas of their body and/or may not allow alcohol consumption. This can be combined with racist, and in some cases 'socio-biological', attitudes that allow many more black players to join British professional football clubs than Asian footballers despite the fact that football plays a major role in the leisure time for many British Asians.

Conclusion

Sivanandan (1990) argues that racism is behind many of the restrictions that ethnic minorities experience within the leisure industries. However, both Sivanandan and Paul Gilroy (1993) claim that there is a resistance to such racism visible in the types of leisure activities taken up, such as music, dance, carnival and sports activities. Referring to 'global cultural styles', Gilroy also comments on how identities are increasingly 'flexible' and are no longer rooted in fixed ethnic and national roots. For example, consider how both rap and Bhangra are influencing and mixing in with other music styles.

● **Synoptic Link**

Apply feminist writer Sylvia Walby's argument and her 'triple systems theory' to the study of leisure activities. She argues that patriarchy, capitalism (and therefore class relations) and ethnicity combine to produce unequal relations between men and women, that is, gender stratification. You might like to read this section again considering and applying Walby's three points. Walby (1990) argues that patriarchy is composed of three elements.

1. Female subordination where institutions such as the leisure industries produce unequal relations between men and women.
2. Female oppression where women experience sexism and racism based on stereotypical ideas and attitudes.
3. Female exploitation where women's skills and labour are not rewarded to the same extent that men experience. For example, consider how male and female tennis players command very different salary structures.

For consideration

1. To what extent do you believe it is possible to separate issues of class, gender and ethnicity when talking about individual participation in leisure-based activities?

2. In terms of leisure activities, is patriarchal control still an issue for women in the 21st century?

What is the relationship between class and culture?

What does this mean?

Writing in 1974, Herbert Gans argued that it is always possible to connect culture and taste to social class. While it might have been possible to connect the type of music people listen to (opera) with a particular class (middle class) at the time Gans was writing, sociologists today have a much tougher job making direct connections between class and culture. Nevertheless, many writers would still argue that even though 'class' is difficult to define, there is a relationship between cultural taste, social class and power which still appears to advantage people from the middle classes.

What is working-class culture?

Zweig (1961) argued that rising living standards in the 1950s were changing the nature of working-class culture. He maintained that a new form of affluent (well-off) worker was emerging in British society and was adopting middle-class tastes, lifestyles and political attitudes. At this time, many working-class families were starting to own cars, fridges, televisions and to go on holiday – for the first time since industrialisation had taken place.

Not all sociologists were happy about these developments. Richard Hogart (1958) commented on the 1950s cultural invasion of American products such as rock'n'roll, American movies and juke boxes into the UK. He argued that these 'imports' were eroding traditional working-class culture in the UK, despite their increasing popularity with British teenagers. However, this view has been attacked by Storey (1993) who argued that such views of working-class culture are nostalgic rather than realistic. He also claimed that working-class culture today, despite its commercial nature, still possesses inventiveness and vitality.

Working-class culture as a form of resistance to capitalism

The Centre for Contemporary Cultural Studies (CCCS) has been strongly influenced by neo-Marxist hegemonic theory (also referred to as culturalism). Their work shows how some aspects of working-class culture resist the dominant values that circulate in capitalist societies.

Richard Johnson (1979) has written about the ways in which working-class adults attempted to organise their own education during the 19th century at a time when there was little adult provision. Paul Willis (1977) has also written about how working class 'lads' actively engaged in resistance to the values of a Midlands comprehensive school. In both cases it is possible to see the active and varied ways in which the dominant cultures within capitalism can be

✓ **Top Exam Hint**

Tell the examiners that 'class' is an extremely problematic term today and one open to a variety of interpretations. In Marx's day to be working class was to be associated with what you produced or manufactured. Working-class lifestyles were traditionally associated with industrialisation. In many modern Western economies few people are employed in manufacturing; more people work in office jobs within one of the service industries such as leisure and tourism and finance. Tell the examiner you are aware of the continually debated nature about what class is and you will be rewarded evaluation marks.

resisted. However, Critcher (1979) shows how some forms of traditional working-class culture can be incorporated or 'tamed' into the mainstream, for example the commercialisation of football today.

Combining class and gender

Much of the work of the CCCS has been criticised for its focus on masculine cultures while denying the importance of both gender and ethnicity in their analysis. Bourke (1994) demonstrates the importance of both class and gender in the development of working-class culture. He notes how, during the 1930s, working-class men were hugely concerned about their physique. He argues that this was partly in response to rising rates of unemployment, which challenged male traditional authority. As a response, their masculinity had to be shown off in other ways.

For women, 1930s cinema and the novel had begun to offer suggestions of a greater degree of freedom in terms of their sexuality. For many working-class women this offered a sense of liberation at a time when to be pregnant while unmarried meant social exclusion from the community.

Middle-class culture

Pierre Bourdieu (1993) argues that regardless of whether it is the ballet, Swan Lake, or a television episode of EastEnders, individuals operate according to a **habitus**, which involves particular responses and particular evaluations of what is on offer. This habitus is the result of socialisation in early childhood and produces reactions that are almost instinctive. Bourdieu argues that a habitus will reflect the social conditions of the person who expresses it.

In what he describes as a cultural field, Bourdieu argues that society is made up of the institutions and agencies, such as newspaper reviews, galleries and museums, which deal with the discussion and evaluation of culture. The habitus of the middle classes will mean they possess the vocabulary required to engage in a discussion that excludes working-class participation.

Conclusion

Bourdieu maintains that in capitalist societies, bourgeois or middle-class culture is awarded greater status and authority while the habitus of the working classes is defined as lacking cultural worth. Taking the museum as an example, he argues that the language, layout and cultural capital deployed by museums mean that many working-class people feel 'inadequate' on entering these and other cultural institutions.

For consideration

1. What forms of traditional working-class culture are now being adopted by the middle classes?

2. How easy is it to divide different forms of cultural activities along gender lines?

➥ Classic Study

Richard Hoggart published *The Uses of Literacy* in 1958. In the first half of this book he describes the richness and energy of pre-Second World War culture in the homes, churches, pubs and other organisations of working-class communities. He believed that in times of high unemployment and little social welfare provision when life was very insecure for the working classes, the culture was necessarily frivolous and possessed a 'living for the moment' element about it. He was concerned at the time about the arrival of radio, which, he feared, would stop working-class people from meeting together to sing their own songs.

✳ Key Ideas

* Bourdieu (1993) argues that cultural capital varies between different cultural fields. In the same way that Marx argued that there is competition between different economic fields, so Bourdieu argues there is competition between different cultural fields with the possession of dominant **cultural capital** determining who wins (the middle classes).

* Claus Offe (1985) criticises the idea that class is a useful concept when evaluating different types of culture. He describes society today as late 'disorganised capitalism' in which fewer and fewer people share the unifying common experience of full-time work, that is, the work experience that for many used to shape the culture of the social classes. With high rates of unemployment, part-time and temporary contracts, what emerge today are a variety of different lifestyles that in turn generate different forms of culture.

66 99 Key Definitions

Habitus is the term used to describe the particular responses and attitudes associated with a particular class.

Cultural capital is the particular cultural skills and knowledge required to appreciate or understand cultural products.

4.15 | How can culture be a commodity?

What does this mean?

Many sociologists argue that now, more than at any previous point in history, culture can be sold in the form of clothes, media products, fashion accessories, leisure opportunities and sportswear – just like any other consumer goods. It is therefore very important to realise how capitalist enterprises have the power to shape the various cultural commodities open to you.

Rupert Murdoch controls 38 per cent of the UK national press and dominates the British pay-TV industries.

More and more owned by fewer and fewer

- With fewer and fewer large companies, the media and cultural sectors of most capitalist economies are dominated by a relatively small number of large companies. These companies often have the ability to exert control over the ways in which cultural markets develop and how goods are marketed. In a deal worth $19 billion, Walt Disney recently took over ABC and Capital combining the might of their film and leisure conglomerate with one of the largest US television networks.

- These large cultural conglomerates can exploit their interests across a variety of cultural products. Rupert Murdoch's News Corporation promotes the image of BSkyB which in turn purchases volumes of stock from Fox Studios, which is owned by News Corporation in the first place. This means that News Corporation's television can be promoted in the various TV listings in the papers owned by Murdoch's companies.

- Golding and Murdoch (1991) argue that the situation regarding the power of these huge companies is helped by the decrease in power in public sector organisations such as the BBC, local libraries and community arts projects which, in recent years receive less funding. In addition to this, the competitive business practices encouraged by government policies, such as privatisation, mean that 'to be big is definitely better'. In other words, competition wipes out smaller but often more exciting cultural industries such as the independent record scene in the 1980s and 1990s.

What is cultural conservatism?

Many writers, poets, painters and actors accuse the entertainment industries of being culturally conservative because of their lack of imagination in commissioning new productions. Because much within the cultural industries is dependent on making huge profits, the decisions made by multinational industries to use 'tried and tested' strategies often produce culturally conservative products. You can see this in the way that both the Hollywood film industry and the British West End theatreland offer guaranteed commercial successes rather than risky but perhaps more challenging (and entertaining) productions.

❝❞ Key Definition

Marxists often use the term **culture industry** to argue that culture has become something that is to be manufactured and sold for profit by media conglomerates. They also argue that the culture industry manipulates the tastes, wants and needs of the masses by promoting a popular culture that is uncritical, superficial and dehumanising.

Business sponsorship affects what we watch and when

With advertising revenue a concern for many television company executives, it is amazing to realise the power that companies like BSkyB exercise. In 1991, the company bought the rights to Premier League soccer with an audience of under one million. This rose to five million by 1996. BSkyB paid £674 million to secure the rights until 2001.

However, these figures pale when compared with the $2.2 billion raised when the television rights for the 2002 soccer World Cup were sold. This means that BSkyB have been able to exert huge influence over the organisation and delivery of sport even to the extent of determining when the games are actually played.

The political economy approach

This approach points out the way that the market delivers cultural goods often in an uneven and unequal fashion. It also argues that the availability of many cultural goods varies according to social background, for example consider how expensive CDs are. This can be seen in the way that many sporting events are only available on satellite or cable networks for which there is a monthly charge. This, in combination with the technology required to engage in many cultural products, means that people lower down the social spectrum may not be able to afford to enjoy the products on offer.

Conclusion

The political-economy approach does, however, have its critics. They argue that while there is no doubt that lack of money means less opportunity to engage in some of the products on offer, there are many people at the bottom of the social structure who do consume cultural commodities; consider the amount of satellite dishes visible in often extremely run-down areas.

Furthermore, while large multinational companies may well control much that takes place they cannot always anticipate the ways in which consumers will respond. Record companies are losing millions of pounds to consumers who use technology available in their own homes to download films and music onto CDs often aided by technology produced by the same companies, such as Sony.

✳ Key Idea

Not all writers are so pessimistic in their views of how audiences are affected by what they see and hear. Morley (1980) argues that audiences can 'decode' or interpret programmes in different ways depending on their class, gender, ethnicity, age, cultural identity, political views and personal experience. All of these act, he argues, as 'filters' and produce different responses in different people. Morley identifies three different types of decoding.

1. Oppositional: this occurs when some audience members reject what they see and replace the intended meaning with a new one that diverges from the message intended.
2. Negotiated: this occurs when audience members twist the intended meaning to make it fit their own views.
3. Dominant: this occurs when some audience members completely accept the dominant or intended meaning of the product and go along with it.

For consideration

1. To what extent do you believe that the range of culture products available is culturally conservative?

2. To what extent does television advertising change according to the programmes being scheduled and what does this tell us therefore about the power that programme schedulers have?

4.16 | What is the relationship between ethnicity and culture?

❋ Key Ideas

- The word 'diaspora' is used to describe the process of cultural dispersal of norms and values that produce new identities. The evidence for this can be seen by the influence of ethnic minorities on the British film and music industries along with the enormous change in eating habits in the UK over the last 30 years. Such ideas can also be linked to the postmodern view that we are living in a rapidly changing and diverse society.

- Winston James (1993) writes that '*although island loyalties still remain, the people of the Caribbean have been brought together by London Transport, the National Health Service and most of all by the...forces of British racism to recognise their common class position...*' (James 1993, page 240). As a response to this racism James argues that a shared oppositional culture emerged around the phrase 'black' in which not only Afro-Caribbean people identified themselves as black but also political activists within the southern Asian communities.

  Stuart Hall refers to the concept of 'cultural hybridity' to describe the process through which a variety of cultural influences are synthesised to produce new cultural forms. Ratansi (1994) shows how postmodernist ideas can be used to explain how ethnicity and cultural imagery are more fluid and flexible in the postmodern world. He argues that these concepts are no longer rooted in traditional social circumstances such as class, ethnic group or economic structure. Ethnic minorities can put together an 'off the shelf' set of images and styles to create new identities.

What does this mean?

Paul Gilroy (1993) suggests that ethnic identities are constantly undergoing change. Ethnicity refers not just to the race of a person but also to their beliefs, customs, religious practices and understanding of belonging and how these interface with their identities. This means that ethnicity is inseparable from what we understand culture to be. Sociologists use the term 'diaspora' to describe the process of cultural dispersal that takes place as a result of the many migrational processes that exist.

The rising status of black working-class fashion and music within Western popular culture now has an enormous influence in many parts of the Western world, aided by the global reach of the mass media and its ability to highlight particular aspects of black style, fashion and music. However, today's 'MTV' generation is not just influenced by Black culture but a diversity of ethnicities, ages and, quite often, sexualities.

The effects of racism on ethnic minority cultures

The experience of migration has a powerful impact on the identities and cultures of those that migrate, those left behind, and those who receive the migrating communities. For many people arrival into a new country can be a negative experience if faced with the racism that many societies inflict. Sometimes the response of the migrating community is to 'turn inwards'. Cashmore and Troyna (1990) have shown how first-generation migrants from southern Asia recreated the institutions and organisations such as temples, mosques, business networks, cinemas and shops necessary to reinforce cultural traditions in new settings in the UK.

Sociologists have been quick to explain the development of 'black subcultures' with distinct styles of dress, forms of music and cultural beliefs as forms of 'cultural resistance' to the racism that many ethnic minorities feel they experience. Stuart Hall (1978) has argued that young black street culture has developed in response to the structural forces of capitalism and the way they affect many ethnic minorities in a negative sense. British capitalism directs many members of ethnic minorities into low-paid work. One response to this is the adoption of 'survival strategies' in which social networks are formed in the street cultures that exist in many inner city areas.

New ethnicities

In an essay called 'New Ethnicities' (1992), Stuart Hall has shown how important changes have taken place in recent years in how we conceive ethnicity. Ethnicity is not just determined by biology or social structure. It is a far more fluid concept and one that Ratansi (1994) argues is being exploited by advertising and the mass media. Individuals can synthesise or create new cultural identities from a variety of different influences around them including the mass media and popular culture.

The film industry in the 1970s used the term 'black' to unite artists and cultural producers from a variety of backgrounds who shared a common interest in opposing racism. Hall argues that in the last 20 years the film and television industries have recognised the far more complex way in which sexuality, class, age and gender interact to create varieties of ethnic cultures and identities.

Style as a political tool

Hebdige (1979) argues that subcultural styles and the creation of identity through group membership can be seen as symbolic ways of resisting the dominant values and ideologies of society. The way people dress, the music they listen to and the ways they speak can be seen as 'symbolic tools' against the powerlessness and alienation that exists for many ethnic minorities.

Kobena Mercer (1995) is one of many sociologists who focus on the idea of cultural resistance. She has noted how ethnic groups often use style as a political tool. Focusing on hairstyles, she shows how identity politics can be played out; for example, the 'Afro' as part of the Black Power movement in the 1960s and 1970s. These were seen to be symbols of pride, unity and difference in what was perceived by many black people as a racist society.

Conclusion

- Mahmood (1996) argues that there is nothing new about the emergence of synthesis or hybrid cultures that some writers talk about. He argues that this process has always existed since migration first started.
- Cathy Lloyd (1993) warns that while the growing diversity of culture and identity is something to be celebrated, it should not stop people from focusing on the inequalities of power that exist for many ethnic groups in different parts of the globe.

✳ Key Idea

Kidd (2003) notes how the term 'wigger' is a contraction of the term 'white nigger' and is used sometimes as a racist insult and sometimes by white lower-middle-class youths to refer to themselves. Wiggers take on and incorporate into their own cultural practices the style adopted by inner city, usually American, black youths. In this case, 'style' includes dress, language, music etc. Some writers argue that this is evidence of postmodernity in the sense that it involves the mixing and playing with traditional ethnic identities in new ways.

For consideration

1. What films or television programmes can you think of that highlight the way that sexuality, age, class and gender can be combined to create a new sense of ethnicity as Ratansi and Hall argue exists today.

2. Think about the many different cultural influences that affect your own culture, such as the food, clothing, music, holidays, sport, television and films. Do these confirm or refute the notion of hybrid cultures?

How do sociologists connect femininity with the culture industries?

✍ Coursework Suggestion

Choose a sample of magazines (national or local) that you can identify as having only female editors. Contact the editors of these magazines and try to secure an interview with them. Evaluate to what extent they edit the magazine using the 'male gaze' referred to in this spread. You could also explore to what extent their job has been made harder by the fact that they are women within a still male-dominated industry.

What does this mean?

Changes in the employment sector over the last 30 years have meant that more and more women are employed in part-time and full-time jobs. Some sociologists argue that they now have more income to spend on popular culture. In other words, women are playing a greater part in the *consumption* of popular culture and the related industries. Evidence to support this view is the increasing amounts of books, television programmes and magazines targeting female audiences along with entertainment that includes the provision of male strippers for female audiences.

Women are also playing a greater role within the *production* of popular culture with more and more women securing positions of seniority within television, the tabloid and broadsheet press and film production. Women also participate on the artistic side of the various industries including those of drama, music, film and literature.

What do feminists say about this?

Feminists note that while women are increasingly taking up senior positions with the media industries, they are still outnumbered by men. For example, by 1998, 29.1 per cent of the BBC's senior executives were women and women made up only 36.3 per cent of its middle managers and senior professionals. They also argue that while women do have increasing earning power it is still less than that of men, and women tend to spend less of their income on their own recreation than men do.

Employment within the industries tends to increasingly focus around part-time and casual contracts, which typically employ more women on lower wages. Finally, much of the imagery used in the promotion of pop bands continues to use women's bodies in, feminists argue, sexually exploitative ways.

Radical feminists point to two disturbing factors affecting women in the cultural industries.

- The commercial market place demands that magazines, films and other cultural products use sex and women's bodies to sell their commodities despite the increasing number of women in senior positions.
- Patriarchal ideology runs so deep within modern societies that both men and women consume culture through a 'male gaze'. That is, men and women take it for granted that women are represented as sexual objects and that it is 'natural' for men to enjoy women in this way.

Writing in 1975, Laura Mulvey believes that the female body is characterised as a sexual toy for men in which certain body types are held up as 'ideal' for other women to strive for.

Romance and competition

Some sociologists have focused on how notions of love, romance and marriage have changed over time within different forms of popular culture. Angela McRobbie (1983) analysed the importance of romance to adolescent girls in her study of *Jackie* magazine. The stories in the magazine tended to reinforce traditional notions of femininity that highlighted the prime role of women as mothers and wives. Typically the stories in *Jackie* were about how to 'get your man' often at the expense of other female friends, students or colleagues. McRobbie argued that these competitive ideas undermined notions of female solidarity by setting woman against woman in the hunt for their man.

Ien Ang (1985) has argued that the popularity of television 'soaps' among many female viewers is based around issues of love, romance and conflict contained not only within the plot lines of the programmes themselves but also within the reality of many of the lives of the women who watch them.

Popular culture and plastic sexualities

Anthony Giddens (1992) refers to the emergence of 'plastic sexualities' where sexual pleasure is separated from the act of reproduction. He argues that it has led to an increase in women's liberation in society. Today, unlike in earlier times, women can openly discuss their own sexual pleasure as a natural and important part of a healthy relationship and not worry about this being considered 'deviant'. Television programmes such as 'Friends' and 'Sex in the City' deal with women's sexuality in a way unheard of in previous generations. In this sense, sexuality is no longer something to be hidden but rather, for Giddens, brings an increased 'democratisation' between men and women within the arena of their private lives.

Conclusion

Most branches of feminism agree that women are still disadvantaged within patriarchal society and that this is reflected in both the consumption and production of popular culture. However, while women were once viewed by many sociological theories as passive victims of the images within popular culture, increasingly they are seen as creative users albeit within a sexist industry.

For consideration

1. To what extent do you think that traditional notions of femininity are still present in television and magazine advertising today?

2. Focusing on different branches of popular culture, how could you apply the ideas of Joan Smith to gender inequality?

⊂⊃ **Classic Study**

Joan Smith (1997) in *Different for Girls* argues that it is culture rather than biology that makes females different from males as it treats them differently because of their different reproductive organs. She makes five claims.

1. Men and women become different because people treat them differently.
2. Being defined as woman is not just a matter of biology but involves moral judgements about how one should behave as a woman.
3. 'Common sense' patriarchal thought sees women as 'biologically different' from men but biologically similar to all other women. This encourages the idea that all women are different from all men.
4. While these views are considered to be 'natural' much research would argue that this is actually a product of 'nurture' or the environment.
5. Science, law and religion are often used as proof to confirm these patriarchal 'common sense' ideologies.

What is the relationship between masculinity and the culture industries?

What do these 'new lad' magazines say about what it is to be male in modern societies?

What does this mean?

Today sexual images of masculinity litter television advertisements, films and girls' magazines in ways previously not seen within British popular culture. With the growth of male lifestyle magazines such as *The Face*, *Arena* and *GQ* and an increasingly male-orientated cosmetics industry, come greater levels of anorexia and bulimia statistics for men – illnesses previously only associated with young females. What does this tell us about the relationships between identities and popular culture?

Men, fashion and identities

Drawing on post-structrual ideas, Frank Mort (1996) focuses on the development of commodities that cater specifically for men's fashion. He contrasts the way that masculinity was represented in the 1950s with the 1980s through fashion, clothes design, advertising and retailing. He argues that there was a movement away from traditional masculinity making it more possible for young men to be increasingly preoccupied with image, style and their appearance. A much wider range of products became available, such as hair gel, moisturisers and deodorants which, for Mort, has meant the development of a wide range of male identities that move away from the image of the white heterosexual male that typified popular culture in the 1950s.

But what is masculinity?

Victor Seidler (1989) argues that masculine identities are associated with the public rather than the private sphere of life. In Western societies the qualities associated with masculinity are characterised by logic, rationality and objectivity. Masculinity is therefore socially constructed to include the qualities of aggression and competition. Seidler argues that women are associated with emotional qualities and subjectivity and caring for others – something that in general men are discouraged from doing.

Marsh et al (1996) connect ideas of competition to the idea that men must be seen to 'prove their manhood' when it comes to male sexuality and sexual behaviour.

'*As part of this competitive struggle men approach sex as something closely connected to individual achievement and something which signifies their position in the pecking order of masculinity. Male sexuality is part of the development of a masculine identity in which sexuality is seen in terms of power and conquest.*'

(Marsh et al 1996, page 284)

Reclaiming what it means to be a man

Robert Bly (1991) believes that behaviour which is now associated with dominant Western ideas of masculinity is out of touch with 'true masculinity'. True masculinity in Bly's terms rests on the idea of 'male instinct'. He argues that men need to 'get in touch' with their masculinity which is wild, primitive and deeply hidden. Bly and his followers organise country weekend 'workshops' where men participate in group therapy exploring the emotional side of what it means to be male.

Constructing 'the new man'

Jonathan Rutherford (1988) argues that masculine identity has traditionally been wrapped up in powerful images of white heterosexuality that is patriarchal in nature. However, these dominant heterosexual images of men have more recently been challenged by images of masculinity conveyed within the media from the gay and black communities and from women themselves, for example many rap videos show women dancing in sexually explicit ways which mock male masculinity. As a result some commentators argue that this has led to a reconstruction by white men about what it means to be male. Those men who are seen to be changing their behaviour by, for example, showing a more emotional caring side have been dubbed 'new men' in the media.

Conclusion

Mort (1996) argues that four factors are responsible for creating a new understanding of how masculinity is portrayed within the culture industries.

1. Traditional forms of employment associated with male masculinity, such as mining and engineering, are no longer secure.
2. Feminist theories on masculinity have encouraged some men to rethink what is means to be 'male'.
3. A consumer boom in the UK during the 1980s allowed those men with sufficient income to spend more on clothes and consumer goods in general, including cosmetics and fashion.
4. This has led to a growth in a new profession of 'cultural professionals' who provide advice and guidance on new trends in consumption, style and fashion, which in turn has led to the publication of style magazines for men.

For consideration

1. What evidence can you find that images of masculinity have changed over time?
2. How do images of masculinity vary in the popular culture of different countries?

✓ Top Exam Hints

- David Beckham, Russell Crowe and Michael Jackson show how the term 'masculinity' is meaningless when referring to popular culture. Mike Featherstone (1991) argues that in postmodernity the construction of 'lifestyles' and creation of 'identities' is based on the type of popular cultural products we consume and the many creative ways in which we use the products on offer. It may be more useful to refer to 'masculinities' rather than 'masculinity' in a postmodern world where the variety of cosmetics, clothes, and images that exist create different images of what it means to be male.

- Many ideas associated within gender studies can be described as 'essentialist'. This means that some argue that there is an 'essential' characteristic to human nature that does not change as a result of socialisation. This can be seen in the work of Robert Bly (1991) who believes that masculinity and femininity are to some extent 'natural'. His ideas can also be described as 'socio-biological' in that they argue for the existence of a biological difference between men and women. Use these descriptive words in the exam to gain extra evaluation marks.

✳ Key Ideas

- The Frankfurt School maintained that the audiences of the various cultural industries are passive victims of a media that is like a 'hypodermic syringe' that pumps ideas into their heads with little or no resistance. In this way masculinity is a creation that serves the interests of those who have much to gain commercially, depending on what image of masculinity is portrayed.

- In contrast to the passive model above, an alternative model for understanding popular culture was provided by Blumler and Katz (1974). Their 'uses-gratifications' approach shows how audiences use the culture industries for specific purposes whether it is to provide background noise, find a specific item of interest or escape from the pressure of their daily jobs. Masculinity is not something that is a product of brainwashing by the media but rather an active choice based on decisions in popular culture taken by its audience.

What is postmodern about leisure and tourism?

What does this mean?

George Ritzer (1993) refers to 'The McDonaldisation' of society. The way in which this hamburger chain prepares food for consumption is used as an analogy for the modern way of life in Western economies that are increasingly adopting American lifestyles and business principles, particularly those focused on the leisure sectors. This analogy provides a picture of a product that is cheap, quickly produced and identical wherever you go. Globalisation in this sense becomes an 'Americanisation' rather than the equal spread of ideas from countries all over the globe.

The growth in leisure complexes like those owned by Disney is one example of Ritzer's ideas in action. The slick and efficient business organisational principals are adopted and replicated around the globe to provide a leisure experience that varies little from one country to the next. However, to what extent is this rather depressing account of leisure and tourism accurate?

The sociology of leisure

Writing in 1993, Rojek argues that it is possible to detect three stages in the development of the sociology of leisure.

1. Popular in the 1970s, an approach developed that focused in the United Kingdom on the development of leisure provision within local authorities. It tended to treat leisure in isolation from other aspects of society such as the family, work and government.
2. Marxists and feminists criticised such approaches and developed a focus that attempted to explain structural inequalities that lead to inequalities of access to leisure facilities, for example the resistance by gyms in the 1970s to cater for women as their clientele.
3. Postmodernists have brought leisure and tourism to the attention of sociologists today by focusing around the issues of the body, consumer culture, and consumption patterns in general. Drawing on swimming as a form of leisure activity, they show how it has been transformed in recent years.

'rather than the physical education of 'serious' swimming in Victorian public baths…swimming has been transformed into water-based fun in leisure pools, with water chutes, slides, wave machines, inflatables, fountains, popular music, aqua-rhythm classes…with laser lights…casually overviewed by spectators in Tropicana restaurants, grazing on fast foods while drinking diet cokes'

(Scratton and Bramham 1995, page 22)

⁕ Key Idea

It is perhaps easy to believe from much of the literature that leisure and tourism is very much a 'global phenomenon', that is, experienced by most people around the globe. Drawing on Marxist theories, this idea is challenged by Lash and Urry (1987) when they argue that in a 'globalised' economy multinational companies have shifted their manufacturing operations to the newly developing countries in South East Asia and South America, where labour power is cheaper. Thus a two-tier form of globalisation takes place producing a 'bourgeoisie' in the West and a 'proletariat' in these developing countries. It is this 'bourgeoisie' that can afford the luxury of time and travel while many others around the world subsidise our lifestyles.

This quote highlights the typical postmodernist traits of diversity, choice, superficiality and a 'pick and mix' consumerism, all of which is focused on this leisure activity.

Post-tourism

Postmodernist Baudrillard (1995) argues that we live in a world where it is increasingly difficult to separate real from simulation. Urry (1990) takes this idea and applies it to the tourist industries showing how package holidays do not convey a real experience of the area visited but rather a simulated holiday bonanza far removed from the lives of the indigenous populations in close proximity of visiting tourists. Tourists instead receive a constructed package of contrived events in an artificial environment. Pessimistically, Urry describes this as 'post-tourism' where people resign themselves to giving up any attempt to seek out authentic cultural experiences.

Figurational sociology and sport

Developing ideas originally found in the work of Norbert Elias, Eric Dunning (1971) argues that as sport has developed over time the toleration for physical violence that existed in pre-modern times has significantly decreased. This forms part of a set of historical processes in which a so-called 'civilisation process' has taken place. Where once an emphasis on force and violence existed, skill has replaced this and is backed up and clearly regulated through codified rules, regulations and sporting bodies.

Conclusion

Remember that the concept of empirical adequacy is a useful evaluative tool in the exams, and refers to the evidence that researchers use to back up their claims. Lee and Turner (1996) argue that many researching academics complain that authors often make claims about the direction all societies are supposedly heading in as securely established fact. However, they have often no empirical support to back up their claims. In other words their claims are empirically inadequate.

☞ **Who is this person?**

Norbert Elias, of Jewish origin, escaped Nazi Germany in 1933 and eventually became professor of sociology at the University of Ghana in the early 1960s. A former lecturer at the University of Leicester, his theories rested on two interests.

- He was concerned to understand processes of civilisation in which he argued that external restraints on behaviour are replaced by individual, moral regulation. That is, people impose upon themselves certain moral guidelines about what is and what is not acceptable behaviour.
- He attacked functionalism and other 'structural' theories, arguing that they tended to treat social facts as 'things' that exist, shape and determine individual action. He claimed that instead we should view social relationships as an endlessly changing fluid process.

These ideas hold within them elements of both post-structural and postmodernist strands of thought. The former because post-structuralists argue that we internalise and moderate our own behaviour in the belief that we are being watched. The latter because of the reference to shifting and fluid relationships between different types of identity.

For consideration

1. To what extent do you believe that package holidays are contrived and artificial?

2. Do we all mean the same thing when we talk about 'genuine' holidays?

4.20 | What do sociologists mean by global culture?

✳ Key Idea

Postmodernists reflect both positive and negative views on the globalisation of culture. The plurality (the huge choice) of cultural meanings on offer as a result of globalisation means that people can 'pick and mix' from an enormous and ever changing set of cultural products in a rapidly changing world. However, viewed in a negative light, postmodernists also argue that this creates uncertainty and cultural disorder in which a stable sense of identity may be difficult to maintain.

66 99 Key Definition

Anthony Giddens (1990) argues that the general term for the increasing interdependence of world society is globalisation. For him, **globalisation** describes the way in which the world has become a single social system as a result of growing ties of interdependence that now affect virtually everyone. These social, political and economic connections crosscut borders between countries and change the fate of those living within them.

What does this mean?

How easy is it to identify a person's culture from the clothes they wear, the food they eat or the music they listen to? The term **globalisation** is used to describe the processes involved in making the world increasingly interconnected. Today's media technology can bring into our sitting rooms music, fashion, style and even religion from other parts of the world; think of the impact that MTV, McDonalds and more recently the Asian cultural explosion has had on the 'British way of life'.

People all around the globe can watch the same live-to-air television report of a battle or earthquake in one part of the world and experience, if only temporarily, the same space and time. David Harvey (1989) refers to this as a 'compression of time and space' in which public events in one part of the world are instantly brought into our own homes.

Different sociologists have different ideas about the relationship between popular culture and the many processes of globalisation. Some sociologists argue that a single 'global culture' (fast food, consumerism, movies) will eventually emerge, while others argue that local resistance to such global influences produces local or regional cultures that are becoming increasingly important.

Globalisation and culture

Three views can often be seen to underpin any discussion around globalisation and culture.

1. The traditionalist view in which some writers argue that globalisation is nothing new but rather the continuation of processes that have existed since great empires first conquered huge parts of the world, for example, the Roman, Chinese, and Ottoman empires. In all cases there was a mass movement of people, cultures, and ideas that affected all those concerned.
2. The globalist view in which *optimistic* globalists argue that the processes of globalisation are unstoppable but also something to celebrate. The merging and mixing of new cultures is an inevitable consequence of the success of business and technology. Such views are supported by those on the New Right. *Pessimistic* globalists, however, argue that while such processes may well be inevitable, they also reflect exploitation by big business and the imposition of Western and/or American ideas on the rest of the world. Many Marxists agree that this is what is happening.
3. The transformationalist view accepts that globalisation is taking place and indeed may well be inevitable. However, it is also more complicated than the first two views might suggest. Quite often a reaction against globalisation at a local level is the resistance of local cultures to any changes that may take place. Such views often talk about 'the global and the local' or 'glocalisation' to refer to these complex sets of interactions.

What is cultural homogenisation?

Many Marxists argue that cultural homogenisation (the wiping out of regional and local cultures) will accelerate as huge media concerns, such as Rupert Murdoch's News Corporation, convince us to consume the same clothes, fast food, popular music and television shows. Stuart Hall (1992) argues there are three possible scenarios that could emerge.

1. Cultural homogenisation occurs when national identities and culture are eroded by the impact of global cultural industries that dominate the mass media.
2. Cultural resistance occurs when national and local cultures strengthen as they resist the impact of cultural globalisation, for example the Welsh insistence on the broadcasting of many programmes in the Welsh language.
3. The emergence of new identities of hybridity occur when new 'hybrid' identities are formed through youth subcultures that fuse different cultural influences from different parts of the world to create new identities.

Conclusion

Globalisation could, on the one hand, mean that traditional forms of popular culture or folk cultures are in decline leading to a 'hybridity' of new cultures and identities through inter-marriage with subsequent generations of all ethnic groups subscribing to values and norms from both their inherited and adopted cultures. This view is pessimistically challenged by Marxists who see the process as one in which a single homogeneous, commercialised global culture reflecting American/Western capitalist ideas may well come to dominate all societies.

☀ Key Ideas

- Robins (1991) attacks the cultural homogenisation thesis arguing that successful global conglomerates will, in time, commercially exploit local cultures and identities rather than attempt to wipe them out. Referred to as 'global localisation', evidence of this can be seen in the way that some fast food chains attempt to incorporate local variations in cuisine into the products they sell at a national level.

- New Right thinker Francis Fukuyama (1992) argues that globalisation is bringing about a 'new world order' where differences between East and West are being settled. With the end of the Cold War in the late 1980s, so-called free market ideas are spreading across the world and creating freedom of choice for many people for the first time in their lives. For example, China is adopting many principles of business and competition in the running of its economy.

- Marxists and neo-Marxists are highly critical of New Right ideas and argue that, far from spreading freedom of choice, what is being spread is the expansion and belief that capitalism can work across the globe. In reality Marxists argue that many parts of the globe in fact provide new markets (and profits) for those in the richer Western economies.

For consideration

1. What evidence can you find to confirm the cultural homogenisation thesis?

2. What evidence can you find to confirm ideas of cultural resistance?

4.21 | What do sociologists mean by proto communities?

A café scene in 1930s Berlin. Are 'proto communities' really a postmodern phenomenon?

What does this mean?

When people talk about the growth of 'café society' they refer to a particular lifestyle associated with specific socio-economic groups; typically middle income and upwardly mobile people in their 20s and 30s. Sociologists are increasingly interested in types of culture associated with living spaces and communities. In the past their focus was on class and on the geographical area in which particular activities might take place, for example John William's (1986) work on football culture and the communities it emerged from.

Since the 1980s, however, approaches that are strongly associated with postmodernism have highlighted a more fluid interpretation of 'community' which is based on individual activities and social interaction. Proto communities are one example of such an interpretation.

Communities in poverty

Brian Jackson's (1968) research created a romantic view of working-class culture in his research on working-class communities in Huddersfield. He argued that poverty brought community members together via the development of informal support networks and trade union membership. Similar work by Young and Willmott (1957) showed how informal networks in East London's Bethnal Green were extremely strong in impoverished working-class communities. However, Crow and Allan (1994) have challenged such romantic views arguing that in any such communities differences in status, job role and gender quite often created tensions based around jealousy and hierarchy.

Proto communities

A more optimistic portrayal of city life is to be found in Raban's (1974) portrayal of city living. Here proto communities are created by individuals in their consumption of particular possessions or the creation of particular appearances. Such communities are described as 'symbolic' in that they *appear* to be in harmony because of the similar tastes and habits adopted.

In this sense, proto communities can be identified in the current trend for American café and sushi bars, shopping in the more up-market high street supermarkets and the increasing fascination with leisure centres and recreational sports such as kickboxing. All of these can be interpreted as 'signs' or 'images' that, in the postmodern sense, give an impression of identity however superficial or temporary to the people who share in the cultures created within them.

Four types of consumers in proto communities

Kidd (2002) offers four different postmodern consumers that can be used to explain patterns of behaviour in proto communities.

1. The passive cultural robot who is 'tricked' by the power of advertising into buying all that is on offer.
2. The creative actor who constructs his or her lifestyle and identity based on the free choice that consumption of cultural goods offers.
3. The deviant consumer who is able to manipulate and interpret the wide variety of cultural messages, signs and commodities on offer to create a new lifestyle that rejects the more dominant capitalist lifestyle.
4. The postmodern consumer concerned only with outer image and not inner substance. This consumer 'picks and mixes' from the variety of meanings and styles on offer creating 'throw away identities' that are created and recreated.

What are oppressive communities?

Bauman (1990) offers a very negative portrayal of postmodern communities that try to create the idea of unity arguing that *'a community without privacy feels more like oppression. And that privacy without community feels more like loneliness than being oneself'* (Bauman 1990, page 106). In this sense it is possible to argue that by attempting to fit into a particular lifestyle adopted by so many others, for example lunching in particular trendy restaurants, an individual might actually end up feeling more alienated or lonely from the experience.

Bauman reasons that it is not always clear who might be considered an 'in group' or 'out group' and boundaries often shift as to what is considered acceptable behaviour. Either way he claims that 'insiders' need 'outsiders' to strengthen the identity and coherence of the 'in-group' in question. This 'in group' might mark itself out by the styles of clothes, patterns of speech, tastes in music or destinations to 'hang out' in. In this sense there is a contradiction in the word 'community', that is, its very existence excludes others who are not within it.

Conclusion

Proto communities can be 'real' or 'virtual' and can include and exclude at the same time. *Real* communities that incorporate cafés, shopping and other lifestyles can be a source of exclusion for ethnic minorities in host countries determined to fit into the new countries they arrive into. *Virtual* communities, that is, cyber communities based around chat rooms, can exclude those that do not possess either the knowledge or the finances needed to operate within their unique environments.

For consideration

1. What kind of consumer would you argue you are?
2. How easy is it to identify yourself with any of the types of people that might be regular consumers in some of the places described in this section?

✍ **Coursework Suggestion**

Create a questionnaire based around Kidd's (2002) model of different consumers. Interview consumers in the types of cafés, shops and restaurants described in this section in an attempt to either prove or disprove the model he writes about. You can analyse your findings by contrasting this model with Marxist or feminist theories that you have looked at in this chapter.

※ **Key Ideas**

- Anderson (1983), a neo-Marxist, argues that the nation state (for example, Germany, India and Japan) is an 'imagined political community'. By this he means that 'community' appears to give the impression that people know each other – something which is impossible if we are talking about the whole population of a country. A variety of methods help create this 'community' including the development of the printed word in a common language and the construction of legends, such as Robin Hood in England, which help us to believe in a common shared past and a 'national anthem'. Applied to popular culture, national sports such as rugby create a sense of unity even though in reality huge differences exist between fans at such sporting events.

- Anthony Giddens' *Structuration Theory* is an attempt to combine macro or structural sociology with micro or interpretive sociology. He argues that people 'interpret' the culture around them, deciding how they will act. But the choices that people make are constrained, determined or shaped by the structures in society that individuals have helped to form; for example the power of record companies to determine the artists and how they might be marketed to us. Some of these structures *constrain*, for example rules and regulations, but others *enable*, that is, without the structure of language we would not be able to communicate with each other or understand the messages hidden in the various forms of popular culture on offer.

What are symbolic boundaries?

What does this mean?

A postmodernist concept, 'symbolic boundaries', has been used by A.P. Cohen (1986) to describe mental constructions or boundaries that people create to help decide who might be or might not be part of a particular community. Because these symbolic boundaries are created by individuals and used against other individuals they possess no objective reality and are hugely subjective; they depend totally on the ideas, values, moods and situation of the person applying them.

Cohen argues that, in the postmodern world in which we live, symbolic boundaries are necessary because of the enormous social changes that have blurred, changed or destroyed the traditional taken-for-granted boundaries that existed between different groups such as those based around class, ethnicity or gender.

Why are symbolic boundaries needed?

Cohen's approach assumes the following three changes have taken place on a global level.

- Uncertainty exists due to the erosion of local, national and international boundaries through processes of globalisation. This interpretation views organisations such as the European Union as meddling in the traditional lifestyles of the members of its constituent countries.
- Uncertainty also exists because of the technological revolution that has taken place over the last 30 years. Previously sheltered communities, and the cultures associated with them, are bombarded by information from anywhere in the world. Such information challenges previous widely held respect for traditional values.
- The growth in tourism and travel on a worldwide basis is viewed as a threat to the linguistic and cultural traditions that separate different types of community. This is seen as a reason why some communities or countries, such as Wales, insist on their languages being taught in schools or broadcast on public service radio and television.

How do communities respond to such changes?

Cohen argues that communities attempt to develop a distinct or separate identity in response to the changes outlined above, albeit in a variety of different ways. In addition to this, individuals may adopt symbols to make their own culture distinct but interpret their symbols differently. Symbols that individuals can interpret, adopt and transform stem from language, religion, moral values, behaviour patterns and dress codes. One example is the way that, as a form of cultural resistance, some black teenagers adopt and enhance American sports wear, body posture and a variety of other accessories, for example the plaster worn on the cheek, to establish an identity in the UK.

✳ Key Idea

Functionalist theorists and those on the New Right would argue that the actions taken by a community to monitor the morals and behaviour of those who live within it ensure the smooth running of the community and therefore benefit all its members. Such thinking flies in the face of feminist ideas, which argue that women are often on the receiving end of any sanctions imposed by the community (often headed by males) and where, in many cases, similar behaviour by males would result in little or no action being taken. For example, many girls are shunned within some communities for having 'love affairs' with boys where little or nothing happens to the boy if the situation is reversed.

Applying symbolic interactionist ideas

When considering the behaviour of particular subcultures, and how and why they interact in the way they do, both Goffman (1959) and Giddens (1984) provide useful tools of analysis.

Erving Goffman argues that members of communities play a variety of different roles. Using what is referred to as the 'dramatic analogy', he argues that social actors operate in 'front' and 'back' regions. The 'front' refers to their identity which they offer to other people they meet, usually strangers. Muslim women, for example, wear a *hijab* in public, which displays little of themselves, but in private they do not necessarily wear it. In this sense they only show, in that role, aspects about their identity they wish to show. Goffman argues that the 'back' region is our true self.

Structurationalist Anthony Giddens develops these ideas contending that some people show more of their true selves in different situations and thus, rather than there being a strong division between front and back regions, this should be viewed more as a gradient that merges between the two.

Communities of surveillance

Many writers such as Crow and Allan (1994) have argued that traditional working-class communities act as prisons for their inhabitants, providing a variety of symbolic boundaries enforced by different behaviour patterns. By adopting ridicule, threats and, in some cases, punishment beatings, strong communities will keep watchful eyes on their inhabitants. Examples of this can be seen in areas such as Northern Ireland but also in some ethnic minority regions where the traditional values adopted by first-generation migrant workers are religiously guarded and enforced on many second- and third-generation members of the community. An alternative to this can be seen in the 'gated' communities that exist in wealthy areas to protect the inhabitants from outside influences or threats.

Conclusion

As well as the boundaries considered by the sociologists mentioned, you should also consider the variables of sexuality and disability both of which can act as mediums for inclusion and exclusion from communities. For example, women may be excluded to varying degrees from some traditional male arenas, such as working-men's clubs or the football community.

✍ Coursework Suggestion

Carry out interviews in your school, college or with your own peer groups; you could use 'snowball sampling' to gain your respondents. Chose as your target groups two distinct subcultures. Attempt to find out what codes of behaviour, styles and taste define what is acceptable and not within the two groups. Try also to find out what happens to those that do not live within the symbolic boundaries being created. Compare and contrast the findings from both groups and apply both consensus and conflict approaches in your analysis of the findings.

✳ Key Ideas

In ideas that reflect elements of poststructuralism (see section 4.10) the increased usage of closed circuit television (CCTV) also acts as an enforcer of behaviour patterns. Members of communities will moderate their own behaviour rather than risk being the object of gossip, or face exclusion from the community entirely.

For consideration

1. How might Marxists explain the operation of different forms of social control on any community of members?

2. Do the 'norms' and 'values' associated with the community represent the 'collective conscience' of the whole (as functionalists argue) or the views of power elites within the community?

4.23 | How can we make popular culture synoptic?

Why is synopticity important for popular culture?

Popular culture provides an ideal chapter to use when revising your synoptic unit. Culture is a key synoptic concept and examiners reward students who can combine one area of sociology with another when discussing a particular sociological issue. For example, is it really possible to talk about inequality or stratification in the UK without making references to the lifestyle and patterns of consumption that different groups in society experience?

How does popular culture link to issues of power?

By the term 'culture' sociologists mean the set of shared values, norms and beliefs of a society or group of people. The word also refers to the shared meanings and symbols (for example language) which people use to make sense of the world they live in. Students can talk about a 'dominant culture' to refer to the main culture in a society whose norms and values are seen to be the most powerful and generally accepted. A study of popular culture can be used to tell sociologists the relationship between the values of those that possess power over others and how, in some cases, the dominant cultural values that exist can be challenged by newer forms of popular culture representing the minority views of members within any society.

How does popular culture link to issues of identity?

There is a huge variety of opinions about the connection between popular culture and identity formation. In the last 25 years we have witnessed a 'cultural explosion' as new forms of technology bombard us with sensory experiences unimaginable a century ago. Videos, CDs, computer games, the Internet, video conferencing – all have the possibility to simulate, stimulate and activate minds and bodies. For some pluralists and postmodernists, this has meant a more informed population with increased choice and diversity and a greater ability to belong. They point to the diversity in newspapers, the range of documentaries available on satellite and cable television and the opportunities of distance learning through organisations such as the Open University. For the neo-Marxists, the picture is less rosy; they refer to this new form of 'mass culture' as 'Americanisation' in which the masses are fed a 'diet of trivia' made up of identical mass-produced goods. Identities can be formed in the process or, from a postmodernist perspective, the variety of cultural products reflect the existence of multiple identities that we all now possess in what they argue is a postmodern world. In some cases, however, traditional identities such as class, gender and ethnicity can be reinforced negatively as well as positively.

How does popular culture link to issues of social inequality and differentiation?

Inequality in society, that is the sets of relationships that revolve around those that have power and those that do not, can be analysed through a variety of different factors that include age, disability, sexuality, class, gender and ethnicity. Popular culture is both produced and consumed by these different socio-economic groups and can provide both inclusion or exclusion. The degree to which these groups can be involved in the various forms of popular culture on offer very often comes down to resources – the affordability of what is on offer. In this sense, popular culture can be directly linked to issues of inequality of wealth, health, opportunity and provision.

How does popular culture link to issues of deviance?

A deviant is somebody who deviates from the norms and values associated with a particular culture. You can use Merton's (1968) strain theory as a way of contrasting different viewpoints held about popular culture with the identities Merton identifies below. He argues that identities can:

- conform: such identities conform to day-to-day norms and values of society that aim to receive material rewards, for example money, a place to live
- innovate: such identities, fearing that, through 'normal' means, 'success' cannot be obtained, will commit acts of deviancy or crime
- ritualise: such identities neither expect nor truly desire material rewards to the extent that the first two do, but slavishly carry out day-to-day tasks
- retreat: such identities struggle with the ambitions, hopes and desires that modern societies require – and 'retreat' often through drug or alcohol abuse
- rebel: such identities reject the values of society wishing a complete change and the adoption of a new value system probably through radical forms of political action including terrorism.

Key points to remember

- Culture is a key synoptic concept that can be used to make connections with *any* area of the sociology syllabus.
- When talking about how society is stratified, it is just as important to look behind closed doors and at the micro-politics of private life. The private consumption patterns or habits of different groups in society tell sociologists a great deal about the ideas and inequalities that exist. Some forms of popular culture, such as rap, voice these inequalities at times when perhaps those in power would rather not hear such opinions.
- Popular culture is also a social construction. Different forms of popular culture can be associated with different groups in society that are classified as deviant, for example some youth subcultures. Historically, some forms of popular culture associated with some deviant groups in the past have become the 'hi-culture' of today, for example, blues and its association with some of the chain gangs in early 20th-century America.

4.24 | Pushing your grades up higher

1. Do not forget that not only are you evaluating the *case studies* you talk about, but also the *theories*. Of course you will do this by contrasting one theory with another, for example a Marxist approach to the issue with that of a functionalist or feminist approach. However, it is also useful to remember three categories when discussing theory.

   - Empirical adequacy: that is, what evidence is there to support the particular theory being discussed?
   - Comprehensiveness: that is, can the particular theory be used in all cases under all conditions?
   - Logical coherency: that is, does the theory logically hold together? One example where perhaps you might argue that a theory is *not* logically coherent is post-modernism. It attacks other theories and metanarratives for offering large-scale explanations. You could argue that there is no logical coherency here because surely post-modernism itself is a theory and therefore subject to its own critique.

2. Show that you are in full command of the various theories when discussing a question. Remember that the theories are 'friends' to be called upon when you feel you cannot write any more. Ask yourself 'how might a feminist, or a post-modernist analyse this particular issue?'

3. Look at the style of writing you use. How do your sentences start? If they just start with 'Postmodernist Baumann' you are losing valuable evaluation marks. Much better to use evaluative phrases such as '*in addition to this* postmodernist Baumann…' or '*in contrast to the above* postmodernist Baumann…'

4. Remember to always back up whatever point you are making with evidence. That evidence *must* be in the form of a case study by a named sociologist.

5. Try to identify the period in which the research was carried out. Of course you are not taking a history exam, but the high-achieving student should be able to tell the examiner which decade the research took place in and, ideally, which half of the decade, and what this means to how useful the study is today.

6. Make sure you answer the question! Read the question thoroughly and plan your answer to make sure your response is coherent and answers the question.

7. When discussing the findings of the case study you refer to you can then gain extra critical evaluation marks by mentioning whether the research was 'quantitative' or 'qualitative'. By doing this, you can then link one particular study to another to build up your argument.

8. When an exam question asks you to discuss the 'contribution' that a particular sociologist has made to an issue, it is important to realise that contributions can be both positive and negative. Remember this, as this will then allow you to fully evaluate the work of the sociologist in question.

9. Always remember and use the concepts of 'validity', 'reliability' and 'representativeness' when discussing the work of other sociologists. By applying these terms you will show the examiners that you are extremely critical.

10. Show that you are aware of *where* (geographically) some of these theories and theorists are coming from. For example, if you talk about Fukuyama, refer to him as 'the American New Right theorist Fukuyama'.

Key points to remember

- You must offer evidence in support of whatever argument you are making; without it the examiners will not reward your argument with marks.
- You must show mastery of the theories when constructing an exam answer.
- Use sophisticated language when criticising the theory, case study or concept. Make sure you start these sentences or paragraphs with those key 'evaluative' phrases.

Frequently asked questions

Q. What do we mean by 'the mass society theory'?

A. These sets of ideas were developed by key writers within the Frankfurt School, who dominated much theorising about the media until the 1940s. This approach argued that as society modernised, the bonds that held it together (such as class) were breaking down. One consequence was that people were increasingly living lives run on very individualised lines rather than focusing on family, friends and the community. People turned to the media for information and understanding rather than turning to family or community members. As a result, each individual is easily manipulated by those people who control the mass media.

Q. What do we mean by 'subcultural theories'?

A. These theories represent a set of views that offer an understanding about the behaviour of groups who deviate away from the norms and values associated with the dominant values of society. There is an interesting contradiction in this because while these groups (quite often sociologists focus on young people) often do not conform to the values of society, they will very strongly conform to the values and ideas of the subculture, for example, ways of talking, dress codes and types of acceptable music within the group. Subcultural theories help sociologists understand the attitudes and behaviour associated with these groups quite often adopting interpretive methods in the process.

Q. What is 'bricolage'?

A. A. Weinstein (1991) uses the term to show how subcultures use styles and symbols from different cultures and in so doing create and define their own social group. This has its roots in 'semiology' (the 'science of signs'), a type of methodology that allows sociologists to read or interpret subcultural styles such as body posture, dress codes or hairstyles and what their underlying meanings might be. Phil Cohen's 1972 study of working-class communities showed how skinhead culture was, in fact, an attempt to recover the loss of dignity associated with what was once an industrialised area of London that became redundant. Skinhead dress (braces, boots and short haircuts) became an exaggerated form of traditional working-man attire. To fight against the hegemony of dominant groups, they reuse past and present cultural symbols in new ways. Rap music culture contains elements of 'bricolage' in that it samples from many different musical elements, takes dance from poor inner city areas of the US and combines this with fashion ranging from sports clothing to jewellery.

Chapter 5

How to be synoptic

Key issues in synopticity

Synopticity is all about making links between the different ideas, concepts and theories that come up in each of the six units in the two-year course.

∞ Methods Link

The OCR specification makes clear that the synoptic paper, among other skills, requires students to understand how issues of methods link to issues of inequality and difference. To explain this, you will need to think throughout your course about the various ways in which problems of measurement and definition and issues of data gathering and analysis might be affected by studying inequality, and how they might, in turn, affect how we study issues of inequality.

✓ Top Exam Hint

The unit that you study on inequality and difference is the highest weighted unit in the A2 year – worth 20 per cent of the final two-year combined grade. Since issues of social inequality and difference are also relevant to many other areas in sociology anyway, given how the subject works, this makes it an important topic for your attention this year. It is actually worth more over all than the personal study. So, make sure you devote your study time accordingly.

What does synopticity mean?

By being **synoptic** we actually mean *being able to tie the whole course together:* being able to see how the whole six modules over the two years link together.

How can you be synoptic?

The idea of synopticity means that, as a student, you should be able to see that the different units and modules of sociology do, in fact, all link together as a whole. It is about looking at the things that join the individual bits up; looking at connections.

The good news is that sociology has always been 'synoptic', even before we actually started using the word. If you want to think like a sociologist then you are going to have to understand that society is interconnected, and therefore that all the different parts of the course are also interconnected. This is simply good sociology anyway.

- In order to be synoptic, the starting point, as usual for sociology, is theory. Theories let us make comparisons between topics – what a theory might say about one aspect of society, such as family, would then probably affect the thinking about another different aspect of society, such as education or the media. Theories let us see that society is interconnected. Theories encourage us to think about the joined up bits of the course, rather than simply see sociology as a series of unrelated topics.
- The other key synoptic tool we have is methods. Each topic or unit in sociology has case studies that are completed using methods. The same issues and problems of research and data gathering exist in many different topics.

Building up and breaking down

Often, students' perception of school is that different knowledge is taught by different teachers in different rooms and that the subjects all have different names and are located in different 'faculties' or 'departments'. It does not look as if there are any common connections, but there are! Learning about chemicals in science would help you in art. Learning about art history might help you in English literature or in history itself. Teachers often encourage us to break down connections because it is always easier to learn something if it is split up into smaller parts.

This is also true for this book. We are pulling sociology apart to show you how it all works. But, once you have pulled it apart, you then need to re-build it again, otherwise it will not work. This means that being synoptic is really important and useful; it will allow us to see how sociology links together. It has always been the case that good students saw and discussed in exams all the connections between the different ideas in sociology. Now, you get rewarded formally for this too.

What synoptic tools are there to use?

We can talk of synopticity in two main senses.

- **Social synopticity** means seeing the connections between the parts of society, and hopefully using sociological theories and ideas in order to do this.
- **Sociological synopticity** means seeing connections between sociological ideas themselves; looking at what might link together different studies or theories or even debates that sociologists might have.

It makes sense to see these two types of synopticity as related. Since everything in society is connected, then everything in sociology must also be connected. Imagine it like this. You leave your house and you go to school one morning. You talk to your friends on the bus about what you watched on television last night. Even in this 'normal' example of life we have a lot of connections going on – family, education and mass media. We should also note that culture tells us we must go to school, and so does the law! Class is a factor here, as is ethnicity; these might affect where we live and also what we might actually watch on television. As you can see, life is one big interconnected whole. In order to do good sociology, you must be aware of this.

In order to try and see how both society and sociology are connected, we can use the following 'tools':

- class
- gender
- ethnicity
- culture
- identity
- location
- globalisation
- age.

The OCR specification for the social inequality and difference topic area says quite clearly that the main focus for the exam is on issues of inequality as it links to class, gender, ethnicity and how these three in turn relate and inter-relate with each other. All these tools above, however, should enable you to evaluate all ideas from any topic, not just the actual synoptic paper.

The specification also makes very clear that synoptic issues of inequality and difference must be understood in the 'context of sociological thought'; in other words, these issues must be related to theories and to methods.

Conclusion

These ideas will allow you to think about how ideas and theories are connected. You can use them to link studies together or to link theories together, both from within the same topic, or from different topics even across the AS and A2 years. You will find that these 'tools' are key concepts that have a massive relevance to every topic in the whole specification.

At the end of the day, all sociology is about two ideas, which are related to each other.

- **Power**: who gets their way in society, and how and why?
- **Stratification**: how is society divided up?

Key points to remember

- Synopticity is a natural part of the 'sociological imagination'.
- Synopticity means making links and seeing connections.
- There are a number of tools or concepts that you can use in order to be synoptic.

● Synoptic Links

- The synoptic exam paper (unit 2539) opens with the following quote: '*You will be assessed on your understanding of the connections between sociological thought and methods of enquiry as they apply to the study of social inequality and difference. You should therefore take every opportunity to include references to aspects of social inequality that you have studied throughout your course.*' As you can see, you are being asked to make links or connections based around the theme of inequality and difference from everything that you have been taught, from any topic, and to consider how both theories and methods deal with and relate to the issue in question.

  Synopticity accounts for 20 per cent of the final grade.

- Do not forget, issues of social inequality and difference are central to how sociology works as a subject. These issues can be seen everywhere – in every theory, and in every topic

✓ Top Exam Hints

- Students get high grades by showing that they are aware of all the inter-connections between the ideas in each topic. They also get high grades for using theories and methods issues in essay questions.

- Use the synoptic concepts on page 174 in longer essay questions as a way to show your understanding of how all sociology is connected.

- Make sure you revise ways in which class, gender and ethnicity might combine together in order to make your answers for this exam sophisticated.

How will your synoptic skills be tested?

What does the specification want you to do? It asks you to be familiar with three things: connections between your unit 2539 topic and other topics; the nature of sociological thought; and how sociologists use methods of enquiry. You will need to use these three things in the exam.

✓ Top Exam Hints

- It is really important that you familiarise yourself with what the exam paper will actually look like – not just for this unit exam, but every exam for every subject. Sometimes just the look of an exam paper can put people off, so know exactly what you can expect before you go into that exam hall. Ask your teacher for a copy of the unit 2539 exam from last year. Make sure it makes sense.

- Try to imagine sociology as being made up of four essential ingredients: theory, key words, named examples and the skill of evaluation. It might make it easier to think about the skill of synopticity as a way to manipulate these four ingredients, to show your understanding of them by connecting them together in different and interesting ways.

Do not forget, like every exam, the unit 2539 paper is asking if you can think about what questions mean and respond accordingly. This is the most important skill to demonstrate in any exam – it is, in fact, the point of the exam. In your enthusiasm to answer the questions, do not forget to do this at all times.

What does this mean?

The skill of synopticity is formally tested in the final, sixth exam, which will be on social inequality and difference. Since this exam paper accounts for 20 per cent of the final A2 grade, synopticity is clearly an important skill.

It might help to think about being synoptic as a two-way process. You can link other topics to the formal synoptic paper (unit 2539), or it can also work the other way round; you can link the synoptic unit to the topic you study in unit 2536 on 'power and control'. This is because, like theory and methods, issues of inequality and difference are vital to the sociological world view as a whole; every topic deals somewhere and somehow with these important issues.

What will the unit 2539 exam paper look like?

The topic of this unit will be on issues of social inequality and difference.

- You are given a choice of one whole exam question from two. Each question is made up of five small questions (a–e) and comes to 90 marks in all.
- The exam paper presents you with two pieces of data to consider. Item A links to question (a), and item B links to question (b).
- The third question on this paper, question (c), asks you to 'identify and explain'. Do not forget that you need to show clearly in your answer to the examiner exactly where you identify and where you explain. Use these words to show him! Here you will need to link social inequality and difference to theory and methods.
- Question (d) starts with the phrase 'using your wider sociological knowledge…'. Do not forget that you can still use the items provided, but you actually need to do much more than this. The mark schemes say that if you rely on the items without adding extra ideas then you cannot score highly. Bring others ideas, studies and theories you have learned into the discussion, but make sure it is all relevant. The use of the term 'wider' in this sense asks you to be synoptic, to see links.
- The last question (e) in this paper is a 44-mark essay question, starting (as unit 2536 does) with the phrase 'outline and assess…'

The OCR mark schemes very clear say that students should '…*take every opportunity to include references to aspects of social inequality that they have studied throughout their course.*'

What sorts of things can you be asked to do?

The skill of being synoptic might require students to demonstrate these links in a variety of different possible ways, such as.

- to link your topic to methods issues, debates and problems
- to link your topic to theories and how they differ in how they see the world
- to link your topic to another topic.

Be careful with this last point. Make sure what you write is relevant to the actual question you are set. Sociology is all connections, especially when thinking about issues of social inequality and difference, but do not go off the point. Answering the question clearly and carefully must come first.

Give them what they want from you! Read the question carefully. Practice making these sorts of links as part of your revision.

Do not let the exam paper confuse you. Remember, other students in the country might have done a different topic to you for one of the units; the exam board will list all the names of all the combinations since when they print the paper they send it to everyone, and they do not know what you have done. There will be some questions on topics you have not studied. Just look for the ones you have done.

Key points to remember

- You can make synoptic links with theory, linking to methods and linking to other topics.
- Synopticity accounts for 20 per cent of the final grade.
- You can practice synopticity skills as part of your revision.

What does the exam board say about synopticity?

We can use the phrase 'drawing together' when referring to the skill of synopticity. It says that you must demonstrate in a clear and obvious way connections between theories, methods and topics, based around the chosen theme of the paper – social inequality.

It also says that synopticity involves using the skills that we call AO2 (see sections 8.2 and 8.5). Synopticity is not just about knowledge and understanding as such, it is more about what you do with your knowledge and understanding, how you manipulate it. The OCR specification refers to these as the 'higher order skills'. This means that synopticity is about the skills of:

- **analysis**
- **interpretation**
- **evaluation**.

∞ Methods Links

- You will need to link social inequality and difference to issues of methods in question (c). So, think about this as part of your revision, make a list of all the ways in which issues of methods, measurement and definition might affect or be affected by the synoptic unit you are studying. Do not let the question surprise you!

- In all sociology, theory and methods are what underpin all sociological thought. They are good ways of making synoptic links, as the exam paper requires. Theories from different topics can be compared with each other, and debates and questions in each topic can be related to the types of methods that sociologists use to find out what they know.

● Synoptic Link

As part of your revision, go over all the studies that you have learned over both years of your course. Hopefully you will have these on revision cards. Make sure you know which ones from which topics might link to other topics. Draw out all these links. They might come in handy for the synoptic exam!

66 99 Key Definitions

Analysis – pulling apart the ideas you have learned and questioning them. Can you apply them?

Interpretation – taking what you have learned and applying it in different ways to other ideas and to questions set.

Identification – thinking about what questions mean and responding accordingly.

Evaluation – assessing the ideas you have learned.

How can we make good use of the synoptic tools?

● **Synoptic Links**

The specification for OCR sociology clearly states that there are core themes that must be taught in the two years of the sociology course. These are socialisation, culture and identity and power and stratification. Along with these, theory and methods are seen as part of the 'core' of all sociological knowledge. These provide you with a sense of the basics. They are the things you need to use in every exam answer as a way of making sense of the whole of sociology, not just simply thinking about topics in isolation from each other.

Try and be synoptic in your unit 2536 exam essay question on 'power and control'. It is a good way of creating a unique and individual answer, and therefore keeping the attention of your examiner. But make sure you do not go off the point. Stick to relevant connections and links only.

✓ **Top Exam Hint**

Use these words, these 'tools', in your essays and longer questions. Use them for depth and detail, but do not forget to define them within the 'flow of your writing'.

What does this mean?

As we have seen from the previous section, it is possible to identify a number of key synoptic tools that run throughout the whole of the two-year sociology course.

The core themes are:

- socialisation
- culture
- identity
- power and control
- social differentiation
- stratification.

However, it is one thing knowing they might exist, but another to get used to using them in an active fashion. This section of the book will try and provide a number of hints that you can follow in order to try and develop your synoptic skills further:

What do the synoptic tools mean?

Let us first define each synoptic tool in turn.

- **Socialisation**: learning about your culture
- **Culture**: the way of life of a group
- **Identity**: knowing who you think you are (and what factors might shape this)
- **Power**: making others do what you want them to
- **Social differentiation**: structured social inequality and difference between groups
- **Stratification**: the process of creating power inequalities through the social hierarchy.

Now that we know what they mean, how might we use them?

What can we do? How can we develop our skills?

- Try to link the idea of power to both macro- and micro-studies in all topics.
- Try to see power as a major theme throughout sociology.
- Take any two random studies from any two topics – can you see a link between them? Use the sociological variables and the synoptic tools to build these bridges.
- Take any of the synoptic tools, and take any two theories. How would the theories compare and contrast over the issue in question? You could link in studies and key words. Try practising writing these things out as if it is an exam essay. Practise writing in a detailed fashion.

- Take each topic and link it to every other topic in turn. For each of the above six synoptic tools, try to make a list of five or six ways in which the topics might connect to each other using these tools. If you revise this, it will really help you in the examination for unit 2539.
- Try to get used to using the synoptic words identified in this spread on a regular basis in essay answers.
- Practise writing introductions and conclusions to essays where you can use these synoptic words as a way to explore the issue in question.
- Use synoptic tools to connect to issues of inequality as part of your revision.
- Use these synoptic tools to help you evaluate a theory or to compare theories with each other.
- Use these synoptic tools to help you to evaluate a case study. Think about how the tools might affect the process of data gathering and data handling.
- When you revise, use the tools to brainstorm what you know in each topic area. Use them as headings to organise your thoughts while brainstorming.

How can we use theory and methods?

You must get used to using theories and methods not just to write about and describe, but also as ways to make links.

- Try to find similarities between the theories in your unit 2539 topic. What ideas do they have in common with each other?
- Take case studies from different theories and show common ideas or points of similarity.
- Take a theoretical idea from one unit, and link it to what the same theory might say in a different unit. For example, what a theory might say about crime, might be linked to what it also says about the family, the media or education, as these things tend to be linked themselves in society.
- Explore the ways that different theories 'see' the same piece of evidence in different ways because they approach it differently. Theories that rely on statistical evidence might draw very different conclusions to theories that rely on more in-depth personal experience that does not lead to generalisation.
- Before you enter the examination, make sure you are well-armed with many methods links that you can use for question (c). Practise making methods links to research examples, theories, and think about how the topic in question poses some interesting methods problems for sociologists wishing to research it (see the Chapter 6 Social inequality and difference for help with this).

Key points to remember

- Try to practise synoptic skills as part of your revision.
- Try to use the synoptic tools in essays for depth.
- Try to use the synoptic tools as a way to organise your thoughts about how topics and studies might connect with each other.

5.4 | How can we write in a synoptic fashion?

What does this mean?

In unit 2539 of the examination, you will be required to demonstrate your synoptic skills. One of these questions will be a 44-mark essay question; you are going to be required to demonstrate synopticity while writing an essay.

What can you do?

- Do not fall into the trap of making links for the sake of it – stick to the question and make it relevant at all times.
- Do not prioritise showing off your synopticity at the expense of actually addressing and answering the question.
- You can be synoptic in essay questions in the power and control unit as a way of showing more depth, but again, the warning about relevance applies.
- For an essay question, you might take any of the synoptic tools (see section 5.3) and try to use them to explore what theories argue.
- Use the synoptic tools and make links between studies within the same topic – you could use them in order to link together what different people say and how they might agree or disagree about a particular issue

✓ **Top Exam Hint**

Do not forget to clearly spell out why you are covering what you are writing in essays, be it synoptic skills or evaluation skills. Think of this as 'signposting' to the reader what you are doing.

Refer to Chapter 8 of this book to see advice on examination skills and on how to write good essays.

To signpost to the examiner that you are making links, there are a number of phrases you might like to practise, such as:

- synoptically speaking …
- we can make a link here between XXX and XXX because …
- thinking about this in a broader context, we can …
- there is an important connection here between …
- if we use our sociological imaginations, we can see a link here between …

Think about how you can use synoptic skills as a form of evaluation in essays (see section 5.3) – this would be two skills for the price of one. Try to make connections to other studies in other topics that might support or disprove what someone might say. Spell out the comparison for good evaluation.

Think about how you might weave synoptic skills into introductions in essays. You might like to try to make links and connections as part of the opening to the introduction. Elsewhere in this book (see chapter 8), this is referred to as the 'opening seductive sentence'. Can you explore interesting links as a way of capturing the attention of the reader at the very start of an essay answer?

Key points to remember

- Try to weave synoptic skills into essays.
- See synoptic skills as a form of evaluation.
- Always use synoptic tools in essays for depth.

5.5 | How do theory and methods allow us to be synoptic?

What does this mean?

We have shown that the best way to learn sociology (as with anything) is to break it down into elements. If you can see what the individual parts are, and see how they then link to each other, you will understand quicker and, ultimately, in more depth. To show that you understand, you must be able to manipulate these different elements or ingredients together.

We have identified four main ingredients of sociology.

1. Theory
2. Key words
3. Named examples – studies or research examples (case studies based on methods)
4. Evaluation.

Although they are as important as each other, and they each can't exist without the others, theory does play a special role in sociology.

Theory is useful for the skill of synopticity. One way of looking at it is to see synopticity as the process whereby you tie together all the different insights that the theories have. How can we do this?

Theory comes up in every topic in sociology, and most, if not all, sociology can be linked in some way to a wider theoretical view. Most of the time, the same theories come up in each topic, with a couple of specialised exceptions. Theories tend to talk about the same sorts of things in each topic – after all, no matter what the topic, the theory demands the same outlook for the whole of society.

We can use theory to link our understanding of the different elements of sociology together.

What does the specification say?

The OCR specification says that the synoptic paper does a number of things. To summarise:

- It allows students to draw out issues of inequality and difference from the whole of the two-year course.
- It locates issues of theory and methods into the context of discussions about inequality and difference.
- It requires that candidates understand the links between theory, methods and inequality; the phrase often used is to understand the 'nature of sociological thought'.
- The unit allows students to think about the major forces that shape the life-chances of the individual.

When using the term 'nature of sociological thought', the specification from OCR is drawing attention to how sociology works as a whole; it is showing that underpinning all sociology are theoretical and methodological debates, no matter which topic you are studying. This will help you to be synoptic since these debates link everything to everything else. The 'nature of sociological thought' includes:

- ideas about social order and social change and social control
- ideas about conflict and consensus in society
- ideas about social structure and social action
- macro and micro perspectives
- the nature of social facts
- the role of values in sociology.

Use these debates and ideas in your work.

How can we think about theory in a synoptic fashion?

Do not forget the synoptic tools (see section 5.1) to link each theory to each of the tools; what would each say? All theory offers ideas and opinions about these issues. Make sure you understand what they have to say. This will help you gain more depth in the exam, especially in essay questions.

Do not forget the key sociological variables (see section 5.3) to link each theory to each of these variables; what would each theory say?

Take any two theories and see how they compare and contrast with each other. Use the tools as bridges that you can build – common ground, or even a 'battle-ground' over which the theories might fight.

To really show your detailed and sensitive understanding of theory, show how theories which might seem or look different are actually very similar. Use the synoptic tools to raise issues over which theories might agree.

How can we think about methods in a synoptic fashion?

Try to get a relevant reference to methods into essay answers. Each 'debate' or 'issue' in each topic usually has a hidden methods issue behind it. The reason why sociologists sometimes disagree is not really over what they say, but how they may have measured or defined or interpreted the thing in question in the first place. The method you use to gather your data will affect what your data looks like, and therefore what you actually find. Quantitative data based on statistics and generalisations will lead to very different answers than qualitative data, which is more about people's feelings.

Key points to remember

- Try to explore different theoretical ideas using the tools available.
- Remember to see sociology as being made up of four ingredients. Try to manipulate these to show your understanding of them by connecting them together in different and interesting ways.
- Practise synoptic skills linked to theory as part of your revision. It is an easy way to get depth and detail into your writing.

● **Synoptic Link**

The synoptic tools are: socialisation, culture, identity, power, social differentiation and stratification. These can best be seen as 'themes' that exist everywhere in every topic. Try to refer to them.

✓ **Top Exam Hint**

The key sociological variables are: class, gender, ethnicity, age, location, globalisation. Try to use them.

School tends to give the impression that subjects and forms of knowledge are separate from each other. Subjects are taught by different teachers in different rooms at different times, and they are broken up into little 'segments' or separate 'parcels' of knowledge. This is also true in sociology – we have different topics with different names. But remember, they are all part of a wider whole; they are all linked.

5.6 | Pushing your grades up higher: what ways are there to demonstrate synopticity?

What does this mean?

This chapter is full of ideas that you can use in order to try to be synoptic. This section is available to print off from the accompanying CD-ROM and contains a checklist of the advice elsewhere over the past few pages. Print it off and use it! Try out the ideas; practise them not just for revision but also throughout the course as a whole.

Remember these 'tricks' and use them.

- We can talk of synopticity in two main senses. **Social synopticity** means seeing the connections between the parts of society and using sociological theories and ideas in order to do this. **Sociological synopticity** means seeing connections between sociological ideas themselves and looking at what might link together different studies or theories or even debates that sociologists might have.
- All sociology is about two ideas, which themselves are related: **power**, who gets their way in society, and how and why, and **stratification**, how society is divided up.
- Remember, one question will link the topic to the previous topics you have studied, one will link it to methods, and the other question will link the topic to theory. This is why the paper is the 'synoptic' paper.
- Make sure you pay attention to the advice given on the exam paper about the point of the synoptic questions. It will stand out on the exam paper since it is written in italic writing directly after each of the three questions you have been set.
- It is really important that you familiarise yourself with what the exam paper will actually look like – not just for this unit exam, but every exam for every subject. Ask your teacher for a copy of the exam from last year. Make sure it makes sense.
- Do not let the exam paper confuse you. Remember, the exam board will list all the combinations since the paper is sent to all students across the country. There will be some questions on topics you have not studied. Just look for the ones you have done.
- As we know that question c will always ask about methods, think about methods, think about this as part of your revision. Make a list of all the ways in which issues of methods, measurement and definition might affect or be affected by the synoptic unit you are studying. Do not let the question surprise you!

- As part of your revision, go over all the studies that you have learned over both years of your course. Hopefully you will have these on revision cards. Make sure you know which ones from which topics might link to other topics.
- Key sociological variables are considered to be 'real'; they affect society and are in turn affected by society. They affect the life and the life-course of the individual. The key variables are: class, gender, ethnicity, age, location, globalisation. Use these variables and apply them to studies. You might try to link studies together from different topics by using these ideas as a link between them.
- Show how the variables link theories together across topic areas.
- Show how the variables link studies together across the topic areas.
- The exam board says that there are core themes that exist in everything you do in sociology. These core themes come up in every topic and most theories and studies can relate to them. We can therefore use them to explore links in a synoptic fashion. The core themes are: socialisation, culture, identity, power and control, social differentiation and stratification.
- As part of your revision, take each and every topic and link it to each and every other topic in turn. For each of the above six synoptic tools, try to make a list of five or six ways in which the topics might connect to each other. If you revise this, it will really help you in the examination for the inequality and difference unit.
- To signpost to the examiner that you are making links, there are a number of phrases you might like to practise using. See section 5.5.

Frequently asked questions

Q. Is synopticity a new thing?

A. It is new for the examination since it has only been a formal requirement since the relatively recent introduction of the Curriculum 2000 specifications. But, in one sense, sociology has always been synoptic. These links and connections have always existed and good students have always seen them and tried to explore them.

Q. Is synopticity hard?

A. It is harder than simply remembering things, yes. But ask yourself, what does simply remembering things actually tell you about learning? Synopticity asks you to use the AO2 skills; to try to manipulate what you know, in order to do more with it than simply repeat it. You could say it is a true test of your sociological imaginations!

Q. Why do we have synopticity?

A. Synopticity is now a requirement of all A2 levels. However, it is very sociological for us to have this! As we have said before, sociology has always been synoptic – mainly because society is itself. The connections we see and try to explore are connections that exist in real life.

Chapter 6

Social inequality and difference

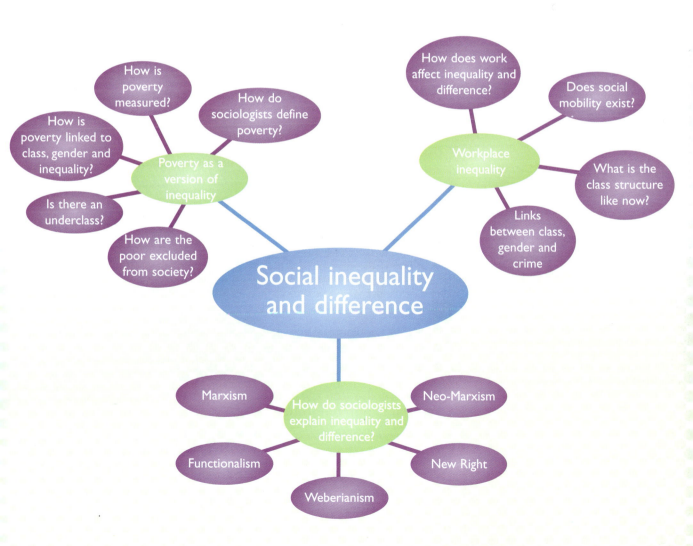

How is poverty measured?

How do sociologists define poverty?

How is poverty linked to class, gender and inequality?

Is there an underclass?

How are the poor excluded from society?

Poverty as a version of inequality

How does work affect inequality and difference?

Does social mobility exist?

Workplace inequality

What is the class structure like now?

Links between class, gender and crime

Social inequality and difference

Marxism

Neo-Marxism

How do sociologists explain inequality and difference?

Functionalism

New Right

Weberianism

 CD-ROM

6.1 Key issues in social inequality and difference

☀ Key Idea

Differentiation refers to the way that social groups and categories of individual are distinguished from one another. Sociologists are increasingly using this term as a general term for social differences such as class, ethnicity, and gender. Differentiation is not the same as stratification because it focuses on differences not inequalities, although difference can lead to inequalities (for example between the able bodied and the disabled). This emphasis reflects the use of the word in postmodernist theory.

❝❞ Key Definition

Sociologists use the term **stratification** to refer to structured social inequalities. Systematic social inequalities can develop and be justified on the basis of any perceived or real characteristic of a group, for example, class, ethnicity, gender, or age.

What are the important issues in social inequality and difference?

All societies have ways of organising and classifying people into different categories or groups. **Differentiation** refers to the processes whereby people are categorised as being different to others, and **stratification** is the process whereby the different social groups that emerge from differentiation are organised into a hierarchy. As a result of this stratification, social inequalities may exist in society. The sociological study of social inequality has changed a great deal in recent years. Below are some of the important issues now facing sociologists in this topic area.

- How many classes are there in British society?
- How do social inequalities and difference shape life chances?
- Which element of social inequality and difference – class, ethnicity, gender, or age – is most important?
- How should sociologists define, operationalise, and measure social inequality?
- Is stratification natural and inevitable or socially constructed?
- How is stratification related to the structure/action debate?

Why are sociologists interested in social inequality and difference?

Sociologists want to know about social inequality and difference because class, ethnicity, gender, and age can have considerable effects on many aspects of our lives. These range from the sorts of jobs we get and how long we live, to our social and political attitudes, to our leisure interests, and even our personal identity.

Sociologists are also interested in stratification because of what it tells us about the structure of society.

- Sociologists agree that social inequality, stratification and difference tell us something about the nature and distribution of power in our society.
- Sociologists agree that social inequality, stratification and difference tell us something about how society holds together (or is integrated).

Of course, sociologists do not agree exactly what it is that social inequality and difference tells us about either power or integration in society, as you will see in this chapter.

What are the key ideas we can use to think about social inequality and difference?

Social inequality and difference is concerned with the divisions and inequalities between different social groups. There are two main types of social division.

- Class: sociologists disagree about how class should be defined, but class can be summed up as referring to a group with a shared economic and social position.

- Status refers to the social prestige a group of people have. This could be social groups such as community organisations, professions, leisure clubs, or categories of people, such as members of ethnic minority groups, or age groups, or those belonging to a particular gender.

New sociologists are more aware of the need to study how class, race and gender inequalities are linked.

What does the exam board say about social inequality and difference?

All students will take the synoptic unit, 'social inequality and difference' (unit 2539). The exam will last for one hour and 30 minutes and will consist of two multi-part data response questions and you must choose one of these. You will be asked to link 'social inequality and difference' to other topics, theories and methods.

Unit 2539 consists of three sections.

- The dimensions of workplace inequality, including contemporary changes in the distribution of wealth, contemporary workplace inequalities, and workplace change and its impact on class formation and identity.
- Poverty as a dimension of inequality, including concepts and measures of poverty, contemporary trends in poverty (class, gender and ethnicity), and theories of culture and poverty including the underclass debate.
- Explanations of inequality and difference, including concepts of class (material and cultural explanations, neo-Marxism and neo-Weberianism, feminist theories), and definitions of race and ethnicity (material and cultural theories, ethnic identities and the impact on inequality).

What are the key problems in social inequality and difference?

As with all other sociological topics, you will find that the key concepts you learn about are contested concepts. This means that there is dispute about what the concepts mean, how they should be defined, and how important they are. There are several key issues which are debated in stratification.

- How do we define and measure class?
- How many classes are there?
- How are inequalities in wealth and income explained?
- Are some explanations of inequality more important than others?

Key points to remember

- Social inequality and difference is a vital topic in sociology because of its focus on power and for what it has to say about the way society is integrated or held together.
- Traditionally sociologists' interest in social inequalities has been focused on class, and there have been different views about how it should be defined and measured.
- Contemporary sociologists are very interested in other aspects of social inequality. Many contemporary sociologists recognise the need to examine how class, gender, and ethnicity are linked, but there is no clear agreement about how they are linked, or whether any one type of social inequality is the most important.

✳ Key Idea

One important concept to remember is the difference between objective and subjective views of class. Objective views of class are the ways that sociologists define a person's class in terms of their employment conditions and income. Subjective class refers to people's own views about social class. The two may vary considerably and both are important. How people think about themselves shapes their behaviour, but so do the realities of their position in the stratification system.

✓ Top Exam Hint

Unit 2539 is the highest weighted unit of the A2 year, worth 20 per cent of the final two-year combined grade. So make sure you devote your study time accordingly.

● Synoptic Link

Issues of social inequality and difference are relevant to many other areas in sociology, which makes it an important topic. You will be asked to make links or connections based around the theme of inequality and difference from everything that you have been taught, from any topic, and to consider how both theories and methods deal with and relate to the issue in question. In particular, you will look at issues of inequality as they link to class, gender, ethnicity and how these three in turn relate and interrelate with each other.

◆ What, when and why?

Postmodernist thought led to a shift away from the focus on inequality to an interest in social differences and the way different identities were created. Postmodernists have argued that people are free to create identities and are largely free from social constraints in doing this. This view has been heavily criticised by sociologists, but many sociologists acknowledge the importance of studying all aspects of stratification and the way that they are interrelated.

How does social inequality and difference link to the AS course?

Why are links to AS important for sociology?

Social inequality and difference is the backbone of the discipline of sociology.

- All sociologists will discuss social inequality (that is, class, ethnicity, gender, or another aspect of stratification) at some stage in their work. The views that a sociologist has will shape the way they see society.
- This, in turn, will shape the sorts of questions that they ask about society.

You therefore need to have a good understanding of social inequality and difference, especially as all students will take module 2539. Remember, you cannot understand sociology properly unless all the parts are linked together carefully, and the concepts of social inequality enable you to link the different topics you have studied together.

Why is social inequality and difference so important in sociology?

Research shows that factors such as class, ethnicity and gender have a huge impact on people's life chances.

Sociological research on social inequality demonstrates that social inequalities are patterned. This means that differences between various social groups in, for example, health, income, or educational level, are systematic and repeated over time with great regularity. However, there are different sociological explanations of these patterns and, indeed, different views about what the patterns look like. Some sociologists see such differences as natural and inevitable, while others feel that differences and inequalities are mainly socially rather than naturally constructed, and reflect differences in power between different social groups.

Social inequality and difference is therefore a vital topic in sociology, because it forms a key part of a sociologists' overall picture of society. The core of any sociological view is its view on power and social inequality and social differences. Different schools of sociological thought tend to produce very different views of the nature of society based upon the way they conceptualise stratification and the stratification system. This means that if we want to evaluate a sociological perspective (such as Marxism, functionalism, Weberianism, feminism, the New Right, or postmodernism) really effectively, we need to have a very good understanding of the way that perspective views social inequality.

● **Synoptic Link**

Social inequality and differentiation has many links with topics you will have studied, such as families and households, individuals and society, or mass media. Make sure that you check through your notes and identify studies which found evidence of systematic social inequalities and differences by class, gender, ethnic group, or age.

What links can be made to social inequality and difference?

There are many links between social inequality and difference and topics such as education and families and households.

- There are (still) big class differences in educational attainment, and class is a key explanatory variable in the work of many researchers, such as Bernstein, Bourdieu (1977), J.W.B.Douglas (1963), Halsey, Heath, and Ridge (1975), and Willis (1977).
- There are many studies on education and gender which demonstrate that students are treated differently on the basis of gender, a process which still leads to inequalities in educational attainment.
- Ethnicity is also a key dimension of differentiation within schools. David Gillborn (2001) argues that schools perpetuate a process of 'institutional racism'. Again, these are processes which lead to inequalities of educational attainment.
- In families and households, the importance of gender is evident in studies of conjugal roles, divorce, and domestic violence.

All of these processes help reproduce inequalities and reproduce social divisions and a hierarchy of class, ethnic, and gender differences

Key points to remember

- Social inequality and difference is taught as a synoptic topic and you will have to make links between it and the substantive topics you have studied, as well as between methods, and between theories.
- Structured inequalities are prevalent in all areas of society, whether we talk about the family, education, religion, power or crime.
- Sociologists argue that an understanding of stratification contributes a vital element to our understanding of how society functions.

☐ Key Fact

'There has been a widening gulf between households in which there are two earners, and households in which there are none (and the latter group of households has increased, owing to both rising unemployment and an increase in early retirement). Indeed, the gap between households in which at least one person has a full-time job, and those without an earner, has widened dramatically. Average incomes have risen in earner households, whereas households without a full-time earner have lower average incomes, in real terms, than in 1979.'

(Crompton 1998, page 220)

✳ Key Idea

Institutional racism refers to the way that the rules and practices of institutions in society may systematically discriminate against groups on the basis of ethnicity. It may well be unintentional. It is a very subtle form of discrimination that is widely misunderstood. Institutional racism can be important in understanding education, crime, work, wealth and poverty.

✓ Top Exam Hint

Use your knowledge of social inequality and difference, and the way it links to key concepts such as power, to evaluate studies and findings in other topics you study. Do not compartmentalise your knowledge and understanding of key concepts in sociology.

How can we find out about social inequality and difference?

How have sociologists tried to measure social inequality and difference?

The main focus in sociological attempts to measure social inequality has been on class. Because class is an abstract concept, it has proved difficult to operationalise and measure it. Most researchers have operationalised class by using occupation as an indicator. It has usually been the occupational title of the head of a household which has been used as a **unit of analysis** to give the class position of a whole family or household. Once occupational data has been collected, researchers then place the occupation in a class category using an occupational classification scheme or scale, of which there are several. Occupational scales are supposed to rank different jobs hierarchically, so that the jobs providing the best life chances are the highest, and those with the least are at the bottom of the hierarchy, although there are numerous criticisms of these scales (see section 6.7).

Sociologists have also tried to measure inequalities in life chances, which are the result of wealth and poverty or gender and ethnic differences. These are generally not so difficult to classify, though there have been many disagreements over the terminology used to define ethnic groups.

What methods do sociologists tend to use to study social inequality and difference?

There are two broad traditions in studies of social inequality and difference. Rosemary Crompton has described these approaches as the **employment aggregate** approach, and the **class formation** approach (1998).

The first of these is the dominant type, and advocates the use of the large-scale survey. This is because the aims of stratification research, to map and measure the class structure, neatly fall into a positivistic framework. Measuring the class structure, and movement and change within it, is only really viable if the research is quantified. Data from occupational classification readily lends itself to quantitative analysis, and quantitative techniques are the best way to display this sort of data. Because of this, the study of the class structure is an area where rigorous and sophisticated techniques of statistical analysis are used in sociology.

However, an alternative approach, aiming to focus on the way classes form as active social groups, can involve using methods more influenced by qualitative approaches, such as case studies or interviewing. These are necessary in order to shed light on the processes by which classes as active social groups can be studied, since it is qualitative methods which best reflect people's motivations and the meanings which social structures have for them.

What problems with definition are encountered in social inequality and difference?

This is a key issue in the study of social inequality and differentiation. As you might remember from a study of theory and methods (see CD-ROM), how sociologists define key concepts can have a big influence on their findings. There are several important problems in defining class.

- There are differences in how class is defined in different sociological theories.
- There is a problem of whether sociologists should use an objective or a subjective definition of class. Objective definitions are the definitions devised by sociologists, which should apply to everyone, regardless of their own opinion. Subjective definitions are the way individuals see themselves. These can be very important, since they can affect people's actions, but sociologists would argue that they may not be sociologically accurate.
- Sociologists disagree as to what should be the unit of analysis of class. Should class be examined on the level of the individual or the family? Whose occupation should be used as an indicator? Some feminist sociologists have argued that in dual career families, the occupations of both adults need to be included as data, and have devised a new scale.
- In terms of other aspects of social inequality, a key issue has been about the construction of ethnic categories and indeed debate over the use of the terms 'ethnicity' and 'race' (see section 6.21). Terms such as 'Asian' have been criticised because they can put groups (for example Bangladeshis and East African Asians) with very different life chances into the same category, thus distorting our understanding of how these groups are stratified.

Key points to remember

- The main focus of sociological interest has been on class, but this is a difficult concept to define and operationalise.
- Two main approaches to the study of class are the employment aggregate model and the class formation model.
- Sociologists do not agree on which model provides the best picture of the class structure. Class is a contested concept.

What does this mean?

Sociologists say that people in society are differentiated. This simply means that society does not classify and identify all people in the same way. For example, society classifies people on the basis of age, and identifies the very young and the very old as being less capable of acting independently. People are also differentiated in other ways which become socially significant, such as in terms of their class, ethnicity or gender. Sociologists claim that the idea that differentiation does indeed occur, is supported by strong evidence of differences in life chances. This leads to the creation of different roles and identities (see sections 6.8, 6.11–6.12, 6.14–6.21).

Sociologists argue that the process of differentiation does not just affect individuals, but also leads to the creation of different social groups based on these processes. These social groups are stratified, which means that they are organised on a hierarchical basis.

What are the main types of social inequality?

Social characteristics such as class, gender, wealth, ethnicity or age, can all be used as factors to differentiate between people, and as a result privilege or discriminate certain groups. All of these types of social differentiation are forms of stratification, but sociologists have until recent years argued that they create two main types of stratification system, **status** systems and class systems.

- In status-based systems, social position tends to be ascribed, that is it is achieved on the basis of fixed characteristics which are difficult to change. Status positions which are shared by a group of people become status groups, such as, for example, women or members of ethnic minorities.
- In class-based systems of stratification, social position can be seen as being something which is achieved, usually through the attainment of educational qualifications or success in a particular job. Class is therefore a form of division which is focused on economic factors.

The position of a class or status group in society is maintained by social exclusion. This refers to the ways that class and status groups have of restricting membership to the group. Exclusionary practices control or limit entry to the group and are usually achieved through the control of economic or cultural resources that lead to membership of the group, for example marriage, educational and professional qualifications, or income or wealth (see also section 6.10).

Sociologists disagree as to which of these elements of stratification is most important, but most would agree that we need to try and understand how both class and status systems are interrelated. This matters since status groups such as gender or ethnicity may also influence a person's chances of success in the class system. (However, see case studies for recent findings on this.) Also, many contemporary sociologists would now argue that theories of stratification have to include gender and ethnicity, and not focus so narrowly on class.

66 99 Key Definition

Status refers to social prestige or reputation. One can have high or low status, based on one's job, gender, ethnicity, or age. People may have various statuses depending on different social situations, for example at work or in a friendship group.

Can people change their position in the stratification system?

Sociological research shows that people can indeed change their position in the stratification system. In terms of class, sociologists have identified two main types of social mobility (movement up or down the class scale).

- Intergenerational social mobility: This measures the changes between different generations, usually by comparing a person's occupational class with that of their father. Many sociologists measure class using the father's occupation on the grounds that this will be the main/largest income (see section 6.7). So if your father was a bus driver and you are a Managing Director then you have undergone upward intergenerational mobility.
- Intragenerational social mobility: This measures the changes in an individual's lifetime. So if a person starts working life as an unskilled factory worker but ends up as a barrister, they have undergone upward intragenerational mobility.

Sociologists refer to the degree of social mobility in a society by the terms **open** or **closed system**. A system which is completely closed is one where there is no social mobility at all, but this is extremely rare. Usually sociologists would refer to a degree of **closure**, and they would be able to quantify the mobility chances for people in that society. An open system or society is one where there is much social mobility. However, it is important to note that for a society to have a truly open stratification system, there must be both upwards and downwards mobility.

Gender and ethnicity may appear to be categories which we cannot change because they are based on natural differences. However, sociologists would point out that both of these are socially-constructed differences and therefore change over time. While only a few people do actually change their sex, sociologists have noted that gender inequalities may be altered by a person's ethnicity and class, and people can use these factors to create different types of gender identity. In the case of ethnicity, sociologists have observed that increasingly people do create a range of identities, or what Hall calls hybrid identities (1992).

Conclusion

- Social differentiation refers to the way that society classifies and identifies people. People and social groups may be differentiated on many different characteristics.
- Social differentiation provides a basis upon which stratification can occur.
- Sociologists argue that there are two main forms of stratification, status systems and class-based systems.

For consideration

1. Is stratification inevitable?
2. Are sociologists guilty of over-generalising when they argue that society differentiates and stratifies on the basis of key social characteristics such as gender, ethnicity, class and age?

☀ Key Ideas

- Sociologists make an important distinction between societies where status is seen to be mainly ascribed, and those where status is achieved. Ascribed status refers to a status which you are born with, and achieved status refers to status which a person gains through their own efforts, for example through gaining a high status occupation. However, sociologists also note that while status in modern society is often achieved, many status distinctions are still ascribed, for example gender, ethnicity and age.

- Social exclusion is a concept which is increasingly being used by sociologists and others. Some sociologists are critical of this tendency, since it can focus more on cultural differences and neglect the economic aspects of structured social inequality.

- An **open** society is one where there is a high degree of social mobility, involving movement up and down the class system. **Closure** refers to a lack of social mobility, and in a completely closed society there would be no social mobility. In reality, sociologists argue that all societies are characterised by degrees of openness or closure.

6.5 | How do sociologists define wealth and income?

What does this mean?

We have seen that sociologists can have different ideas about what **wealth** and income mean, and that this, in turn, can lead to very different research findings. In everyday language, we often do not bother to distinguish between wealth and income. However, for the purposes of sociological research it is important to be aware of the differences between the two, and to understand what we mean by the term 'wealthy' and to consider how we would define the category of 'the wealthy'. The reasons why these issues are important will be examined in more detail later on. First, we need to examine how sociologists have defined wealth. Sociological definitions of wealth indicate that it consists of different things.

Wealth is a general term, and refers to the value of the assets or property that a person owns. Usually it is expressed in terms of a cash value – the amount of money a person would have if all their property were sold. Wealth can therefore include the value of a house, land, money in the bank, the ownership of shares, as well as cars, furniture and other goods that a person has for their own use.

These forms of wealth are often broken down into various sub-categories.

- Productive property: this refers to things that can generate an income, such as shares, the ownership of companies, or property or land that is rented.
- Consumption property: this refers to goods bought for personal use, but which can be sold to raise cash, for example cars, personal home, furniture, and so on.

Another way of categorising wealth is in terms of marketable and non-marketable wealth.

- Marketable wealth refers to any goods or objects that can be sold to raise cash.
- Non-marketable wealth refers to salaries, incomes, or pension schemes.

Lastly, there is the term 'income'. Income refers to money received on a regular basis. The most common form of income is a salary or wage received in return for paid work; this would be called earned income. However, regular interest on a savings account would also be an example of income, but this would be called unearned income.

Why do these differences matter?

There are two main reasons why these definitions are important; one empirical, and the other theoretical.

- Empirical issues are concerned with methods. The issue with wealth is that if we want to examine wealth accurately, we need to be rigorous in defining it. This is because the way we define wealth will shape the way the statistical data is portrayed. Sociologists want their knowledge of wealth to be valid.
- In terms of theory, these different definitions are also important, and form the subject of debate between different theoretical perspectives. Marxists, in particular, argue that the most important form of wealth is productive wealth. This is because Marxists argue that ownership of the means of production forms the basis of class formation and the source of class conflict. Differences in wealth in terms of consumer goods are therefore not so important. What is more important is the structural relationship between the ruling class and their ownership of the source of all wealth – the means of production.

Measuring wealth

One more point needs to be made about how we define wealth. When some people are judged to be wealthier than others, the judgement will always be made in terms of the standards of a particular time and place (and society). It can therefore be difficult for researchers to decide and agree upon a point at which a person can be considered to be wealthy.

Conclusion

How sociologists define wealth is a complex matter, and has important consequences for the picture they provide of social inequalities. It is also important to remember that wealth is a relative concept; a person or group can only be judged to be wealthy in relation to other groups. Wealth then, like poverty (as will be explained later), is a relative concept.

For consideration

1. What do you think is the most advantageous sort of wealth to have?

2. As there are now millionaires being created every week through the lottery and television game shows, does this mean that as a society we are becoming wealthier?

6.6 | Who has the most wealth?

What does this mean?

Defining wealth can be a complex process, but this has not prevented sociologists from trying to find out who has most wealth. Sociologists want to know not simply which individuals have the most wealth, but whether and why it is concentrated among particular social groups.

This is important because if wealth is predominantly the possession of certain social groups it means that they can prevent other social groups from having access to wealth. This process is termed 'social closure'. It is also important because the possession of wealth frequently allows those with wealth to have power. If the distribution of wealth and power are highly skewed towards certain social groups, it will mean that other social groups have less power and wealth.

How much wealth do you need to be wealthy?

According to UK government statistics in 1994 (ONS 1998), the top 1 per cent of the population owned personal wealth worth over £500,000, and held 40 per cent of their wealth in shares. This figure could possibly be used to mark the boundary between the 'wealthy' and the 'normal'. This is a tricky point, but as John Scott (1999) has noted, it is impossible to draw with complete accuracy a line above which an individual is wealthy, and below which they are simply 'rich' or 'fairly well off'. This reminds us again that wealth is a relative concept, and that what counts as wealth changes over time, and is socially constructed.

Who has the most wealth?

Finding out how wealth is distributed in British society provides an excellent example of why sociological research is necessary. A common perception is that inequalities in wealth in contemporary Britain have declined, and that there is more equality. However, empirical research indicates that this is not so, and, in fact, inequalities of wealth have increased over the last decade or so. The following statistics give some indication of the extent of inequality over the last decade.

- According to government statistics (ONS 1998), 53 per cent of the financial wealth in the UK was owned by 5 per cent of the population in 1994.
- In the same year, the wealthiest 1 per cent of the population owned 19 per cent of all marketable wealth; the top 10 per cent owned 51 per cent.
- The least wealthy 50 per cent of the population own 10 per cent of the UK's wealth.

So who are the wealthy?

Marxist sociologist John Westergaard (1976, 1995) argues that the wealthy in British society form a ruling class consisting of between 5 and 10 per cent of the population. For Westergaard, these people are the owners of the means of production.

However others claim that the upper classes have fragmented (split into smaller groups). John Scott (1999), for example, takes a more Weberian view of class (he therefore identifies a more fragmented class structure) and argues that there is a capitalist class in Britain, but that this constitutes about 0.1 per cent of the population, and consists of four types of capitalist. Some sociologists have even argued that there is a trans-national capitalist class, consisting of the executives of trans-national corporations. Trans-national corporations are companies that have branches in many different countries.

Conclusion

Sociologists may not always agree about exactly where to draw a line between 'the wealthy' and the rest of us, but it is clear that considerable inequalities exist in British society. Equally, while sociologists disagree as to the precise composition of the wealthy, elite groups can be identified. As we have seen, though, sociologists disagree as to the best way of explaining the existence and social role of such groups. The next section will explore this issue in more detail.

✓ Top Exam Hint

In evaluating the idea that wealth and power are inevitably linked it is a good idea to use contemporary views on stratification. These increasingly accept that it is important to understand how class, race, and gender are interrelated and crosscut each other.

● Synoptic Link

Being wealthy provides many advantages. In the study of crime and deviance, for example, sociologists have found that the crimes of the wealthy are under-reported and that the wealthy often escape the attentions of the law.

For consideration

1. Does the ownership of wealth always give its owner power?

2. Do the very rich in Britain form a ruling class?

How do sociologists explain inequalities in wealth and income?

⁙ Key Ideas

Meritocracy: functionalists claim that industrial societies offer everyone an equal opportunity to succeed and gain the best jobs. This idea implies that wealth is distributed fairly. Functionalists argue that inequalities of reward (pay) are needed in order to motivate people to compete and work to gain the highest paying jobs.

Value consensus: inequalities arise from the different values placed on certain roles, but there is a consensus in society about these different values.

● Synoptic Link

Functionalists see the education system as a key mechanism for creating social mobility and meritocratic role allocation. This means that industrial societies are indeed stratified, but stratification occurs on a meritocratic (fair) basis because people's occupational role is decided by how well they do in what functionalists see as an entirely fair and open education system.

❝❞ Key Definition

Meritocratic allocation means that people are appointed to jobs on the basis of their merit (how good they are) and there is open competition for all jobs.

Market situation: this means that different levels of skill can demand different wages from the market.

Functionalists argue that inequalities in income and wealth reflect the skill and effort required for particular jobs.

Marxists argue that inequalities in income and wealth are the result of the two-tier class structure (bourgeoisie and proletariat) and the inequalities in power which it inevitably creates. People are either owners or workers and their class position (and income) is determined by this relationship to the means of production.

What does this mean?

Sociologists have identified regular patterns of inequalities of wealth (see section 6.5) and there are also marked inequalities in income. Differences of wealth between different social classes are marked. There are also clear differences in income between different classes, as different occupations receive different rewards. In addition, there are marked differences in income and wealth on the basis of gender and race. Sociologists may draw on several theoretical approaches in order to explain these patterns of difference.

How do functionalists explain inequalities in wealth and income?

Functionalists such as Davis and Moore (1967) and Melvin Tumin (1967) argue that differences in wealth and income reflect the need to offer higher incentives to those undertaking the most demanding occupations. Differences therefore reflect the supply and demand for different jobs and are based on the assumption that there is a **meritocratic allocation** of jobs. Talcott Parsons argues that there is **value consensus** on what are the functionally most important jobs in a society. Functionalists argue that as there are so many roles in society, inequality is inevitable. Selection for these roles is done on the basis of merit and so the inequalities are legitimate as there is equal opportunity to find one's role in society. These views are virtually identical to the view of the New Right (see section 6.16), and other sociologists such as Peter Saunders are in general agreement with it. See section 6.14 for more information on functionalist explanations.

How do Marxists explain inequalities in wealth and income?

Sociologists working in or influenced by the Marxist tradition, such as John Westergaard (1976, 1995), or more contemporary Marxist-influenced theorists like David Harvey (1990) would be highly critical of the functionalist approach. They would argue that meritocracy is a myth, and that the higher incomes paid to professionals and managers simply reflect the power of the capitalists to pay higher wages to those who are key workers. This also has the effect of dividing the working classes (all those who do not own the means of production) preventing them from realising that they all have a common interest in seeing the end of capitalist exploitation. This means that they are weaker as a social or political force, because they do not campaign together against their employers.

In terms of wealth, while capitalism does lead to large differences in consumption property, the most important form of property, productive property, remains firmly in the hands of the capitalists, and this is still true today. In fact, there is now a greater concentration of productive wealth than there was in the 19th century when Marx was writing. See section 6.14 for more information on Marxist explanations.

How do Weberians explain inequalities in wealth and income?

Weber provides a more complex approach to class and inequalities in wealth and income than Marx. Weber saw inequalities in income and wealth as resulting from several factors and believed that Marx's two-tier class system was an inadequate description of class and therefore wealth. He saw class as a group of people who share the same **market situation**, and therefore life chances. Weber also argued that the ability of groups of workers to exclude others from doing their job was important in explaining inequalities in wealth and income. Social groups can use various strategies and resources to help them achieve this. Weber agrees with Marx that one good way to achieve this is to be a capitalist (own the means of production) so that other people have to work for you. See section 6.15 for more information on Weber's view of class.

However, there are other strategies that can be used to exclude others who are competing for the same work. For example, skilled professionals can achieve a significantly higher income than manual workers. Weber does not follow the functionalists and say that this is because the professional really is more skilled and more deserving than the manual worker. On the contrary, Weber takes the view that the professional is able to achieve a higher income and gain more wealth because of the limited supply of people qualified to apply for professional jobs. They can therefore demand higher wages from the market for their skills.

Professionals and workers can create shortages of people qualified to do a job by forming trade unions or professional groups. These can then operate to exclude certain categories of people. This can occur on the basis of status, (for example gender, race, age or religion). If workers do this, they limit the supply of labour for their occupation, and thus their income (and wealth) will rise since it is in short supply. See section 6.15 for more information on Weberian views.

Conclusion

So sociologists have a number of ways of explaining inequality. The different explanations also lead to different explanations of the causes of poverty and to different views about the workings and effectiveness of the welfare state. You will have to evaluate these views carefully in order to discover which theory you think is most accurate. In doing this, a good starting point is to think which theory has the most accurate view of power.

For consideration

1. Which of the following is most important in determining a person's wealth: class, race or gender?

2. Functionalists claim that without high rewards for the best jobs, people would not want to do them. Do you agree with this idea?

66 99 Key Definitions

Weberians argue that inequalities in income and wealth are the result of the use of exclusion strategies by workers acting collectively to protect their own interests.

✳ Key Idea

For Weber, society, and in particular the distribution of power and inequality, can be likened to a 'market'. He refers to the process of difference or social stratification as giving people 'marketability'. This is both an individual and a group location in society, showing how people compete with each other for socially desirable positions, however they might be defined in society. The New Right often use an image of competition between people in the class system similar to this idea of a 'market'.

✓ Top Exam Hint

When you are evaluating these competing explanations of inequality it is a good idea to use a key concept such as power to start reflecting on the accuracy of the different views. Functionalists, for example, seem to assume that we all have an equal amount of power, and we all have a chance to achieve wealth. Other theories would be more critical of this assumption.

☀ Key Ideas

- **Alienation** is a Marxist term used to describe how people are increasingly removed from the creative side of work. Workers lose control over the products they make; they are not producing for their own use and the products profit goes to the owners of the means of production. Repetitive work under these conditions reduces work satisfaction and can produce feelings of anxiety, lack of pride in work, frustration and powerlessness.

- **Deskilling** is a term coined by Braverman, which argues that capitalists need to extract the maximum labour from workers for the least expenditure. As a result, jobs are broken down and skilled workers become replaced with less-skilled workers. An example of this would be the replacement of craft workers with production line processes. Deskilling leads to alienation.

- **Postmodernists** have argued more recently that work-based inequalities are of little importance and that sociologists' attention should be focused on the differences in identity which individuals are able to create through buying the many sophisticated consumer goods made available by advanced capitalist society (see section 6.22).

∞ Classic Study

Neo-Marxist Braverman's *Labour Process Theory* (1974) looked at how alienation at work covered more and more sectors of the working world in the latter half of the 20th century. He used the word 'proletarianisation' to describe how workers were being affected by the pressure to accept lower incomes, fewer hours of work, reduced job security, degraded job conditions and fewer opportunities for career development, promotion and training.

What does this mean?

Most theories of inequality see the role of work as having an important influence on social inequalities and differences. By work, sociologists refer to paid employment, or people's jobs and occupations. The sort of work a person does will both reflect their position in society and their class, ethnicity and gender and, at the same time, it can also have a powerful influence on their life chances.

How does work influence inequality and difference?

Functionalists argue that work leads to unequal rewards, but that these are needed in order to provide the motivation for individuals to apply for jobs with a greater degree of responsibility or skill. If such jobs were given the same level of reward as less demanding jobs, people would be unwilling to take on higher level positions. Functionalists argue that there are equal opportunities to gain the top jobs as appointment is by merit (meritocracy) and there are laws in the UK to prevent racial or sex discrimination.

Marxists argue that work (or the division of labour) is vital in creating and maintaining inequality in capitalist societies. Class differences arise from the relationships formed in the course of production. These are class relationships between owners and workers (or bourgeoisie and proletariat, see section 6.14) and are characterised by class conflict. The two have different goals; owners want to increase profits and get the maximum effort for the least cost, while workers want to get the best possible wage for the least effort. Workers enter an exploitative relationship because they do not receive the full value of their labour. This can lead to **alienation** and **deskilling**. Some Marxists have argued that capitalism is race and gender blind, that is, that it does not discriminate on the grounds of race or gender, only class. Other sociologists have seen this as a major criticism of Marxism, arguing that discrimination on the basis of race/ethnicity or gender are distinct forms of exploitation which are the result of cultural beliefs. This indicates that inequality cannot be understood by simply examining economic factors and relationships.

Weberians argue that many inequalities are created in the workplace. This can be the result of economic (or material) factors, which are mainly the result of the supply and demand for particular skills. Weber pointed out that those sharing similar positions in the workplace can form trade unions or professional associations to promote their own interests. However, status differences, such as those based on gender or ethnic difference, could result in discrimination and inequality in the workplace, and these were based on cultural differences.

Feminists have argued that the workplace is patriarchal and that there has been a long history of the exclusion of women from paid employment. This has had an important impact on gender inequality, and although women's position in terms of inequality has vastly improved in some ways over the 20th century, significant inequalities remain (see section 6.10) and work is a gendered activity. Feminists such as Crompton, Le Feuvre (1996) and

Hartmann (1982) have argued that women are pushed towards certain roles and denied access to the jobs which will enable them to survive independently.

How has the world of work changed?

Functionalist and Marxist theories of inequality and stratification were developed in the 19th and 20th centuries. Since then the world of work has changed a great deal. There has been a change from what sociologists term a **Fordist** system of production to a flexible **post-Fordist** system. Fewer manual workers are needed, and those that remain are required to be flexible in work practices. Until the late 20th century, people's (typically men) identities and class were tied to the job they did. They were expected to work in the same profession for their entire adult life and the job they did defined their identity and lifestyle. In modern economies, the workplace has become much more fragmented and insecure and people do not expect to stay in the same career for life. This makes it difficult to define somebody's identity by the work they do and also hinders career progression as skills bases change with each new role (Sennett 1998).

The shift to a post-Fordist system of production has been accompanied by an increase in service sector jobs such as shop work and call centres, and a decline in the manufacturing sector. It has also led to flexible working conditions. These changes reflect the pressures of competition in a global economy (see section 6.18). In terms of inequality they have led to several important changes.

- In recent years inequalities have widened, not decreased. Since 1977 the proportion of the UK population with less than half the average income has increased by more than three times (Crompton 1998).
- There has been an increase in part-time work and the casualisation of many jobs (temporary and short-term contracts), whereby they are paid at lower rates and with fewer benefits (Pinch 1993).
- Historically, women's role and identity was confined to the 'private', unpaid world of the home, and men dominated the 'public' sphere of work. More women now work, but there is still a gender gap and inequalities persist..
- In 2003, 68 per cent of white women and 80 per cent of white men were employed, as opposed to 25 per cent of Pakistani and Bangladeshi women and 61 per cent of Pakistani and Bangladeshi men. Marxists argue that ethnic minorities are more likely to be in temporary work; as the female reserve army of labour ran out, so capitalists turned to immigration to fill the gap.

Conclusion

Changes in the organisation of work have had an important influence on inequalities and identity.

- The decline in manufacturing has led to the fragmenting of class structure and a decline in class identity.
- There has been an increase in social inequalities and a polarising of wealth.
- These changes have also resulted in a restructuring of gender relations and identities as more women enter the labour market (see also section 6.20).

For consideration

1. Why has there been a decline in class identity at the same time as inequalities in wealth have increased?

66 99 Key Definitions

Fordism is a production system where goods are mass produced in a standardised way. The term is based on the factories established by Henry Ford in the early 20th century to produce his cars. Workers worked on production lines and specialised in certain activities.

Post-Fordism refers to more recent production systems, typified by Japanese firms, where a standard car model, for example, can be endlessly modified to produce many different versions. This allows customers to have much more choice and leads individuality and diversity in style. It also helps sell more products.

Key Facts

- The highest paid workers in 2002 (general managers in large companies and organisations) earned an average of £2079 per week compared with £205 per week for checkout operators.
- In 1981, 32 per cent of men worked in manufacturing. In 2001, only 22 per cent of men worked in manufacturing. The area where employment has increased is in financial and business services, where there was a rise from 11 per cent to 19 per cent in male employment, and from 12 per cent to 18 per cent for females.
- Only 9 per cent of men undertake part-time work, as opposed to 43 per cent of women.
- Women form 69 per cent of administrative, secretarial, customer and personal service roles.
- In 1991, women's pay was 77.8 per cent of men's pay on average. In 2001, women's pay had increased to stand at 81.6 per cent of men's pay; an improvement, but still some way from being equal (Denscombe 2003)

Source: Equal Opportunities Commission 2003

● Synoptic Link

Changes in work have an important influence on families and family incomes. As Crompton notes, the increase in dual income households has led to a polarisation between two-, one-, and no-income families. In 1995, average incomes for earner households had risen, but in households without a full-time earner, incomes were lower in real terms, than they had been in 1979 (Crompton 1998).

6.9 | How do sociologists define poverty?

Charles Booth (pictured) and Seebohm Rowntree conducted studies into poverty in the 19th and 20th centuries.

What does this mean?

You might think that it is a waste of time trying to define poverty since it is so obvious what it is. People who take this viewpoint, though, very often define poverty in broad terms as 'not having enough money to live' or 'being in a situation of starvation with no money to buy food'.

Some sociologists have taken a view similar to this, but nowadays there are probably more that disagree with this viewpoint. In fact, defining poverty is quite difficult. This is because even if we agree with the view above that poverty is 'not having enough', how we define 'enough' will depend on the expected standards or norms in our society.

Even if we are talking about something basic such as food, people might disagree about how much is 'enough', given that people eat and need varying amounts depending upon age, health, gender and so on. If we broaden the question out to consider other needs, such as shelter and clothing, matters become even more complicated. So, poverty is actually very complex – it can mean different things to different people, and for sociologists this raises difficult questions about how to define and measure it.

How do sociologists define poverty?

There are two main definitions of poverty: absolute poverty and relative poverty.

- **Absolute poverty** centres around biological needs and is the idea that there are absolute, defined minimum standards of income or food needed for a person to survive. This is sometimes called subsistence poverty. Subsistence means that a person has enough food and other resources to continue to exist, or in other words, to remain alive. Using this definition a person is only considered to be in poverty if they cannot subsist, that is, do not have enough food or money to survive. Sociologists such as Booth and Rowntree used absolute definitions of poverty.
- **Relative poverty** centres around social needs and is a different idea of poverty. This view suggests that a person is in poverty if they have less than the accepted minimum standard in their society. For example, in contemporary British society, it is now the norm to have accommodation with electricity, hot and cold water, an indoor toilet, and a bath or shower. A relative definition of poverty would suggest that these are essentials and those without them live in poverty. Sociologists such as Townsend and Mack and Lansley use this definition of poverty.

Sociologists can use either of these definitions to produce a 'poverty line'. This is a way of defining the level of income at which poverty starts; above the line an individual is out of poverty, below the line an individual is in poverty. This sounds straightforward, but it is not easy to decide where this line should be drawn.

Why is it so difficult to measure poverty?

- One reason, which we have already identified, is because not everyone agrees on what would count as a minimum standard, whichever definition is being used.

- Another problem is that living standards can change as a result of both increases in wealth and changes in attitude and fashion.
- Thirdly, it is difficult for researchers to make objective judgements about what things count as essentials.
- David Piachaud has also argued that Townsend's deprivation index is a subjective measure (1987). Piachaud questioned why and how Townsend picked twelve items to be the key indicators of poverty. In the case of food, for example, Piachaud points out that tastes have changed since the 1960s and many people may actually choose not to eat meat. Townsend may therefore be imposing his own value-judgements as to what is an essential item.
- Researchers Mack and Lansley (1985) developed this criticism, and constructed a deprivation index by asking respondents to comment on what items were considered 'essentials', rather than deciding themselves. All items that over 50 per cent of respondents believed to be essential were included in the index, and individuals lacking three or more were classified as poor by the researchers. In 1990, they found that the number of people in poverty had risen to 20 per cent of the population.

Where does all this leave sociology?

There are many different explanations for poverty within sociological debates. Put simply, these explanations can be divided into those that are **system-blaming** and those that are **individual-blaming**. Marxist and Weberian theories fall into the first group, whereas the ideas of the New Right fall into the second. Present-day 'New Left' (New Labour government) thinking seems to have adopted a combination of both these approaches.

Conclusion

The idea of absolute poverty is useful to the extent that it provides fairly easy solutions to poverty: provide all with the means of subsistence. However, it can be hard to reach a consensus as to what the 'essentials' are, and this definition neglects the way standards of living are socially constructed.

Relative poverty, while it recognises that poverty is socially constructed, still relies on the value-judgements of researchers as to what is 'necessary', and it seems to imply that poverty can never be eradicated as long as inequality persists. New Right sociologist Marsland (1996), for example, argues that relative poverty is simply a measure of inequality which will always exist unless a society achieves equal income distribution. Which of these views sociologists think is more adequate will ultimately depend on their own values.

It is also difficult to make comparisons between definitions of poverty because of the wide number of different indices and definitions used to measure poverty.

For consideration

1. Is it possible to eradicate poverty?
2. Is it possible to measure poverty objectively?

⮞ Classic Study

Peter Townsend's studies of poverty: Townsend (1979) rejected the idea that poverty in 1950s Britain was a thing of the past. He conducted research in the late 1960s and argued that poverty actually affected an estimated 22.9 per cent of the population. He believed that poverty was not an absolute term and had to be seen as relative and non-material. He argued that it involved an inability to participate in the lifestyles considered normal in any particular society, and devised an index of twelve key essentials to calculate poverty. This index included not having a joint of meat on a Sunday, not having a daily cooked breakfast, not having a holiday, not having sole use of indoor facilities (toilet, bath, sink, cooker), not having fresh meat on four days a week.

66 99 Key Definitions

System-blaming – this theory argues that society creates poverty due to inequalities built into the make-up of the structure of society in the first place.

Individual-blaming – this theory argues that people make lifestyle and personal choices that might sometimes lead to poverty. A good example of this view is the idea of a 'cycle' or 'culture' of poverty – the view that values such as 'welfare dependency' are transmitted through families across the generations through socialisation.

✓ Top Exam Hint

When you are evaluating different studies of poverty, make sure that you discuss the methods used by the various researchers, showing how these shape researchers' views on the extent of poverty. Remember to use key methodological terms like validity, reliability, representativeness and operationalisation.

6.10 | How is poverty linked to class, ethnicity and gender?

✳ Key Idea

Poverty and inequality are related, but they are not the same. Poverty can be defined in either absolute or relative terms. Relative poverty is not the same as inequality. As indicated previously, relative poverty can be defined in several ways, but it is always a standard of living considerably below the average. Inequality simply means a difference between, for example, two income levels, and does not necessarily entail poverty.

❝❞ Key Definition

Ethnicity refers to the shared cultural characteristics and identity of a group, which could be a religious or a nationally based group. It is often used as an alternative to race.

▢ Key Facts

A 2003 Equal Opportunities Commission study showed that the unemployment rate for the white population in Britain is 4 per cent for women and 5 per cent for men. The average corresponding rates for all other ethnic groups is 10 per cent for women and 12 per cent for men, with Pakistani and Bangladeshi groups rating the highest unemployment levels of 15 per cent for women and 16 per cent for men.

In Britain, full-time female employees earn an average of 18.8 per cent less per hour than male employees.

Source: Equal Opportunities Commission 2003

What does this mean?

Until fairly recently sociologists tended to focus on studying how poverty was linked to class, but there has been increasing recognition that poverty is also linked to gender and **ethnicity**. Feminist Harriet Bradley has argued that sociologists have to focus on the way that the different dimensions of inequality interact together. For example, middle-class women, although they still earn less than their male counterparts, are much less at risk of falling into poverty than working-class women.

How is class related to poverty?

Class differences do not cause poverty. However, if you are in the lowest social class, you will have a much greater chance of falling into poverty than a person from a higher socio-economic position. This is because poverty is caused by factors such as unemployment and low wages and these factors are strongly associated with lower socio-economic classes. Westergaard and Resler (1975) go so far as to suggest that class inequalities caused by the capitalist system are the real reason for the existence of poverty. However, it would be wrong to say that a person's lower social class caused their poverty, because not all people in the same social class will be in poverty. Social class systems therefore create inequality, but not necessarily poverty.

How is ethnicity related to poverty?

Ethnicity is also closely linked to poverty. Some ethnic minorities have higher chances of being unemployed or in low-paid work, and are therefore more highly represented among the poor.

- Scott and Fulcher (1999) note that two-thirds of Pakistani and Bangladeshi families are in the bottom fifth of the income distribution in Britain.
- Asian women are disproportionately likely to be in low-paid 'home work' (work carried out in their own home).
- Ethnic minorities are disproportionately likely to be unemployed. There are differences among different ethnic minority groups. In 2000, the government Labour Force Survey found unemployment levels of 5 per cent of white people, 8 per cent of Asian Indians, and 17 per cent of Pakistanis and Bangladeshis.
- There is also a mass of evidence showing inequalities in health (including high infant mortality rates), and poor housing conditions among some ethnic minorities.

How is gender linked to poverty?

Women are more likely than men to find themselves in poverty. This is mainly because of women's structural position in society. There are various reasons for this.

- More women are heads of lone-parent families than men. This often puts women in a situation where they are dependent upon benefits and cannot gain employment because of childcare responsibilities.
- Women are more likely to be in part-time or low-paid employment because of discrimination, inequality, and the demands of their roles as housewives and mothers. This has consequences for their pensions in later life, and also means that they do not get many welfare benefits that are dependent upon the worker being in full-time employment. Also, low pay is, of course, one of the main causes of poverty (Glendinning and Millar 1994).
- The British welfare system has been based largely on a model where contributions made by those in work count towards their benefit. In this model, if women work less, their contributions and therefore benefits will be less.
- Women live longer than men. They are more likely to end up living on their own, and the longer they live, the more any private savings will dwindle, leaving them to survive on the basic state pension.

Feminists such as Arber and Ginn (1991, 1995) have documented the 'feminisation of poverty', which suggests a growth in female poverty. However, studies by Lewis and Piachaud (1992) point out that 61 per cent of the adults on poor relief at the beginning of the 20th century were women, and Oppenheim (1993) calculates that in 1991 62 per cent of those dependent on state benefits were women, showing that women have always been in poverty. There is therefore a need for an awareness of the extent to which women suffer from poverty rather than how much this has grown. It remains the case that women are still more at risk of falling into poverty than men.

Conclusion

In order to explain the findings presented in this section, sociologists have to draw upon the theories of social inequality and stratification which are discussed elsewhere in this chapter (see sections 6.14–6.16 and 6.20–6.22). However, sociologists need to remember the following key points when trying to understand how poverty is best explained.

- Poverty is caused by many factors, such as low wages, sickness or unemployment. There is no single cause of poverty.
- Poverty is not caused by a person's class, ethnicity or gender, but all of these aspects of inequality are strongly linked to poverty.
- In order to understand poverty and inequality, it is necessary to examine how class, ethnic, and gender differences are interrelated (see sections 6.20–6.24).

For consideration

1. What do sociologists mean when they say that poverty is being feminised? Do you think this is really happening?
2. Why is the disadvantage and high risk of poverty faced by some ethnic minorities not shared by all ethnic minority groups?

◆ **What, when and why?**

- Feminism became prominent in sociology in the 1960s and 1970s. This happened because more women were going into higher education and getting into academic careers. These women were critical of much academic sociology, seeing it as male dominated and out-of-date.
- In the 1960s and 1970s, many sociologists focused on class inequalities and saw poverty as being caused by the operation of the class structure. This meant that ethnicity and racism were not seen as the cause of inequality and poverty. Sociologists are now more aware of the ways that these two aspects of stratification are distinct yet interact to create powerful effects.

✳ **Key Idea**

Sociologist Harriet Bradley has been strongly influenced by feminism and has a particular interest in stratification. She is one sociologist who has argued that sociologists now have to focus on understanding how different aspects of stratification (class, race, gender) work as a system.

How are the poor excluded from society?

What does this mean?

In recent years sociologists and policy makers have started to use the term **social exclusion**. This term refers to inequalities in a broader sense than the notion of poverty. It also refers to the idea that poverty is not just an economic phenomenon.

- Social exclusion refers to the way that some groups in society are excluded from activities and opportunities that the majority are able to partake in. Examples of social exclusion would include the way that being poor excludes people from education and employment opportunities, from the chance of applying for housing, and from participating in politics and decision-making.
- Equally, social exclusion can mean that some social groups are more likely to be the victims of crime.
- Social exclusion is a complex idea, since those at the top of the social hierarchy can also be excluded, in their case, by their wealth. Examples of this are the way that the rich are able to exclude themselves from social institutions by using private services such as health, education, or even living in separate and guarded residential areas.

How are the poor excluded from society?

Some of the ways in which the poor can be excluded have been briefly indicated above, but this needs further explanation. The poor can be excluded from employment opportunities because applying for jobs often involves expense, for example for travel or interview clothes. Additionally, those who do not have access to a computer or a telephone cannot easily look for jobs. For the homeless, lack of an address makes it difficult to even apply for welfare benefits. Another example of social exclusion occurs in education where non-attendance rates and educational failure rates can be high among particular socio-economic groups and some ethnic minority groups.

As we have mentioned though, social exclusion is not just an economic phenomenon. One of the important aspects of the idea of social exclusion is that it indicates how exclusion in one area can have further consequences. In this way, social exclusion can be seen as having some similarity to the idea of multiple deprivation.

What theoretical perspective does the idea of social exclusion come from?

The concept of social exclusion has its origins in the work of Emile Durkheim. The French sociologist Emile Durkheim (1858–1917) was one of the main founders of functionalism. Durkheim noted that a lack of shared norms (anomie) led to a lack of social integration, and this could cause instability. More recently various sociologists including Anthony Giddens and Amitai Etzioni have taken up the idea. Giddens is associated with the 'Third Way', a set of ideas that advocate an approach to welfare emphasising individual responsibilities as well as rights, and a greater role for **welfare pluralism**. Etzioni is the founder of 'communitarianism' and recommends that social policies need to be aimed at recreating community networks in order to create more opportunities for self-help.

Conclusion

Social exclusion is a popular concept in contemporary social policy. Sociologists from many different perspectives could undoubtedly agree that the poor are excluded from a whole range of activities that the majority of society partakes in.

However, those sociologists who are more influenced by Marxist, conflict, or feminist theory treat the concept critically. They believe that the main causes of exclusion are indeed economic, and so to focus on policies which will attempt to re-integrate the poor or the excluded into the mainstream, without making any allowance for economic inequalities, are bound to end in failure. It can also be argued that policies aiming to eradicate social exclusion are likely to become rather authoritarian and intolerant of cultural differences. After all, as conflict theorists would point out, trying to integrate a society through shared values and culture does not preclude the possibility of conflict, since the cultural values will be those of the dominant group. Functionalists, of course, take the view that societies can be integrated by a shared culture.

How keen sociologists are to use the concept of social exclusion then, will depend upon which sociological perspective they find most convincing.

✓ **Top Exam Hint**

Use the comments here about the Durkheimian origins of social exclusion in your evaluation of the concept of social exclusion. Durkheim is a functionalist, so his view of a socially integrated society assumes that consensus is achievable. A criticism of this view and of social exclusion, therefore, is that it masks differences in power between different social groups. There may be considerable disagreement about the values that society should be integrated around. This can also mean disagreement about which groups and values should be included in the consensus.

◆ **What, when and why?**

The idea of communitarianism is associated with the work of American sociologist Amitai Etzioni (1995), and has been very influential throughout the 1990s. Communitarianism is the belief that modern society (particularly modern American society) can only be preserved and further developed by returning to the certainties of the older values of community and family.

For consideration

1. Are the rich socially excluded from society?

2. Is a truly socially inclusive society possible? What would it mean?

Changes in the class structure: is there an underclass?

66 99 Key Definition

Underclass: a group at the bottom of or 'underneath' the class system. Take care of this concept though, as there is no clear agreement as to exactly who fits into the underclass. Critics have also pointed out that the term is more about a moral judgement and evaluation of certain types of people, than a rigorously objective sociological term (see Lydia Morris's comments below). It is also worth linking the underclass to the idea of moral panics – perhaps the debates about the underclass are themselves a moral panic?

What does this mean?

There are several theories regarding the causes of poverty. Theories tend to be split along structural or cultural lines; for example, are the poor the poverty-stricken victims of a society which should help them or an idle group to be motivated into working? In recent years some sociologists have taken the second view and argued that a new class is developing at the bottom of the class system. This class has been called the **underclass**. The underclass has been defined in different ways, but it is often seen as consisting of the long-term unemployed, those living continuously on welfare benefits, the homeless, and broadly, the 'poorest of the poor'.

The cultural approach: the underclass

The idea of an underclass was developed and used by several sociologists in the 1980s. One of the most important of these sociologists was Charles Murray. Murray published an article in the *Sunday Times* in 1988, arguing that there was an urban 'underclass' in the USA and that a similar group was developing in the UK. He argued that this group had several key distinguishing features.

* The underclass included a variety of types of people: the unemployed, young single parents, drug addicts, those involved in petty crime and a high proportion of young black males.
* It promoted 'a dependency culture'; an unwillingness to take personal responsibility for their wellbeing, and a dependency upon state benefits to survive.
* The underclass has been created by the welfare state. Murray argued that by the late 1980s, governments in the USA and the UK were providing an over-generous welfare system, so for many of those at the bottom of the stratification system, there was no incentive to work.

Some New Right theorists argue that those in the underclass have a certain way of life and attitudes that make them dependent, and which create a culture of poverty and stop them from breaking free from poverty. Oscar Lewis (1961, 1968) studied the poor in Mexico and Puerto Rico and developed the 'culture of poverty' thesis, arguing that the poor have particular norms and values including resignation to their situation. This 'culture of poverty' is passed between generations.

How can we evaluate this concept?

Many criticisms of cultural or dependency theories point back to the definitions of class (see sections 6.1 and 6.4) and argue that using the category of underclass involves putting people into a common class. However, the underclass has come to include many different groups who are likely to be in poverty for different reasons. Equally, it is possible to be a criminal or a drug

Charles Murray is an American academic. He is usually associated with the New Right and became well-known in the 1980s following the publication of his controversial pamphlet on the underclass.

addict, and to be fairly well-off financially. Critics therefore conclude that the underclass is not bound together by a shared market and work situation, one of the key ways contemporary sociologists use to define a class.

The structural approach

American sociologist, William Julius Wilson (1987), disagreed with the idea of a culture of poverty and dependency and argued in his book *The Truly Disadvantaged* that although there was an 'underclass' their position was the result of a lack of power in the face of economic and social structures of disadvantage.

Lydia Morris (1994) argues that this idea of the undeserving poor is a very old one. Morris states that the identification of such a group, and its labelling as a scapegoat for society's ills, is a form of social exclusion which reflects the fears and concerns of the dominant classes in capitalist society. Morris argues that the concept came about when globalisation was leading to important changes in the UK labour market (the late 1980s), in particular a decline in manual work and the growth of a large service sector. These changes have helped to fragment the class structure and inequalities in wealth have become increasingly polarised. Morris argues that the concept of an underclass is useful, as long as it is seen as a cultural category, rather than an economic category. Morris suggests that the concept is more helpful for showing how dominant and mainstream groups use cultural values as a basis for excluding and stigmatising those who are considered to depart from the norm.

Townsend (1979) argues that in a capitalist society the poor are excluded from employment opportunities available to others, and poverty will only be resolved through radical social policies to redistribute resources. In the 1980s and 1990s, New Right initiatives also saw changes to the labour market which introduced flexible working conditions such as less specialisation, part-time work and short contracts which provided less job security and fewer opportunities to find well-paid work. At the same time, many welfare provisions still rested on the claimant being in full-time work, so groups of people were excluded from benefits (single-parents/elderly people). Benefit provision also became subject to tighter eligibility tests. Townsend (1991) argues that it is these kinds of policies that have created an underclass, and a radical change in policies is necessary to redistribute wealth.

Conclusion

Sociologist Rosemary Crompton (1998) suggests that it is best to resolve this debate by referring back to, and using, basic concepts.

- Those arguing for the existence of an 'underclass' are in fact referring to differences in status, not class.
- However, economic class differences are often the basis on which status differences are created.
- Contemporary sociologists therefore need to focus more on the ways that class and status divisions are linked and interact together.

For consideration

1. Do any value judgements enter the underclass debate?

2. Can new classes be created?

✳ Key Ideas

- **Dependency theorist David Marsland (1989)** has argued that welfare provision should be minimal and used only as a last resort. He believes that welfare provision merely serves to stop the poor from fending for themselves and detracts from the services of other welfare providers such as the family and community.

- **American sociologist Wilson (1987)** produced a structural explanation of the underclass in the USA, similar to that of Morris. His focus was on the black community and he argued that the cause of the underclass was due to social isolation, including:

  - historical discrimination leading to the growth of a black underclass in cities supported by white fear

  - the change from a manufacturing to a service economy in cities, reducing job prospects for young, unskilled males

  - migration of working- and middle-class black Americans from the city into the suburbs leaving the very poor in the centre.

☐ Key Fact

Other researchers have argued that there is no empirical evidence to suggest that people from such categories do share a similar set of cultural values (Dean and Taylor-Gooby 1992, Heath 1992). In fact, these researchers have found that the very poor, and those living on benefits, are generally keen to escape from poverty and find a well-paid full-time job. There was therefore no evidence at all of a dependency culture.

◆ What, when and why?

Old 'heavy industries', such as iron and steel manufacturing and coal mining, were dying out as a result of foreign competition. This led to high levels of male unemployment, but more part-time work for women, and a growing service sector.

6.13 | How can we measure social inequality?

Does the wealth achieved by winning the lottery make the winner upper class?

∞ Methods Link

The problems of measuring and operationalising class show how sociologists' findings are always dependent on their theoretical views and definitions. Marxists and Weberians, for example, define stratification and class in particular ways. Feminists are highly critical of both approaches, arguing that they reflect malestream approaches to stratification and neglect the employment of women.

✓ Top Exam Hint

Remember, classes and occupations are not the same thing. Sociologists use occupation to *indicate* class position only.

What does this mean?

The idea of class inequality means that there are systematic differences and inequalities in the life chances of different social groups. Sociologists have devised a number of different ways of trying to measure these inequalities.

How can we measure stratification?

The main type of stratification which sociologists have tried to measure is class. To achieve this, sociologists have had to pick an **indicator** of class and then measure inequalities in terms of these indicators.

The most commonly-chosen indicator has been occupation. Sociologists have created several occupational **class scales**. Most sociologists using these occupational scales have been influenced by Weber's idea of life chances and market situation, and they have tried to rank the different social classes in order of life chances. All of these scales have therefore ended up with the top social class groups consisting of professional occupations such as lawyers and accountants, intermediate groups consisting of administrative and clerical workers, and lying below these, skilled and unskilled manual workers.

Sociologists using the various occupational class schemes would argue that the scales are valid measures of the class structure because they have revealed systematic differences between each group. For example the Registrar-General's scale has consistently revealed health inequalities in terms of infant mortality and mortality rates. However, other sociologists have been critical of occupational scales.

Are there any problems with these ways of measuring stratification?

It has been argued that occupational scales do not produce a valid measurement of social class. To understand these criticisms you need to remind yourself about the concepts of operationalisation and validity.

Since class is an abstract concept, sociologists can only study it by operationalising the concept in terms of an indicator. In the case of the occupational class schemes discussed here, the chosen indicator is occupational title. Occupational titles can then be graded in terms of their market situation and working conditions. This means that sociologists are interested not just in how much a person earns, but in all their rewards, privileges and conditions, such as hours worked, holiday entitlement, and whether they have authority over others in their job.

Those using occupational scales claim that they can produce a valid picture of the class structure. However, critics argue that the picture that emerges may not be valid for the following reasons.

- Not everybody has a job. The unemployed, royalty, the very rich, the retired, and housewives, will all be excluded from occupational scales. So how can their class be measured?
- Occupational scales confuse class with subjective views of status. For example, vicars are in Class 1 in the Registrar-General's scale, but their earnings are the same as those in many manual jobs.
- Marxist's such as John Westergaard (1976, 1995) argue that occupational scales either leave out capitalist owners or put them into the same group as professionals such as managers or accountants. Marxists argue that this completely distorts and misunderstands the nature of the class structure, which is defined as the relationship to the means of production, not as differences in market and work situation.
- Feminist sociologists, such as Arber and Ginn (1991), have argued that basing the class of households on the occupation of the male neglects the growing importance of women's paid employment. They contend that women's incomes can make a significant difference to household income and life chances, and sociologists therefore need to examine joint incomes. They also argue that most occupational scales represent a 'malestream' view of class, and present a sexist bias by using only the occupation of men or 'breadwinners'.
- Occupational class scales do not show us how factors such as gender, ethnicity and age, affect or crosscut class differences. For example, having a professional job may benefit your life chances generally, but this advantage will vary depending on your ethnicity, your gender, or your age.
- Occupational class scales produce a static picture of the class structure. They do not show how a person's class may change through their life.

Rosemary Crompton argues that research based on occupational scales shows us data about 'employment aggregates', and is useful because it tells us about patterns of inequality. However, we must not confuse occupation with class relationships, or with status groups, and we need other research methods (such as qualitative data) to find out about the social groups and relationships which they create.

Conclusion

- You will have to apply your knowledge of theory and method to evaluate attempts to measure stratification in sufficient detail.
- Theoretical differences in defining class will lead to differences in how class is operationalised and measured.
- Occupational scales lack validity, focus on structure rather than action, and are static.
- Occupational scales only attempt to measure one aspect of stratification.

For consideration

1. What factors apart from occupation could be used as indicators of class?
2. Which provides a better unit of analysis for class, the individual or the household?

Class scales

The Registrar-General's Scale (devised by the government)

I	Higher professional/managerial (e.g. doctors; company directors)
II	Lower professional/managerial (e.g. police; managers)
III N	Supervisory and lower/routine non-manual
IIIM	Skilled manual
IV	Semi-skilled manual
V	Unskilled manual

The National Statistics Socio-Economic Classification (a new scale which the government devised to replace the RG Scale and used in the 2001 census)

1. Higher managerial and professional
2. Lower managerial and professional
3. Intermediate
4. Small employers and self-employed workers
5. Lower supervisory, craft and related
6. Semi routine
7. Routine
8. Long-term unemployed or never worked

Goldthorpe's Class Scheme (although revised during the 1980s, this scheme identifies the three key classes).

Service class
1. Higher professionals, higher administrators, managers of large industrial concerns, large proprietors
2. Lower professionals, higher-grade technicians, lower-grade administrators, managers in small businesses and supervisors of non-manual employees

Intermediate class
3. Routine non-manual, e.g. clerical and sales personnel
4. Small proprietors and self-employed artisans
5. Lower-grade technicians and supervisors of manual workers

Working class
6. Skilled manual workers
7. Semi-skilled and unskilled manual workers

The Surrey Occupational Class Scale (Developed by Sara Arber, Angela Dale and Nigel Gilbert of the University of Surrey, this aims to avoid the sexist biases of other scales. It classifies women on the basis of their occupations and takes account of the gendering of occupations, as is clear by the splitting of class 6 into two categories.)

1. Higher professional/administrators/ managers and large proprietors
2. Employers and managers
3. Lower professional
4. Secretarial and clerical
5. Foremen and self-employed
6a Sales and personal services
6b Skilled manual
7. Semi-skilled
8. Unskilled

What do Marxists and functionalists say about social inequality and difference?

What does this mean?

Marxism and functionalism both provide well-known structural theories of society. They arrive at very different explanations of social inequality and difference, reflecting their respective consensus and conflict approaches to society.

What do functionalists say about inequality and difference?

Functionalists think of inequality in terms of the concept of stratification. This refers to a continuous hierarchy of occupational ranking. They are aware that the many different occupations in a complex modern society can be ranked in terms of both their prestige and their different privileges and rewards. Functionalists see these different ranks as being like strata, or layers of rock in the earth, arranged in a hierarchy. The layers are all different, but they are closely packed together and all are needed to be in place if the earth's crust is to be stable.

What is the purpose of inequality and difference in modern society?

Functionalists argue that stratification and social inequality is a functional prerequisite. A prerequisite is something which is essential, or 'pre-required', in order for something else to happen. Functionalists argue that stratification is essential for several reasons.

- It enables society to maintain a set of common values. The rewards given to only some members of society help to reinforce social values and create an incentive for others to aspire to the same goals and values.
- In modern society it becomes a key mechanism for what functionalists call **role allocation**. Role allocation refers to the part that people play in society, particular the work they do.

Davis and Moore argue that inequality and difference is essential for efficient role allocation (1967). They say that all jobs can be ranked in terms of their functional importance. The most important jobs have to be more highly rewarded than the lesser jobs. They claim that if this did not happen then there would be no incentive for people to compete or go to any effort to gain the top jobs. Stratification, or structured inequality, is therefore functionally necessary to motivate and reward people to aspire to the most important jobs. This is why top surgeons earn more than factory workers. Davis and Moore argue that this leads to a meritocratic system, which is essential if structured inequality is to be seen as legitimate. If it is believed that people are recruited to the top positions or roles in society through fair and free competition, inequality will be accepted by the rest of the population.

66 99 Key Definitions

Functionalists use the term **role allocation** to refer to the way that jobs are distributed in modern industrial society. Functionalists say that the most efficient way for jobs to be distributed in modern society is by having a meritocratic education system, as this makes the best use of the talents and abilities that exist in any population. In this respect, and in terms of the belief in meritocracy, the views of the new right are very similar to functionalism. The New Right (for example Saunders, Murray, Hayek) believe that inequalities are both inevitable, due to varying skills and abilities, and necessary for a competitive economy.

What do Marxists say about inequality and difference?

Marxists define inequality and difference in terms of class differences. Two main classes are identified.

- The Bourgeoisie: these are the owners of the means of production. The means of production is anything that people use to make wealth, such as land, a factory and the equipment in it, or an office. Because the bourgeoisie are the owners, Marxists say that they do not need to work in order to earn a living; rather other people work for them.
- The Proletariat: members of this group do not own the means of production and therefore have to work for the bourgeoisie to earn a living.

Marxists therefore define classes as groups of people with a shared economic position. People are either owners or workers, and Marxists say that an individual's class position is determined by their relationship to the means of production. This just means whether they are owners of the means of production or are workers. Marx was aware of other classes, such as the petty bourgeoisie who are owners of small businesses, but saw these groups as being less important than the two main classes. Marx argued that these two classes would polarise. By this he meant that the economic inequalities between the bourgeoisie and the proletariat would tend to increase. This would lead to increasing class conflict, and eventually to revolution.

Some sociologists argue that Marxist theory on class is not relevant to our understanding of contemporary society, because the process of polarisation has not occurred, and instead societies like Britain have actually seen the growth of a large middle class of white-collar workers and professionals. Also it is argued that Marx's view of the relationship between class consciousness and identity was mistaken. Marx believed that the proletariat should become aware of exploitation and their shared class position.

Conclusion

The following points indicate some of the key areas of criticism made of both theories.

- Are we as free as functionalist theory or as constrained as Marxist theory imply?
- The identification of only two classes by Marxists is often considered to be too simple (see section 6.16).
- Both theories provide structural views focusing on material (economic) differences. Other theories argue that cultural differences can be equally important (see section 6.15).

For consideration

1. Which concept gives a truer picture of inequality in contemporary Britain, class polarisation or meritocracy?

2. How could the functionalist approach to stratification explain why top sports stars and musicians are so highly paid?

✓ Top Exam Hint

There are three key criticisms that can be made of the functionalist approach.

1. Critics of functionalism argue that there is no consensus on which jobs are the functionally most important in our society; compare this with Parsons' view in section 6.7.
2. There is much evidence (see section 6.17) that ascribed characteristics are still important in determining occupational role, not merit.
3. Functionalist accounts of structured inequality and difference focus mainly on occupational ranking. Other forms of structured inequality (gender, ethnicity) appear to be neglected.

☐ Key Facts

ONS (The Office of National Statistics) figures from 1997/8 showed that professionals had a participation rate of 80 per cent in higher education, compared with 19 per cent for those from a skilled manual background. The participation rate for all social classes was 34 per cent. Participation rates measure the proportion of people from different social classes currently enrolled on full-time higher education courses.

'Of the top 200 schools in Britain in 1996 (in terms of A level performance), all but twenty-two were in the private sector. The private sector accounts for only 7 per cent of the school population, but for over half of the entrants to Oxford and Cambridge universities.'

Rosemary Crompton (1998, page 221)

How does Weber explain social inequality and difference?

☞ Who is this person?

Max Weber (1860–1924) was one of the chief founders of modern sociology along with Durkheim and Marx. Weber had a wide range of academic interests, and held academic posts in law, economics, and political economy before ending his career as Professor of Sociology at the University of Munich in 1918. One important contribution he made was the '*verstehen approach*', which is the idea that sociology has to be aimed at understanding the motives and views of individual actors.

✳ Key Idea

Weber defines the difference between class and status in the following terms.

'*With some over-simplification, one might thus say that "classes" are stratified according to their relations of production and acquisition of goods; whereas "status groups" that are stratified according to the principles of their consumption of goods are represented by special "styles of life".*'

(Max Weber in Gerth and Mills 1948)

In other words, two groups of people may have similar incomes (for example, junior police officers and university lecturers) but lead very different lifestyles, mix with different groups of people, and have a different status in society.

Weber's view of Marxism and its emphasis on structural factors is an important contribution to our understanding of inequality and difference, since how people think about structures will affect their behaviour.

What does this mean?

Max Weber was a German sociologist famous for arguing that sociology had to focus on the experiences and motivations of individuals. This made him critical of approaches such as Marxism which put too much emphasis (in his opinion) on structural factors.

How did Weber define social inequality and difference?

Weber (1948) recognised the importance of the difference between owners and workers (bourgeoisie and proletariat) but argued that differences *within* the working class were also significant. Weber defined class in terms of a person's situation in market terms. Clearly, different types of workers can gain very different levels of pay and working conditions, and Weber thought these were more important than Marx did. Defining class in this way allowed Weber to identify important differences in the class structure. He identified four main classes: the propertied upper class (owners); the property-less white-collar workers (managerial, administrative, and clerical workers); the petty bourgeoisie (self-employed workers and small business owners); and manual workers.

Classes, therefore, are simply groups that share a similar market situation (or position) and **life chances**. They may not necessarily have shared values or group identity.

However, Weber, in contrast to Marx, argued that three types of structured social inequality, or stratification, were important in modern capitalist societies: class, status and party. He was keen to point out that stratification in modern society could occur on the basis of non-economic factors.

Status groups are competitive, and aim to achieve 'social closure', which means that they try to monopolise privilege and to exclude other groups from their position of privilege. Weber also observed that status could cut across class differences or even divide a class group, for instance through the adoption of different values, lifestyles, or consumption patterns.

The final aspect of structured inequality identified by Weber, 'party', can be defined as a group that forms in order to gain power, and in so doing reflects and promotes the interests of any social group. Organisations such as trade unions or professional groups, or groups like Greenpeace or Outrage! are all examples of party. They reflect the idea that status groups, as well as economically-based class groups can form a basis for political action.

What does the Weberian approach tell us about structured inequality in modern capitalist societies?

There are several reasons why Weber's theories of structured inequality are still of importance and relevance today.

- Weber's theory shows that structured inequality can be achieved in terms of social (or cultural differences) as well as economic divisions.
- Weber's focus on intermediate groups in the class structure indicates the importance of differences in market situation and a variety of forms of payment or reward. It therefore focuses on position rather than the relationship between different classes.
- Weber's analysis reminds us that we should understand that the boundaries between class groups will inevitably be 'fuzzy' because they involve the attempt to distinguish different positions in the labour market on the basis of levels of income.
- People may define themselves in terms of any or no aspect of stratification, so we should not be surprised if people do not think of themselves as members of a certain class.
- Class and stratification (structured inequality) still have a vital influence on people's life chances, but in an affluent society we can use Weber's idea's about status groups to remind ourselves that people may create their identity more around consumption patterns than class groups.
- Class differences in the 20th century developed in a different way to that suggested by Marx. Some sociologists influenced by Weber argued that rather than polarisation occurring, more and more people were becoming middle class, a process called 'embourgeoisement'.
- Sociologist David Lockwood (1958) has synthesised elements of Weber's analysis with Marxism and has defined class in terms of 'market situation', 'work situation' and 'status situation'. This analysis has been used by Lockwood and other neo-Weberian sociologists to analysis class structure in contemporary Britain.

Conclusion

Weber's theory of inequality and difference shows us that theories of class are also always theories about power.

- Weber's theory suggests that there are other sources of power besides economic power, for example culture and cultural differences.
- Weber's theory therefore provides some useful insights into the nature of gender and ethnic differences in modern societies.
- However, critics might argue that Weber's theory does not provide any way to distinguish between the relative importance of the different types of inequality.

For consideration

1. How would a sociologist influenced by Weberian theory describe and explain the social position of sports and pop stars?

2. How can class be crosscut by status?

❝❞ Key Definition

Life chances are the opportunities, advantages and disadvantages that a person will have in life, depending upon their social position. Weber does not ignore the idea of natural differences between people, but he maintains that our chances in life will vary, regardless of individual talents, according to our social position. A good example of the way life chances influence the course of our life is given by mortality statistics which show that life expectancy in Britain varies systematically according to class.

Market situation refers to the supply and demand for certain skills, which therefore affects wage levels for any particular job. **Work situation** refers to the degree of authority a person may have in their job, whether they are responsible for others, or whether they carry out orders. **Status** refers to the degree of social prestige which is attached to an occupation.

✳ Key Ideas

- Weber defined status as an '*effective claim to social esteem*' (1948), which can refer to either positive or negative levels of social respect. Status may be related to ethnicity, gender, caste group, religion, attendance at a particular school or university, the values or lifestyle of a group, or membership of a particular occupational group, for example, surgeons, barristers.

- The idea of embourgeoisement claimed that middle-class values and standards of living were being adopted by more and more people in the middle of the 20th century. This was not an idea developed by Weber, but rather by sociologists influenced by functionalism, although it does reflect Weber's focus on the importance of the intermediate classes. Neo-Weberian sociologist John Goldthorpe tested the theory in a famous study 'The Affluent Worker' and found little evidence for the view that the working classes and middle classes were becoming identical.

How do neo-Marxists and the New Right explain social inequality and difference?

Neo-Marxist Erik Wright is Professor of Sociology at the University of Wisconsin-Madison.

☞ Who is this person?

Erik O. Wright (born 1947) is one of the few contemporary sociologists who claims to actively work on class analysis in the Marxist tradition. He studied at the Universities of Harvard and Oxford, before studying for a PhD at the University of California, Berkeley.

✳ Key Ideas

- Maybe the best way to think about Wright's ideas is to see the class structure as a web or map, rather than simply as a vertical ladder. For example, there are four levels of power or ownership: *full, partial, minimal* or *none*. Secondly, there are three aspects of modern work that might be controlled: *labour power, means of production, investment*.

- These three aspects of power and the four levels of control create a highly complex picture of class – much more so than traditional Marxism where either you do or don't own the means of production. In a sense, Wright's ideas are more Weberian as they see the complexity of class in modern society and the complexity of power through ownership, but also (with the rise of the managerial workforce) the partial power of control *without* ownership.

What does this mean?

Sociological theories are frequently modified to take into account criticisms made against them and to make them more up to date. Marxist-influenced sociologists have, for example, tried to develop an explanation of social inequality which is able to account for the expansion of the middle classes, rather than the allegedly simple polarisation of bourgeoisie and proletariat. Marxist ideas have been criticised for their failure to account for the rise of the middle classes in the 20th century, and so neo-Marxists have tried to offer new explanations of contemporary class structure. These can be usefully contrasted with the views of New Right sociologists, who argue that capitalism creates opportunities and high levels of social mobility.

How have neo-Marxists explained social inequality and difference?

Erik Wright (1997) argues that class is the most important type of structured inequality in modern capitalist societies. Wright argues that capitalist production leads to exploitative relations between different groups in the production process (in the workplace) based on the type of control that different groups have over production. Wright identifies three types of resources to control: investment, the means of production, and labour power. There are, however, four levels of control: full, partial, minimal and no control. The capitalist class has full control over all of these dimensions while the working class has control over none of them. This means that other groups are in an intermediate position, having one or two types of control.

Wright's analysis claims that class in capitalist society is more complex than Marxist theory of ownership/non-ownership originally acknowledged. He argues that intermediate groups in the class structure occupy contradictory class locations. By this Wright means that those in intermediate positions have the power to exploit others, while at the same time they are themselves exploited by the capitalist class. For Wright this is an important point to make, because it is this focus on exploitation that helps to preserve the Marxist orientation of his approach.

Wright argues, for example, that managers within a large corporation make decisions about investments and 'hiring and firing', but they are also employees themselves and do not have complete control over the means of production (factories, offices, machinery). More junior white-collar workers will exercise authority over 'labour power' by, for example, supervising manual workers, but have even less control over the means of production than higher level managers. These workers are therefore located in between the bourgeoisie and the proletariat. However, there are also contradictions within the ownership class. A self-employed owner of a small business owns the means of production, but may not have any employees and therefore has less power and control over others than the non-owner manager in a large business.

What has the New Right said about inequality and difference?

New Right thinkers claim that social inequality and difference are not only inevitable, but also beneficial to the efficient functioning and growth of a capitalist economy. New Right sociologists have not produced the sort of rigorous definitions of structured inequality produced by Marxists or Weberians, but they make important claims about its place in modern society. Sociologist Peter Saunders is one researcher influenced by New Right ideas. He puts forward the following points.

1. Saunders (1990) argues that the key source of differentiation in contemporary society is in consumption patterns, and not relations of production or differences of market situation. By consumption patterns, Saunders means the difference between those who rely on state services for housing, health and education, and those who purchase these services privately. It is these 'consumption cleavages' which are increasingly the most important form of inequality in contemporary society.
2. Saunders (1996) claims that while there is an economic elite, its power is limited. Most managers and directors are company employees not owners, and have worked hard to gain their positions. Differences in society are the result of **equal opportunity**, so those in higher classes deserve greater rewards. New Right sociologists therefore agree with the functionalist idea of meritocracy. Saunders argues that there is considerable mobility in Britain. He contends that ability and motivation are the key factors determining class position (see section 6.8).

Conclusion

Many criticisms have been levelled at these two theories. However, the following represent some of the most important points made.

* It can be argued that Wright's scheme ends up measuring an occupational hierarchy (not relations as he claims), and is therefore closer to Weber than to Marx.
* New Right theories assume that individuals are free to make choices, a point which goes to the extreme of denying that structural constraints exist.
* New Right thinkers, like functionalists, believe in meritocracy. Although Saunders would contest the point, arguably the evidence does not support this view.

For consideration

1. What evidence could be given to reject the view that social position is mainly determined by ability and effort?
2. Do people's subjective views of their class matter? If so, why?

❝❞ Key Definition

Equality of opportunity: Saunders puts forward three types of equality.

* *Formal or legal equality*: all members of a society are judged by the same laws and regulations and are treated on the basis of their actions (that is, breaking the law), rather than who they are.
* *Equality of opportunity*: all members of society have the same chance to succeed or fail based on their individual talents. This society is a meritocracy.
* *Equality of outcome*: an egalitarian society where all members are 'handicapped' to start at the same position, and achieve the same results. Saunders rejects this type of equality as unjust as people have to be treated differently in order to equalise their starting positions. He argues that 'positive discrimination' is an example of such treatment.

Other New Right sociologists argue that a combination of these economic trends and a decline in cultural and moral values standards leads to the creation of an underclass (see section 6.12).

◆ What, when and why?

The New Right is a political ideology rather than a sociological theory, but it is important because it has been so influential in British society. Prime Minister John Major clearly expressed one key belief of the New Right, when in 1990 he said that we live in a classless society.

Prime Minister John Major argued that in the 1990s Britain was a classless society. Peter Saunders argues that our position in the class structure is purely the result of individual ability and effort.

6.17 | Does social mobility exist?

Pupils at Harrow. Do state school pupils have an equal chance of making it to the top?

66 99 Key Definition

Social mobility refers to movement within the class scale. Mobility may be upwards or downwards.

✳ Key Idea

It is important that sociologists consider movement both up and down the class scale in order to measure the extent of mobility in a society. There may be a lot of upward movement for groups lower down, for example, but if this is not matched by downward mobility for those in higher groups, it means that more room has been created at the top, but it also means that those in the higher groups still have a better chance to maintain their position of relative privilege.

What does this mean?

Social mobility is the term sociologists use to refer to the process whereby people change their class position. There has always been debate about how much social mobility there is in British society and this section will examine the different viewpoints on this issue.

Why is social mobility important?

Studying social mobility enables sociologists to measure one aspect of structured inequality, class, by quantifying the amount of movement up and down the class structure. Estimating the degree of social mobility therefore enables sociologists to comment upon the degree of openness or closure exhibited by the class structure. It is important to have this information in order to be able to judge whether a society is meritocratic or not.

Social mobility is also important because when mobility is restricted, it means that a class boundary becomes a firmer social barrier. When mobility rates are less restricted the opposite occurs. This means that social mobility has a key role in constructing the boundaries between different social classes. It is also important because people's subjective perceptions of social mobility influence the extent to which class membership becomes seen as an important part of their identity.

How is social mobility measured?

There are two main forms of social mobility, relative mobility and absolute mobility.

- Relative social mobility means measuring the relative chances of those from different social classes of moving to a higher-class group. Relative chances means the chances of one class compared to those of another class.
- Absolute social mobility refers to the amount of movement in a class structure. This means the total number of people who have moved up or down the class scale.

Sociologists also distinguish between intergenerational social mobility and intragenerational mobility. Intergenerational mobility is social mobility between different generations, for example whether a son or daughter has moved up or down compared with their parents. Intragenerational mobility measures the degree of upward or downward movement an individual experiences within their own lifetime.

How much social mobility is there in Britain?

There have been several large-scale studies of social mobility in Britain and numerous analyses of secondary data. The main findings of these studies can be summarised as follows.

- The 1972 Oxford Mobility Study conducted by a team led by neo-Weberian John Goldthorpe (1980) found high rates of absolute mobility, but, importantly, it also found big differences in relative mobility rates between different social classes.
- The Oxford study took Weber's two elements of work and market situation and combined these into a single class scale. It identified three classes – service, intermediate and working class – and found that the relative chances of a person reaching the service class depended upon the class of their father. Of those with fathers in the service class, 55 per cent gained service class positions themselves, while for those from an intermediate class origin the figure was 25 per cent, and for those with a working class father the figure was 14 per cent. This meant that a boy from the service class had about three and a half times more chance of ending up in the service class compared with a boy from a working-class background.
- More recent research by Gordon Marshall (1988) also found big differences, and calculated that those from a service class origin were around seven times more successful in gaining a service class position than someone from the working class.
- These results have been criticised by Peter Saunders. Using data from the National Child Development Study (NCDS) (1996), he argues that absolute mobility is a more important measure, and that there has been a considerable increase in this, with 52 per cent of those in the sample of around 11,000 had experienced some upward intragenerational mobility. On the basis of the NCDS data, including tests of ability, Saunders concludes that British society is a meritocracy and that effort and ability, not class of origin, are the key determinants of success.
- In response to Saunders, it may be agreed that effort and ability are important, but so too is the class of origin in determining class destination. Marshall and Swift found that 43 per cent of men from the service class as opposed to 15 per cent of men from the working class, all educated up to A Level standard, reached service class destinations (1993, 1997).

Conclusion

Sociologists need to remember that society and social change are linked in a two-way relationship, and we need to be aware of both.

- The occupational structure has changed, and there are fewer manual jobs.
- Absolute mobility has indeed increased, but this is because of the changes in the occupational structure.
- Crompton (1998) argues that people are probably more aware of changes in absolute mobility, hence the common belief in meritocracy.

For consideration

1. What problems are posed by using different scales to measure social mobility?

2. What is reflexivity and how is it demonstrated in the conclusion above?

↩ Classic Study

The 1972 Oxford Mobility Study

This study was conducted by a team of sociologists led by John Goldthorpe at Oxford University. The study used a sample of 10,000 men between the ages of 20 and 64. The class background of these men was analysed and compared with the class background of each man's father. Although revised during the 1980s, this scheme provides a key to the three key classes – service, intermediate, and working class – referred to in Goldthorpe's studies.

● Synoptic Link

You might draw links here between social inequality, class and education. For example, Basil Bernstein (1990) argues that middle-class children use the same language as that of teachers and so perform better than working-class children with their restricted codes. Boudon (1974) argues that middle-class children tend to do better and aim higher because their social structure (family, friends) encourages this.

☐ Key Facts

The proportion of service sector jobs in the UK increased by 36 per cent between 1978 and 2000. Between 1978 and 2000, manufacturing sector jobs decreased by 39 per cent (Bilton 2002, page 304). This is important because it suggests that one reason why mobility has increased is simply because the occupational structure has changed. It is therefore not necessarily best seen as an increase in the openness of the class structure.

What is the class structure like now?

Sociologists argue that the decline of manufacturing industry in the UK has led to a big change in the class structure.

What does this mean?

In previous sections we have looked at two of the most important theories on class structure to be developed in the late 20th century (see sections 6.15 and 6.16). It has been found that there is insufficient evidence to support either theory. This section suggests that in fact what has happened in the late 20th century is that the class structure has fragmented.

What is the class structure like now?

In the 1970s and 1980s, studies of social mobility by sociologists such as John Goldthorpe and others (1980), suggested that in reality what had happened to the class structure was best described by using a visual image; the class structure had developed into a diamond shape. This meant that it had a large extended middle, and two shorter and narrower ends. The upper and working classes had shrunk and the middle classes had expanded. This does not mean that the embourgeoisement thesis was correct, though, because the differences between those in the middle and other classes were still significant. However, it did mean that class differences were becoming more blurred, as class was crosscut by status divisions. Note, however, that contemporary sociologists, such as John Scott, would point out that the upper class has now fragmented into several distinct sections.

More recently other sociologists have added to and qualified this picture of the changing class structure. Some, influenced by postmodernism, have suggested that class is no longer important as a determinant of life chances (see sections 6.21 and 6.22). Others have argued that class remains an important structure in contemporary society. For example, Rosemary Crompton (1998) argues that class remains an important structural force shaping life chances, but that it has changed over the second half of the 20th century, with class divisions becoming much more blurred than they used to be.

Crompton suggests that to fully understand what has happened to the class structure, we have to look at class as an objective structure as well as looking at how people view class subjectively. Crompton says that both of these two senses of class are linked.

What has happened to the class structure?

In terms of objective class, Crompton argues that the UK class structure has undergone a number of important changes since the late 1970s. In the workplace manual jobs have declined and technological changes have created new types of work and new jobs. This has led to an increasingly large 'middle' section of the population, although it has many sub-divisions within it in terms of income and lifestyle. At the same time, the old-fashioned manual working class of the early and mid-20th century, employing men in heavy industries such as steel manufacturing, coal mining and shipbuilding, has died out. This process can be described by the term **class fragmentation**.

This aspect of change draws mainly on the objective sense of class, referring to changes in the way that people work and what they do to earn a living. However, Crompton argues that changes in objective class have had a big impact on people's subjective views about class. Whereas in the early and mid-20th century it was more common to find people describing themselves as members of a class, now class fragmentation has led to another process: individualisation. This means that people now see themselves as individuals rather than as members of a class. A sense of class is therefore now less likely to exist and less likely to have an influence on a person's identity.

However, these changes do not mean that class has disappeared. Objective class, or 'employment aggregates' still remain, but they do not necessarily create social groups which people feel a sense of belonging to. Crompton's strategy of considering both the subjective and objective aspects of class structure enables us to understand that the objective structures of class can change and by doing so, can effect changes in the way people see their class position.

Conclusion

Crompton's summary of changes in the class structure sheds considerable light on the way the class structure has changed, and allows us to draw several key points in conclusion.

- Both embourgeoisement and proletarianisation theories were wrong and in recent years the class structure has fragmented.
- This has been caused by changes in the occupational structure and changes in technology.
- In order to fully understand these changes we have to be aware of both subjective and objective aspects of class and the way that these different views of class are interrelated.

66 99 Key Definition

Class fragmentation: this means that the traditional working-class communities of the early and middle 20th century, exemplified by mining villages or working-class areas in big cities, are largely gone, as these social groups and identities have been fragmented by social change.

◆ What, when and why?

Crompton claims that the class structure and stratification changed in the late 20th century as a result of several factors. Occupational change has occurred, with the development of a large service sector creating many jobs requiring little training. Technological change has meant the decline of many manual jobs and the creation of new jobs and professions. Changes in gender relations, with more women working, have led to important differences between households. Political decisions and policies on issues such as taxation and welfare benefits also had an important influence on shaping inequalities.

☐ Key Facts

Since 1977, the proportion of the UK population with less than half the average income has trebled (Rowntree 1995). This demonstrates that class differences are widening.

The effect of class origin on class destination does seem to have weakened over the last 20 years according to Marshall et al.

'The odds [chances] *of a man reaching the middle classes from a Class 1 or Class 2 background have been approximately halved, relative to those for a man from an unskilled background.*'

Marshall (1997)

For consideration

1. Who can best describe your class position – you or a sociologist?

2. Which theory of class do you think is best able to explain the changes described here?

6.19 | What has happened to class: are we all middle class now?

What does this mean?

In the 1960s some sociologists argued that the differences between the middle classes and the working classes were disappearing. One of the key reasons why this claim was put forward was that some sociologists thought that poverty and inequalities in wealth were being eradicated as incomes and the average standards of living rose. It was suggested that the population was becoming increasingly middle class in its attitudes, and in terms of its income and wealth. This process was called 'embourgeoisement'. This claim is still important as some sociologists argue that increasing affluence means that class differences are disappearing or becoming less important.

What evidence would be needed to support this theory?

Most contemporary sociologists have used definitions of class which are based on Weber's ideas (see section 6.15). They would therefore argue that to test the embourgeoisement thesis (or theory) we need to look at several key areas:

- Economic relationships and factors: these would include not just how much people earn, but how hard they have to work to get their reward, as well as any perks or benefits, and the amount of authority they have at work. The embourgeoisement thesis also suggested that the working class would share middle class attitudes to work. It was assumed that the middle classes were more involved in their work and gained more satisfaction from it, whereas the working class had a more instrumental attitude to work (they aimed to make as much money as possible from it and were less concerned about 'satisfaction').
- Norms, values, and social relationships: the idea of embourgeoisement assumed that the working class would increasingly have friends from outside their own class as both middle and working classes started to share similar incomes and lifestyles. There would be more social mixing. The research also aimed to find out whether different social classes have distinctive sets of norms and values.
- Image of society: the embourgeoisement thesis suggested that both working and middle classes would have a similar outlook on society. Unlike the 'us and them' (conflicting) views of the past, a fairer and more affluent society would lead to a more harmonious view of society on the part of both the working and the middle class.
- Political attitudes: the embourgeoisement thesis suggested that the political attitudes of the working class would become similar to those of the middle classes.

What evidence has sociological research identified?

In the 1960s a team of sociologists led by John Goldthorpe and David Lockwood decided to test the theory by conducting a large scale research project (see Classic study). The researchers picked Luton as a good place to do the research, reasoning that its growing working class population and full employment in skilled manufacturing work would make it a place where, if embourgeoisement was occurring, they would find evidence of it. In fact though, the research team found very little evidence to support the thesis.

Economically, workers still had very instrumental attitudes towards their work. In terms of their social relationships, very few of the sample mixed with people from other social classes. In terms of 'image of society', the affluent workers viewed society in terms of what the researchers termed a 'pecuniary model', in other words, in terms of money; 56 per cent of the workers saw society in this way. The middle class in contrast, were acutely aware of positions in a hierarchy, and sometimes put more emphasis on this rather than on the level of financial reward they received. Politically, the affluent workers mainly expressed a different set of interests and values from the middle class, with the majority voting for the Labour party (the traditional party of the working class). The researchers noted though that support for Labour owed less to a sense of 'class loyalty' and more to a perception of self-interest – they thought they would personally benefit more from Labour policies.

In fact the research found that there were only two limited ways in which the working and the middle class were becoming similar:

- Both classes had a home-centred and 'privatised' (individual, private) lifestyle
- Both classes were becoming increasingly instrumental in their attitudes to work, as white-collar workers were joining trade unions to help improve their pay and working conditions.

Conclusion

The Affluent Worker study is a classic study in sociology and it tells us at least three things about social inequality and difference in contemporary society:

- How researchers define and measure class will have a big impact on their view of the class structure.
- The so-called 'affluent workers' may have been much better off than their parents' generation, but this did not make them middle class.
- In the late 1960s, Britain was not becoming an increasingly middle class society. This suggests that levels of income and wealth may improve over time, but important differences and inequalities can remain.

For consideration

1. How important are economic factors in defining class?

2. The Affluent Worker study focuses in detail on people's attitudes about class. Is class just a matter of attitude?

⤳ Classic Study

This study was based on questionnaire and interview research conducted with a sample of 229 manual workers and 54 white collar workers. The workers were drawn from three large factories in Luton; The Skefco Ball Bearing Company, Laporte Chemicals, and the Vauxhall Car Plant. The findings of the research were published in the book, *The Affluent Worker in the Class Structure*, by Goldthorpe et al (1969).

⚭ Methods Link

How concepts are operationalised is very important in sociology. The embourgeoisement thesis provides a good example of why sociologists need to think carefully about how class should be defined. Advocates of the embourgeoisement thesis were suggesting that the most important aspect of class was income or wealth, but as we have seen, many sociologists argue that class is more complex than this, and Goldthorpe and Lockwood define class here in terms of market and work situation (see sections 6.4, 6.5 and 6.6)

☐ Key Facts

- Over the course of the 20th century the proportion of the UK population working in manual occupations has declined.
- Routh (1980) estimates that in 1911, 79 per cent of the workforce consisted of manual workers. By 1975, however, manual workers composed on 55 per cent and, by 1994, 46 per cent of the work force.

Sociologists argue that this means that the class structure is inevitably affected by changes in the occupational structure.

What has happened to class: are we all working class now?

What does this mean?

The theory that the population in the UK was becoming more working class, (although it was also considered to be occurring in other societies, such as the USA) was developed in response to the embourgeoisement thesis in the 1970s (see section 6.19). This alternative theory was called '**proletarianisation**', and its supporters claimed that in fact, rather than the population becoming increasingly wealthy, the inequalities between workers and the **bourgeoisie** were widening.

As we have already seen in section 6.14, this theory of inequality is associated with Marxist sociologists such as Braverman. This theory focuses on the position of **white-collar** or clerical workers, and argues that they are being 'pushed' down into the working class. The theory suggests that this process will go on, leading to the sort of class polarisation envisaged by Marx (see section 6.14).

What evidence would be needed to support this theory?

The theory of proletarianisation suggests that the pay and skill levels associated with occupations in the middle of the class structure are gradually being eroded. If a process of proletarianisation was occurring then, it should be possible for researchers to observe the following features:

- A decline in the pay differentials between manual workers and white-collar workers and professionals.
- A decline in the benefits and perks available to white-collar and professional workers.
- A decline in the amount of skill required to do white-collar jobs, making them easier to do and requiring less training.

What evidence have researchers identified?

One important study arguing against proletarianisation is David Lockwood's study, *The Black Coated Worker* (1958). Lockwood argued that while the differences in pay between manual workers and white-collar workers did indeed decline in the early 20th century, there were still important differences between them. These included differences in promotion prospects, job security, and other benefits such as holidays, time off and differing health risks in their workplaces. This is now a very dated study, but it is very important because it argued that class is composed of two key elements; market situation and work situation (see Key Idea), and this is something which many sociologists still believe has to be taken into consideration.

More recent studies, such as those of Stewart et al (1980) and Marshall et al (1988) echo Lockwood's findings. Stewart's study makes the point that many of those working in white-collar jobs later move up the class hierarchy, and so in some ways the issue of whether white-collar jobs are being proletarianised is irrelevant, since they still form an important gateway for those hoping to progress to higher and better paid-professional positions.

Marshall's research in the 1980s claims that clerical workers are not deskilled. However, Marshall's research used the approach of asking clerical workers themselves whether they thought that their work needed more or less skill than it had when they began working. It is of course possible that the respondents are wrong, or are making a judgement on the basis of a short range of experience. Marshall, however, does note that the 1980s saw the beginning of a big change with the development of relatively low-skilled jobs in the service sector, such as shop assistants and call centre operators. Marshall argues that in terms of pay and conditions, these jobs cannot be seen as being similar to the bulk of middle-class occupations. This does not support the idea of proletarianisation as it applies only to a small section of service workers, but it does indicate that class is changing (see section 6.19).

Conclusion

These studies provide useful material with which to evaluate the proletarianisation thesis. The following points can be made in conclusion:

1. These studies are now slightly dated. However, more recent evidence suggests that important differences between white-collar jobs (including other middle-class professions) and working-class occupations persist and are significant.
2. There was a decline in the pay of white-collar workers in comparison to the wages of skilled manual wages in the 20th century. Even today, wage differentials between white-collar workers (and many lower professions such as social workers, teachers, and nurses) and skilled manual workers are narrow; indeed, some skilled workers can earn more than these occupations.
3. Nevertheless, Lockwood's classic study illustrates that determining class position involves examining more than just pay. Status is also important. On this basis, the case for proletarianisation is unconvincing.

✳ Key Ideas

- Deskilling is an idea devised by Marxist Harry Braverman (1974). He argued that manual working class jobs were being deskilled, that is, were continually being simplified by the introduction of modern technology. This would have the effect of lowering wages and Braverman claimed of 'proletarianising' the bulk of the work force in capitalist societies. This has not happened, because while technology simplifies some jobs, it also creates new ones, of varying levels of skill.

- The distinction between market and work situation as elements of class is a vital one in sociology. Lockwood is drawing on Weberian theory and suggests that sociologists can identify classes by using these two indicators. Market situation refers to the ability of an individual to gain high rewards for their work. It does not just refer to wages though, and can include a range of perks and benefits. Work situation refers to the amount of authority a person has in their occupation, or their ability to avoid being closely supervised by others. Lockwood says that class is the sum of both of these things.

☐ Key Fact

In the late 1980s, Marshall et al (1988) pointed out that the routine non-manual category consisted of 39 per cent of women workers and only 6 per cent of male workers. This suggests that this type of work is heavily gendered.

For consideration

1. Is computer technology deskilling white-collar jobs?

2. Having read this section, which theory of class do you find more useful – Marx or Weber?

6.21 | How does ethnicity shape our life chances?

What does this mean?

You may have noticed that the theories of social inequality considered earlier in this chapter generally seem to have little to say about inequality and differences in life chances which are based on **ethnicity** or **race**. This neglect has been the source of many debates in sociology. In this section we will look at the nature of ethnic inequalities and consider how they are best explained.

What is the evidence about ethnic inequality?

Sociological researchers have identified a number of key inequalities in the present-day UK, which vary according to ethnic origin.

- Scott and Fulcher (1999) note that two-thirds of Pakistani and Bangladeshi families are in the bottom fifth of income distribution in Britain.
- Ethnic minorities are disproportionately likely to be unemployed, although recorded unemployment levels vary among different ethnic minority groups. In 2000, the government Labour Force Survey found unemployment levels of 5 per cent for whites, 8 per cent for Asian Indians and 17 per cent for Pakistanis and Bangladeshis.
- A recent Department for Education and Skills study (2003) showed that in 2002–3, black Caribbean pupils were three times more likely to be permanently excluded from school than white pupils, and that black, Bangladeshi and Pakistani pupils consistently performed less well than white pupils at all levels. However, Chinese and Indian pupils were shown to outperform all groups.

How do sociologists explain these inequalities and differences?

Modernist sociological theories have offered a number of ways of trying to explain these inequalities.

- Marxists argue that inequalities between different ethnic groups are caused by relations of production. In other words, Marxists acknowledged that these inequalities exist, but they are not caused by cultural and ethnic differences themselves, but simply by the fact that ethnic minority groups occupy the less skilled positions in the working class. This sort of approach was reflected in work by sociologists such as Castles and Kosack (1973).
- Functionalists argue that ethnic inequalities have been the result of low skill levels among migrant ethnic minority labourers. They take the optimistic view that such inequalities are therefore not the result of discrimination and in time would decline as ethnic minorities worked their way up the career ladder.
- Weberian-influenced sociologists, such as Rex and Moore (1967) and Rex and Tomlinson (1979), argue that ethnic minorities form a secondary labour market (they are in the worst jobs, less pay, worse conditions, least

security), due to the lower levels of their skills, but also due to their lower cultural status. Weberian theory therefore acknowledges that cultural discrimination exists and that stratification is not purely economic; the existence of status groups, such as those based on ethnicity, shows that stratification also occurs on the basis of cultural factors.

Critics have argued that Marxist explanations do not treat ethnicity as an important factor in its own right (because they are mainly interested in economic differences) and that Marxist theory has been 'race blind'. Functionalism has been considered unduly optimistic in light of continued and, in some cases, worsening inequalities on the basis of ethnicity and in so doing appears to neglect the reality of racial discrimination. Weberian-based explanations seem more promising due to the acknowledgement that status differences on the basis of culture can complicate class differences.

More recently, sociologists have been influenced by postmodernism and have recognised that ethnic differences co-exist alongside and are shaped by class and gender differences. This can have the effect of fragmenting ethnic identities, since members of ethnic minorities in different class positions may feel that they have less in common, or may have cultures which are highly differentiated by their class positions. Equally, gender divides women from the same ethnic group. Because of this, sociologists like Stuart Hall (1992) and Tariq Modood (1988), argue that people's identities are no longer shaped in a simple way by their ethnicity. Rather than being 'black', or 'Asian' for example, people may consider that they are 'Black British' or 'British Asian'. Hall and others refer to these as 'hybrid identities' and suggest that we are witnessing the development of 'cultural hybridity' in the contemporary UK.

Conclusion

Some sociologists (including those influenced by postmodernism) have argued that ethnicity is indeed an important aspect of stratification in its own right, and not just a side effect of economic inequality.

- Tariq Modood (1988, 1990) has argued that social inequality and difference involves economic and cultural elements. In particular he emphasises the need to examine how inequalities between ethnic groups are shaped by class, colour, and creed (religion).
- This means that sociologists need to acknowledge that there are important differences between ethnic minority groups – they are not all the same. Certainly in general they suffer discrimination, but this can vary according to other factors, for example, class position.
- Sociologists have therefore more recently been concerned to examine the way in which ethnicity is crosscut by other aspects of stratification, such as gender, class, and even age (see section 6.11).

● Synoptic Link

Remember to use ethnicity to see the links between different topics. Inequalities between ethnic groups are also clearly demonstrated in the study of figures on differences in educational attainment.

✓ Top Exam Hint

If you get questions on inequality and ethnicity in the exam, use the material here but also remember to apply material from sections 6.5, 6.6, 6.9–6.11, 6.13 and 6.19, in order to create a full and detailed evaluation.

✳ Key Ideas

- Some sociologists have argued that there is a black 'underclass', which is even more exploited and deprived as a result of both economic and cultural (status) discrimination (see section 6.12).

- **Theories of Ethnicity**
  Some theoretical approaches have pointed out that ethnicity can only be understood by linking it to other forms of stratification. Robert Miles (1989) for example, has suggested that ethnic minorities are members of a combined category which he terms 'racialised class fractions'. This term acknowledges that many ethnic minorities are part of the working class, but at the same time are separated from the white working class by their ethnicity.

For consideration

1. Are ethnic identities changing in contemporary Britain?

2. What is racism?

Why are gender differences and inequalities in life chances important?

What does this mean?

Just as was the case with ethnicity, most of the sociological theories considered earlier in this chapter neglected to consider the role of gender in social inequality. For a long time in sociology, gender differences and inequalities were not questioned or studied very seriously. More recently, since the 1970s, some sociologists have argued that gender inequalities are less important than class inequalities. In this section we will examine the extent and causes of gendered inequalities and differences in life chances based on gender.

What evidence is there about gender differences and inequalities?

Despite years of political campaigning by feminists, considerable gender inequalities persist in British society.

- Women are more likely to be in part-time or low-paid employment than men. According to the Equal Opportunities Commission (2003), 43 per cent of women and only 9 per cent of men work in part-time employment, and 79 per cent of those employed in administrative or secretarial jobs are women.
- Research by Crompton and Jones (1984) indicated that clerical work is a mainly female occupation. 70 per cent of workers in Crompton and Jones' study were female and they found that they were less likely to gain promotion than men.
- Despite recent improvements in women's employment opportunities, researchers have noted the existence of a '**glass ceiling**' restricting female promotion to the highest levels in business (Crompton 1998).
- More women head single-parent families than men and single-parent families tend to have lower incomes than families with two parents. Equally, women are more at risk of falling into poverty than men (Arber and Ginn 1991 and 1995).

How do sociologists explain these inequalities?

Modernist sociological theories have tended to explain gender inequalities and differences in terms of other factors, such as class, or have argued that they are not as important as other forms of structured inequality.

- Marxist theories tended not to question women's role in society too closely until the development of Marxist-feminism in the 1970s. However, early Marxist-feminists such as Rowbotham (1973) argued that gender stratification was actually caused by capitalism, and believed that gender inequalities were functional for capitalism. Gender inequalities help capitalism by providing a reserve army of labour (women) and by maintaining and reproducing labour power (caring for men, bringing up children).

- Functionalist theories of structured inequality also tended to see gender inequalities as either an inevitable outcome of role allocation, or took a more progressive view believing that gender inequalities would gradually decline as social change created new norms and values regarding women's role in society. In the 1970s, legislation such as the **Equal Pay Act** and the **Sex Discrimination Act** helped give this explanation credibility.
- Weber's concept of status, and his distinction between class, status and party, suggests that cultural differences (including gender) can be seen as a basis for structured inequality. In the 1980s, Weberian sociologist John Goldthorpe (1984) argued that gender was a distinct aspect of inequality. However, Goldthorpe used this point to argue against feminist claims that his methods for defining and measuring class were sexist. Goldthorpe suggested that the class of a household was best indicated by the occupation of the head of household, who should be the main wage earner. Feminists saw this method as sexist, since it meant that the earnings that women brought into families, and the class position which their occupations gave them, were often neglected. In response Goldthorpe argued that a woman could be the head of household, but the key point was that class inequalities were more important than gender inequalities.
- Feminists such as Hartmann (1981) argued that there was a 'dual system' of exploitation in capitalism. While Marxist theory explained how it was that there are winners and losers, Hartmann argued that it could not provide an explanation as to who took up those positions. Hartmann argues that gender and racial hierarchies have to be examined in order to do this. More recently, Catherine Hakim has argued that women's inequality in the workplace is largely the result of the choices that women make (1995). Hakim argues that many women choose to work part-time and these women are frequently, 'less committed' to work and career than full time workers (who are often male).

Conclusion

Contemporary sociologists are in general more likely to be critical of all of these previous positions, and would want to recognise that gender and class inequalities are linked and can interact with each other.

- Gender is as an important element of social inequality.
- The concept of patriarchy helps to explain why gender divisions and processes of gendering arise.
- It is also increasingly recognised that women's experience of gender inequality interacts with other elements of inequality, such as class, ethnicity, and age.

For consideration

1. Is the family (a key area for gender relations) becoming more democratic?
2. How are women's experiences of gender inequalities influenced by class, ethnicity and age?

✳ Key Ideas

Rowbotham argued that patriarchy operated within the capitalist system. She analysed male and female work and found that the division between work (outside of the home) and leisure (in the home/after work) did not exist for women, as the home was also a workplace for some women. This unpaid work allows capitalism to continue as children (the new workforce) learn from this behaviour.

∞ Methods Link

The debates about gender and inequality are good examples of how sociologist's theoretical assumptions shape their findings. Goldthorpe and others following his approach refused to operationalise class in terms of gender. Feminists have been keen to challenge this and have developed alternative ways of measuring inequality.

✓ Top Exam Hint

Use feminist theories as a way of criticising other sociological theories for their male bias.

● Synoptic Link

Crime and education are also aspects of social life which are heavily gendered. Crime is a predominantly male activity, and women's crime is generally restricted to particular types of non-violent crime. The education system can be seen to be gendered, and helps to push women into certain subjects, which reinforces later work roles and choices.

| # Is feminism still relevant?

Key Definition

Postfeminism is the idea that we live in a time after feminism. This assumes that feminism has declined or even disappeared as a significant social and political theory because it is not needed as women now have equality with men. However, this is a highly selective view and there is a great deal of sociological research which indicates that women are still some way off achieving equality with men. Also as a sociological theory feminism remains important although it has fragmented into a number of sub-branches, e.g. black feminism, triple systems theory feminism, and postmodern feminism.

Key Ideas

In the 1960s second wave feminists came up with the slogan that 'the personal is political'. This meant that that the details of our personal lives and identities are in fact the outcome of political power and political struggles. The fact that as men and women we have different life chances is an illustration that this is the case. Walter's adherence to parodying of 60s and 70s feminists leads her to reject the idea that 'the personal is political' (she says we need to separate the personal and the political). Yet this is an excellent sociological insight. All aspects of our gendered identities are socially constructed, and so all aspects of our lives are indeed political.

What does this mean?

In contemporary society, where women in many if not most areas of life appear to have attained equality, many people might argue that feminism is a political theory which is now dated and irrelevant to our lives. This has been referred to as **postfeminism**.

Is feminism still needed?

Susan Faludi's book *Backlash* (1992) suggested that there has been a reaction against feminism. Faludi suggested that the general cultural climate in the 1990s was one which claimed that women had achieved equality with men, but were no better off, and in fact, were worse off. Although women had won the right to work outside the home on equal footing with men, they still had to care for the home and children so, in effect, had two roles. This, critics argued, meant that women were overworked and children neglected. Therefore, it was often concluded, women should return to their traditional roles and positions. According to this view (which Faludi was highly critical of), feminism was a failure and a sham.

Other writers though, have argued that whilst there has been much positive change, feminism is still important. One example is the writer Natasha Walter, whose book, *The New Feminism*, expresses a common contemporary view of what feminism should be (1998). Walter argues that the feminism of the 1960s and 1970s, with its motto that 'the personal is political', was doomed to failure. Walter feels that the feminism of the 1960s and 70s was too puritanical. Walter is referring to some feminists' criticisms of women who wished to wear make-up or adhere to anything remotely resembling a traditional female role; e.g. housework, having a boyfriend, and so on.

Is patriarchy still relevant?

Catherine Hakim (1995) has argued that feminism over-emphasises the effects of patriarchy in society. She refers to this as the 'myth' of patriarchy. She maintains that although women may have suffered discrimination in the past, theories of patriarchy are misleading. Hakim claimed, for example, that many women choose to work part time so they can still perform household duties. Also, as women can choose whether or not to have a child in today's society, the expense of child-care does not prevent women from entering the workplace.

Walter is also critical of the concept of patriarchy, suggesting instead that the key issue in gender relations is in fact much simpler; it is equality. Walter identifies several areas where equality between men and women needs to be increased in order to achieve equality; work (pay and conditions), sharing the duties of childcare, responsibility for domestic work. Walter also notes the continued prevalence of domestic violence (see section 2.17). Dobash and Dobash (1979), for example, point out that when women are the victims of rape, murder or assault, it is usually a family member that is the criminal, and more often then not the husband. The family is the most likely source for such crimes, rather than society as a whole, as is more generally feared. More recently, Heidersohn has referred to crime in which women are the victims of men, such as rape and domestic violence. She calls this gendered crime and argues that such crimes are often 'hidden' in official statistics and many go unreported as they occur in the home and may be committed by family or friends.

However, Walter argues that ultimately women today have a tremendous amount to thank feminism for. She takes the view that there has been nothing less than a gender revolution over the course of the twentieth century, and the contrasts between the experience of her generation (born in the late 60s) with that of the generation living in the 1920s are enormous. Having said this, Walter presents what some might see as an over optimistic view of women's current freedoms and of the future:

"I don't think about the fact that I wear comfortable clothes, that I drink in bars, that I work, that I can love a man outside marriage. Yet all these everyday transformations, as well as others – that I use contraceptives, that I work at a newspaper, that I got a degree from a university, that I am paid much the same as my male colleagues, that I own a flat – were only brought to me after the struggle and argument of previous feminists. …. In another hundred years we will see women and men sitting together in equal numbers in Parliament. We will see men carrying their babies in slings to their workplace crèches…" p256–7

Walter concludes that feminism is still needed, but if it is to be popular and successful, feminists have to cease focusing on personal issues such as how women express their sexuality and their personal relationships with men, and focus instead on clear cut political issues which will promote equality between men and women. Walter's position is very similar to that of a liberal feminist and Liberal feminists would share Walter's optimism about the inevitability of progress expressed in the quote above.

Conclusion

This may seem an appealing contemporary analysis of feminism. However, several points can be raised in criticism of Walter's analysis.

- Walter presents a narrow view of what feminism was in the 1960s and 70s. Arguably she is just reflecting a common stereotype and a parody of radical separatist feminists. Moreover, even if some feminists had unusual values, this does not invalidate their analysis.
- Walter's rejection of patriarchy is perhaps too hasty. Patriarchy is a theoretical concept which helps to explain inequality – it is patriarchal culture which leads women to be positioned as worth less than men. It is unclear how else Walter would explain economic inequality (Walby, 1990).
- Walter's view of gender inequality as simply being a matter of economic inequality gives us a narrow and impoverished understanding of gender. The 1960s radical feminists were right to see gender inequality as being linked to culture; so women's inequality has got something to do with our society's rules about femininity and sexuality and the personal is indeed political.

For consideration

1. What is the difference between feminism as a political theory and as a sociological theory?

2. In what ways are women still discriminated against by patriarchal culture?

How far have we come since the equal rights legislations of the 1970s?

☞ Who is this person?

Natasha Walter is a freelance journalist. She studied at the elite universities of Cambridge and Harvard before entering journalism, where she has worked for various publications including The *Independent* and *The Guardian*. Sociological critics from various perspectives might observe that her sense of considerable freedom (see quotation opposite) is not unrelated to her elite position and elite education which gives her power which other women do not have. Perhaps this is why she neglects cultural aspects of patriarchy and focuses on economic freedoms.

✓ Top Exam Hint

In discussing the continued relevance of feminism evaluate Walter's assessment by showing how feminism is useful as a sociological theory. Feminism as a sociological theory aims to explain women's position in contemporary society. Walter is writing from a political perspective and is advocating a certain form of feminism as a political strategy. This is very different from the aims which sociologists have. If you can show the difference between these two views you will demonstrate that you have a sociological imagination.

What are the links between class, gender and ethnic inequalities?

◆ What, when and why?

Modernist sociology developed in the 19th century. Modernist sociologists were optimistic that sociology could help bring about social change and improvement and would identify the truth about the social structures governing our lives. Postmodernism developed around the 1970s and 1980s when social progress seemed much harder to have faith in, given the troubled history of the 20th century. This led to a general scepticism about the possibility of progress and universal truth and, at the same time, changes in the division of labour and in the class structure made belief in the relatively simple categories of modernist theories less credible.

✳ **Key Idea**

Walby's six social structures are as follows.

1. The patriarchal mode of production where women's labour is exploited within the household by men.
2. Patriarchal relations in paid work where women are segregated and paid less.
3. Patriarchal relations in the state where the state operates in the interests of men rather than women.
4. Male violence against women through rape, sexual, emotional and physical assault.
5. Patriarchal relations in sexuality where men's sexuality is viewed completely differently to that of women.
6. Patriarchal relations within cultural institutions and the creation through the media, education and religion, of masculine and feminine identities.

What does this mean?

In recent years sociologists have become interested in examining how the different aspects of social inequality are related and in finding out whether any particular type of inequality is most important. Modernist sociologists have argued that class is the most important type of structured inequality, and other types, such as ethnic or gender divisions, are less important. Sociologists influenced by postmodernism, though, have argued that all the different aspects of inequality are linked together in complex ways. This section examines these viewpoints.

How do sociologists explain the links between class, gender and ethnicity?

For traditional or modernist sociological theories (for example Marxism, Weberian theory, and functionalism), the central divisions in modern society are class divisions. These are seen to have a determining influence on an individual's life chances rather than gender or ethnic inequalities. Indeed, some sociologists argued that other inequalities were the result of class inequalities, as, for instance, Marxist sociologists Castles and Kosack claimed in their study of the position of ethnic minority migrant workers (1973).

More recent sociological perspectives have seen these claims as over-generalisations. In the 1980s, some feminists criticised the idea that women's life chances could be predicted simply from the class position of their husband, pointing out that women's own employment could make a significant difference. **Third wave feminists** argued that women's experience also varied according to their ethnicity. In the 1990s, Sylvia Walby claimed that there were, in fact, three systems stratifying women's experience: class, gender, and race (1990). Walby argues that all three of these elements of stratification are important, but that they form an overlapping network of structures which shape life chances. She identified six patriarchal structures which constrain women (see Key Idea). Walby argues that patriarchy has adapted to fit the limited civil rights women gained in the 20th century, and shifted into the workplace as well as the home. Although women do work and participate in public life, Walby argues that they are still under-represented in higher levels of society.

This triple-systems approach argues that class, gender and ethnicity intersect, both in the life of the individual and over time in the history of the whole society. Therefore, the intersections of these structures of power and difference are both 'macro' and 'micro' at the same time. Walby also makes the important point however, that at times these structures might actually curtail each other. For example, severe class inequality might reduce the effect of patriarchy.

Sociologists influenced by postmodernist ideas have also been highly critical of modernist sociological theories of inequality and difference. Postmodernist influenced approaches vary, but there are several key points they all make.

- Postmodernists have been highly critical of general, overarching theories and claims, such as the claim that class is the key determinant of life chances.
- Postmodernists have argued that it is more important to examine diversity and the differences within the groups identified by sociologists, for example differences within classes, ethnic groups, and gender groups. This helps us to understand the complexity and plurality of contemporary life.
- This has led sociologists to look at the complex ways in which class, ethnicity, gender and age are linked. This can mean that more complex patterns are identified, for example gender is less of a disadvantage to white, middle-class women than to working-class women, or can be yet another basis of discrimination for women from ethnic minority groups.
- Postmodernists have argued that society should be looked at in terms of the categories and ideas which people themselves use to explain things. This means examining how people themselves define gender, ethnicity or class, and how they perceive it affecting them.

Which is more important, inequality or difference?

The differences between modernist and postmodernist approaches to inequality are considerable.

- Modernist theories suggest that inequality is the result of social structures, and that these powerful forces shape our lives. These structures are largely, though not exclusively, the result of economic power resulting from a position in the division of labour. Modernist theories then argue that inequality is the key feature of modern societies, and the most important concept to grasp in order to understand them.
- Postmodernist theories claim that what is most important in social inequality are cultural differences. Postmodernists argue that these are socially constructed and vary tremendously in different cultures. They therefore have to be studied on a more individual basis. Postmodernists place much less emphasis on structural economic differences, indeed, in the most extreme examples, they neglect them. Contemporary societies can be best understood by examining the way culture leads to the construction of social differences.

Conclusion

Sociologist Harriet Bradley offers some useful points to consider in evaluating these differing views.

- There is no way to determine whether it is inequality or difference which is the most important form of stratification.
- Both cultural and economic aspects of inequality are important.
- Bradley suggests that sociologists need to look at class, ethnicity and gender as interacting dynamics.

For consideration

1. Can individuals choose their own identity?
2. Does social change mean that we can now ignore older theories of stratification, such as those of Marx and Weber?

❑ Key Fact

The Equal Opportunities Commission's *Facts about women and men in Great Britain 2003* highlights Walby's point that women are underrepresented in society. It states that in 2003 only 18 per cent of MPs were women and only 31 per cent of women were in managerial or senior official roles, as opposed to 69 per cent of men.

❝❞ Key Definition

Third wave feminism developed around the 1980s when black feminists argued that previous generations of feminism had neglected to consider other dimensions of inequality, such as race. For example, ethnic and gender inequalities are linked, since life chances for women will depend on their ethnicity as well as their gender. Equally, where white feminists claim to speak for all women, black feminist arguments are seen as separate from the norm and only concerning black women (Aziz 1997). Heidi Mirza (1997), in fact, argues that black feminism should be separate as it can contribute a different aspect to feminism. Third wave feminism has therefore contributed to the idea that different forms of inequality are linked together in more complex ways.

✳ Key Idea

Power is important in terms of both cultural and economic approaches to stratification. In both cases, the ability of individuals or groups to gather and use cultural and/or economic resources to differentiate themselves from others is vital. Arguably, postmodernist approaches to stratification and differentiation neglect power, while modernist approaches have sometimes exaggerated the constraining influence of power differences.

✓ Top Exam Hint

Use postmodernist approaches to evaluate older debates about stratification such as those on embourgeoisement and proletarianisation. Postmodernist theories suggest that the class structure is best seen as fragmented, something which the modernist theories neglected in their over-emphasis on stability and structures. However, you must not forget the criticisms of postmodernism, and here Bradley's synthesis may be a very useful way to conclude.

How does social inequality and difference affect our identity?

What does this mean?

Social inequality and difference are things which can have a big impact upon our identity. The classical sociologists, Marx, Weber, and Durkheim, were interested in this question, and they suggested that in modern society people could be alienated, experience feelings of isolation and individualism (anomie), or become very strict and self-denying (Weber's Protestant ethic). Sociologists are now especially interested in the ways that stratification affects our identity, but they have developed these ideas in new directions.

What do sociological theories say about social inequality and identity?

Marxism

In Marxism, identity was seen to follow on very simply from class position. Other types of identity, such as gender or ethnic identity, were relatively neglected, since Marxist theory assumed that the most important aspect of stratification was class – other factors could only have at best a secondary influence. According to Marxist theory, the prospects for identity in capitalist society were not good. People would lead lives and develop identities stunted by the inequalities created by capitalism, and would be alienated.

Functionalism

Identity in functionalist theory is seen as something which in modern society is achieved not ascribed. Functionalists therefore have a very optimistic view of the way that individuals can shape identity in modern society. They do recognise some differences, such as gender roles, but tend to emphasise how roles are now much more flexible and are the outcome of consensus rather than being imposed through social control.

Weberiansm

Weber's work on stratification is important partly for raising the importance of status differences and so reminding sociologists of the complexity of social inequality. However, Weber is also important because the concept of status brings the idea of culture into stratification. By including status differences in his account of stratification, Weber shows us that it is not just economic differences which should be taken into account. This is because status differences, such as those between different ethnic groups or those arising from gender differences, reflect cultural beliefs. Weber's analysis shows us that identity depends on cultural as well as economic factors, and that while in many ways we can create our identity, there are also important structural constraints.

What do contemporary sociologists say about social inequality and identity?

Contemporary sociologists have noted that the late 20th century was a time of considerable social change. Ideas drawn from two new theories, postmodernism and post-structuralism, have had a particularly strong influence in sociology. This has led sociologists to turn away from economic differences, and to focus more on the way that culture can be used to actively create identity and differences. A well-known example of such a view is apparent in Pakulski and Water's book, *The Death of Class*, 1996 (see also section 6.24).

While many sociologists have been highly critical of these new approaches, they have nevertheless borrowed insights from them. Many would agree that care has to be taken not to over-generalise, as traditional theories of stratification sometimes did. This means that there has to be recognition that class, race, gender and age, are all important aspects of social inequality, and may be linked in complex ways (see section 6.14). As Bradley has argued (1998), sociologists now recognise the need for better ways of theorising stratification. Several key changes seem to have occurred in relation to social inequality and its relation to identity.

- The class structure has fragmented in the sense that class no longer seems to form a key aspect of people's self-identity.
- Gender identities are now considered to be much more flexible and varied. Sociologist Bob Connell (1987) has argued that genders have to be seen as constructed and as involving a range of masculine and feminine identities. These may vary, for example, on the basis of class, age, or ethnic origin.
- Ethnic identity is changing in the UK, as those from immigrant backgrounds form hybrid identities.
- Sociologists are also keen to explore new aspects of stratification and identity, such as the way that age groups can shape identity and inequality.
- Giddens (1990) argues that social change has led to a society where we can now be said to be living in a post-traditional social order. People's identity is no longer constrained by traditional rules, and they are able to create and mould a 'plastic identity'.

Conclusion

As a result of changes in society and sociology, many sociologists would argue that sociologists need to do at least three things to study stratification properly.

- Develop new theories of social inequality and identity.
- Examine the way that groups and their cultures can create social exclusion and stigmatised identities.
- Examine the way that stratification and identity are shaped by globalisation.

For consideration

1. Are people free to choose their identity in contemporary society?

2. How does a person attain a high status identity in contemporary society?

✳ Key Idea

Postmodernists have suggested that identities are no longer constrained by social structures such as class, race and gender. They have argued that people are now free to construct their identity as they wish. As social structures have fragmented, people are strongly influenced in doing this by the mass media. Post-structuralism is a theoretical approach which has turned attention to culture, identity, and differentiation, pointing out that people are able to use culture and cultural symbols as a way of actively creating identity.

✓ Top Exam Hint

Remember that the structure/action debate is directly relevant to these debates about identity and stratification. Point out this link and use it to make criticisms of both perspectives. For example, postmodernism puts too much emphasis on action and neglects the importance of structures, and modernist theories can neglect the importance of reflexivity.

❝❞ Key Definition

Hybridity refers to the creation of a new identity which is the product of a mixture of two different cultures. For example, a person whose parents are from Bangladesh, but who was born in the UK, might describe themselves as a 'British Asian' (see Hall 1992, and also M. Song in Abbott 1998).

6.26 How can we make social inequality and difference synoptic?

Why is synopticity important for social inequality and difference?

Synopticity refers to the way that different topics are linked together. Examining how social inequality and difference runs through the different topics you have studied will help improve your understanding of each of these topics. The unit 2539 exam will ask you to make synoptic links to other topics you have studied in AS Sociology and to Theory and Method (see CD-ROM). This section will therefore look at a few of the ways in which social inequality and difference is linked to some of the main topic areas and core themes.

How does social inequality and difference link to families and households?

There are many relevant links between social inequality and difference and families and households. The family is a highly gendered institution as contemporary studies of conjugal roles have demonstrated. This differentiation is also reinforced and reflected in social policies which privilege men and have tended to assume that women's place is in the home, looking after children and dependants. In this chapter (see sections 6.11 and 6.12) the influence of women's work on household incomes is seen by Crompton as reflecting the changing role and importance of women's position in the stratification system. As many sociologists now argue, class and gender are both important aspects of social inequality, and both of these structures have a big impact on the family, and the family is a key site where gendered identities are created.

How does social inequality and difference link to education?

It would be very hard to understand education without an understanding of social inequality and difference. One of sociologists' key interests in the sociology of education is to explain the varied patterns of educational attainment which have been observed. Systematic differences in attainment occur on the basis of class, ethnicity and gender. Inequality is also an important issue in the meritocracy debate, where the opposed claims reflect different views of the stratification system. Educational policies since the 19th century have reflected the idea that different social classes exist and require different types of education. Differentiation in terms of ethnicity and gender is also relevant to the issues of institutional racism and to the gendering of the curriculum. The education system is a key site where class identities, and ethnic and gendered identities, are created and reinforced.

How does social inequality and difference link to theory and method?

Theory and methods are linked to social inequality and difference very simply in some ways, because different theories provide competing descriptions and explanations of social inequality and difference. If you know the theoretical approach taken by a sociologist, you should be able to make a fairly accurate prediction of what they will say about social inequality.

In terms of methodology there are important issues about how class is operationalised and measured, as well as issues about how class relates to structure and action (see section 6.1 for more on the latter). For example, feminists have argued that many sociological views of stratification have neglected women's role in social inequality and difference. This claim has led to debates about whether women are a class and how women's class position is best identified and operationalised. In the case of race and ethnicity, some sociologists have argued that theoretical perspectives such as Marxism were 'race blind' since racial and ethnic differences were seen to be based primarily on class position, not race or ethnicity itself.

How does social inequality and difference link to culture and identity?

Sociologists often argue that cultures enable social groups to become integrated around unifying beliefs or values. However, cultures can also promote social inequality and difference. In British culture, for example, there are important rules based on social differences such as gender, age, class, and ethnicity. Those who do not maintain cultural rules may find that they are socially excluded. Social inequality and difference, therefore, is very much concerned with cultural differences and the cultural bases of inequality and stratification, and is not simply about economic differences. The way that cultures differentiate people also has an important impact on identity. In order to attain a favourable identity in British society, a person must follow certain cultural rules, and failure to do this can lead to social exclusion.

Key points to remember

- Theories of social inequality and differentiation are one of the key ways that sociologists try to explain how societies are integrated or held together. This topic is therefore relevant to all other topic areas.
- Different sociological theories describe and explain social inequality and differentiation in very different ways. However, this provides you with lots of ideas and material for debating and to use for evaluation.
- Do not forget to link social inequality and differentiation to issues of culture and identity (a core theme). Social inequalities shape our identity and the identities which are available to us, and also reflect cultural rules.

✓ **Top Exam Hints**

- Use the concept of power to evaluate different explanations of social inequality. Marxist and feminist views of power tend to see it as something which is unequally shared out. This helps to explain the continuity of inequality. Functionalists, though, claim that power is equally shared and do not believe that there are any major conflicts of interest in capitalist society. These views led the theories to reach very different conclusions about the nature of social inequality and difference.
- Identify key studies for each of these topic areas which demonstrate the importance of social inequality and difference.

6.27 | Pushing your grades up higher

1. Identify and learn five key facts about the extent of inequalities in contemporary Britain. The A2 exam does of course give you more marks for interpreting, evaluating, applying and analysing your knowledge, but it is easier to do all these things when you have a sound base of knowledge.

2. Remember to point out that social inequality and differentiation in contemporary society have changed considerably in recent years. Use this point to evaluate older studies.

3. Make a habit of reading from a range of textbooks to gather different points of view and fresh insights and data. Also read a few articles on this topic. Your teacher will be able to point you towards relevant articles in books of readings or magazines such as *Sociology Review*.

4. Make your own glossary of terms for this topic, taking care to explain the terms in your own words. This will be better than just using glossaries from textbooks because you will have to think carefully about the terms to do this. You should understand something better if you have written about it yourself. Keep adding terms to your glossary for as long as possible – the more you stretch yourself the better.

5. Make your own summary chart about social inequality and the other topics you have studied. Use a piece of A4 paper in landscape format. You should make a column on the left to put down summaries of each of the major theories of social inequality. Add other columns such as, 'view of the class structure', 'key strengths', 'criticisms', 'links to other topics', and any others you think are important. The rows cutting across the columns will be for the main theories. You should have at least five rows so that you can include the following theories: Marxist, Weberian, Functionalist, Feminist, Postmodernist.

6. Make a list of all the things which you do not think you fully understand about this topic. Compare your list with other students and with the help of your teacher have a lesson when you try to iron out these problem areas.

7. Obtain a copy of last year's exam paper, the mark scheme for the exam, and the subsequent chief examiner's report. Study these carefully to see exactly what was required in order to do well.

8. Organise a time when you can make your own presentation or talk about one aspect of this topic to another student studying sociology. This is a good way of finding out if you really do understand the topic well. You could try this in class and give the talk to a group of students.

9. Make a second glossary. This one should be for non-technical (that is, non-sociological) words which you have had to look up in the dictionary. Make sure that every time you find a word that you do not know the meaning of in the course of your reading for sociology you look it up in the dictionary and record and define it. This will expand your general vocabulary and improve your communication skills, which are vital in a subject like sociology.

10. Make it a priority to work on your language skills, especially essay writing. Use any specialist books you can find in your school or college library. Ask friends and teachers for advice on essay writing and try to look at other people's essays. Find good examples of essay writing and analyse them, identify their strengths and try to use similar techniques and styles in your own work.

11. Do not use personal pronouns in your essays, for example 'I' as in 'I think that…' Use impersonal pronouns such as 'It' as in 'It can be argued that…' This is the conventional style for academic essays because it makes your essay sound more reflective and objective.

12. Always make sure that you evaluate ideas, theories, concepts and studies explicitly. This means that you need to make it clear how and why you are criticising something and tell the reader of your work/essay why your point is relevant. For example 'This is relevant since…' or 'This helps answer the question because…'. Do not assume that your point will be obvious or clear to the reader unless you have made an effort to make sure that it is. Also remember that in long essay answers you are trying to construct an argument in response to a question. This means that you need to present a number of points which support your conclusion.

Key points to remember

- Demonstrate your understanding by using sociological terms.
- Work hard to develop a good essay style and explain why your points are relevant.
- Try to show that you are aware of social change and the impact it may be having on social inequality and difference.

Frequently asked questions

Q. Why are sociologists always worried about social inequality and difference?

A. Sociologists are certainly interested in social inequality because they see it as an important aspect of society, although they have very differing views about how and why it is important. Sociologists are not necessarily 'worried' about social inequality. Some sociologists, such as functionalists, see it as a beneficial feature which is essential if modern industrial societies are to continue to function effectively.

Q. Why do sociologists spend more time talking about class than anything else?

A. Even if this was true in the past, it is almost certainly no longer the case. Sociologists are now increasingly aware that class is only one element, although a very important one, of social inequality in contemporary societies. They are therefore keen to explore the links between class and other forms of social inequality such as gender, ethnicity and age. Moreover, as we discussed in this chapter, there are many sociologists who dispute the importance of class in contemporary society. So despite the popular image of sociology, which sees it as dominated by 'radical' and 'left wing' ideas, it is actually a very diverse discipline. Sociologists nowadays are just as likely to spend more time talking about culture, gender, identity or globalisation. Which one of these they talk about will vary from individual to individual. Of course, they might also be talking about all of these, as sociologists are very aware of the way that social life is influenced by all of these factors!

Q. Why is social inequality and difference synoptic?

A. What sociologists want to understand is how society is organised and functions, and this involves having to see how different elements of society influence each other. In AS and A2 sociology you learn about individual topic areas, but it is important to see how they link together. For example, we can better understand the differences between and within families and households once we have an understanding of social inequality. Ideas about social inequality and difference help us to understand gender differences in the family. Social inequality can explain class differences between families, or the way that family structures and the sharing of resources varies according to the ethnic group involved. A person's role in the family will also depend upon their age.

So social inequality is a very important topic which can link together all of the different topic areas which you have studied in sociology. It will provide you with various ways of explaining the different patterns of social inequality that are revealed by sociological research, for example, inequalities in health, official statistics on crime, or patterns of educational attainment.

Chapter 7

A2 personal study:
a practical guide (Unit 2538)

 **CD-ROM** **7.1**

Key issues in the personal study

What is the personal study?

The A2 personal study is for Unit 2538 of the second year course. Many schools and colleges start preparations for the personal study towards the end of the AS year. The final deadline will be set by the school or college that you attend, but the personal study is sent to the Awarding Body for examination by May of each year.

The personal study itself is an individual piece of research, written up in a format prescribed by the examination board. The personal study counts for up to 15 per cent of the final A2 mark, and is optional. You can either do the personal study or sit an examination on theory and methods (Unit 2537). The aim of the personal study is to replicate the aims of the examination paper on methodology, but in a practical setting. It shows you 'hands on' what research design is like, and as such, what the many problems are with research. The personal study builds on the work carried out for the Research Report at AS level (Unit 2535) and the emphasis is on piloting or trialling a research design, and evaluating the pilot. You will gain marks for the design of your study, rather than the data you collect.

What should the personal study look like?

The personal study should ideally be word-processed, since it will save time later on. You will probably be drafting each part or chapter of the personal study so often that not to word process it and save each draft as a separate file would be a waste of your time in the long run. Your personal study must follow these criteria.

- It is recommended that the personal study is between 2000 and 2750 words long.
- The choice of topic to research is up to you, although you must follow the guidance of your teachers.
- Although the choice of topic is yours, you must make sure that you are safe at all times while carrying out your research and that those you study are also safe.
- For ethical reasons, the Awarding Body will not want you to research a 'vulnerable group' without really thinking and explaining how you can do your research in an ethical fashion.
- You must follow, and show that you are following, the British Sociology Association's (BSA) ethical guidelines for research practice.
- The personal study is divided up into 9 sections: title; contents; rationale; research; evaluation; bibliography; appendix; research diary; annexe.
- The personal study must have a bibliography of all sources used.
- You are required by the Awarding Body to keep a research diary, and to include it with your final project.

∞ Methods Link

A pilot study is a much shorter version of the study, that you try out before the main research in order to test your method. You can make last minute changes and evaluate what you have done.

✓ Top Exam Hint

You need to complete a proposal for your personal study before you undertake it. This is then submitted for approval by the exam board, OCR. It should include the aims, research methods and techniques you plan to use. The personal study advisor will provide advice on your proposal and you should take this into account when undertaking your pilot. This proposal should also be included in the appendix of the main project once completed.

✍ Coursework Suggestion

The annexe includes all the raw data gathered by you during the course of you piloting your method. The annexe MUST be kept, in case it is requested by the exam board, but it is not actually sent up by your teachers unless it is requested for examination purposes. However, you will need to include one blank copy and one completed copy of your research device (questionnaires, etc.).

Why is a diary important?

A research diary is important for two reasons.

1. It is an examination requirement that you submit it with your finished piece of work.
2. It will be useful for you to keep a diary, especially when it comes to writing up the final sections of your project, as it charts your 'journey' from start to finish.

Use the diary for the following, and make sure that you keep it safe and use it right from the start.

- The most important use of the diary will be as a place to log or record problems and issues with your research as you carry out the collection of your data.
- Make a list of all the problems that occurred and mistakes that you made and solutions you think would be useful to a full-blown study; you can use these in the evaluation chapter. If you do not record them, you might be in danger of forgetting them once the end of the project is in sight. Keep a record of what you are doing and how you think it is going
- Record in your diary any books you use or refer to. Make sure you note the author, title, date it was published and what pages you used.
- Record in your diary any other sources such as newspapers or websites you used. This way you will have a running record of everything you looked at ready for the bibliography at the end of the project.
- Record feedback you get from teachers. If you have an individual appointment with your teacher for advice or support, make a note of the issues raised.
- From time to time, maybe at the end of each week, make a quick note of what you have done during that period of time.

Key points to remember

- You will be asked to keep a diary.
- You can choose what to do, with the guidance of your teacher.
- The Awarding Body decides what the sections of your project should be.

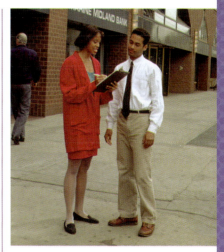

The personal study is an opportunity for you to find out what it feels like to conduct real research.

✓ **Top Exam Hint**

The ethical guidelines provided by the BSA are available from the British Sociological Association website. To access the website to to www.heinemann.co.uk/hotlinks.

Make sure that you follow the guidelines and show that you are doing so in order to gain important evaluation marks. You might like to quote from the guidelines as long as you fully reference what you use.

7.2 | How is the personal study written up?

Part of getting the best grade you can in personal study, as in any examination, is to give the examiners what they want. There are some very simple tips and tricks to follow when writing up your personal study to make it as clear and well presented as possible. This is discussed below.

What does the personal study need to look like?

Make sure your personal study is word-processed, the pages are numbered and that the chapters are in order. The following advice will help you with your presentation.

1. Do not use an arty font or spend ages making a front page. Make it look simple and professional and include the title and your name.
2. Look at how this book and others like it reference the names of sociologists. Look at how our bibliography is presented, and copy the same format.
3. You need to put all quotes in inverted commas.
4. If you are producing quantitative data, make sure that all graphs etc are clearly labelled and each graph has a discussion along with it. They should also be placed within the text.
5. If you are producing qualitative data, put all quotes from your respondents in inverted commas. Change their name for ethical reasons, and say that you are doing this. Make sure you present what they say exactly how they said it in order to make it valid.
6. Always refer back to your aim at every opportunity. Show that everything is relevant to the main focus of what you are trying to do.
7. Make sure you read through your personal study when it is finished, and check your grammar and spelling.

How should it be presented?

- Print it off and treasury tag it all together in the top corner.
- Make sure you include a photocopy of your diary in the appendix.
- The appendix should include a copy of the original proposal for your study.
- Include a contents page.
- Keep a copy printed off and a copy saved to disk just in case.
- Add one blank copy of your research device (i.e. questionnaires, interview schedule, observation schedule, content analysis grid) and one completed copy where applicable.

What should the appendix be used for?

An appendix is a section at the end that allows you to include extra background information. The appendix is not actually marked as such and it is not included in your word count.

- Do not overdo it with an appendix. Only put things in if you need them.
- Make sure a copy of the proposal is included – this is an exam board requirement.
- Do not include something in the appendix instead of putting it in the main project. This is a waste since it can only get marked if it is in the main part of the project itself.
- You may like to include letters asking permission from organisations you might have needed to contact during the course of your research.
- You need to show an example of one questionnaire completed by a respondent but there is no need for you to put every single one in.
- You need to type up (**transcribe**) one interview, if applicable, and present it here to show that you took the research experience seriously.
- You might like to include notes from doing the actual research, although this should all really be included in the diary in the first place.
- Do not include all your data as this will make the project too bulky.
- Include a copy of articles and newspaper sources used. If you need to use them, perhaps in your rationale as a secondary source, then quote from them and fully reference them.

Key points to remember

- Make it look professional.
- Make sure you present your findings clearly, follow the advice above.
- Make sure everything is fully referenced.

❝❞ Key Definition

When we say '**transcribing** an interview' we mean the process of typing up a record of the conversation that took place. Interviews may be tape-recorded or recorded in note-form and permission should be gained from the respondent beforehand. You need to write about this in the methodology chapter and it might be the case that the presence of a recorder actually affects the outcome of the interview in some way. Make sure you transcribe it exactly as it was said, including all the words and noises and half-finished sentences. People do not speak in a perfect way so do not try to fake an interview – it will be easy to spot.

What does each of the chapters do?

What does this mean?

The OCR examination body has pre-set the sections or chapters of your project and you must follow these. Each section does a different thing, and it is important that you find ways to link the sections together so that the project as a whole flows.

1. Front page (title page)
2. Contents page
3. Rationale
4. Research
5. Evaluation
6. Bibliography
7. Appendix
8. Research diary

The main section of the written study is parts 3–5: the rationale (introduction), research and evaluation.

- Rationale – this should include your aims, background focus, methodology and sampling procedures. In other words, this is your justification for why you propose to do what you are doing.
- Research – this should cover piloting, interpretation of the evidence and tentative conclusions.
- Evaluation – this should include your assessment of the overall strategy and design, and ideas for future development of the study.

These sections will help you to structure what you do, how you present it to the reader, and will help you to communicate your ideas more logically. Remember: the aim of the personal study is for you to show your understanding of both the practical and theoretical aspects of pilot research design, and how they both relate together.

What is the rationale?

The rationale is the introduction. As the name suggests, it is where you tell the reader what you are going to be doing and how you will be doing it. In the rationale you are required to state your aims clearly and concisely, and to explain what the point of the research is going to be. Your aims should have a clear, narrow focus as this will be a small-scale pilot. If you are producing quantitative data you will need to clearly state your **hypothesis** in this section.

Background focus

You will also need to include a paragraph about a previous, related study as a background focus to your pilot. You should show what another sociologist has done on the topic that you have chosen. You might present some ideas that you are going to update, or ideas that you will disagree with during the course of your research. This must all be relevant to the point of your particular research. This section 'sets the scene'.

Methodology

As part of your rationale you will need to discuss your methodology. Arguably this could be seen as the most important section of all. After all, the point of doing the personal study is to show how much you understand about the process of carrying out a research pilot. In this section you present your method, sampling techniques, procedures, access and ethical issues. You should discuss strengths and weaknesses and explore the problems and solutions you might encounter when conducting your pilot. Write this in the future tense – you have not done the method yet.

What is the research section?

The research section is where you show and comment upon your findings – the data you have produced. It is vital that you analyse and interpret what you have found, and that you evaluate it. Do not just present it as a fact and not provide any commentary. Go back to your aim and link back to your background focus. What have you found? What do you think it all means?

What is the evaluation section?

The purpose of the evaluation section, the last section of your piloted project, is to take the findings of the previous section and to think about the success of the research as a whole. What did you find? What does it mean? Are there any problems with what you found? Could it have been done any differently? Are there recommendations for any future research? The purpose of a pilot is to review the effectiveness of your strategy and design, and to identify what would need to be changed for a full-blown study.

How are the marks divided up between the sections?

The whole study is marked out of a total of 60 marks, and the marks themselves are divided by the three assessment objectives of the course:

AO1: knowledge and understanding = 28 marks
AO2 (a): analysis and interpretation – 16 marks
AO2 (b): evaluation = 16 marks

Key points to remember

- Evaluation is important to your project and should flow throughout.
- Each section is marked in a specific way.
- Show your 'thinking out' (your reasons and decisions) all the way through.

66 99 Key Definitions

- A **hypothesis** is a statement that can be tested. It should not be a question and it should be as clear as possible. You will need to define carefully any problem words that you use in this statement so the reader understands what you mean.

- **Primary research** means you gather the data yourself. The data would not exist if you did not undertake the project.

- **Secondary data** means you use data gathered by others. The data existed before you carried out the project.

✓ Top Exam Hint

Make sure you get the rationale to a reasonable standard before you do anything else with your personal study. Until your aims are clear, there is no point trying to go any further.

✍ Coursework Suggestions

- Evaluation is very important when you write up your personal study. You must show the difficulties and problems you face, and what possible solutions you should investigate. You must make sure that the project becomes like an ongoing discussion of what you are thinking and what you are trying. Research is like problem-solving, so show the process that you are going through for as many evaluation marks as possible.

- Although your piloted research should be mainly based on **primary research**, you can use a small amount of **secondary data** in order to back up what you find, or to compare and contrast with your findings.

How do you decide what to do?

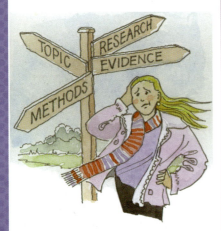

Producing a successful personal study is often a result of finding a clear route through the process of planning your research, carrying it out and writing it up. Do not make the point of your research too complicated or confused, or you will not know what direction to turn in.

✍ Coursework Suggestions

- Most ideas for the personal study that work well are very simple. Do not take on too much. Decide on clear aims, a method that is suitable and a theory that you can see through the eyes of. If you cannot explain your idea in very simple terms, then you might not really understand what you are doing. Do not fall into this trap early on. Spend some time, but make sure you understand what you are doing and what the point of it is. Otherwise, you simply will not be able to write a sensible and meaningful rationale.

- Many students take an old sociology study and play around with it. You could see if it is still true today. You could use a different variable by taking an existing piece of sociological research that did not look at ethnicity or gender and do the research again with the new variable. You could change the location. Take a piece of research done in one location, and try it in another.

What does this mean?

Getting started is the hardest thing about the personal study. Because the decision of what to do is so open, it is very difficult to narrow down the options and to make a decision. Do not worry about this, and most importantly, do not make a quick, rushed decision and then regret it later.

It is also important that your idea is not too big. A real problem every year for many students is that they simply try to do too much, or to take on too many ideas. Aim for a straightforward idea, but try to find something you will be interested in doing. After all, you will be working on this piece of work for a considerable period of time. Make sure you are not going to get bored.

What will you need to decide?

In order to progress, you are going to have to make a few decisions.

- What topic area in sociology will you study? Do you choose a topic you have studied at AS, at A2 or something different?
- What method will you use to test your hypothesis?
- What will your hypothesis be?
- What type of data will you try to produce – quantitative or qualitative?
- Who exactly will you study? Where will you find these people? Will they actually allow you to do your research? How will you gain access to them?
- What theoretical ideas will be most closely associated with your project?

The question is, where do you start? What decision comes first?

Where do you start?

Here are some ideas to consider in helping you to get started.

- What have you enjoyed most in sociology so far? What debates or topics or even theories have interested you most? Can you link a project to one of these?
- You could update an old study that you have been taught and which has interested you. You might wish to see if it is still true, or to try and prove it wrong.
- You could work backwards. Do not think about the topic, but think about the method you might use. Are there any methods you might prefer? You simply might be more interested in them. Are there any methods you just would not want to use? Why?
- Is there a theory that you have enjoyed over the past year? You could try to conduct a piece of research into an idea or concept that the theory is associated with.

- What sorts of people would you enjoy studying the most? Who can you easily get access to?
- Think about what issues are current in the media. Might they form the basis of a project?

What sources can help?

In order to make a decision on what kinds of sources to use, you might try to get hold of the following.

1. A sociology textbook is the simplest source to use. Are there any ideas you are interested in? Use the contents page and the index to find an interesting topic.
2. What about the web? Are there any interesting news stories that you might like to investigate?
3. Can your teacher show you some old projects? Clearly, this project must be your own work, but if you look at what others have done you might see what sorts of things people do each year.
4. Do you get a free local newspaper sent to your home? Do you ever read It? Maybe there are some items of local interest that you could investigate?

Once you have your idea, you will find the rest of the project much easier, but take your time. It is important to get this first stage right.

Key points to remember

- Think about what issues you have enjoyed the most.
- Think about what method and theory you might like to use.
- Make sure you have an ethical idea.

∞ Methods Link

Make sure that whatever you choose to do, it is ethical. Make sure your idea is not going to put you or others in danger and think very hard about the ethical nature of covert methods. Consider the BSA guidelines carefully.

✓ Top Exam Hint

Don't forget: your proposal decisions will be checked very carefully by both your teachers and the exam board through the proposal you submit.

✍ Coursework Suggestion

Do not forget that running throughout this book are these margin boxes with personal study hints and ideas for you to try. You can print them off from the CD-ROM that accompanies the book so you can find them all easily. Also remember that the AS book in this series also has many other ideas for you to think about.

7.5 | How do you decide what method to choose?

What does this mean?

Once you have decided on your aims (what you want to find out) you need to give some serious consideration to the method(s) you want to use. You will need to think about the topic, the data you want and the potential success of anything you try and do.

Your reasons why you have chosen your method(s) should appear in some detail in your methodology section.

What choices do you have available?

The personal study only requires you to choose one or two methods. You must think of the following issues when choosing a method.

- How much time do you have available?
- What other resources might you need – dictaphone, photocopier, computer, video camera?
- Where would the method need to be carried out? For example, if you are doing interviews, would you need a quiet room somewhere?
- What data do you need? Do you need to produce quantitative data or do you need detailed information about people's thoughts and feelings?
- Do not forget that some methods have sensitivity and ethical issues. Can you guarantee to limit or at least to reduce these as much as possible?
- All methods have strengths and weaknesses, but can you make sure that the strengths outweigh the weaknesses?
- You could try and work backwards. Do not think about what method(s) to choose, but rather, what methods you can rule out. Do not forget to have a brief discussion in your methodology chapter not only about those methods you have chosen, but also an analysis of why you rejected others. This is good for evaluation marks.

You will need to answer all these questions in order to be able to decide what to use and why to use it. These questions will also help you in your methodology chapter since you will be required to provide an extended discussion of your choice of method and the reasoning and thinking behind it.

You will also, at all times, need to show your thinking. The personal study should be written as if it is a discussion of the problems involved in doing and planning research, as well as actually showing what you did do.

What methods are available?

There are many methods available to the researcher, and each has its own strengths and weaknesses. You have the following to choose from.

You must decide on what method to adopt and there must be clear reasons for your choice. What sort of data do you want to produce and why?

∞ Methods Link

Remember that many feminist thinkers have rejected quantitative data, feeling that qualitative data is better for 'empowering' those that you study, as people are **reflexive**. If you are going to take a feminist approach in your project, you will need to consider this and discuss it in some depth in your methodology and rationale chapters.

✳ Key Idea

Reflexive/reflexivity

This term is used by Anthony Giddens (1990) to refer to people's capacity for reflection and action. The idea suggests that far from acting passively, human beings have lots of knowledge about how society works, and they use this knowledge in their everyday lives. In this context, the idea implies that interviewees can interact with and question the interviewer, based on their knowledge of society, and therefore empower themselves in the interview situation. Equally, interviewers can use their knowledge of society to direct research. In this way, sociology is constantly evolving. You should consider how your research design will contribute to this by being reflexive and evaluating your pilot, thinking about your method(s) and whether respondents were being honest or telling you what you wanted to hear, for example.

- Questionnaires/surveys: you need to think about whether the questions should be open or closed or both.
- Interviews: they could be structured, semi-structured or unstructured.
- You might wish to do joint interviews (interviews with more than one person).
- Rather than joint interviews you could choose a focus group or interview.
- Covert methods might be unethical, but are there ways in which you might use them?
- Observation: could be participant or non-participant.
- You could study media products using content analysis or semiology.

What will you need to write about?

Whatever method you choose, you will need to be able to justify its use and choice. You will always need to consider and write about the key methodological issues of reliability, representativeness, generalisability and validity.

You will need to write about the following in the methodology section of the rationale.

- Why is your choice the most appropriate for your study?
- How will you carry it out?
- What potential problems can you predict?
- How will you solve potential problems, such as researcher bias?
- How will you gain access to those in your sample?
- How did you choose your sample? What sampling technique or sampling frame did you use?
- Why did you reject other methods?
- Why are you producing the type of data you are creating?
- Make sure you discuss issues of reliability and validity.

Key points to remember

- All methods have both strengths and weaknesses.
- Show your thinking and problem-solving when you write up your method choice in the rationale.

🖎 Coursework Suggestion

Do not forget that every method has problems and you will need to think about these in advance of your actual choice to make sure it is still the most suitable option. Think about PETS: practical issues, ethical issues, theoretical issues and sensitivity issues. How do these relate to your choice of method? Think about probability/non-probability, researcher bias, objectivity and so on.

∞ Methods Link

The Surrey University website has some really useful articles about doing research and using methods that you might find helpful. The website can be found at www.heinemann.co.uk/hotlinks and you will need to look at the sociology homepage to find *Social Research Updates*. This is a series of printable articles by researchers about the process of research. Do not forget to write published material in your own words and reference clearly the names of the authors in your methodology section. Use your diary to take notes and put the full reference in the bibliography.

What goes in the rationale?

What does this mean?

The rationale is like the introduction. As the name suggests, it is where you tell the reader what you are going to be doing and how you will be doing it. In the rationale you are required to state your aims or hypothesis clearly, and to explain what the point of the research is going to be. Do remember however, that OCR suggests this section should be between 500 and 750 words.

What do you need to do?

Be very clear about your aims and objectives. State them as clearly as you can and as early as you can in this opening chapter. Try to really find the easiest description of what you are doing and then explain it in more depth. Say what you think the point of the research would be; in other words, why is it sociological? Why is it interesting?

To illustrate your reasons for choosing your topic you might be able to find a statistic as a secondary source to show that the project has some significance or relevance to modern-day society. Perhaps this could be a government official statistic?

Equally, you might be able to find a newspaper source that links your project to 'real-life'. This could be from a national newspaper or a local one. You could find both in order to try to locate the research into both regional and social contexts.

What must you include?

The OCR specification states that the rationale should include the following:

- a statement of your central research issue or hypothesis to be addressed;
- a clear, concise statement of your justifications for carrying out this study;
- a description, explanation and justification of your research design and the procedures you will use (methods).

You should also take into account the following points.

- Make sure you define all key terms as clearly as possible. This process is known as **operationalisation**.
- Are there names of key sociologists who are important to this research? People you are following, testing, trying to prove right or wrong? Briefly mention them here.

✓ Top Exam Hints

Try the website of National Statistics. It is full of official statistics, organised under topics.

Try *The Guardian* website. There will be lots of searchable detailed articles and the site organises news stories from *The Guardian* around topics and ongoing debates.

These websites can be accessed at www.heinemann.co.uk/hotlinks.

Do not forget those sociological variables – class, gender, ethnicity, age, location, globalisation etc.

66 99 Key Definition

To **operationalise** is to define clearly what is meant by a term and how you intend to use it. This must be made clear in your rationale right from the start.

How should it be written up?

Avoid making lists. Treat the rationale as an extended discussion but try to keep it to one side of typed writing (500 words). It should be a short and clear introduction to what will be coming next. The rationale will have to be written in the future tense as it is written before you have carried out the actual data gathering.

Key points to remember

- Make it clear and to the point.
- Make sure it is obvious what you will be doing and how.
- Make sure your aims have a narrow, clear focus.

7.7 | How do I build a brief background focus?

What does this mean?

As part of the rationale, you have to show what other sociologists have done on the topic you have chosen. You might present an idea that you are going to update, or that you will disagree with during the course of your research. This must be relevant to the point of your particular research and should place your study in context.

What do you need to do?

- You should start by reminding the reader of your aims. This is important, as it will make sure that you link your background focus back to your aims. Remember, this is a 'literature review'. This means it provides the background focus to the study. You must make sure that you use this background focus in the results section.
- Once you have discussed your aims, try to link them to theory. Briefly state your chosen theoretical perspective.
- Make sure that the example you provide is fully referenced in the bibliography.
- Identify a study that most links to your project. It might be that you are doing something different from the named study you have chosen, but that it still links to it. Explain how it links to what you are going to do, as well as providing a brief discussion of what it has to say.
- You might find a named study or example of something your project disagrees with. Spell it out here and show how your project is trying to be different.
- It is important that you do more than simply list all these ideas. Discuss them and show how they compare and contrast.
- Show how your background focus is relevant to your aims, and, most importantly, how what you are doing is similar to and different from the ideas you have presented here.

How should it be written up?

Think of this part of the rationale as basically a small essay. Write it with an introduction, main body and a conclusion. Make sure that it really is, however, a 'literature review' – a background focus. This should help 'set the scene' for your pilot study and is part of your reasons for carrying out your study.

Key points to remember

- Make sure it is a genuine context – it is just the background for your study.
- Try and present ideas that both complement and contrast with what you think you will find.
- Make sure that you use this literature review in the research section, to help you to be evaluative of your findings.

7.8 | How and where do I explain my methodology?

What does this mean?

Arguably this could be seen as the most important part of the rationale. After all, the point of doing the personal study is that you need to show how much you understand about the process of carrying out the pilot. In this section you present your method(s). You should discuss strengths and weaknesses and to explore the problems and solutions you will have when conducting your research.

What do you need to do?

You will need to explain in very precise terms why you are going to use the method that you have chosen. Think of this as an exercise in problem solving. You will need to explain every aspect of your method, why you have chosen it and how you will try to carry it out. Discuss what problems might be involved and how you might solve them.

- Try to locate your project within a theoretical perspective such as **positivism**, **interpretivism** or **realism**. What does your methodology imply you are trying to do, and what sort of knowledge are you trying to explore? Why have your chosen one over the other?
- Explain very briefly, as part of this discussion, why you have not chosen the alternative methodology? Why have you rejected it? Remember, every decision to do one thing, is a decision to reject something else!
- Link the methodological tradition you are locating yourself in with the type of data you will produce. Say why this is the right sort of data for what you want to find.
- Next think about your chosen method(s) and link it to your aims. Start by explaining what the strengths and weaknesses are of the method(s) in general and then go on to explain how these strengths and weaknesses apply in the case of the particular research you will be carrying out.
- Give a sense of why you are not choosing some methods that still might be relevant. Be careful here. Do not just list all methods and reject them in a simplistic way. Clearly some would not be appropriate depending on what you are trying to do, but there are always choices. So, why have you made the decisions you have?
- Remember to offer solutions as to how you will try and overcome problems, such as ethical issues or bias, in the evaluation section.
- Think about your sample. What method of sampling will you choose? Why is it the right choice? Explain exactly how you will carry it out.
- How will you gain access to your sample? Explain how and try to predict potential problems with this.
- Actually show your method in the appendix. Explain why you have chosen the questions you have.
- Try to give a sense of exactly how you will carry out the research, in as much depth as possible.

Things to think about

To explain exactly what you will be doing, think about these issues.

- How will you introduce the aims of the project to your respondents?
- How will you settle and put your respondents at ease?
- If you are recording an interview, how will you explain this to the respondent so they are comfortable?
- Where (what location) will you carry out your research? What are the advantages and disadvantages of this?
- How will you prompt the respondent if you need to? Will you have back-up questions?
- How will you ensure confidentiality?
- How will you treat your respondents with sensitivity?
- How will you try to act and speak when you are with your respondents?

Key points to remember

- Justify every aspect of the strategy and design.
- Every decision to do something is also a decision not to do something else. Make this clear

7.9 | How do I show my results? What goes into the research section?

What does this mean?

Once you have carried out your method, you will be left with lots of data. The question is, what do you now do with it? How do you present your results, and what do you do with them? Here is where you present and analyse your results.

How you present your results differs according to whether you have produced quantitative or qualitative data, but there are some general pointers to follow first.

- Make sure you label everything, even quotes and graphs. It should be obvious what everything means.
- Do not let the 'facts speak for themselves'. They do not. You will need to work quite hard now to explain to the reader what you think you have found out.
- Make sure you start this chapter by reminding the reader of your aims, and link all your findings to each of your aims.
- Make sure that it is clear you have kept to the BSA guidelines in relation to confidentiality and anonymity. Say this at the start. Change people's names, the name of places you went to, etc.

What do I do with quantitative date?

If you have produced quantitative data you will need to present this as tables, graphs or charts. Make sure each has a title, and make sure they mean something by always offering an interpretation. Try to relate variables to each other, rather than simply presenting each separate question as a separate graph. Make sure you comment on each graph. What does it mean? Why do you think you got the answers you did? Make sure you conclude, and use your literature review (background focus) as a resource through which to interpret what you have produced. Evaluate your results. Are there reasons why you might have produced the data that you did?

What do I do with qualitative data?

Make sure you quote directly from those you studied, in *exactly* their own words. Put these in quotation marks to make them stand out. Quotations are not included in your word count, but you don't need to include everything your interviewees said. If you need to shorten what people say then put in omission marks (…) to represent a cut.

Most importantly, comment on them. Compare what respondents say; try to look for patterns, confusions, contrasts. Link what they say to what sociologists in your background focus say. You are advised to provide a sample transcript in the appendix to assist the examiner in judging whether it is an effective research tool.

Make sure that you reflect upon why you think people said what they did. Finally, make it obvious who is saying what. You can identify them by giving them a number or changing their names.

Key points to remember

- Do not just let the facts speak for themselves. They do not.
- Make sure you use your literature review from the rationale as a comparative tool to analyse the results with.
- 'Bounce' results off each other: make comparisons and contrasts, look for patterns and contradictions. Do more than simply show them!

※ **Key Idea**

When you decide to choose some comments over others, you are actually being selective and therefore biased. You have no choice since you cannot show everything, but what about the things you leave out? If someone has decided they are relevant to say to you, do you have the right to cut them? You are setting the questions and then choosing what bits of the answers you like the best. This is called the 'imposition problem'. Try and evaluate your research within this concept.

Where and how do I make conclusions?

What does this mean?

You need to make conclusions in both the research and evaluation sections. There are, in fact, a number of different issues you will need to conclude, now that you have carried out your research, interpreted your data and reflected upon the experience.

What different conclusions are there?

With hindsight, now it is all over, you need to decide

- whether your method was the most appropriate choice
- whether your data was the most appropriate choice
- whether your theory was the most appropriate choice
- what you think your results mean
- how your results compare with each other
- how your results compare with your background focus
- what your results mean for your aim
- how successful the research carried out was
- whether the sampling technique was the best choice
- whether the problems outweighed the solutions or vice-versa
- what you would do differently and why
- what would need to be changed for the real study
- how you think this research might be of benefit to sociology.

You are going to need to develop an answer for each of these questions although, as you can see, they overlap quite considerably. Some of these should be discussed in the research chapter, and some in the evaluation chapter. Some might be appropriate for both, as follows.

How do you conclude in the research chapter?

In the research section you are required to come to some sort of conclusion about the nature of your findings. You will need to answer the following in a clear way.

- Refer to your hypothesis and establish what you have found.
- What do you think your results mean?
- How do your results compare with each other?
- How do your results compare with your background focus?
- What do your results mean for your aim?

In a sense, it does not matter what data you find; it is what you think about your method and how well or badly it went that is more important since the point of the pilot is for you to demonstrate how much you know about methods.

○─○ Methods Link

Try to write in such a way that you are able to show the big difference between what the textbooks say about methods, and what it is like in real life when you try to do research. Show that research is an unpredictable business, full of unexpected problems and difficulties.

You will need to approach your conclusions with sensitivity and maturity.

- Do not make massive generalisations that you cannot support given the size of your sample.
- Do not gloss over any problems; be honest and reflect upon them.
- Do try to think about how the data you produced is selective. You have asked certain things and got what you were looking for. This is called the imposition problem and you might like to reflect upon this.
- Do think about the validity, reliability and representativeness of your research.

How do you conclude in the evaluation chapter?

You will need to answer the following in a clear way.

- How successfully was the research carried out? Refer to reliability, validity, ethical issues.
- Was the sampling technique the best choice?
- Did the problems outweigh the solutions or vice versa?
- What would you do differently and why?
- What would need to be changed for the real study?
- Do you have recommendations for further research?

The point of this chapter is to pull it all together and then to push it all forward, into the future. Try to think about what happens next. What would you do differently? Reflect upon the experience of trying to be a sociologist. How did it make you feel? How did others respond to you? Did they take you seriously? Do not forget to record these feelings in your research diary at the time and refer to your diary in the evaluation chapter.

Key points to remember

- Think about the different sorts of issues you will need to draw a conclusion about.
- Do not forget that concluding comments appear both in the research and evaluation chapters.
- Try to be reflective and self-critical at all times for those important evaluation marks.

What goes in the evaluation chapter?

What does this mean?

The purpose of the evaluation chapter, the last section of your project, is to take the findings of the previous chapter and to think about the success of the pilot as a whole. What are your conclusions? What did you find? What does it mean? Are there any problems with what you found? Could it have been done any differently?

What do you need to include?

For this final chapter it should already be clear to the reader from the previous chapters what you have done and what you have found. You should start the chapter by once more reminding the reader of your original aims and also that this is a pilot.

Since this is the last chapter of the project, it is time to take stock, to assess how you felt the pilot went, what problems really got in the way and how you feel about the actual experience. The worst evaluation you could write would simply gloss over problems and just say that it went well. This is totally unrealistic. Just think of it like this. The examiners know you will have problems and will have made mistakes; they understand that research is an unpredictable and complicated business, so show them how this was true for you. They are actually giving you marks for admitting mistakes, as long as these are not too trivial and as long as you offer solutions.

✍ Coursework Suggestion

You could write this section under the headings of the previous sections, or under the sub-headings you have used throughout. Use these as side-headings through which to organise your thoughts.

Evaluation of the methodology

- Were your aims reasonable?
- What would you change?
- Was your method the right choice?
- Did you measure what you set out to measure?

Evaluation of the research section

- Did the strengths outweigh the weaknesses or the other way around?
- Was it the right choice of method? Would you still use this for the full-blown study?
- Did the sampling work as it was intended to? Would it be changed?
- Were the problems you predicted actually present, or were there unforeseen problems that occurred?
- What would you do differently?
- What went well?
- Is your method valid?
- Is your method reliable?

- Is your method representative?
- Were there any issues with objectivity?

Please note that you still need to include evaluation all the way through the project, as well as in this section. Like a good essay, don't leave all the evaluation until the end. Also at the start of the evaluation section, make sure that you make a comment on the nature of your sample. Discuss in some detail what sorts of people responded – what the 'make-up' of the sample was. Did you have any **non-responses**? Was there any **sample attrition**?

Make sure that you fully discuss ethical issues. You must include a brief discussion in your methodology of how you will try to avoid ethical problems, but in this chapter you should go back to these and think about whether or not you were successful. Do some of the BSA guidelines conflict and contradict with other more practical problems?

- Might informed consent lead to a Hawthorne effect where respondents do what they think you want them to?
- Respecting confidentiality might mean there are some things you cannot write up in your project.
- Some people might ask you to turn off your tape recorder. What will this do for your data?
- Some questions might be uncomfortable and might lead to sensitivity problems.
- People might not respect you since you are young; they might not take the research seriously.
- You might have an imposition problem since you are going to be setting the questions and therefore getting what you want from people. Consider what you do not ask. Are you just collecting data in a biased way to prove you are right?
- Did you lead people towards certain answers? Did you have interviewer bias?

Key points to remember

- Evaluate under the headings of the previous chapters.
- Discuss ethical issues.
- Do not forget to finish the project and establish what you would do differently for the full-blown study.

---

66 99 Key Definitions

- **Non-response** means, quite literally, potential respondents who do not take part – they 'do not respond'. If too many respondents drop out, then this might affect your data.

- **Sample attrition** refers to the situation of people dropping out during the course of the research. They have taken part in some aspects, but have left before the end. It is a bit annoying when this happens, but remember those BSA guidelines. People have the right to refuse! Make sure you discuss this in the results.

✓ Top Exam Hint

Reflect upon who was in your sample by thinking about the key sociological variables – class, gender, ethnicity, age, location etc. Did you get the people you wanted to? How might these variables affect their answers?

✍ Coursework Suggestion

As we have said before, research is a messy and unpredictable business and the general rule is that what can go wrong probably will go wrong. If you are reading this before carrying out your research do not start to get worried. This is just how it is, so you must reflect this reality in what you comment on in this chapter.

✳ Key Idea

The British Sociological Association (BSA) says that research must allow respondents:

- to choose freely to be involved
- to not be harmed or upset in anyway
- to have their privacy respected
- to understand what they are volunteering for
- to understand they can say 'no' at any time
- to understand what the point of the research is.

7.12 Pushing your grades up higher

In this section we will simply summarise the key points from this chapter. Follow the advice this book gives you and make sure you use this as a checklist. This information is also available on the CD-ROM to be printed off. Use it as a checklist and keep it in your folder. Tick off each piece of advice once you feel you have successfully completed it.

- Make it look professional and check your punctuation, spelling and grammar.

- Make sure everything is fully referenced.

- Make sure you get the rationale to a reasonable standard before you do anything else with your personal study. Until your aims are clear, there is no point trying to go any further. Make sure it is obvious what you will be doing and how.

- Always refer back to your aims at every opportunity; show that everything is relevant to the main focus of what you are trying to do.

- Try to find the simplest, shortest and clearest way to explain what you are doing, in as ordinary a language as possible. You will need the sociological depth, but try also to be as clear as possible.

- Do not forget those sociological variables – class, gender, ethnicity, age, location, etc.

- Make sure you define all key terms as clearly as possible. This process is known as 'operationalisation'.

- Do not forget that every method has problems – you will need to think about these in advance of your actual choice to make sure it is still the most suitable choice.

- You will always need to think and write about the key methodological issues of reliability, representativeness, generalisability and validity.

- Show your thinking and problem-solving when you write up your method choice in your methodology section.

- In the research chapter, go back to your literature review – what have you found and how does it link to your background focus? What have you found and what did they find? Do you agree or disagree and why might this be the case?

- Make sure you present your findings clearly, follow the advice given.

- Follow, and show that you are following, the British Sociology Association's (BSA) ethical guidelines for research practice.

- The Surrey University website has some really useful articles about doing research and using methods that you might find helpful. The website can be found at www.heinemann.co.uk/hotlinks and you will need to look at the sociology homepage to find *Social Research Updates*.

- Try the National Statistics website at www.heinemann.co.uk/hotlinks. It is full of official statistics, organised under topics. You are sure to find something interesting here.

- Try *The Guardian* website at www.heinemann.co.uk/hotlinks. There will be many searchable detailed articles and the site organises news stories from *The Guardian* around topics and ongoing debates.

- Research is a messy and unpredictable business and the general rule is that what can go wrong, will go wrong. But, don't worry. You should reflect this reality in what you comment on in the evaluation chapter. Evaluate your project in every chapter. Think of your project as an exercise in problem-solving. What are you trying to do, and how? What are the problems and difficulties that might get in the way? What are you going to do about them? If you write like this, then it will tie the project together since it will be full of self-reflection and criticism.

Key points to remember

- Try to see your project as an exercise in problem-solving.
- Use your aims all the way through the project as a way of being relevant and clear, and bringing it all together.

Frequently asked questions

Q. How do I decide on what to do?

A. This is the most difficult part of the project. Once you have the idea, then you can really make a start but until you do it is very difficult to know where the inspiration might come from. Think about what you would find the most interesting. Do not do something because it is the first thing you have thought of. You will be working on your personal study on and off for a few months so it must be able to keep you interested and motivated. Look at textbooks and think about the sorts of things that sociologists do. Make sure your aims are focused, simple, clear and concise – do not take on too much.

Q. How should my personal study be presented?

A. Word-process everything since you will probably re-draft your work a number of times, it is a false economy to do anything else. Read through your work when it is finished to make sure it reads as one document. Make sure that all sources are fully referenced in a bibliography. Number all the pages. Do not use bulky folders, just treasury tag it all together. Follow the sections provided by the exam board. Include a contents page, a bibliography and your research diary. Do not overdo it on the appendix if you have one.

Q. What should go in the appendix?

A. You should include one blank copy and one completed copy of your questionnaire or an interview schedule. Transcribe one interview, but do not include every single one. Include your research proposal that you submitted to the exam board.

Chapter 8

A2 examination skills

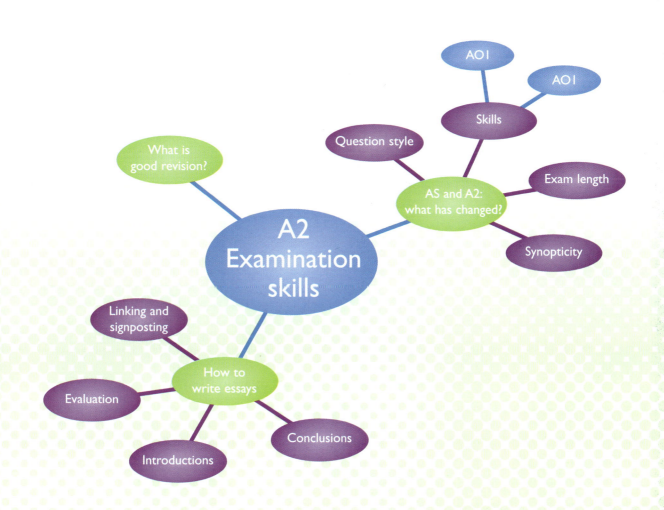

8.1 Key issues in developing good exam skills. What will the exam look like?

What does this mean?

It is important to know the sort of examination you are working towards. You already have an idea of what sociology exams look like, since you have already taken AS exam papers. Let us remind ourselves what the AS exam consists of.

- Unit 2532 (individual and society) was an hour long and you chose one question from two 4-part questions.
- Unit 2533 (culture and socialisation) was one hour and 30 minutes long and you could choose either one or two 2-part structured questions from a choice of 4 different topics, all within this general, overall theme.
- Finally, if you did the exam rather than the coursework for the methods part of the course (unit 2534) you had an hour examination using one data response question.

The A2 examination is similar in that different modules or 'units' ask for different things from you, both in terms of time and in terms of what the paper actually looks like. You will need to tackle the different types of questions in slightly different ways.

- Unit 2536 is on the theme of 'power and control' – the paper is one hour and you answer a traditional essay question (called an 'unstructured' essay question). Each topic has two choices, and you are required to answer **one** from the following topics: crime, education, health, popular culture, welfare and social policy, and protest and social movements.
- For unit 2537 (if you do not do the coursework this year) you will have an examination on applied sociological research skills, as you possibly did for the AS course. This examination is an hour and 30 minutes long and you answer two questions. One question is a data response, and one is a discussion about research design.
- Finally, unit 2539 is what we call the 'synoptic' exam and it is on the theme of social inequality and difference. This exam is one hour and 30 minutes and you answer **one** from two data response questions. You use the theme of inequality and difference in order to explore wider issues about inequality, methods and how these issues link to everything else you have studied over the past two years (see chapters 5 and 6 for more details).

How different is the A2 examination?

Clearly, the questions are asking you to produce more-detailed pieces of writing, that is more-extended discussions of ideas and concepts, but you are still basically manipulating the same elements or ingredients as before. You still have:

- theory
- key words
- named examples
- evaluation.

The ingredients of sociology remain the same, but you are now required to do different, or at least more-detailed, things with them. You have, after all, had an extra year by the end of the course with which to become accustomed to using them. You are now being asked to:

- write more
- produce more depth
- show more evaluation
- show more connections between ideas and issues.

What tricks are there to writing a good answer?

You are expected to produce a more-detailed response. This is not the same thing, though, as simply writing more words, although in the case of the longer essay questions on units 2536 and 2539 you will need to do this as well. You are actually being asked to consider things more fully; to show a deeper insight, a more-rounded understanding. You should not just compare theories with each other, but go further and try to see how and why theories say what they do.

Some of the following ideas might help you to make a more-detailed answer.

1. Try to think about the underpinning debates that most theories battle over.
   - macro/micro
   - freewill/determinism
   - feminism/malestream
   - consensus/ conflict.
2. Try to show that you can link theories to the political ideologies and values that underpin them. Show the bias at work in the views they have of society.
3. There is usually a hidden methods issue behind most sociological questions. For example, this might be an issue of how we might measure or define something. Try to spell this out in your writing. This is what we refer to as a synoptic skill and is formally tested by question (c) on the final synoptic paper on inequality and difference. But, remember: methods links are everywhere.
4. Try to locate the theoretical ideas in the time period that they come from. What theories propose are a reflection of when they were written and what society was like at that time. It may very well be different now. If you think this, then say it. Be confident enough to say that you think something is out-of-date, as long as you say why.
5. Make a distinction between social problems and sociological problems.

As you can see, A2 answers are about depth. They are about looking at things in more detail and showing more understanding and sensitivity.

Key points to remember

- The A2 exam asks you to use the same basic ingredients of sociology as the AS exam.
- The A2 course requires you to look at issues in more depth.
- The A2 course asks you to be more sensitive to the underpinning reasons behind why theories say what they do, rather than simply learn them off by heart at a surface level.

✓ **Top Exam Hints**

- A really important way to make sure you produce a good exam answer is to make sure that you do a very quick plan of your time in the exam, and that you also plan your answers. In section 8.3 of this book, you will find some advice on how to do this.

- Use these four ingredients as a simple way to quickly plan essay answers under timed conditions: theory, key words, named examples, evaluation.

- Divide up a piece of A4 paper into four boxes – one for each of the ingredients. Make a list of the ideas that you will need to use to answer the question and then number them. This is a very simple yet effective way to plan an essay.

- Use these ingredients (theory, key words, named examples, evaluation) as a checklist through which to evaluate your own answers. Re-read your work and try to see how much of each ingredient you use and how evenly spaced throughout your answers they are.

Writing a good exam answer is like being a juggler, you need to keep lots of ideas and concepts going all at the same time.

What skills are needed for the A2 course?

What does this mean?

When you learn sociology, as with all other subjects, you are not just learning a body of knowledge, but you are practising what to do with it. The exam asks you not only to remember things, but also to be able to do things with this knowledge. To truly show and prove that you understand something you need to be able to manipulate it..

Therefore the A2 exam is different from the AS exam in terms of *skills*. A skill is a practised ability; you are able to show the degree of ease with which you can do the required task. In A2 sociology, you are required to know about sociological ideas, and you are also asked to show the ease with which you can do things with the ideas.

What skills are important?

The OCR sociology specification divides up skills into three main areas:

- Assessment Objective 1 (AO1) – the skills of knowledge and understanding
- Assessment Objective 2a (AO2a) – the skills of interpretation and analysis
- Assessment Objective 2b (AO2b) – the skill of evaluation.

What is knowledge and understanding?

The OCR specification says that the skill of knowledge and understanding can be seen as three related elements.

- **The nature of sociological thought**: how we use ideas to think about society; theories, macro- and micro-perspectives; how values might affect sociological thinking; looking at order and control and power; looking at how sociological ideas might affect and influence social policy.
- **Knowledge and understanding of methods and research skills**: how sociologists create data; the strengths and weaknesses of their methods of data collection; problems in carrying out research etc.
- There are important themes that run throughout all sociological thinking which students need to both know and understand – power, control, socialisation, identity, culture, inequality etc. These are important since they are the 'tools' that sociologists use to think about the world they are studying.

What are interpretation, analysis and evaluation?

These skills, arguably, are harder than those of knowledge and understanding, and in some senses they are much more 'creative' and 'imaginative'; they also probably take longer to get to grips with and to feel comfortable in demonstrating.

Students need to be able to show they can:

- take ideas, theories and pieces of data/sources and show what they mean, and relate other sociological ideas to them

Like every other skill, you have to train to do well in sociology. You need to practise the action you are trying to perfect so that it can then actually become a skill. A skill is simply something that you can demonstrate with some ease. You are trying to pass exams by showing what you know, so get used to manipulating the ingredients of sociology as much as possible.

✓ **Top Exam Hints**

In AS, the emphasis was more upon AO1, but in A2, you will need to have a much more developed sense of AO2.

- discuss the strengths and weaknesses of ideas, theories and research
- organise evidence in such a way as to make an argument
- understand the role of values and bias in the arguments of others
- use theories and concepts to understand different topics and issues.

As you can see, these skills are very *active*; they are about you being able to use sociological ideas in various ways.

What other important elements make up A2 sociology?

You will need to get used to being much more free thinking this year. You should be able to see the connections and interrelationships between the ideas from one topic and another, and see the connections between aspects of society. Sociology has always been like this – there have always been lots of connections between the ideas and the topics, but at A2 sociology you will actually be tested on this. This is called **synopticity**.

There are also some very important 'integral elements' in the whole of your sociology course, which must be a foundation for everything that you do. These are theories, methods, key concepts and the connections between topic areas using these. As you know, sociology has a number of ingredients and you are being assessed on the ease with which you can show your understanding of them, their connections and and how you can manipulate them into an exam question answer.

Finally, the OCR specification identifies two 'core themes'. These will underpin all that you do. They are the things that make sociologists see society how they do. The core themes are the ideas of *socialisation, culture and identity*, and the ideas of *differentiation, power and stratification*. These exist everywhere in all sociology – in every theory, every case study and every topic.

What does the specification say about 'skills'?

The OCR specification identifies specific 'skills' that concern how sociology students acquire and handle what we refer to as 'evidence'. This is important for sociology as a whole and equally important in the exam given the synoptic emphasis on research methods. To summarise, you are required to show that you can:

1. assess the nature of evidence
2. evaluate different ways of investigating society
3. evaluate the over-all design of an enquiry
4. interpret data
5. apply theories and concepts to data and evidence
6. identify significant trends from data
7. organise your ideas in a logical and well-structured fashion

These skills are important for the research methods papers at both AS and A2 levels, but are also vital for the data response questions that you might answer in the A2 examinations.

Key points to remember

- There is more to 'doing sociology' than just remembering and repeating things.
- Evaluation is a really important skill at A2.
- You must make sure you understand what the A2 exam requires of you to be able to demonstrate that you can manipulate sociological ideas.

● **Synoptic Link**

Use the terms that the exam board says are 'themes' in order to be synoptic. These themes or 'synoptic tools' include socialisation, culture, identity and power, inequality, stratification, differentiation. Try to see how they underpin every topic, both at AS and at A2.

8.3 | How should I divide up my time in the exam?

What does this mean?

It is important to remember that examinations are not really about how much you know, or how much you can remember, but rather, they are more about what you can demonstrate. They are about what you can get out of your head and onto that exam paper, as long as it is relevant. You must always actually directly address and answer the question set. You will be required to demonstrate a number of things:

- how much you know
- how much you understand
- how you can interpret exam questions
- how you can apply your knowledge
- how you can evaluate
- how you can directly answer the questions set.

This last skill or technique is really important. It does not matter how good you are at the other skills listed, if you cannot give the examiners what they want from you, you will not do yourself justice. A key factor in providing good examination answers is to think about the time on offer.

What should you do at the start of the exam?

During the first few minutes of the examination, spend the time thinking. Read the paper. You must not simply rush into the exam, turn over the paper and start writing without fully considering the questions in front of you. Spend time now, to save time later on.

1. *Do not start writing straight away!* This is hard, especially when you see lots of others people around you in the hall doing just this. Be brave – you have a plan! When you do start putting pen to paper it will be to quickly plan first. Spend time now to get it right. Remember though that you have roughly a minute per mark for each question, so don't dwell for too long on your plan.

2. *Do read the questions.* Read all of them, and more than once. Highlight the key words of the question. Think about the command words of the title; what is it actually asking you to do? Look at the key words in the titles; which words will need defining in your answer? What theories would be associated with the words? What other issues link in?

3. *Now check the items on the paper (if they are provided).* Read them two or three times. Get a pen and highlight key words. Look at the author and the date, if it is provided. What does this tell you? While you are reading the items, make some notes on the item at the side. What does it mean? What key words come to mind? Do you know of any studies that might agree or disagree with the item? What would theories say?

✓ Top Exam Hints

- Try getting past exam papers from your teacher and practise this advice over and over again.

- *Do have a watch in front of you.* This is an obvious piece of advice, but an absolutely essential one! Make sure you know how long you have and how long to spend on each question. Look at your time. Do not assume that your watch and the exam hall clock will say exactly the same time.

4. *Make a choice of essay question (if applicable).* Consider both the questions. Do not assume you know what they mean and fall into the trap of writing what you *think* you are being asked, rather than what you are *actually* being asked.

5. *Now start quickly brainstorming.* Start by remembering the key sociological variables: class, gender, age, culture, identity, location, ethnicity, and globalisation. How might these help in your answers? What about the synoptic words (see section 5.4). How can they be applied? Think about the studies you have learned.

6. *Finally think about the introduction and the conclusion.* Think about the formula for writing good introductions and conclusions (see section 8.6). Start to think about what the question is asking you, and what your approach will be to tackle it.

All this can be achieved in a few minutes, but you must make sure that you practise doing it a few times before you actually have to do it for real.

What about the rest of the time?

The unit 2536 paper is only an hour long, whereas unit 2539 is one hour and 30 minutes. Both require you to write an essay style answer. For unit 2536 you spend the whole hour writing the essay, including your planning time, but for unit 2539 you have:

- Two items. You will need to go through these once you have read and re-read the questions.
- The first two (6 mark) questions refer you to the two items provided. Make sure that you lay your answers out so that it is clear what two separate points you are making. You can probably aim to answer these in about 6 minutes each – a minute per mark.
- Question (c) will be a methods question since this is a major synoptic link, and it is worth 12 marks. Use about 12 minutes to answer this. Present it clearly so that you 'identify' and then 'explain' the first point, leave a space, and then do the same for the second. You might actually like to write the words 'identify' and 'explain' to make sure you are answering the whole of the question. This is vital.
- Question (d) asks you to use 'wider sociological knowledge' and, in doing so, to be synoptic. Make sure you practise this as part of your revision and that you can do this in about 22 minutes (remember: it is worth 22 marks so should take a minute per mark).
- The final essay question should take you about 44 minutes to complete as it is worth 44 marks.

As you can see, you do have time but make sure you use it wisely and follow these guidelines.

Key points to remember

- Do not start writing straight away.
- Make sure you create a simple, quick plan.
- Make sure you think about what the questions are asking you to do.

✓ **Top Exam Hints**

- There are two final things that you need to remember to do with your time:

  o You will need a couple of minutes at the end to actually read through what you have produced.

  o If the unit you are sitting has a long 'essay style question' then you will need to spend about 40 minutes on the actual essay question, including a few minutes at the start planning the answer in a little bit more depth than you did at the start. If you are doing unit 2536 make sure you make a careful and considered choice and use the first few minutes of planning wisely. You will not have any data supplied to look at in the form of an extract or Item, so concentrate instead on the key words in the essay and establish what it really wants from you.

- Use the four ingredients of sociology as a way to plan your essay answers. Divide up a piece of A4 paper into four boxes, one for each of the ingredients. Make a list of the ideas that you will need to use to answer the question and then number them. This is a very simple yet effective way to plan.

- Another thing you can try while writing homework or class essays is to use your revision cards as a plan. Put all the theories and case studies onto cards and then sort them into those that are relevant for the essay title you are writing. Simply arrange them on the table in the order you think flows best, and then you can start writing. Simple!

8.4 | How do I write good essays?

What does this mean?

The purpose of an essay-style question is to allow you to enter into an extended discussion of what you have learned in your two years of sociology. There are some important elements to writing good essays:

- being able to understand sociological ideas
- being able to describe sociological ideas in an accessible fashion
- being able to manipulate sociological ideas together in order to form an answer to a specific question
- being able to structure your answer in a clear and logical way
- being able to communicate effectively in writing.

A good essay must provide an answer to the question set. The answer should take all the relevant sociological elements and put them together in such a way that a logical and sensible answer emerges. You are showing the reader that you have understood the point of the question and what sociologists would think about the issue in as clear a fashion as possible.

What are command words?

All essay questions and, in fact, all exam questions of any sort, are made up of two important elements.

- **Key sociological words**: these are important sociological ideas that will need to be defined in the introduction and then used throughout the answer to demonstrate your relevance in answering and addressing the question set.
- **Essay command words**: these are the words in the title that tell you what sort of essay is required from you; they tell you what the point of the essay is.

Command words do different things as you'll see below, and the point of writing an essay is that you give the reader what the question asks you to give them. You can identify what this is through the command words. In unit 2536 and unit 2539 section (e) the questions will always contain the same command words; 'Outline and assess…'

Outline: this term indicates that you are required to enter into descriptions of ideas and concepts. You should show good knowledge and understanding. This part of your answer should be quick, short and to-the-point.

Assess: this term indicates that you are being asked to do more than simply show knowledge. Here you are being asked to do things with the knowledge you have – to manipulate it in some way. This term shows that you are being asked to sum-up and weigh-up evidence for different view points and evaluate the ideas you are using.

It is important that you do what is being asked of you. You should think about what the essay question (or whatever exam question it might be) is actually asking from you.

What makes a good answer?

Good answers to essay questions should follow this checklist.

- Does the introduction answer the question set and use the key words from the title?
- Does the main body start in a logical place?
- Does the main body address and answer the question set?
- Does the main body use the command words and the key words from the title?
- Is the order logical?
- Does the answer flow? Is there linkage between paragraphs?
- Are key terms used for depth throughout the answer?
- Are key terms defined within the flow of the writing?
- Is the content up-to-date and relevant to the question set? Is it clear that your writing answers the question?
- Does evaluation run all the way throughout the answer?
- Are enough studies and theories used for depth?
- Does the conclusion sum-up the argument and debate and does it answer the question set?
- Are spelling, punctuation and grammar satisfactory?
- Does the essay draw out synoptic links (for unit 2539)?

Key points to remember

- Essays must actually answer the question set.
- Exam questions show you what they want from you by the command words they use.
- Essays must follow the checklist above in order to produce a good answer.

How can I show good evaluation skills?

What does this mean?

By evaluation we often mean criticism. In sociology, we mean something more specific:

- making criticisms
- pointing out that there might be problems in evidence
- showing that there are comparisons between ideas
- showing that there are contrasts between ideas
- saying what is good about an idea
- saying what is useful about an idea
- having an opinion, which we can backup with evidence.

Evaluation is a really important skill, and it is actually very hard. In fact, along with learning about strange new theories, it is having to be evaluative that students often find quite challenging if they are new to sociology. But, do not worry. In time, students actually end up liking evaluation – it is a really important thing to be able to do, and something that few other subjects really focus on. What more could you want than to have the opportunity to actually criticise what you are learning?

Why is evaluation important?

Sociology is marked and assessed according to certain skills, as set out by the examination boards. We collect these skills together, and call them 'Assessment Objectives' (AO). There are two sets of skills, evaluation being very important for the second set:

- **Assessment Objective 1**: knowledge and understanding
- **Assessment Objective 2(a)**: interpretation and analysis
- **Assessment Objective 2(b)**: evaluation.

The first set of skills are the main focus for the AS course, and the second set become more important as you move from AS to A2.

Even if you end up doing the exam and never thinking about sociology again, and even if you forget in time the ideas you were taught, evaluation skills will be really important for the rest of your life. (See section 8.8).

How can you be evaluative?

It might be useful to identify different types of evaluation that you might like to try. These could act as a checklist that you might use to think about the quality of the answers you are producing.

✓ Top Exam Hints

- In the exam, some questions require you to be more evaluative than others. Questions that ask you to 'assess' are asking you to be evaluative.

- Evaluation will also give you depth and detail in any question that is not simply a short-answer question. If you can show an awareness of why two theories or two studies disagree, then this is understanding as well as evaluation.

☀ Key Idea

This emphasis upon evaluation is central to what C. Wright Mills calls the 'sociological imagination' – the distinctive worldview that sociology gives us.

1. Use theories to criticise other theories.
2. 'Think through the eyes of theories'. Imagine what it would be like to think in a particular way.
3. Make methodological criticisms; attack a study for how it carried out its research.
4. Use 'real life' examples. Argue that an idea or theory might not be true or might be true because an event in the contemporary world provides us with evidence that we can use to access what sociologists are saying.
5. Use historical examples to support or criticise a theory for saying something whereas history might agree or show something else has happened.
6. Some named sociologists did research in order to 'prove' or 'disprove' other research; make sure you spell out these links.
7. Use synoptic tools to think about a theory or study: link an idea to class, gender, culture, identity, power etc, and in doing so you can discuss it in more depth, and in interesting ways.
8. Make a note of when the idea, study or theory was invented. If it was a long time ago, this will help you to think about its use today.
9. You could say not only what is bad about an idea, but also what is good about it.
10. You could try and point out political biases and value judgements behind the theory. Some ideas might be left or right wing, and this might affect how the proponents see society.
11. Another really impressive thing to do is to try to 'assess the contribution' made to sociology by a theory. Try to say what we would miss or lack if the idea had not been invented in the first place.

Conclusion – thinking like a sociologist

As you can see, evaluation is really important for your exam, and also really important if you want to think like a sociologist.

Key points to remember

- Make sure evaluation runs all the way throughout essay answers. Do not just leave it until the end.
- Make sure that you try to use different types of evaluation – vary it a bit.
- Try to spell out evaluation, do not assume the reader can recognise it. Make it obvious by using signposted phrases (see section 8.7).

✓ **Top Exam Hint**

Use the ways of evaluating on this page. Try them out and see if they work for you. They will take time to master, but will improve your exam answers once you have.

8.6 | How can I write good introductions and conclusions?

What does this mean?

Something that many students find difficult is the beginning and end of their essay answers. This is actually quite a hard skill to master, but it is an important one.

- The introduction is the first thing to write. Where do you start? How can you get over having a blank sheet of paper staring back at you? The introduction is the first thing to be read by the examiner, so it has got to be interesting; you need to make an impact right from the start.
- Since the introduction is first, you will need to explain what your answer is all about – this means that you need to know what you are going to write, before you actually write it. In other words, you will have to plan before you write the introduction (see section 8.3 for information on how to make a plan).
- You will need to address the question all the way through your answer, but you must actually answer the question finally at the end in the conclusion.
- The conclusion has to pull together all the interwoven threads of your essay in a concise, reasoned judgement of the initial question.

What do essays do?

Think about what the purpose of an essay is. Its purpose is to answer a question, but also to take the reader along a journey to the answer at the end. Your job is to be the guide, but to a certain extent you are also the referee between different sides. You must get the reader to the end, but then weigh up the battle and decide on the winner if you can.

In essence you need to do four things when writing an essay:

- say what you are going to write
- write it
- remind the reader what you wrote
- decide on what the answer to the question is.

Are there any tricks to introductions?

In order to get the introductions and conclusions right, there are a number of things you can do. The following structures or formulae will help you write good introductions and conclusions.

For introductions, you must make sure that you do the following.

- Begin with an opening 'seductive sentence or phrase' that awakens the interest of your reader; a sentence that takes the essay title and explains how and why it is an 'important' title for sociology or even for society. You might try to link the title to a current world event or show why the title is sociologically significant. 'Seduce' your reader; show them it is worth reading your answer by giving them a taste of what is to come.

- Re-write the aims of the essay in your own words. You might start this by saying 'the aim of this essay is to…'. Show that you understand the point of the question. You can demonstrate here what you think the different interpretations of the question are.
- Define the key words from the question. Not the command words (see section 8.4), but the key sociological words. Show that you understand what the words mean and how they link to the debate in the title. You might also want to think about other key words that link to the title and define these as well. Show your reader what you think the question is about in as clear a way as possible.
- Give a sense of essay order and structure. Say what you will be looking at first, second, third etc. Show what the main disagreement is and say which side you will look at first. You might like to link these 'sides' of the answer to different theories or to different sociologists.
- Raise potential problems or issues that underpin the essay title. Most have these; for example, a problem defining a word or a problem measuring something. Spell these out for evaluation marks at the start of your answers.

Make sure that the introduction sets the scene of the essay. Its purpose is to explain to the reader what you understand to be the point of the question. What do you think you are being asked to do? What are the key sociological issues that are part of the question?

Are there any tricks to conclusions?

For conclusions, you must make sure that you do the following:

- In order to make it obvious to the reader, you could start the conclusion by saying 'In conclusion…'.
- Briefly summarise what the general argument is. Remind the reader what they have read, but only as a short sentence or two. Do not repeat too much, and certainly do not make lists.
- Explain why there might be different sides to the debate you have described. Why are the sociologists disagreeing? What are they disagreeing over exactly?
- Actually answer the question set – make sure you outline and assess.
- Suggest ways forward. What have sociologists not looked at? Can we combine ideas together?

The point of the conclusion is to do more than just summarise; it should directly comment on the extent to which the question is answerable. Avoid ambiguous statements such as 'the answer will depend on the type of sociologist or theory'. Avoid this; your examiner will have heard it all many times before. Show exactly what the disagreement is, rather than simply say that there is one. Of course the examiner will know that there is a debate, otherwise how could you write the essay in the first place?

Key points to remember

- Plan the essays before you start writing, so you can make sure that the introduction and the conclusion link together.
- Follow the formulae given in this spread.
- Practise writing introductions and conclusions as part of your revision.

✓ Top Exam Hints

- Once more the four key ingredients of sociology come in here. Use them in your introductions as a way of getting depth, especially the idea of having to define key words right from the start.

- Try practising only writing the introductions and conclusions to essay answers. Time yourself. You could try to write six introductions and conclusions in a one-hour period.

- Many students ignore introductions and conclusions. They go straight into the main body of the essay, and actually disregard answering the question at the end. Another common mistake is that students spend too long on the introduction; they actually introduce the introduction. Go straight into explaining what you think the point of the title means. Be direct, but also be thorough.

8.7 How can I get my essays to flow?

What does this mean?

A good essay is a discussion rather than a list of points. It is important that you can move from point to point in a smooth way. Your essay should have a structure and an order that is not just a random list of unconnected points.

What tricks are there?

Try the following ideas.

- Make sure you always plan your answer (see section 8.3). An effective way to do this is to use the four ingredients of sociology (see section 8.1) and to brainstorm what ideas link to your title. Number the ideas in the order you wish to present them before you start.
- You could always start with the 'for' argument and then do the 'against' and show that this is what you are doing. This is a simple but effective structure for some essays to show an argument.
- You could say 'referring back to the question' as a way to show the reader when you are addressing the question.
- You could start the main body with a paragraph on the theory that agrees the most, and then link this to a relevant study.
- You need to make sure that evaluation runs throughout the answer, not just at the end.
- Use the command words from the title over and over again to link what you do back to the title (see section 8.4).
- Use the key sociological words from the title that you defined at the start of your introduction throughout the answer, in order to link what you do back to the title (see section 8.6).
- You might like to try to spell out comparisons and contrasts between ideas or thinkers in order to connect the different ideas you are using together.

What are 'signpost phrases'?

In order to develop and to show the reader that you have good evaluation skills, you might wish to use certain sorts of phrases that allow your answers to show evaluation, sound sophisticated and clearly allow your answers to flow from one point to another. Such signpost phrases might be:

- the relevance of this is …
- this is similar to/different from xxx because …
- the implication of this is …
- this can be applied to …
- the usefulness of this is …
- this is confirmed by …

- a strength of xxx is …
- the main problem with this is …
- this can be seen by …
- I disagree because …
- this assumes that xxx is true, however …
- this makes little sense because …
- this lacks evidence because …
- this does not take into account …
- this is questioned by …

For conclusions (see section 8.6) you might like to use these phrases:

- to sum up …
- having weighed up …
- the balance of the argument suggests that …
- the weight of the evidence suggests that …
- to conclude, …

These phrases will give your answers an important 'gloss'; they will allow you to link your points together rather than simply jumping from point to point. Remember, it must be an ordered discussion rather than simply a list of points.

These phrases will also help your evaluation skills. It is much better to spell out evaluation than to simply **juxtapose**. In other words, it is better to evaluate ideas, rather than simply placing opposite ideas together and leaving it up to the reader to figure out that they are opposite to each other. Spell everything out as much as you can. This is how you get good marks in essays.

Key points to remember

- Do not make lists, but try to make points connect with each other.
- Use the signpost phrases.
- Make sure you plan so you do not forget something and then end up just adding it in when you do think of it later during the writing of the answer.

✓ **Top Exam Hint**

Think of other phrases that allow your essays to flow from point to point.

● **Synoptic Link**

- Some of these 'signpost phrases' can also be used to demonstrate good synoptic skills in your writing. You can actually start sentences by saying 'synoptically-speaking …' to really highlight to the reader what you are doing.

- Remember, you do not have to wait until the unit 2539 exam in order to demonstrate your ability to write and think in a synoptic fashion; to make relevant and interesting links between ideas and topics. This is an important sociological skill even if it was not actually being tested in the exam. By doing this you can create a wider answer and can also provide a more original answer to gain your reader's interest.

❝❞ **Key Definition**

To **juxtapose** means to place two opposites together without commenting on why they are opposites.

8.8 | How will my essays be assessed?

What does this mean?

In order to produce a good essay answer you need to understand what you are being required to do. You need to understand how you will be assessed and what your examiners are looking for. Then you can give it to them.

What skills are important in essay writing?

As we have discussed elsewhere, the A2 examination is based upon three sets of skills:

- **Assessment Objective 1**: knowledge and understanding
- **Assessment Objective 2(a)**: interpretation and analysis
- **Assessment Objective 2(b)**: evaluation.

Each of these skills asks different things of you.

- **Knowledge**: What do you know? What ideas have you learned?
- **Understanding**: How much do you understand the ideas you have learned?
- **Analysis**: Can you pull the ideas you have learned apart? Can you question them?
- **Interpretation**: Can you take what you have learned and apply it in different ways to other ideas and to questions set?
- **Evaluation**: Can you **assess** the ideas you have learned?

How will I be assessed?

The two types of questions we can refer to as being 'traditional' essay questions appear on units 2536 and 2539. Unit 2536 is worth 15 per cent of the A2 grade, whereas the synoptic unit 2539 is worth 20 per cent.

For unit 2536 you will be asked to answer a single essay question which will start with the term 'outline and assess'. This will be worth up to 60 marks. Within this 60 marks:

- there is up to 28 available for knowledge and understanding (AO1 skill);
- up to 16 for interpretation and analysis (AO2 (a) skill);
- and, again, up to 16 for the separate skill of evaluation (AO2 (b) skill).

The OCR examination board marks your essays in a series of 'bands' or 'grade descriptors' that describe, in a qualitative fashion, what the marks might actually mean about the quality of the answers you are producing.

For the AO1 skill (knowledge and understanding):

- 0 = no evidence of the skill in question.
- 1–7 = limited evidence of the skill. Too much commonsense and not enough sociology; too much description; limited knowledge.

Do not try to guess what the exam questions might be or what the examiners want. Concentrate on reading the questions and really understanding what they are actually asking you to do. Take your time.

✓ **Top Exam Hint**

While answering exam questions, it is important to think what the skills you are being asked to display might be. Think about the command words (see section 8.4) being used. What does the question want from you?

❝❞ **Key Definition**

To **assess** means to weigh up; to consider all the views on and interpretations of something.

- 8–14 = limited evidence of the skill. Some basic relevance; lack of depth and lack of examples. Too few points explored.
- 15–21 = reasonably good levels of depth, detail and knowledge shown. Largely relevant. Some good use of key terms and most aspects of the question explored.
- 22–28 = a wide answer. Clear and detailed. Lots of ideas, discussed in a relevant fashion. Few if any spelling and grammar mistakes.

For the AO2(a) skills (interpretation and analysis):
- 0 = no evidence of the skill in question.
- 1–4 = limited interpretation. Maybe only one side or point covered, maybe a limited problem with accuracy.
- 5–8 = limited. Some basic and relevant material chosen and used.
- 9–12 = broad skills employed – balanced and quite sensitive. Appropriate analysis.
- 13–16 = detailed. The title is addressed throughout. Relevant and appropriate material selected throughout; focuses on a number of balanced points.

For the AO2 (b) skill (evaluation):
- 0 = no evidence of the skill in question.
- 1–4 = limited. Too much commonsense and not enough sociology; maybe anecdotal and only one point of evaluation offered.
- 5–8 = limited. Some basic evaluation, but largely simple juxtaposition. Does not flow through the whole answer.
- 9–12 = broad skills employed – largely balanced and quite sensitive. Good conclusion.
- 13–16 = detailed. The title is addressed throughout. Strong conclusion. Sophisticated evaluation.

In the synoptic unit 2539, the final essay-style question is worth 44 marks from the total 90 marks available for the paper as a whole. This paper does more than unit 2536, and combines the essay question with some short answer and data response questions.

The 44-mark essay-style question also starts with the command words 'outline and assess' but is marked slightly differently from the 60-mark questions in unit 2536. It is marked twice; once for knowledge and understanding (out of 20) and once for evaluation (out of 24). This is significant as it shows that on the synoptic paper evaluation is more important than knowledge.

Key points to remember

- Make sure you understand what the marks are given for so you can give the examiners what they want from you.
- Make sure you understand what the different skills mean, since you will be asked to demonstrate them.
- Make sure you understand what makes a good exam answer, so you can provide it.

✳ **Key Idea**

Philosopher Nietzsche referred to philosophy as the 'art of mistrust' and the same can be said for sociology. Evaluation is important to how sociologists think about society, and what they make of the ideas of other sociologists. Evaluation is an important skill for you to show in your exam. You will be assessed on it.

✓ **Top Exam Hint**

How do you demonstrate, as it says here for 13–16 marks, 'sophisticated evaluation'? One simple way to do this is to use the key signpost phrases as described in this book in section 8.7. Another way is to use evidence to support the points you make in your answer.

8.9 | What makes good revision?

What does this mean?

Many students take revision for granted. It is assumed that students know what to do when they are 'revising' and that they know how to do it. Perhaps this is not the case. We should think hard about revision; what is the purpose of it and what are the best ways of going about it?

What makes good revision?

Learning is not the same for everyone. We might learn in different ways, and we may need to revise in different ways too. Each of us will find some ways of working and studying easier than others, but we should experiment and try them all out to see what works best.

Think about how you learn best.

- Do you find it easier to remember when you write things down?
- Do you need to colour-code revision notes to help you think about them?
- Do you need to shorten your notes? Are there just too many to learn without doing so?
- Do you need to write things out from your head, not just read them?

We are all different learners, and it is important to remember this. You must find out what works for you; this might be different from what works for other people. But you must also make sure you experiment with different types and techniques of revision. Otherwise how will you really know which method actually suits you the best? Despite the fact that we are all different, there are some basics that we can use as a starting point in order to think about good revision.

Some things that you should do:

- make sure that you engage in what is called 'active' revision, which is about writing and doing (not passive reading, which really is not the most effective way to revise)
- make sure that you have all the notes from your folder shortened, perhaps onto index cards ready to revise from
- think about evaluation skills while you revise; practise making lists of how theories and thinkers would criticise each other
- practise past exam papers obtained from your teachers
- try to revise by manipulating the four key ingredients of sociology (see section 8.1); try to link theories to words to studies etc.

Some things you should not do:

- do not simply rely upon reading as revision; it is not effective since it is too passive
- leave sorting out and shortening down your notes until the end of the course; making notes is not really revision; do not fool yourself into thinking that it is
- do not see revision as a process of putting things into your head; see it as a process of taking things out of your head and putting them onto paper. This is after all what you are doing in the exam, so it is what you should be doing in the revision also!

Conclusion

Think about learning to drive a car. You do not sit in your kitchen and look out of the window at the car. You get in the car, and you actually drive; you practise the thing you are actually being tested on. It should be the same in exams. Practise past papers; practise writing things from memory.

Experiment with all these ideas and try to find what works best. Make sure you do this early on in your course, especially for mock or trial exams. Do not leave revision until the final examination; it might be too late then for you to experiment with different revision methods. You do not want to be experimenting with revision before the real exam and you should already know what works best for you.

Key points to remember

- Make sure your revision is 'active'.
- Make sure you practise past essay questions.
- Make sure you find what works for you!

Frequently asked questions

Q. Why is evaluation so important this year?

A. Evaluation is important for four reasons: it is a higher-weighted skill than at AS in the exams you will be sitting; it is an important ingredient in the writing of a quality essay answer; it is vital for a detailed piece of coursework; and finally, it is an essential part of being synoptic.

Q. What does a good essay look like?

A. A good essay is really about how you manipulate the four key ingredients of sociology that we have spent so much of this book demonstrating to you. A good essay should start by clearly showing the reader that you understand the point of the question and that you can clearly define the key terms in the question itself. You should then start with the theory most associated with the 'for' side of the answer, and write about the theory in depth using the key words. This enables you to show knowledge and understanding, but it is vital that you spend some time relating this back to the topic or issue of the question itself in order that it is relevant. You must provide studies or named examples as evidence of this theoretical point of view, and then proceed to show comparisons and contrasts with other theories on the same issue. Ensure that you use the key words at all times for depth. Finally, summarise and try to solve the issue – actually answer the question, whatever it was.

Q. How can I revise essay technique?

A. There are a number of different things you can do. You can brainstorm essay questions, five to ten minutes per title, as if you were in the actual exam. Use the four ingredients of sociology in order to think about what content should go in each answer. You can also practise simply writing introductions and conclusions for each essay title, following the formula presented in this chapter. Finally, make sure you practise timed essay questions. Nothing can substitute for practice according to the timed conditions of the real thing.

Bibliography

Abbot, D. (1991) *Culture and Identity*, London, Hodder and Stoughton.

Abbott, P. and Wallace, C. (1990) *An Introduction to Sociology*, London, Routledge.

Airchison, D. and Carter, 1 (1990) 'Battle for Language', *Geographical Magazine*.

Allen, H. (1987) *Justice Unbalanced: Gender, Psychiatry and Judicial Decisions*, Milton Keynes, Open University Press.

Althusser, L. (1971) *Lenin and Philosophy and Other Essays*, London, New Left Books.

Althusser, L. (1971) 'Ideology and Ideological State Apparatuses' in *Lenin and Philosophy and Other Essays*, London, New Left Books

Appadurai, A. (1992) 'Disjunction and Difference in the Global Cultural Economy ' in *Theory, Culture and Society* 7, 295-310

Arber, S. and Ginn, J. (1991) *Gender and Later Life*, London, Sage.

Atkinson, J. M. (1978) *Discovering Suicide – Studies in the Social Organization of Sudden Death*, London, Macmillan.

Aziz, R. (1997) 'Feminism and the Challenge of Racism' in Mirza, H. (ed) (1997) *Black British Feminism: A Reader*, London, Routledge.

Baldwin, J. and Bottoms, A.E. (1976) *The Urban Criminal*, London, Tavistock.

Ball S. (1994) *Education Reform: A Critical and Poststructuralist Approach*, Buckingham, The Open University

Ball, S. (1981) *Beachside Comprehensive: A Case-Study in Secondary Education*, Cambridge, Cambridge University Press.

Ball, S. (1990) *Politics and Policy Making in Education*, London, Routledge.

Ball, S. (ed.) (1990), *Foucault and Education and Power: Discipline and Knowledge*, London, Routledge.

Barker, M. (1981) *The New Racism*, London, Junction Books.

Bauman, Z. (1996) ' Culture on Praxis' in S. Hall and P. du Gay (eds) *Questions of Cultural Identity*, London, Routledge.

Beck, U. (1992) Risk Society, London, Sage.

Becker H S (1971) 'Social class variations in the teacher-pupil relationship' in

Becker, H. (1963) *Outsiders*, New York, Free Press.

Bernstein, B. (1975) *Class, Codes and Control*, London, Routledge and Kegan Paul.

Biggs, S. (1993) *Understanding Ageism*, Milton Keynes, Open University Press.

Bilton, T. et al, (2002) *Introduction to Sociology*, London, Palgrave.

Blair, T. (1993) *Why Crime is a Socialist Issue*, New Statesman.

Blanchflower, D. and Sargent, J. (1994) cited in Bovey, *The Times*, 20 March 1994.

Bordua, D. (1961) 'Delinquent Subcultures: Sociological Interpretations of Gang Delinquency' in *Annals of the American Academy of Political and Social Science 338*.

Bouden, R. (1974) *Education, Opportunity and Social Inequality*, New York, John Wiley and Sons.

Bourdieu P. and Passeron J.C. (1977) *Reproduction in Education, Society and Culture*, London, Sage.

Bourdieu, P. (1986) *Distinction: A Social Critique of the Judgement of Taste*, London, Routledge

Bowlby, J. (1946) *Forty Four Juvenile Thieves*, London, Tindall and Cox.

Bowles, S. and Gintis, H. (1976) *Schooling in Capitalist America*, London, Routledge and Kegan Paul.

Box, S. (1983) *Crime, Power and Mystification*, London, Tavistock.

Boyd, W. L., and Gibulka, J.G. (1989), *Private Schools and Public Policy: International Perspectives*, London, Falmer Press.

Bradley, H. (1996) *Fractured Identities: Changing Patterns of Inequality*, Cambridge, Polity Press.

Braverman, H. (1974) *Labor and Monopoly Capital*, New York, Monthly Review Press.

Britton, A (1989) *Masculinity and Power*, Oxford, Blackwell.

Burkitt, I. (1991) *Social Selves: Theories of the Social Formation of Personality*, London, Sage.

Campbell, A. (1981) *Girl Delinquents*, Oxford, Blackwell.

Castells, M. (1997) *The Information Age: Economy, Society and Culture*, Oxford, Blackwell.

Castles, S. and Kosack, G. (1973) *Immigrant Workers and Class Structure in Western Europe*, Oxford, Oxford University Press.

Chambliss, W. (1973) 'Vice, Corruption, Bureaucracy and Power' in Chambliss, W. (ed) *Sociology Readings in the Conflict Perspective*, pp353-378, Reading, Mass, Addison-Wesley.

Chambliss, W. (1988) *On the Take: From Petty Crooks to Presidents*, Indianapolis, Indiana University Press.

Chibnall, S. (1977) *Law and Order News*, London, Tavistock.

Clarke, J. (1975) 'The Skinheads and the Magical Recovery of Community' in Hall and Jefferson (eds) *Resistance through Rituals: Youth Sub-cultures in Post War Britain*, London, Hutchinson.

Clark, J (1996) 'Insights: Gender and Education Revisited', *Sociology Review*, vol. 5, no. 4.

Clarke, M. (1990) *Business Crime*, Oxford, Polity Press.

Cloward and Ohlin (1961) *Delinquency and Opportunity*, New York, Free Press.

Cohen, A. K. (1955) *Delinquent Boys*, New York, Free Press.

Cohen, P. (1984) 'Against the New Vocationalism' in Bates et al (1984) *Schooling for the Dole?*, London, Macmillan.

Cohen, S. (1973) *Folk Devils and Moral Panics*, London, Paladin.

Coleman, J., and Hoffer, T., (1987) *Public and Private High Schools: the Impact of Communities*, New York, Basic Books.

Commission for Racial Equality (1998) Education and Training Factsheet

Commission for Racial Equality (1999) Housing and Homelessness Factsheet

Connell, R. (1987) *Gender and Power*, Oxford, Polity Press.

Crewe , I. (1992) 'Changing Votes and Unchanging Voters' in Electoral Studies, Dec.

Croall, H. (1992) *White Collar Crime*, Milton Keynes, Open University Press.

Crompton, R. and Jones, G (1984) *White-collar Proletariat: Deskilling and Gender in the Clerical Labour Process*, London, Macmillan.

Bibliography

Crompton, R. and LeFeuvre, N. (1996) 'Paid employment and the changing system of gender relations: a cross-national comparison', *Sociology*, vol. 30, no. 3.

Crompton.R. (1998) *Class and Stratification*, Cambridge, Polity Press.

Cully, L. (1986) *Gender Differences and Computing in Secondary Schools*, Loughborough, Department of Education, UK

Davies, B. (1989) *Frogs, Snails and Feminist Tales: Pre-school Children and Gender*, Sydney, Allen & Unwin.

Davis, K. and Moore, W. E. (1967) 'Some Principles of Stratification', in Bendix and Lipset (1967) *Class, Status, and Power*, London, Routledge and Kegan Paul.

Davis, M. (1990) *City of Quartz*, London, Verso.

Dean, H. and Taylor-Gooby, P. (1992) *Dependency Culture*, Hemel Hempstead, Harvester-Wheatsheaf.

Deem, R. (1990) 'Women and Leisure', *Social Studies Review*, vol. 5, no. 4

Denscombe, M. (2003) *Sociology Update 2003*, Leicester, Olympus Books UK.

Department of Social Security (DSS) (1997, 2001) *Households Below Average Incomes: A Statistical Analysis 1978-1994/5*, London, The Stationary Office.

Derrida, J (1991) *A Derrida Reader: Between the Blinds*, Hemel Hempstead, Wheatsheaf.

Devine, F (1992) *Affluent Workers Revisited: Privatism and the Working Class*, Edinburgh, Edinburgh University Press.

Donald, J. and Rattansi, A. (eds) (1992) *'Race', Culture and Difference*, London, Sage.

Douglas, J. (1967) *The Social Meanings of Suicide*, Princeton, New Jersey, Princeton University Press.

Douglas, J.W.B. (1964) *The Home and the School*. London, MacGibbon and Kee.

Durkheim, E. (1979) *Suicide: A Study in Sociology*, London, Routledge and Kegan Paul. (First published 1897).

Eisenstadt, S. (1956) *From Generation to Generation*, Chicago, The Free Press.

Equal Opportunities Commission (1993) *Facts about Women and Men in Britain*, 2003, Manchester, EOC.

Esping-Anderson, G. (1990) *The Three Worlds of Welfare Capitalism*, Cambridge, Polity Press.

Etzioni, A., (1995) *The Spirit of Community*, London, Fontana.

Falk, P. (1994) *The Consuming Body*, London, Sage.

Featherstone, J. and Hepworth, M. (1991) 'The Mask of Aging and the Postmodern Life Course' in M. Featherstone et al. (eds) *The Body: Social Process and Cultural Theory*, London, Sage.

Featherstone, M. (1990) *Consumer Culture and Postmodernism*, London, Sage.

Finn, D. (1987) 'Leaving School and Growing Up' in Bates et al (1987) *Training Without Jobs*, London, Macmillan.

Fitzgerald, M. and Hough, M. (2002) Policing For London Survey, http://www.policingforlondon.org/

Foucault, M (1997) *Discipline and Punish*, London, Tavistock.

Foucault, M. (1978) *History of Sexuality*, Vol 1, London, Penguin.

Gans, H. (1974) *Popular Culture and High Culture*, New York, Basic Books.

Gardner H. (1995) Cracking Open the IQ Box in Fraser S., (eds) *The Bell Curve Wars*, London, Basic Books

Garfinkel, H. (1967) *Studies in Ethnomethodology*. Cambridge, Polity Press.

Gelsthorpe, L. and Louck, N. (1997) *Understanding the Sentencing of Women*, Home Office Research Study 170.

Giddens, A (1990) *The Consequences of Modernity*, Cambridge, Polity Press.

Giddens, A. (1999) *Runaway World*, The BBC Reith Lectures, London, BBC Education.

Gill, Owen (1977) *Luke Street*, London, Macmillan.

Gillborn and Gipps (1996) *Recent Research on the Achievements of Ethnic Minority Pupils*, London, HMSO.

Gillborn D. (1990) *Race, Ethnicity and Education: Teaching and Learning in Multi-ethnic Schools*, London, Unwin Hyman.

Gillborn, D. (2002) *Education and Institutional Racism*, London, Institute of Education, University of London.

Gillborn, D. & Youdell, D. (2000) *Rationing Education: Policy, Practice, Reform and Equity*, Buckingham, Open University Press.

Goffman, E. (1959) *Presentation of Self in Everyday Life*, Harmondsworth, Penguin.

Goldthorpe, J.H., Llewllyn, C. and Payne, C. (1987) *Social Mobility and Class Structure in Modern Britain*, Oxford, Clarendon Press.

Goffman, E. (1963) *Stigma: Notes on the Management on Spoiled Identity*, Harmondsworth, Penguin.

Goldthorpe, J. (1980) *Social Mobility and Class Structure in Modern Britain*, Oxford, Clarendon Press.

Goldthorpe, J. (1984) *Women and Class Analysis: a Reply to the Replies*, Sociology, Vol 18, No 4.

Goldthorpe, J. et al (1969) *The Affluent Worker in the Class Structure*, Cambridge, Cambridge University Press.

Gordon, D. (1976) 'Class and the economics of crime' in Chambliss and Mankoff (1976) *Whose Law? What Order?* New York, John Wiley.

Griffin, G. (ed) (1995) *Feminist Activism in the 1990s*, London, Taylor and Francis.

Hall, S. (1992) 'New Ethnicities' in Donald, J. and Rattansi, A. (eds), Race, *Culture and Difference*, London, Sage.

Hall, S. et al, (1978) *Policing the Crisis, Mugging, the State and Law and Order*, London, Macmillan.

Hall, S. (2000) 'Who Needs Identity?' in Du Gay, P., Evans, J. and Redman, P., (eds) *Identity of a Reader*, London, Sage.

Halsey, A. H., Heath, A. and Ridge, J.M. (1980) *Origins and Destinations*, Oxford, Clarendon Press.

Hannerz, U. (1996) Soulside: *Inquiries into Ghetto Culture and Community*, New York, Columbia University Press.

Hargreaves, A. (1995) 'Kentucky Fried Schooling", *The Times Educational Supplements*, Issue 4109

Hargreaves, D.,(1967) *Social Relations in a Secondary School*, London, RKP. Social Trends 27 and 29 (1999). London, HMSO.

Heath, A. (1992) 'The Attitudes of the Underclass', in Smith, D.J. (ed), *Understanding the Underclass*, London, Policy Studies Institute.

Heaton T., & Lawson, T. (1996) 'Education and Training', Macmillan, London

Hebdige, D. (1979) *Subculture: The Meaning of Style*, London, Methuen.

Hechter, M. (1976) *International Colonialism: The Celtic Fringe in British National Development*, London, Collins.

Heidensohn, F. (1996) *Women and Crime*, Basingstoke, Macmillan.

Heidensohn, F. (2002) 'Gender and Crime' in *Oxford Handbook of Criminology*, 3rd edition, Maguire, M., Morgan, R., and Reiner, R. (eds), Oxford, Oxford University Press.

Held, D. (1980) *Introduction to Critical Theory*, London, Hutchinson.

Held, D. (1995) 'Liberalism, Marxism and Democracy' in S. Hall et al. (eds) *Modernity and its Future*, Cambridge, Polity Press.

Herstein, R. & Murray, C.A. (1994) *The Bell Curve: Intelligence and Class Structure in American Life*, New York, The Free Press.

Hey V (1997) *The Company She Keeps: an ethnography of girls' friendship*, Buckingham, Oxford University Press.

Hirschi, T. (1969) *Causes of Delinquency*, Berkeley, California, University of California Press.

Hobbs, D. (1986) *Doing the Business*, Oxford, Oxford University Press.

Hoggart, R. (1957) *The Uses of Literacy*, London, Chatto and Windus.

Holdaway, S. (1983) *Inside the British Police*, Oxford, Blackwell.

Home Office, (2002) *Race and the Criminal Justice System*, London, HMSO.

Howarth, C. et al (1999) *Monitoring Poverty and Social Exclusion 1999*, York, Joseph Rowntree Foundation.

Jenkins, R. (1996) *Social Identity*, London, Routledge.

Jones, A. (1993) 'Becoming a "girl": post-structuralist suggestions for educational research', in *Gender and Education*, vol. 5, no. 2.

Jones, S. (1994) *The Language of the Genes*, Harmondsworth, Penguin.

Joseph Rowntree Foundation (1995) *Inquiry into Income and Wealth*, York.

Karabel, J., and Halsey, A .H. (eds) (1977), *Power and Ideology in Education*, New York, Oxford University Press.

Karstedt, S., and Farrell, S. (2003) Paper presented to the British Academy Annual Conference, Sociology and Social Policy Section.

Keddie, N. ed. (1973) *Tinker, Tailor*, Harmondsworth, Penguin.

Kellner, D. (1997) ' Culture' in D. Owen (Ed.) *Sociology after Postmodernism*, London, Sage.

Kellner, D. (2002) *Marxian Perspectives on Educational Philosophy: from Classical Marxism to Critical Pedagogy*, London, Collins.

Kelly, A. (1985) *The Construction of Masculine Science*, British Journal of Sociology of Education, Vol. 6, 133-54.

Kelly, A. (1987) *Science for Girls*, Milton Keynes, Open University Press.

Kenway, J. (ed.) (1994), *Economising Education: The Post Fordist Directions, Geelong, Aus, Deakin University*.

Kirby, M. (1996) *Sociology in Perspective*. Oxford, Heinemann.

Kluckholm, C (1951) ' The Concept of Culture' in D. Lerner and H. D. Lasswell (eds) *The Policy Sciences*, Stanford, Stanford University Press.

Lacan, J. (1977) *Ecrits: A Selection*, London, Tavistock.

Lash, S., and Urry, J., (1994) *Economies of Signs and Space*, London, Sage.

Lea, J. and Young, J. (1990) *What is to be Done about Law and Order? Crisis in the Nineties*, London, Pluto Press.

Leach, E. (1964) *Rethinking Anthropology*, London, Althone Press.

Lewis, J. and Piachaud, D. (1992) 'Women and poverty in the twentieth century,' in Glendinning, C. and Millar, J. (eds) *Women and poverty in Britain: The 1990s*, Hemel Hempstead, Harvester Wheatsheaf.

Lewis, O. (1961) *The Children of Sanchez*, New York, Random House.

Lewis, O. (1968) *La Vida*, Harmondsworth, Penguin.

Lockwood, D (1958) *The Blackcoated Worker*, London, Allen and Unwin.

Lombroso and Ferrero (1895) 'The criminal type in women and its atavistic origin' in *The Female Offender*, London, Fisher Unwin, reprinted in *Criminological Perspectives* (eds) McLaughlin, Muncie, Hughes, London Sage, 2nd edition 2003.

Mac an Ghail, M. (1994) *The Making of Men: Masculinities, Sexualities and Schooling*, Buckingham, Oxford *University Press*.

Marris, P. (1996) The Politics of Uncertainty, London, Routledge.

Marsh, I. (ed.) (1999) *Sociology: Dealing with Data*, Harlow, Longman.

Marshall et al (1988) *Social Class in Modern Britain*, London, Hutchinson.

Marshall, G., Swift, A., and Roberts, S. (1997) *Against the Odds?*, Oxford, Clarendon Press.

Marshall, G. and Swift, A. (1993)' Social class and social justice', British Journal of Sociology, June.

Marsland, D. *Welfare or Welfare State?*, Basingstoke, Macmillan.

Matza, D. (1964) *Delinquency and Drift*, New York , John Wiley and Sons.

McLeish, D. (1993) *Key ideas in Human Thought*, London, Bloomsbury.

McRobbie, A. (1978) 'Working Class girls and the culture of femininity' in *Women Take Issue: Aspects of Women's Subordination*, Birmingham, Women's Study Group/Centre for Contemporary Cultural Studies.

Mead, G. H. (1934, 1967) *Mind, Self and Society*, Chicago, University of Chicago Press.

Mead, M. (1935) *Sex and Temperament in Three Primitive Societies*, New York, Morrow.

Mednick, S., et al (eds), (1987) *The Causes of Crime: New Biological Approaches*, Cambridge, Cambridge University Press.

Merton, R. (1968) *Social Theory and Social Structure*, New York, Free Press. (Originally published 1949).

Miles, R. (1989) *Racism*, London, Routledge.

Miller, D. and Swanson, D. (1958) *The Changing American Parent*, New York, Wiley.

Miller, W. (1958) *Lower Class Culture as a Generating Milieu of Gang Delinquency*, The Journal of Social Issues, 14, 3, 10.

Mills, C. Wright, (1980) *The Sociological Imagination*, Harmondsworth, Penguin.

Mirrlees-Black, C, et al., (1998) *The 1998 British Crime Survey*, London, Home Office.

Mirza, H. (1992) *Young, Female and Black*, London, Routledge

Mirza, H. (ed) (1997) *Black British Feminism: A Reader*, London, Routledge.

Modood, T. (1988) 'Black Racial Equality and Asian Identity', *New Community*, 21 (2), pp183-193.

Modood, T. (1990) 'British Asian Muslims and the Salman Rushdie Affair', Political Quarterly, 61 (20), pp143-160

Moore, R. & Hickox, M. (1992) 'Education and post-Fordism: A new Corresponsance' in Brown, P. and Lauder, H (eds), *Education for Economic Survival: From Fordism to Post-Fordism*, London, Routledge.

Morgan, R. (2002)'Imprisonment – A Brief History, The Contemporary Scene, and Likely Prospects' in *The Oxford Handbook of Criminology*, 3rd Edition, Oxford, Oxford University Press.

Morris, L. (1994) *Dangerous Classes: The Underclass and Social Citizenship*, London, Routledge.

Morris, T. (1957) *The Criminal Area*, London, Routledge and Kegan Paul.

Muncie, J., and McLaughlin, E., (1996) *The Problem of Crime*, London, Sage.

Murray, C. (1989) *The Emerging British Underclass*, London, IEA.

Newburn, T. (2002) 'Young People, Crime, and Youth Justice', in *The Oxford Handbook of Criminology*, Oxford, Oxford University Press.

Nixon, S. (1996) *Hard Looks*, London, UCL Press.

Oakley, A. (1981) *Subject Women*, Oxford, Martin Robertson.

Oppenheim, C. (1993) *Poverty: The Facts*, 2nd ed, London, Child Poverty Action Group.

Pakulski, J. and Waters, M. (1996) *The Death of Class*, London, Sage.

Parsons T and Bales R F (1955) *Family, Socialization and Interaction Prcoess*, New York, The Free Press.

Parsons, T. (1954) *Essays in Sociological Theory*, New York, The Free Press.

Parsons, T. (1973) *The American University*, Cambridge, Mass., Harvard University Press.

Patrick, J. (1973) *A Glasgow Gang Observed*, London, Methuen.

Pearce, F. (1976) *Crimes of the Powerful. Marxism, Crime and Deviance*, London, Pluto.

Pearson, G. (1983) *Hooligan: A History of Respectable Fears*, London, Macmillan.

Pfohl, S. (1992) *Death of the Parisite Café: Social Science (Fiction) and the Postmodern*, Basingstoke, Macmillan.

Phillips, Z., and Bowling, B. (2002) *Racism, Ethnicity, Crime, and Criminal Justice*, in The Oxford Handbook of Criminology, Oxford, Oxford University Press.

Pinch, S. (1993) 'Social Polarisation: a comparison of evidence from Britain and the United States' in *Environment and Planning*, Vol 25, No 6, pp779-95.

Plummer, K. (1979), 'Misunderstanding Labelling Perspectives' in Downes, D., and Rock, P., (eds) *Deviant Interpretations*, London, Martin Robertson.

Pollak, O. (1950) *The Criminality of Women*, Philadelphia, University of Philadelphia Press.

Pring, R. (1990) 'Spanning a Deep Cultural Chasm' *The Guardian*, 13th February 2001.

Bibliography

Pryce K. (1979) *Endless Pressure*, Harmondsworth, Penguin.

Radford, T. (2003) 'Meet criminals who cost the UK £14bn : the middle class', *The Guardian*, 12th September 2003.

Reay, D., David, E.M., Ball, S. (2004) *Degrees of Choice*, Stoke-on-Trent, Trentham Books.

Reiner, R. (1994) 'Policing and the Police', in Maguire, M., et al (eds) *The Oxford Handbook of Criminology*, Oxford, Oxford University Press.

Reiner, R. (1996) 'Crime and control: an honest citizen's guide', *Sociology Review*, vol 5, no 4.

Rex, J. and Moore, R. (1967) *Race, Community and Conflict*, Oxford, Oxford University Press.

Rex, J. and Tomlinson, S. (1979) *Colonial Immigrants in a British City*, London, RKP.

Robertson, R. (1992) *Globalisation*, London, Sage.

Rose, S., Lewontin, R., and Kamin, L. (1984) *Not in Our Genes*, Harmondsworth, Penguin.

Rosenthal, E. and Jacobson, L. (1968) *Pygmalion in the Classroom*, London, Holt Rinehart and Winston.

Routh, G. (1980) *Occupation and Pay in Great Britain*, 1906-79, London, Macmillan.

Rowbotham, S. (1973) *Woman's Consciousness*, Man's World, Harmondsworth, Penguin.

Saunders, P. (1990) *Social Class and Stratification*, London, Routledge.

Saunders, P. (1996) *Unequal but Fair? A Study of Class Barriers in Britain*, London, IEA.

Savage, M. et al (1992) *Property, Bureaucracy and Culture: Middle Class Formation in Contemporary Britain*, London, Routledge.

Savory, C. (2002) *Colleges and Curriculum 2000*, London, NATFHE/Institute of Education.

Scott, J. and Fulcher, J. (1999) *Sociology*, Oxford, Oxford University Press.

Segal, L (1990) *Slow Motion: Changing masculinities, Changing men*, London, Virago.

Sharpe, S. (1976) *Just like a Girl*, Harmondsworth, Penguin.

Shaw and McKay (1942) *Juvenile Delinquency and Urban Areas*, Chicago, University of Chicago Press.

Sklair, L. (1993) *Sociology of the Global System*, Baltimore, John Hopkins University Press.

Smart, C. (1989) *Feminism and the Power of the Law*, London, Routledge.

Smith, D.J. and Gray, J. (1983) *Police and People in London*, London, PSI.

Smith, R., and Wexler P. (1995), *After Postmodernism; Education, Politics and Identity*, London, Falmer Press.

South, N. (2002) 'Drugs, Alcohol and Crime' in *The Oxford Handbook of Criminology*, Oxford, Oxford University Press.

Spender, D.(1983) *Invisible Women: The Schooling Scandal*, London, Women's Press.

Stephens, P. et al (2001) 'Teacher Training and Teacher Education in England and Norway: Competent Managers and Reflective Carers.' Paper presented at the Annual International Seminar, Department of Educational Studies, University of York, 16th June 2001.

Stewart, A. et al. (1980) *Social Stratification and Occupations*, London, Macmillan.

Strinati, D. (1995) ' Postmodernism and Popular Culture', *Sociology Review*, April.

Sutherland, E.H, (1949) *White-collar Crime*, New York, Holt, Rinehart and Winston.

Taylor, I. Walton, J., and Young, J. (1973) *The New Criminology*, London, Routledge and Kegan Paul.

Taylor, P. (1997) *Investigating Culture and Identity*, London, Collins Educational.

Thomas, W.I. (1909) *The Child in America*, New York, Alfred Knopt.

Thompson. K,. (ed and transl), *Readings from Emile Durkheim*, London, Routledge.

Thornton, S. (1995) *Club Cultures, Music Media and Subcultural Capital*, Cambridge, Polity Press.

Tomlinson, S (1983) *Ethnic Minorities in British Schools,* London, Heinemann.

Tomlinson, S. (1980) *Educational Subnormality: A Study in Decision Making*, London, Routledge.

Townsend, P. (1979) *Poverty in the United Kingdom*, Harmondsworth, Penguin.

Wagner, P. (1994) *A Sociology of Modernity: Liberty and Discipline*, London Routledge.

Walby, S. (1990) *Theorising Patriarchy*, Oxford, Blackwell.

Walby, S. (1997) *Gender Transformations*, London, Routledge.

Wallerstein, I. (1991) 'The Construction of Peoplehood: Racism, Nationalism, Ethnicity' in Balibar, E., and Wallerstein, I. (eds) *Race, Nation, Class*, London, Verso.

Walmsley, R, Howard, L., and White, S. (1992), *The National Prison Survey 1991: Main Findings*, Home Office Research Study No 128, London, HMSO.

Weber, M. (1948) 'Class, status and party', in Gerth, H. and Mills, C.W. (eds) *1948 From Max Weber*, London, Routledge.

Westergaard, J. (1995) *Who Gets What? The Hardening of Class Inequality in the Late Twentieth Century*, Cambridge, Polity Press.

Westergaard. J. and Resler (1976) *Class in a Capitalist Society: A Study of Contemporary Britain*, Harmondsworth, Penguin.

Williams, P., and Dickinson, J. (1993) 'Fear of Crime: Read all about it? The Relationship between Newspaper Crime Reporting and Fear of Crime', *British Journal of Criminology*, No 33, pp33-56.

Williams, R. (1990) *What I Came to Say*, Cambridge, Cambridge University Press.

Williams, R.(1981) *Culture*, London, Fantana.

Willis, P. (1977) *Learning to Labour: How Working Class Kids Get Working Class Jobs*, London, Saxon House.

Willis, P. (1990) *Common Culture: Symbolic Work at Play in the Everyday Lives of the Young*, Milton Keynes, Open University Press.

Wilson, J.Q. and Kelling,G.L. (1982) 'Broken Windows: The Police and Neighbourhood Safety' in *The Atlantic Monthly*, March 1982, pp29-38.

Wilson, W. J. (1987) *The Truly Disadvantaged: Inner City Woes and Public Policy*, Chicago, University of Chicago Press.

Wright, C. (1992) 'Early education: multiracial primary school classrooms' in D. Gill, B. Mayor, M. Blair (eds) *Racism and Education: Structures and Strategies*, London, Sage.

Wright, E. (1997) *Class Counts*, Cambridge, Cambridge University Press.

Young, J. (1971) *The Drugtakers*, London, Paladin.

Young, J. (1988) 'Radical Criminology in Britain: the Emergence of a Competing Paradigm' in *British Journal of Criminology*, 28, 2, 289-313.

Young, J. (2002) 'Crime and Social Exclusion' in *The Oxford Handbook of Criminology*, Oxford, Oxford University Press.

Index

A

A2 examination
  AS to A2 transition 11–20, 192–3, 272–3
  Assessment Objective 1 (AO1) 72, 77, 127, 274, 286–7
  Assessment Objective 2 (AO2) 72–3, 77, 127, 274, 286–7
  essays assessment 286–7
  unit 2536 power and control 18, 272
  unit 2537 applied sociological research skills 18, 19, 272
  unit 2538 personal study 18, 19, 245–70
  unit 2539 social inequality and difference 18, 19, 178–9, 191, 272
  unit examination times 16
absolute poverty 206–7
Affluent Worker study 227
age 56–7
alienation 204
Althusser, Louis 100
Anderson 167
Ang, Ien 159
anomie 59
Anti-Social Behaviour Orders (ASBOs) 57
AS examination
  AS to A2 transition 11–20, 192–3, 272–3
  unit 2532 individual and society 272
  unit 2533 culture and socialisation 18, 272
  unit 2534 data response question 272

B

Ball, Stephen 104–5, 118
Baudrillard, Jean 144, 146–7, 149
Becker, Howard 40–1, 68–9, 104
Bernstein, Basil 24, 112, 113

bibliography 291–4
'black' as unifying term 157
Bly, Robert 161
Booth, Charles 206
Bourdieu, Pierre 153, 170
bourgeoisie 217, 228
Bowlby, J 24
Box, Steven 37, 51, 57
Bradley, Harriet 208–9
Braverman, Harry 229
bricolage 149
'bricoleur' 146
'broken window thesis' 65
business sponsorship 155

C

'café society' 166
cannabis 60, 68–9
capitalist, types of 200
Carlen, Pat 43
Centre for Contemporary Cultural Studies 79, 132, 139, 148–9, 152–3
Chambliss, William 37
Chicago 58
chivalry thesis 54–5
Cicourel, Aaron 61
Clarke, Michael 51
class
  crime and deviance 50–1
  current position 224–9
  definition differences 195
  education 112–13
  fragmentation 225
  leisure 150
  market and work situation differences 229

Index

middle class 226–7
popular culture 149, 150, 152–3
poverty 208
social inequality and difference 208, 212–13, 224–9, 236–7
underclass 212, 238
working-class 112–13, 152–3, 228–9
class formation approach 194
class scales
Goldthorpe's Class Scheme 215
National Statistics Socio-Economic Classification 215
ranked by life chances 214–15
Registrar-General's Scale 215
Surrey Occupational Class Scheme 215
closure 197
Cohen, A P 168–9
Cohen, Albert 46–7
Cohen, Stanley 61, 65, 66–7, 128–9
Coleman, James 56
'collapse of the economy of truth' 106–7
commodification 137
commodity fetishism 137, 142
communitarianism 63, 211
communities
'gated' 169
of surveillance 169
oppressive 167
poverty 166
proto 166–7
working-class 169
Comte, Auguste 14
content analysis 129, 131
control 108
control theory 62–3, 64–5
corporate crime 50
crime and deviance 21–74
age 56–7
class 50–1
control theory 62–3, 64–5
culture 70
definition problems 26
definitions 28–9
different route to common goal 46–7
disorderly behaviour 62
drugs 68–9
education 24, 121

ethical issues 27
ethnicity 52–3
families 24
feminism 42–3
functionalism 34–5, 60
gender 54–5
households 24
identity 70
interactionism 40–1, 61
key issues 22–3
location 58–9
Marxism 36–7, 61, 64
mass media 66–7
measuring 26
neo-Marxism 38–9
New Left realism 44–5, 64, 65
New Right realism 45, 65
official statistics 25, 32–3, 43
phenomenologism 61
popular culture 171
postmodernism 48–9
qualitative methods 27
racial discrimination 52–3
realism 44–5
region 58–9
self-report studies 26, 33
social control 60–1
social inequality and difference 71
solutions 64–5
synopticity 70–1
theory, methods and methodology 25, 26
victim surveys 26, 33
'zero-tolerance' 62–3, 65
Crime and Disorder Act 1998: 57
criminalisation 37, 60
criminals, born or made ? 30–1
Croall, Hazel 50
Crompton, Rosemary 193, 213, 215, 224–5, 232
Croydon 58
cultural absolutism 135
cultural capital 153
cultural conservatism 154
cultural deprivation theory 116
cultural elitism 135
cultural homogenisation 165
cultural images 126

cultural imperialism 143
cultural products 126
cultural relativism 135
cultural transmission 103, 120
culture
   education 79
   industry 154
   social inequality and difference 241
   types of 132
   and see popular culture
Curriculum 2000: 94–5

D
Davies, B 81
Dearing, Sir Ron 94
deskilling 204, 229
deviance amplification 67
deviance *see* crime and deviance
discourses 144
disorderly behaviour 62
drugs 68–9
Dunning, Eric 163
Durkheim, Emile 34–5, 59, 62, 98, 210–11

E
economic determinism 139
education 75–124
   'alienation' 101
   changes currently 118–19
   class 112–13
   comprehensive system 88–9
   crime and deviance 24, 121
   cultural bias 112
   culture 79
   Curriculum 2000: 94–5
   definition problems 81
   economy of the UK 90
   ethnicity 116–17
   family 78
   feminism 102–3
   formal 82–3
   functionalism 82, 87, 98–9
   gender 114–15
   higher, expansion of 113
   'in-school' factors 110–11
   informal 82

intelligence 84–5
interactionism 104–5
key issues 76–7
marketisation 119
Marxism 82, 87, 97, 100–1
mass media 78–9
measuring 80–1
National Curriculum 114
New Right realism 118
other types 96–7
'out-of-school' factors 110–11
parental choice 92–3
politics in UK 86–93
postmodernism 97, 106–7
privately-sponsored academies 118
public schools 83
religion 78
secondary socialisation 78
social control 100–1
social inequality and difference 78, 121, 240
socialisation by education 78
socialisation of pupils 108–9
state 82–3
synopticity 120–1
theory, methods and methodology 80–1
tripartite system 86–7
vocationalism 90–1
youth 79
Education Act 1944: 86–7
Educational Reform Act 1988: 92–3
elaborated code 113
Elias, Norbert 163
embourgeoisement 219
empirical adequacy 163
employment aggregate model 194
Equal Pay Act 1970: 232–3
equality of opportunity 221
essentialism 42, 161
ethical issues 27
ethnicity
   crime and deviance 52–3
   education 116–17
   leisure 151
   life chances 230–1
   popular culture 149, 151, 156
   poverty 208

Index

social inequality and difference 208, 230–1, 236–7
Etzioni, Amitai 62–3, 211
examination skills 272–90
  analysis 274–5
  command words 278–9
  essay conclusions 282–3
  essay introductions 282–3
  essay writing 278–9, 284–5
  evaluation 20, 73, 274–5, 280–1
  grade improvement 72–3, 122–3, 172–3, 186–7,
    242–3, 268–9
  interpretation 274–5
  key issues 272–3
  knowledge and understanding 274
  'outline and assess' essay questions 19
  revision 288–9
  'signpost phrases' 284–5
  time division 276–7
  underpinning debates in sociology 273

F

false needs 139
Falud, Susan 234
families
  crime and deviance 24
  education 78
  social inequality and difference 240
Farrell, Stephen 51
Farrington 24
feminism
  chivalry thesis 54–5
  crime and deviance 42–3
  different theories 102
  education 102–3
  female under-achievement 114
  glass ceiling 232
  legislation 232–3
  liberal 140
  Marxist 140–1
  patriarchy 102, 120, 141, 234, 236–7
  popular culture 158–9
  postfeminism 234
  radical 140
  relevance currently 234–5
  social inequality and difference 204–5, 234–5
  third wave 236–7

Weberianism 233
  women as victims 43
Ferguson, Marjorie 140
figurational sociology 163
film industry 157
focus group 92
'folk devils' 56
Fordism 106, 205
Foucault, Michel 49, 144–5
Frankfurt School 134–5, 139, 161
Fukuyama, Francis 165
functionalism
  crime and deviance 34–5, 60
  education 82, 87, 98–9
  popular culture 142, 148
  social inequality and difference 202, 204, 216–17,
    230–1, 238

G

Gardner, Howard 85
'gated' communities 169
gay/lesbian culture 145
Gelsthorpe, Lorraine 43
gender
  crime and deviance 54–5
  education 114–15
  leisure 150–1
  life chances 232–3
  popular culture 150–1
  poverty 209
  social inequality and difference 209, 232–3, 236–7
gender blind 42
gender socialisation 103
Giddens, Anthony 159, 164, 167, 169, 254
Gillborn, David 81, 105, 117, 119
Gilroy, Paul 145, 156
Girls into Science and Technology (GIST) 114
glass ceiling 232
global culture 164–5
global village 143
globalisation 164
Goffman, Erving 169
Goldthorpe, John 219, 223, 233
Gordon, David 36
Gramsci, Antonio 38, 135, 138

H

habitus 153, 170
Hakim, Catherine 141, 234
Hall, Stuart 38, 53, 145, 156–7, 165
Hartmann 233
Hawthorne effect 27
Hebdige, Dick 147, 149
hegemony 38, 138
Heidensohn, Frances 42–3, 54–5
heterosexuality 145
Hey, Valerie 81
'hidden curriculum' 99, 100, 103
high culture 136
Hirschi, Travis 62
Hobbs, D 33
Hoggart, Richard 153
homosexuality 28–9
households
    crime and deviance 24
    social inequality and difference 240
hybridity 239

I

iceberg principle 32
identity 93, 170, 241
ideology 138
illegitimate opportunity structure 46
imposition problem 194
'in-school' factors 110–11
indicators 214
individual-blaming 207
individualisation 48
institutional racism 53
intellectual snobbery 134
intelligence 84–5
interactionism
    crime and deviance 40–1, 61
    education 104–5
intergenerational social mobility 197
interpretive sociology 260
interpretivism 27
intragenerational social mobility 197
IQ (intelligence quota) 84, 87

J

James, Winston 156
Jameson 146
Jones, Trevor 117

K

Karstedt, Susanne 51
Kidd, Warren 133

L

labelling theory 40–1
Lawrence, Stephen 53
Lea, J 64
leisure
    class 150
    ethnicity 151
    gender 150–1
life chances
    class 218–19
    ethnicity 230–1
    social inequality and difference 199, 230–1, 232–3
Liverpoool 59
location 58–9
Lockwood, David 228–9
Lombroso, Cesare 30, 54
low culture 136

M

malestream 42, 141
marginalisation 44–5
market situation 202–3
Marsland, David 213
Marxism
    crime and deviance 36–7, 61, 64
    education 82, 87, 97, 100–1
    feminism 140–1
    popular culture 136–7
    social inequality and difference 202–3, 204, 216–17, 230–1, 238
masculinity 160–1
mass culture
    negative use of phrase 134–5
    popular culture 143, 144
mass media
    crime and deviance 66–7
    education 78–9
    popular culture 128, 165
mass production 143

Index

Matza, David 47
'McDonaldisation' of society 162
McRobbie, Angela 140, 141, 148, 159
Mead, George Herbert 104
Mednick, Sarnof 30–1
Mercer, Kobena 157
meritocracy 202
Merton, Robert K 35, 46, 171
middle class 226–7
Miller, Walter 46
Modood, Tariq 231
moral panics 67
Morley 155
Morris, Lydia 213
Mort, Frank 160
Murray, Charles 212
'myth of education' 100

N
National Curriculum 114
National Deviancy Conference 39
nature/nurture debate 31
neo-Marxism
    crime and deviation 38–9
    popular culture 134–5, 138–9
    social inequality and difference 220–1
New Left realism 44–5, 64, 65
New Right realism
    crime and deviance 45, 65
    education 118
    social inequality and difference 221
News Corporation 154, 165

O
occupational crime 50
Offe, Claus 153
open society 197
oppressive communities 167
organic analogy 35
'out-of-school' factors 110–11
Oxford Mobility Study 223

P
parental choice 92–3
parity of esteem 87, 94
Parsons, Talcott 24, 98

patriarchy 102, 120, 141, 234, 236–7
Patrick, James 27
Pearce, Frank 37
personal study
    appearance and presentation 246, 248–9
    appendix 248–9
    background focus 258–9
    chapters/sections 250–1
    conclusions 264–5
    diary, importance 247
    evaluation chapter 250, 251, 265–7
    key issues 246–7
    marking 251
    methodology 260–1
    methods 254–5
    rationale chapter 250–1, 256–7
    research chapter 250, 251, 262–5
    starting 252–3
    and see A2 examination unit 2538
phenomenologism 61
pluralism 142–3
polarisation of identities 48
policing as contribution to crime 32
popular culture 125–74
    as commodity 154–5
    Centre for Contemporary Cultural Studies 139, 148–9, 152–3
    class 149, 150, 152–3
    crime and deviance 171
    definition problems 131
    definitions 132–3
    ethnicity 149, 151, 156
    feminism 140–1, 158–9
    Frankfurt School 134–5, 139, 161
    functionalism 142, 148
    gender 150–1
    global culture 164–5
    high culture 136
    identity 170
    key issues 126–7
    low culture 136
    Marxism 136–7
    masculinity 160–1
    mass culture 134–5, 143, 144
    mass media 128, 165
    measuring 130–1

neo-Marxism 134–5, 138–9
pluralism 142–3
postmodernism 146–7, 162–3
poststructuralism 144–5
power 170
proto communities 166–7
racism 156
social inequality 170–1
synopticity 170–1
theory, methods and methodology 130–1
working-class culture 152–3
youth and culture 128–9
youth subcultures 148–9
positivism 260
post-Fordism 106, 205
postfeminism 234
postmodernism
crime and deviance 48–9
education 97, 106–7
leisure 162–3
popular culture 146–7, 162–3
social inequality and difference 204, 239
tourism 162–3
poststructuralism 144–5
poverty
class 208
communities 166
definitions 206–7
ethnicity 208
gender 209
measuring 206–7
social exclusion 210–11
social inequality and difference 206–9
power 93, 108, 170
primary socialisation 78, 108
privately-sponsored academies 118
proletariat 217, 228
proto communities 166–7
public schools 83

Q
qualitative methods 27

R
racial discrimination 52–3
racialised class fractions 231

racism 156
realism 44–5, 260
reductionism 31, 37
reflexivity 67, 254
region 58–9
relative poverty 206–7
relativism 147
religion 78
restricted code 112, 113
Ritzer, George 162
Robins 165
role allocation 216
Rowbotham, S 233
Rowntree, Seebohm 206
Rutherford, Jonathan 161

S
sanction 28–9
Saunders, Peter 221, 223
schools
comprehensive 88–9
grammar 86
other 96–7
public 83, 96–7
religious 97
secondary modern 86
'sink' 93
technical 87
Scott, John 200, 201
secondary socialisation 78, 108
Seidler, Victor 160
self-fulfilling prophecy 104
self-report studies 26, 33
semiology 129, 131
'sets' 88
Sex Discrimination Act 1975: 232–3
Sheffield 59
'signpost phrases' 284–5
simulcra 147
situational deviance 28–9
six social structures 236–7
Smart, Carol 43
Smith, Joan 159
social capital 56–7
social control, agencies of 60–1, 100
social disorganisation 58–9

Index

social exclusion 210–11
social fragmentation 48
social inequality 170–1
social inequality and difference 189–244
    AS course links 192–3
    class 208, 212–13, 224–9, 236–7
    crime and deviance 71
    culture 241
    definition problems 195
    definitions 196–7
    education 121, 240
    ethnicity 208, 230–1, 236–7
    families 240
    feminism 204–5, 234–5
    functionalism 202, 204, 216–17, 230–1, 238
    gender 209, 232–3, 236–7
    households 240
    identity 238–9, 241
    income 198–9
    investigation 194–5
    key issues 190–1
    life chances 199, 230–1, 232–3
    Marxism 202–3, 204, 216–17, 230–1, 238
    measuring 214–15
    neo-Marxism 220–1
    New Right realism 221
    postmodernism 204, 239
    poverty 206–9
    social mobility 197, 222–3
    stratification system 197
    synopticity 240–1
    theory, methods and methodology 194–5, 241
    underclass 212–13, 238
    wealth 198–9, 200–1
    Weberianism 203, 204, 218–19, 230–1, 238
    work 204–5
social mobility 197, 222–3
social structures, Walby's six 236–7
social synopticity 177
socialisation by education 78
socialisation of pupils 108–9
sociological synopticity 177
state education 82–3
status 196
stratification 197, 214, 238
'streams' 88

Street-Porter, Janet 158
Strinati, D 146
'strong on law and order' 65
Stuart, Andrea 141
subculture 46
Sutherland, Edwin 50
symbolic boundaries 168–9
synopticity
    crime and deviance 70–1
    education 120–1
    key issues 176–7
    popular culture 170
    social inequality and difference 240–1
    synoptic skills 15, 175–88
    synoptic tools 180–1
    synoptic writing 182–3
    theory, methods and methodology 184–5
system-blaming 207

T
Taylor, Ian 39
Technical Vocational Educational Initiative (TVEI)
    114
techniques of neutralisation 46–7
theory, methods and methodology
    crime and deviance 25, 26
    education 80–1
    popular culture 130–1
    social inequality and difference 194–5, 241
    synopticity 184–5
third wave feminism 236–7
'tough on crime, tough on the causes of crime' 44, 65
tourism 162–3
Townsend, Peter 207, 213
tripartite system 86–7
triple systems theory 151

U
underclass 212, 238
unit of analysis 194
unstructured interviews 80

V
value consensus 58
victim surveys 26, 33
vocationalism 90–1

Index

W

Walby, Sylvia 102, 141, 151, 236–7
Walter, Natasha 234–5
Walton, Paul 39
wealth
    social inequality and difference 198–9, 200–1
    statistics 200, 200–1, 205
Weber, Max 199, 203, 218–19
Weberianism
    feminism 233
    social inequality and difference 203, 204, 218–19, 230–1, 238
welfare pluralism 210–11
Westergaard, John 201
white-collar crime 50–1
'wigger' 157
Williams, Raymond 132–3

Willis, Paul 24, 39, 79, 101, 149
Wilson, James Q 45
Wilson, William Julius 213
working class 228–9
working-class culture 152–3
working-class under-achievement 112–13
Wright, Erik O 220–1

Y

Young, Jock 39, 44, 64, 68–9
youth
    education 79
    popular culture 128–9
    subcultures 148–9

Z

'zero-tolerance' 62–3, 65

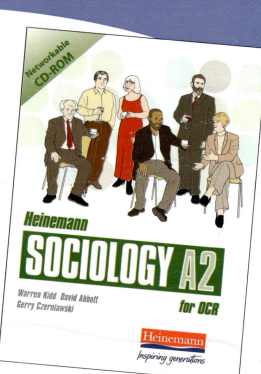